The Jurisprudence of Style

In the contemporary domain of American legal thought, there is a dominant conception in which lawyers and judges craft their argumentative practice. More colloquially, this is called "thinking like a lawyer." Despite the widespread popularity of this conception, it is rarely described in detail, much less given a name. Justin Desautels-Stein tells the story of this curious absence in American Legal Thought, and why that story matters. Drawing upon and updating the work of Harvard Law School's first generation of critical legal studies, Desautels-Stein develops what he calls a jurisprudence of style. In doing so, he uncovers the intellectual alliance, first emerging at the end of the nineteenth century and maturing in the last third of the twentieth century, between American pragmatism and liberal legal thought. Applying the tools of legal structuralism and phenomenology to real-world cases in areas of contemporary legal debate, this book develops a practice-oriented understanding of legal thought.

Justin Desautels-Stein is Associate Professor of Law at the University of Colorado Law School.

Cambridge Historical Studies in American Law and Society

Recognizing legal history's growing importance and influence, the goal of this series is to chart legal history's continuing development by publishing innovative scholarship across the discipline's broadening range of perspectives and subjects. It encourages empirically creative works that take legal history into unexplored subject areas, or that fundamentally revise our thinking about familiar topics; it also encourages methodologically innovative works that bring new disciplinary perspectives and techniques to the historical analysis of legal subjects.

Series Editor

Christopher Tomlins, *University of California, Berkeley*

Previously Published in the Series:

Angela Fernandez, *Pierson v. Post: The Hunt for the Fox*
Rebecca E. Zietlow, *The Forgotten Emancipator: James Mitchell Ashley and the Ideological Origins of Reconstruction*
Robert Daniel Rubin, *Judicial Review and American Conservatism: Christianity, Public Education, and the Federal Courts in the Reagan Era*
Matthew Crow, *Thomas Jefferson, Legal History, and the Art of Recollection*
Oren Bracha, *Owning Ideas: The Intellectual Origins of American Intellectual Property, 1790–1909*
Anne Twitty, *Before* Dred Scott*: Slavery and Legal Culture in the American Confluence, 1787–1857*
Leia Castañeda Anastacio, *The Foundations of the Modern Philippine State: Imperial Rule and the American Constitutional Tradition in the Philippine Islands, 1898–1935*
Robert Deal, *The Law of the Whale Hunt: Dispute Resolution, Property Law, and American Whalers, 1780–1880*
Sandra F. Vanburkleo, *Gender Remade: Citizenship, Suffrage, and Public Power in the New Northwest, 1879–1912*
Reuel Schiller, *Forging Rivals: Race, Class, Law, and the Collapse of Postwar Liberalism*
Ely Aaronson, *From Slave Abuse to Hate Crime: The Criminalization of Racial Violence in American History*
Stuart Chinn, *Recalibrating Reform: The Limits of Political Change*
Ajay K. Mehrotra, *Making the Modern American Fiscal State*
Yvonne Pitts, *Family, Law, and Inheritance in America: A Social and Legal History of Nineteenth-Century Kentucky*
David M. Rabban, *Law's History*
Kunal M. Parker, *Common Law, History, and Democracy in America, 1790–1900*
Steven Wilf, *Law's Imagined Republic*
James D. Schmidt, *Industrial Violence and the Legal Origins of Child Labor*
Rebecca M. McLennan, *The Crisis of Imprisonment: Protest, Politics, and the Making of the American Penal State, 1776–1941*
Tony A. Freyer, *Antitrust and Global Capitalism, 1930–2004*
Davison Douglas, *Jim Crow Moves North*
Andrew Wender Cohen, *The Racketeer's Progress*
Michael Willrich, *City of Courts, Socializing Justice in Progressive Era Chicago*

Barbara Young Welke, *Recasting American Liberty: Gender, Law and the Railroad Revolution, 1865–1920*

Michael Vorenberg, *Final Freedom: The Civil War, the Abolition of Slavery, and the Thirteenth Amendment*

Robert J. Steinfeld, *Coercion, Contract, and Free Labor in Nineteenth Century America*

David M. Rabban, *Free Speech in Its Forgotten Years*

Jenny Wahl, *The Bondsman's Burden: An Economic Analysis of the Common Law of Southern Slavery*

Michael Grossberg, *A Judgment for Solomon: The d'Hauteville Case and Legal Experience in the Antebellum South*

The Jurisprudence of Style

A Structuralist History of American Pragmatism and Liberal Legal Thought

JUSTIN DESAUTELS-STEIN
University of Colorado

CAMBRIDGE
UNIVERSITY PRESS

CAMBRIDGE
UNIVERSITY PRESS

University Printing House, Cambridge CB2 8BS, United Kingdom

One Liberty Plaza, 20th Floor, New York, NY 10006, USA

477 Williamstown Road, Port Melbourne, VIC 3207, Australia

314–321, 3rd Floor, Plot 3, Splendor Forum, Jasola District Centre, New Delhi - 110025, India

79 Anson Road, #06-04/06, Singapore 079906

Cambridge University Press is part of the University of Cambridge.

It furthers the University's mission by disseminating knowledge in the pursuit of education, learning, and research at the highest international levels of excellence.

www.cambridge.org
Information on this title: www.cambridge.org/9781107156654
DOI: 10.1017/9781316661444

First published 2018

Printed in the United States of America by Sheridan Books, Inc.

A catalogue record for this publication is available from the British Library

Library of Congress Cataloging-in-Publication data
Names: Desautels-Stein, Justin, 1975– author.
Title: The jurisprudence of style : a structuralist history of American pragmatism and liberal legal thought / Justin Desautels-Stein, University of Colorado.
Description: Cambridge, United Kingdom; New York, NY, USA : Cambridge University Press, 2018. | Series: Cambridge historical studies in American law and society | Includes bibliographical references and index.
Identifiers: LCCN 2017036749 | ISBN 9781107156654 (alk. paper)
Subjects: LCSH: Law – Philosophy. | Structuralism. | Liberalism. | Pragmatism | Law – United States – Philosophy.
Classification: LCC K230.D47 A33 2018 | DDC 340/.1 – dc23
LC record available at https://lccn.loc.gov/2017036749

ISBN 978-1-107-15665-4 Hardback

For Amy

Contents

Acknowledgments

This book has its beginnings in a law school class with Roberto Unger. The name of the course was *Contemporary Legal Analysis*, a survey of Unger's book *What Should Legal Analysis Become?* Never before had I found a course either so confusing or so enriching. It was one of those classes that forever changes the way you put the world together, as this book attests. At the same time, I was taking a course on rational choice theory with Amartya Sen, in which he introduced the class to Richard Posner's work on pragmatism and economics. A short while later, David Kennedy showed me a draft for his forthcoming *Dark Sides of Virtue*, a work of another pragmatist variety. Further still, Unger ended his course with an ode to William James. Pragmatism, it seemed, was everywhere a Cambridge fog. It was this amorphous and plentiful pragmatism that sparked my first interest in James, Dewey, and Rorty, and their legacies in law. I am grateful for my teachers' willingness to put up with all of those early questions.

After graduation, my interests in pragmatism continued with David Kennedy's ongoing support. His Institute for Global Law and Policy was an early and lasting site for intellectual warfare of the best kind, and I'm sure that my work was bettered with his generosity. After arriving in Boulder, I was lucky to find in Pierre Schlag, Jack Schlegel, and William Simon a trio of commentators who seemed willing to read just about anything I'd send their way. This was, and still is, deeply appreciated. Over the past few years a new and formidable influence on my approach has been that of Chris Tomlins. His theorization of legal history and all of his work in the *Law as . . .* symposia have been tremendous and a real benefit to my intellectual development. Last in this list of signal figures is Duncan

Kennedy. It is difficult to characterize the immensity of Duncan's impact on this book, both in substance and in style. His endless energy and willingness to dig out my many mistakes have been indispensable, just as have been his warmth and encouragement.

Along the way, there have been friends, readers, and commentators in too many venues to adequately address. But among those that have helped make this book a better one (I hope), and in addition to those I have already mentioned, are Paulo Barrozo, Jon Baker, Charles Barzun, Arnulf Becker Lorca, William Boyd, Ming Hsu Chen, Amy Cohen, Adrienne Davis, Dan Ernst, Maks del Mar, Frank Garcia, Ben Golder, Bernard Harcourt, Janet Halley, John Haskell, Martti Koskenniemi, Alex Kinsella, Andrew Lang, Doreen Lustig, Sam Moyn, Fernanda Nicola, Amy Ostdiek, Umut Ozsu, Ben Moritz, Kristina Moritz, Akbar Razulov, Annelise Riles, Brishen Rogers, Spencer Weber Waller, Catherine Wells, Emilyn Winkelmeyer, and Ahmed White. For helpful research assistance, I thank James Kin, Ethan Tacket, Alec Gibson, Daniel Chavez, and Michael Gannon.

Finally, my deepest gratitude goes to my children, Dakota and Noah, my wife, Amy, and my parents. In its fundamentals, this is a book about the quest for harmony in law, and the illusions that haunt that quest. But it is in the company of my family that I have learned harmony's most crucial lessons, and for that I am forever grateful.

Overture

There was once a Madman, a Madman with news. That news, as Friedrich Nietzsche famously relayed it in 1882, was that God had died. "*We have killed him*," reported the Madman. "All of us are his murderers!"[1] Of course, this was not just any old news. It was *good news*. The Madman continued, "Is not the greatness of this deed too great for us? Must not we ourselves becomes gods simply to seem worthy of it? There has never been a greater deed; and whoever will be born after us – for the sake of this deed he will be part of a higher history than all history hitherto."[2] Realizing his own divinity, the Madman believed that Man's truly autonomous dispensation was, apparently, *finally*, about to begin.

Unsurprisingly, the reports of God's demise turned out to have been false.[3] Writing a few years later in 1966, Michel Foucault suggested that the Madman had been a little confused in his initial reporting. He had been mad, after all, and Foucault knew a thing or two about madness. It was not that God had died, for God had never lived. What the Madman might have been better off saying, what he had likely seen through the fog on that dark and stormy night, was the murder of *Man*, not God. In glimpsing the eclipse of a perspective from which to master the universe, the Madman had mistaken God for the Subject, the autonomous, rights-bearing individual. It was the murder of the Subject – a particular

[1] *The Portable Nietzsche* (Walter Kaufman, trans.) (New York: Penguin Books, 1982), p. 95.

[2] Id. at 96.

[3] Despite his madness, even the Madman knew he'd gotten it wrong. Id. at 96. For Nietzsche's part, putting God in the ground wouldn't be easy: "'Reason' in language – oh, what an old deceptive female she is! I am afraid we are not rid of God because we still have faith in grammar." Id. at 483.

image of the human being – that the Madman had borne sure witness yet failed to accurately explain. This, at any rate, is a reading of Foucault's reading of that ghastly event in 1882.[4] Sadly (or happily), the view from 2018 suggests that whatever that Madman had really seen, it was not the murder of God *or* Man. They are both alive and well.[5] Perhaps, in retrospect, we might say that Nietzsche and Foucault were sensing similar disturbances, and that it had been the death of neither God nor Man. Rather it was *liberalism* they saw on the march to the gallows, a perplexing and enchanting view of the universe nowadays attributed to a Trinity of John: Locke, Mill, Rawls.[6] And while liberalism may have been knocking on death's door back in 1882 and 1966, it did not die then and it is not dead now. Nevertheless, the Madman's whispers insist on a coming end, that liberalism lives on borrowed time.[7]

This book tells an untold story of how liberalism has lived on, refusing to die, even when its friends and enemies were sure of its imminent demise. The context in which I tell the story of liberalism's uncanny survivability is Law.[8] One way to get a handle on this legal context of liberalism, or what I will call throughout this book "liberal legal thought" or "liberal legalism," is to approach it colloquially. In this vein it is useful to invoke the familiar phrase "thinking like a lawyer." For law school graduates and

[4] Michel Foucault, *The Order of Things: An Archaeology of Human Sciences* (New York.: Vintage Books, 1994), p. 385.

[5] For discussion, see Terry Eagleton, *Culture and the Death of God* (New Haven, CT: Yale University Press, 2015). The Columbia Center for Contemporary Critical Thought has recently hosted a fascinating seminar series on each of these thinkers. The series on Nietzsche is available at http://blogs.law.columbia.edu/nietzsche1313/, and the Foucault series is available at http://blogs.law.columbia.edu/foucault1313/. See also Bernard Harcourt, Radical Thought from Marx, Nietzsche, and Freud, through Foucault, to the Present: Comments on Steven Lukes' In Defense of False Consciousness, 2011 *University of Chicago Legal Forum* 29 (2011).

[6] See, e.g., John Locke, *Two Treaties of Government* (Peter Laslett, ed.) (Cambridge: Cambridge University Press, 1988); John Stuart Mill, *On Liberty and Other Writings* (Stefan Collini, ed.) (Cambridge: Cambridge University Press, 1989); John Rawls, *A Theory of Justice: Revised Edition* (Cambridge, MA: Harvard University Press, 1999).

[7] A recent and repeated example is Mark Lilla, The End of Identity Liberalism, N.Y. Times Sunday Review (November 18, 2016), SR1.

[8] Interventions in a similar spirit include Duncan Kennedy, *A Critique of Adjudication* (Cambridge, MA: Harvard University Press, 1999); Roberto Unger, *What Should Legal Analysis Become?* (London: Verso, 1996); Bernard Harcourt, *The Illusion of Free Markets: Punishment and the Myth of Natural Order* (Cambridge, MA: Harvard University of Press, 2012); Paulo Barrozo, The Great Alliance: History, Reason, and Will in Modern Law, 78 *Law and Contemporary Problems* 235 (2015).

law professors alike, legal education ought to produce, at the very least, the ability to think in this way. Unfortunately, very few of us have much of an idea of what this ubiquitous phrase is really supposed to mean. Perhaps thinking critically, or instrumentally, or being good at problem solving, or something like that. What I will suggest is that in the United States of today there is no single way in which to think like a lawyer, and that throughout American legal history there have been many ways to do so.[9] Liberal legal thought is one of these ways, if not the dominant way of thinking like a lawyer in the United States. And as I will argue, there are actually three distinctive ways in which liberal legal thought manifests itself. I will call these the classic, modern, and pragmatic structures of liberal legal thought.

But first things first: What is liberal legal thought?[10] Now, I recognize the extent to which the term liberalism is bandied about. It might refer to the discredited theory of American history developed by Louis Hartz, it might refer to the unfashionable economic theory of Friedrich Hayek, it might refer to the middlebrow politics of Barack Obama. It might refer to much more. In this work, however, I define liberal legal thought by way of three foundational theses.[11] In their differing ways, these three theses constitute the underlying and ordering grammar of each of the three structures of liberal legalism (classic, modern, pragmatic).

The first is *the thesis of free competition*. It holds that society is an artificial architecture, supported by the organic will of autonomous, rights-bearing individuals. Founding society on the autonomous, rights-bearing individual is both natural and just. Society comes into being as a derivative *good* to the extent that the clash of individual wills yields natural outcomes. There is no a priori definition of the good superseding the right of individuals to pursue, in contest with one another, their own private notions of the good life. The second is *the thesis of social control*. It holds

[9] One especially helpful collection is David Kennedy and William W. Fisher III, *The Canon of American Legal Thought* (Princeton, NJ: Princeton University Press, 2006).

[10] At the level of liberal political theory, useful examples include Pierre Manent, *An Intellectual History of Liberalism* (Rebecca Balinski, trans.) (Princeton, NJ: Princeton University Press, 1996); Alan Ryan, *The Making of Modern Liberalism* (Princeton, NJ: Princeton University Press, 2012); James Kloppenberg: *The Virtues of Liberalism* (New York: Oxford University Press, 1988); Alasdair MacIntyre, *After Virtue: A Study in Moral Theory* (University of Notre Dame Press, 2007).

[11] For earlier work, see Justin Desautels-Stein, The Market as a Legal Concept, 60 *Buffalo Law Review* 387 (2012); Justin Desautels-Stein, Race as a Legal Concept, 2 *Columbia Journal of Race and Law* 1 (2012).

that the contest of individual wills cannot result in a stable environment in which individuals are capable of freely pursing their will. Free competition does not merely yield a derivative good, left to its own devices. It yields chaos, and in the end, it yields a society devoid of the competitive impulse initially understood as the good fruit of an autonomous individualism. The thesis of social control, as a result, holds it as a necessary correlative of the rights-bearing individual that a police power define the proper scope of the contest of individual wills. Society is still artificial, individual right is still organic. But in order to realize good competition in society, so holds the thesis of social control, individual rights must be constrained by the police power.

In liberal legal thought, these two theses exist in a state of *antinomy*. This word comes from the Latin *anti-nomia*, "against law." What it means here is a conflict between the two founding theses of liberal legalism, a situation in which it impossible to choose rationally between either of the imperatives without doing violence to the other. While I see this antinomy as fundamental to the language of liberal legal thought, it is worth emphasizing here what I will emphasize repeatedly. It does not follow that in establishing this basic antinomy in liberal legalism that I am also establishing an antinomy in all of American Legal Thought, or American Law, or any other such thing. It is a mistake, in other words, to understand the structure of liberal legalism as synonymous with any of these abstractions. Sure, they *could* refer to the same thing. But nothing I'm saying here demands that identity. Furthermore, the antinomy of liberal legalism is historically situated. As I argue in this book, there is nothing timeless about the antinomy, and it manifests itself differently in different substructures of thought. Time, in other words, is for real. And if time is for real, nothing transcends it. There is nothing timeless and eternal about the antinomy between the theses of free competition and social control. At least, I don't think there is.

The structure of liberal legal thought might be pursued through the demolition of any number of possible doctrinal sites. International law has proved, in my opinion, a particularly fruitful front.[12] Here, however, I focus on the construction of the market in liberal legal thought, and there is a plurality of legal bodies relevant in such a pursuit. Rather than take our received organizations for what constitutes a "body of law,"

[12] Justin Desautels-Stein, International Legal Structuralism: A Primer, 8 *International Theory* 201 (2016).

however, I follow the lead of Foucault and emphasize a different, structural composition of the market – the market as a legal concept.[13] And so, while the doctrines of nuisance, takings, due process, and anticompetitive behavior might traditionally "belong" to those bodies of law called property, constitutional law, and antitrust, I place these legal concepts in the orbit of a larger legal concept, that of the market – the market as rendered as a legal concept in the language of liberal legal thought.

Beyond the antinomy between the theses of free competition and social control is the third thesis in the grammar of liberal legal thought. This is *the thesis of naturalizing juridical science*. This third thesis is of another sort than the first two, and as a consequence I approach it rather differently. That approach begins in a mathematical milieu, but it only begins there so as to make a quick exit. For all we need to know of math is that it has for centuries presented scholars of all sorts with a gold standard for analyzing what we can call "natural reality."[14] The idea is that there is a natural reality and a human reality, and the aspiration is to create a correspondence between our human representations and the facts that exist independently of those representations in the natural world.[15] The best understanding we have of natural reality is mathematical, as it is in our mathematical statements that we express the purest match between human representation and natural fact. Through the mathematical lens, according to this view, humanity sees nature as God sees it, independent of

[13] Foucault explains, "One stands back in relation to this manifest sea of concepts; and one tries to determine according to what schemata . . . the statements may be linked to one another in a type of discourse; one tries in this way to discover how the recurrent elements of statements can reappear, dissociate, recompose, gain in extension or determination, be taken up into new logical structures . . . " Michel Foucault, *The Archaeology of Knowledge: And the Discourse on Language* (New York: Pantheon Books, 1972), p. 60. "This dispersion itself – with its gaps, its discontinuities, its entanglements, its incompatibilities, its replacements, and its substitutions – can be described in its uniqueness if one is able to determine the specific rules in accordance with which its objects, statements, concepts, and theoretical options have been formed: if there really is a unity, it does not lie in the visible, horizontal coherence of the elements formed; it resides, well anterior to their formation, in the system that makes possible and governs that formation." Id. at 72.

[14] Georg Lukacs, *History and Class Consciousness: Studies in Marxist Dialectics* (Rodney Livingstone, trans.) (Cambridge, MA: MIT Press, 1999), pp. 112, 129.

[15] See, e.g., Janice Thomas, *The Minds of the Moderns: Rationalism, Empiricism, and Philosophy of Mind* (Montreal: McGill University Press, 2009); Louis Loeb, *From Descartes to Hume: Continental Metaphysics and the Development of Modern Philosophy* (Ithaca, NY: Cornell University Press, 1981); Daniel Coquillette, *Francis Bacon* (Stanford, CA: Stanford University Press, 1992).

time and context. In this way, as Max Horkheimer and Theodor Adorno suggested, "In their mastery of nature, the Creative God and the ordering mind are alike."[16]

As the story of liberalism unfolds, the mathematical reality of nature discloses a fundamental harmony. For math is, as expressed in phrases like the "golden ratio," a harmonious architecture of natural essence.[17] However, if mathematics represents the purest form of humanity's capacity for representing a natural reality, and if "mathematical procedure became a kind of ritual of thought,"[18] non-mathematicians have long been jealous. As Christian monks in Europe discovered new forms of music, for example, a centerpiece was the concept of harmony.[19] In contrast with mathematical harmony, musical harmony traveled in two directions, horizontally and vertically. In its vertical dimension, a series of single pitches was in harmony if played simultaneously (the pitches are stacked on top of one another on the staff, creating a chord). In its horizontal, temporal dimension, a musician achieves harmony sequentially, playing particular pitches in an appropriate order. If the order of things is violated and a wrong pitch follows, the result is *dissonance*. If the correct pitch follows, the dissonance is *resolved* in a harmonious *consonance*.[20] Either in its vertical dimensions or in its contrapuntal form, we can ask, from what resource does the musician decide what counts as a harmonious order, or what counts as having resolved dissonance into consonance?[21]

[16] Max Horkheimer and Theodor Adorno, *Dialectic of Enlightenment: Philosophical Fragments* (Stanford, CA: Stanford University Press, 2007), p. 6.

[17] As Ian Stewart explains in his enjoyable tour of math's greatest hits, mathematical equations "reveal deep and beautiful patterns and regularities. They are valid because, given our basic assumptions about the logical structure of mathematics, *there is no alternative*." In *Pursuit of the Unknown: 17 Equations That Changed the World* (New York: Basic Books, 2012), p. viii. For a popular tour of the golden ratio, see Mario Livio, *The Golden Ratio: The Story of Phi, the World's Most Astonishing Number* (New York: Broadway Books, 2002).

[18] Horkheimer & Adorno, supra note 16, at 19.

[19] Of course, the concept of harmony dates far earlier than the late middle ages. J. Peter Burkholder et al., *A History of Western Music* (New York: W. W. Norton & Company, 2014), p. 13. But the point here is to emphasize the conception of harmony that comes to attend a Cartesian mindset, rather than a Platonic one. Id. at 85.

[20] Conventionally, music is dissonant when the combination of two or more tones, either contrapuntally or harmonically, create an experience of tension and lack of stability. Conversely, music is consonant when a combination of two or more tones create the reverse experience of stability and wholeness. *The New Harvard Dictionary of Music* (Don Randel, ed.) (Cambridge, MA: Harvard University Press: 1986), pp. 197–199.

[21] Arnold Schoenberg, *Theory of Harmony* (Roy Carter, trans.) (Berkeley: University of California Press, 1983), pp. 19–22.

Traditionally, that resource was math.[22] The program is clear: If music is to represent a natural reality, and if natural reality is a mathematical harmony, then music must reflect mathematical harmonies as well. Small wonder that the prayer of the German masters was to hear in the mathematical fabric of counterpoint the murmurs of God's own breath.[23]

What is interesting for our purposes about the shift from mathematics to music is that we are also shifting from the "natural sciences" to art. For music is an art, not a science, yes? (We can see how and why the question of musical taste has for so long been so thorny: if harmony is a matter of natural reality, and if you dislike harmony, something is wrong with you. Hence, the Church's early take on dissonant intervals and what it condemned as "the devil's tone".)[24] But let us turn to an indisputable "art," that of painting. Once again, Christian painters in Europe increasingly found themselves with math envy. Their representations just didn't represent very well. The figures were too flat, the dimensions out of whack, the scenes not lifelike. And yet, what was painting about if not the revelation of a natural order, a natural law? If it was to succeed in this mission, painting would become more "realistic," and if it was to become realistic, it would need to achieve greater degrees of harmony. The key to a harmonious painting, a realistic painting (notice that these terms are becoming duplicative), was geometry.[25] As Samuel Edgerton suggested in his history of the use of mathematics in pictorial representation, the Renaissance master's desire was to reveal – on the canvas – the harmony between geometrical perspective and divine revelation. "Linear perspective, then,

[22] See, e.g., Gareth Loy, *Musimathics: The Mathematical Foundations of Music* (Cambridge, MA: MIT Press, 2006).

[23] Although I am much more in mind of Bach's use of counterpoint here, it is interesting to consider Adorno's well-known interest in Beethoven's later symphonies as a key for critical theory. For discussion, see Peter Gordon, The Artwork Beyond Itself: Adorno, Beethoven, and Late Style, in *The Modernist Imagination* (Warren Breckman et al., eds.) (New York: Berghahn Books, 2008). For a classic discussion of counterpoint, see *The Study of Counterpoint from Johann Joseph Fux's Gradus ad Parnassum* (Alfred Mann, trans.) (New York: W. W. Norton & Company, 1971).

[24] Howard Goodall, *The Story of Music: From Babylon to the Beatles: How Music Has Shaped Civilization* (New York: Pegasus Books, 2013), p. 35. See also Graham Phipps, The Tritone as Equivalency: A Contextual Perspective for Approaching Schoenberg's Music, 4 *The Journal of Musicology* 51 (1985). On taste, a classic treatment is Eduard Hanslick, *The Beautiful in Music: A Contribution to the Revisal of Musical Aesthetics* (Gustav Cohen, trans.) (Indianapolis: The Liberal Arts Press, 1957).

[25] Leonard Goldstein, *The Social and Cultural Roots of Linear Perspective* (Minneapolis: MEP Publications, 1988), p. 71; John Berger, *Ways of Seeing* (New York: Penguin Books, 1990), p. 16.

with its dependence on optical principles, seemed to symbolize a harmonious relationship between mathematical tidiness and nothing less than God's will. The picture, as constructed according to the laws of perspective, was to set an example for moral order and human perfection."[26] In his wonderful tour of the philosophy of vision, Martin Jay makes a similar point:

> With the differentiation of the aesthetic from the religious . . . perspective was free to follow its own course and become the naturalized visual culture of the new artistic order. What makes it especially important is that it functioned in a similar way for the new scientific order. In both cases space was robbed of its substantive meaningfulness to become an ordered, uniform system of abstract linear coordinates. As such, it was less the stage for a narrative to be developed over time than the eternal container of objective processes.[27]

It would take us too far afield to engage the debate in whether what I am about to say about painting applies in the same way to music and math. For as painting developed in Renaissance Italy, something critical came into view about marshaling geometry and perspective in the service of "the real."[28] These tactics, these tools of precision, were insufficient. A discovery that assisted in bridging this gap was this: In order to create a "truly" "lifelike" representation, the painting needed to drench its geometry in *illusion*. This was *trompe l'oeil*, as put to marvelous effect in paintings like Leonardo da Vinci's *Mona Lisa*.[29] In order for the painter to set that "example for moral order and human perfection," he would assault the eye with a left-right combination: the promise of analytical precision shrouded in fog and obfuscation. It was precisely in this blending that the image most successfully constituted its aim: a harmonious conjuring of the real.

On the way toward understanding the third thesis in liberal legal thought, we have very quickly touched on the distinction between natural reality and human reality, as negotiated in painting and music, by way of an analogy to a harmonious model of natural reality. I will call

[26] Samuel Edgerton Jr., *The Renaissance Rediscovery of Linear Perspective* (New York: Basic Books, 1975), p. 24. See also Samuel Edgerton Jr., *The Mirror, The Window, and the Telescope: How Renaissance Linear Perspective Changed Our Vision of the Universe* (Ithaca, NY: Cornell University Press, 2009).

[27] Martin Jay, *Downcast Eyes: The Denigration of Vision in Twentieth-Century French Thought* (Berkeley: University of California Press, 1994), pp. 52–53.

[28] Martin Kemp, *The Science of Art: Optical Themes in Western Art from Brunelleschi to Seurat* (New Haven, CT: Yale University Press, 1990).

[29] Ernst Gombrich, *Art and Illusion: A Study in the Psychology of Pictorial Representation* (Princeton, NJ: Princeton University Press, 2000), p. 221.

this negotiating strategy *the naturalizing sensibility*.[30] As I will argue, this naturalizing sensibility is critical in understanding the structure of liberal legalism, and in particular, the thesis of naturalizing juridical science. The thesis of naturalizing juridical science, in other words, is a direct associate of the naturalizing sensibility at work in the arts and sciences.[31] As Gerald Postema has said, in its Renaissance life jurisprudence aspired to be "a science, a matter of knowledge and of theoretical understanding,

[30] Throughout this book I take care with terms like structure, style, and sensibility. "Sensibility" is its own special case. When I use it in describing the naturalizing sensibility, the antinomian sensibility, and the sensibility of American Pragmatism, I mean to very explicitly distinguish these usages from the styles of liberal legalism. That is, if I use "sensibility," I am describing a disposition external to the structure of liberal legal thought. If I use "style," I am referring to a pattern of argumentative practice internal to that structure. I take the meaning of "sensibility" largely from Pierre Bourdieu's discussion of "disposition." *Outline of a Theory of Practice* (Cambridge: Cambridge University Press, 2009), p. 72.

[31] I should clarify that my reference to "naturalizing juridical science" is only dimly related to what Brian Leiter means in his arguments for "naturalizing jurisprudence." See Brian Leiter, *Naturalizing Jurisprudence: Essays on American Legal Realism and Naturalism in Legal Philosophy* (New York: Oxford University Press, 2007). As I discuss throughout this book, I locate the thesis of naturalizing juridical science in the grammar of liberal legal thought and focus on its role in harmonizing apparent antinomies in the structure of that language. My usage is semiotic. Leiter, in contrast, offers a theory of naturalizing jurisprudence as a proposition about the desirability of immersing adjudication in Quine's theory of "empirical inquiry in the natural and social sciences." Id. at 31. Leiter explained, "Naturalism in philosophy is always first a methodological view to the effect that philosophical theorizing should be continuous with empirical inquiry in the sciences. The naturalist, following Quine, rejects the idea that there could be a 'first philosophy,' a philosophical solution to problems that proceeds *a priori*, that is, prior to experience." Id. at 34. As a variation of Quine's naturalism, Leiter's naturalizing jurisprudence is probably best understood as a rebellious descendent of the Cartesian paradigm, rather than as its equivalent. For an introduction to naturalist philosophy and the squabbles over Descartes, see Jack Ritchie, *Understanding Naturalism* (Stocksfield, UK: Acumen Publishing, 2008). See also Alexander Rosenberg, "Disenchanted Naturalism," in *Contemporary Philosophical Naturalism and Its Implications* (Bana Bashour and Hans Muller, eds.) (New York: Routledge, 2014). In contrast with Leiter's view, Roberto Unger's understanding of naturalism is the one underwriting my own account of naturalizing juridical science. Unger writes, "The mistake of naturalism lies in making a promise it cannot keep: that a mind embodied in a dying organism will see the world as if that mind were universal spirit; that it will grasp the world as the world really is, through progressive convergence to the truth; and that the reward of its disinterestedness will be its penetration into the inner nature of reality, not all at once, to be sure, but slowly and cumulatively ... From the standpoint of the naturalistic error, our inevitably controversial ideas about society and culture appear to be less reliable and less penetrating than our disinterested ideas in science about nature and the universe, driven by our theories, developed with our instruments, and vindicated by our experiments." Roberto Unger, *The Self Awakened: Pragmatism Unbound* (Cambridge, MA: Harvard University Press, 2007), pp. 21–22.

not merely an applied art or practice of prudence innocent of theory."[32] In the context of liberal legal thought, naturalizing juridical science holds that legislation is political and discretionary, that adjudication is impersonal and constraining, and that in order to maintain this distinction, the work of adjudication must prove a natural harmony between the imperatives of the first two theses.

The work of proving the natural harmony between the theses of free competition and social control must be that of a juridical science, which is simply one way of saying that the work of a court should look as harmonious as it can. If the third thesis falters, if the agent doing the work of legal science loses faith in the project of harmonizing the first two theses, there would seem to be two consequences, one following from the other. The first consequence is that there would be no hiding from the raw antinomy between the two theses; or to use our musical language, the dissonance of the theses fails to find its proper resolution in consonance; or to use our painterly language, the image of law in liberal legal thought would break with the real, failing to offer that "example of moral order and human perfection." The second consequence would be that, having failed in the project of crafting a legal order that might reflect a natural one, law dissolves in the acid of politics, and with it, the rule of law.

Given this understanding of naturalizing juridical science, the stakes for liberal legalism in maintaining the integrity of its third thesis are high. Nevertheless, in its history since the Civil War, the third thesis of naturalizing legal science has had its ups and downs. In music and painting and in so much else, the naturalizing sensibility that had developed since the Renaissance slammed into a new sensibility coming into its own at the turn of the twentieth century. Often called "modernism," this was an artistic sensibility directed at undermining the idea that there were natural laws of harmony, in music, in painting, and in law. Because this new view, at least for present purposes, exposed the internal and ideological antinomies in representational efforts at demonstrating a natural harmony, I call it the antinomian sensibility.[33]

[32] Gerald Postema, "Jurisprudence, the Sociable Science," in *Metaphilosophy of Law* (Pawel Banas et al., eds.) (Oxford: Hart Publishing, 2016), p. 10.

[33] Some might suggest that I simply call this a "modern" sensibility. I prefer antinomian because of the chiastic gloss of my argument, as well as the fact that modernism, modernization, and modernity all refer to various and distinguishable aspects of that period. Furthermore, for reasons of clarity of exposition I need to keep the antinomian sensibility analytically separate from the "modern" style of liberal legal argument. On the meanings of the modern, see Hannah Arendt, *Between Past and Future: Six Exercises in*

As I discuss below, a "classic" style of liberal legal thought flourished between 1870 and World War II. It was a classic style in the sense that it approached the naturalizing sensibility in a way that very closely emulated that of the musicians and painters, blending an appearance of logical precision with *trompe l'oeil*. In the classic liberal style the name for this blending is "legal formalism."[34] When music and painting encountered the antinomian sensibility of artists like Stravinsky and Kandinsky, music and painting changed.[35] So too, in the context of liberal legalism, when lawyers, judges, and law professors encountered the antinomian sensibility in the guise of a "critical realism," did legal thought change.[36] What eventually emerged was a second structure of liberal legal thought, what I call its "modern style." The modern style had already, in fact, been around for a while. But it only came into dominance by the middle of the twentieth century. Like the classic liberal style, the modern style had its own way of navigating the three constitutive theses of liberal legal thought. Jettisoning old preoccupations with formal logic, this style combined the application of social science expertise and *trompe l'oeil*. The name for this modern blending is "legal functionalism."[37] Both legal formalism and legal functionalism shoulder the same task: naturalizing the apparent antinomy between the theses of free competition and social control, resolving their dissonance into a harmonious consonance.

The modern style of liberal legal thought triumphed until the last third of the twentieth century, at which time it entered something of a crisis. And once again, it was not a crisis for law alone. This was the time of the

Political Thought (New York: Viking Press, 1961); Fredric Jameson, *A Singular Modernity: Essays on the Ontology of the Present* (London: Verso, 2002); Theodor Adorno, *Negative Dialectics* (New York: Seabury Press, 1973); Marshall Berman, *All That Is Solid Melts into Air: The Experience of Modernity* (New York: Penguin Books, 1988); Carl Schorske, *Fin-de-Siècle Vienna: Politics and Culture* (New York: Vintage Books, 1981).

34 See, e.g., Pierre Schlag, Formalism and Realism in Ruins (Mapping the Logics of Collapse), 95 *Iowa Law Review* 195 (2010).

35 See, e.g., Paul Griffiths, *Modern Music and After* (New York: Oxford University Press, 2010); Peter Burger, *Theory of the Avant-Garde* (Minneapolis: University of Minnesota Press, 1984).

36 I follow Duncan Kennedy in his distinction between a realism that was largely negative in its critical orientation and a sociological/legal process approach that was reconstructive. While Kennedy's name for the latter is "social legal thought," I call it legal functionalism, and we both distinguish it from realism. See Duncan Kennedy, "Three Globalizations of Law and Legal Thought," in *The New Law and Development: A Critical Appraisal* (David Trubek and Alvaro Santos, eds.) (Cambridge: Cambridge University Press, 2006). For a different version of the story, see Brian Tamanaha, *Beyond the Formalist-Realist Divide: The Role of Politics in Judging* (Princeton, NJ: Princeton University Press, 2009).

37 See, e.g., Robert Gordon, Critical Legal Histories, 36 *Stanford Law Review* 57 (1984).

culture wars, the science wars, the war in Vietnam, the rise of neoliberalism, the fall of OPEC, the fall of the IMF, the rise of minimalism, the rise of the postmodern, the rise of the contemporary.[38] In the context of liberal legal thought, it was a time of despair: its third thesis was suffering an all-out assault, left, right, and center. The naturalizing juridical science of the modern style was shown up as either outright ideology or just mistaken.[39] But if the third thesis collapsed, as I suggested above, liberal legal thought might collapse with it. It certainly looked as if it would collapse, as if it were dying (there's that premature obituary again – remember, Foucault's 1960's comment about God's murderer being murdered happens here). But it didn't.

Enter *American Pragmatism:* an entrance with consequences as dramatic as they were long-lasting.[40] There is quite a lot to say about American Pragmatism, and an initial clarification is that when I say that American Pragmatism enters the legal scene, I am not referring to the philosophy of the American pragmatists, Charles Sanders Peirce, William James, John Dewey, George Herbert Mead, Richard Bernstein, Hilary Putnam, or Richard Rorty.[41] True, just as "liberalism" comes with baggage, so too does "pragmatism."[42] As I discuss later on, there is a meaningful relation between philosophical pragmatism and what I am calling American Pragmatism (in capitals), but it is the latter and not the former that is both the star of the show and its villain. As for what I mean by American Pragmatism, I characterize it as a cultural sensibility with five features. When it "arrived" on the "scene" Pragmatism was not fully formed, and I do not know when its mature formation may have taken place. But at least here in 2018, American Pragmatism is all grown up.

38 See, e.g., Fredric Jameson, *The Cultural Turn: Selected Writings on the Postmodern, 1983–88* (London: Verso, 1999); David Harvey, *The Condition of Postmodernity: An Enquiry into the Origins of Cultural Change* (Malden, UK: Blackwell, 1990).

39 See, e.g., Costas Douzinas et al., *Postmodern Jurisprudence: The Law of Texts in the Texts of Law* (New York: Routledge, 1993); Catherine MacKinnon, *Toward a Feminist Theory of the State* (Cambridge, MA: Harvard University Press, 1991); Richard Posner, *The Economics of Justice* (Cambridge, MA: Harvard University Press, 1981); Richard Epstein, The Static Conception of the Common Law, 9 *Journal of Legal Studies* 253 (1980).

40 My rendition of American Pragmatism owes much to Unger, Self Awakened, supra note 31, and Fredric Jameson, Postmodernism, or, *The Cultural Logic of Late Capitalism* (Durham: Duke University Press, 1997).

41 See, e.g., *A Companion to Pragmatism* (John Shook and Joseph Margolis, eds.) (Malden: Blackwell, 2006).

42 Justin Desautels-Stein, At War with the Eclectics: Mapping Pragmatism in Contemporary Legal Analysis, 2007 *Michigan State Law Review* 565 (2007); Justin Desautels-Stein, Pragmatic Liberalism: The Outlook of the Dead, 55 *Boston College Law Review* 1041 (2014).

Its first feature is flatness or depthlessness. This is a view about the value of offering higher-order meta-proposals or deeper discourses for social change. You shouldn't do it. In whichever register you like, whether it is up in the clouds or deep in the earth, the only place from which you should think about solving our collective problems is right here. On the flat surface of the particulars and not on the abstract level of generalities, totalities, and continuities – this is the front from which our first-order solutions to particular problems ought to be launched.

A second feature is eclecticism or pastiche. At a prior point in time (the validity of which we can never be sure), humans had faith in very particular modes of being. Perhaps, in a political thematic, people once believed that the only role for government was the protection of a very small sphere of individual rights. At another moment, they may have had faith in a view of the state that had a much larger mission and enjoyed a warrant to plan and regulate society. In the pragmatist sensibility, faith in any single view of the state is pure fantasy. What we need to do – *what works* – is borrow. We borrow the outlooks of the dead, we borrow the methods, techniques, solutions, we borrow whatever, from wherever, so long as the job gets done. And if you are skeptical, if you are freaked out about Trump or were freaked out about Obama, don't worry, this is all a work in progress. Not the cunning of reason, mind you, just slow trial and error. But take note: our pragmatic eclecticism is not ideological, there is no manifesto here; manifestos are fantasies for fanatics. Pragmatism is humble, problem-solving at work, practical, piecemeal, forward-looking, experiential learning.

A third feature of American Pragmatism is its relation with time. *When* is pragmatism? Is it "modern"? Is it "contemporary"? If "modern" suggests an antinomian stance, a subversive hostility, a manifesto, then pragmatism is definitely not that. Is it "contemporary"? Well, if that means something happening right now, sure! If it means a constant sense of renewal, renewal repeating, definitely! Or, to put this differently, we can say that American Pragmatism views itself as occupying an everlasting present, a present that is simultaneously always happening and new, in Hal Foster's words, new "in the sense that, in its very heterogeneity, much present practice seems to float free of historical determination, conceptual definition, and critical judgment."[43] With its dismissal of the "grand narrative" or "totalizing" account of a "modern" or a "contemporary," American Pragmatism is at once wildly historicist and militantly

[43] Hal Foster et al., Questionnaire on the Contemporary, 130 *October* 3 (2009).

ahistorical. The pragmatist narrative is, therefore, a progress narrative of a new and different kind.

In its first three features, American Pragmatism strikes a pose. It rejects both higher-order proposals for social change and deeper discourses intending to explain structural congruence. It rejects faith in any single view of the social world, demanding the swift exit of all grand theory, mission, and manifesto. It rejects the possibility of historical narratives or totalities. What American Pragmatism embraces is a flat, ad hoc, highly contextual approach to problem-solving; an approach that borrows relentlessly, copying-and-pasting from whatever sources look fit for duty; a view of history in which time is radically historicized, producing a progress narrative peculiarly pragmatic.

These three features combine with a fourth, and that is its glorification of technology in the name of populism. In the pragmatist sensibility, as good an insult as any is to call someone an intellectual. Intellectualism, on this view, suggests detachment from if not a disdain for those considerations that really matter "on the ground." Intellectuals are too wrapped up with views of the world already rejected: higher-order proposals, totalizations, grand narratives, and the like. These intellectual playthings are irrelevant to the real work of getting the job done, and undermine our basic commitments to social equality. (Of course, American Pragmatism's relationship with an egalitarian principle is tentative and qualified; equality only matters when it is practical.) For example, isn't it better to take problem solving away from intellectuals and give it to the "common people"? Are not social media and crowd sourcing far superior to the intellectual cadre in its capacity for innovation and its deployment of every voice wishing to speak? What was responsible for the so-called Arab Spring? The intellectual ramblings of the elite or the social action that takes place in the real world, i.e., Twitter and Facebook? For American Pragmatism, the answers are obvious. *So long as* the masses are focused on the totalizing grand narrative of pragmatism, everything will in the end be better for it.

Finally, a fifth feature of American Pragmatism is its worship of a commodified nature. Later, I will defer to Fredric Jameson's analysis of the postmodern as the wholesale consumption of the natural by the social. Here, I briefly illustrate the idea by way of Richard Posner's work on pragmatism.[44] Posner's main target is legal pragmatism, but given his

44 Richard Posner, *Law, Pragmatism, and Democracy* (Cambridge, MA: Harvard University Press, 2005).

discussions of what he calls an "everyday" pragmatism, and his effort to distinguish that everyday pragmatism from a philosophical pragmatism, I think it is relevant here. Posner has argued that a pragmatic judge is the judge who seeks what is reasonable given the particulars in a given situation. Yes, the judge ought to also consider principles and precedent, but only to the extent that these formalities are pressed into the quest for reasonableness. But, Posner asks, how will the judge know if his decision is reasonable? Is it simply a matter of his ideology, or what he ate for lunch? No, the pragmatist judge seeks out the most reasonable decision, and then unpacks reasonableness in the language of economic efficiency. As it turns out, what is reasonable is what is most efficient in terms of the allocation of wealth and resources. In this view, American Pragmatism's love affair with practicality and ad hoc problem solving is funded by an economic worldview in which, to use Arthur Okun's phrase, the transformation of nature into a great vending machine is complete.[45]

If this is a snapshot of the American Pragmatist sensibility in 2018, it is time to make way for *Pragmatic Liberalism*, the third and contemporary structure of liberal legal thought. As I mentioned above, at around the time in the 1970s when the modern liberal style was falling apart, American Pragmatism was beginning its legal turn. Now, this might mean that pragmatism was influencing the whole of the legal process in the United States, its institutions, its doctrines, and so on. And while this might be right, this is not my claim. The legal turn I am interested in is much more specific, and it involves the intersection between American Pragmatism and liberal legal thought. That critical intersection, which ended up rescuing liberal legalism from another Madman's eulogy, resulted in a third structure of liberal legal thought: pragmatic liberalism. The fundamental shift away from the classic and modern styles and into the pragmatic style relied on a surgical operation on the crucial third thesis of liberal legal thought.

The reason American Pragmatism was perfectly suited to resuscitate liberal legal thought was that American Pragmatism had a conspicuous way of dealing with the antinomian sensibility[46] – and it was precisely the return of the antinomian that was causing so much trouble for

[45] Arthur Okun, *Equality and Efficiency: The Big Tradeoff* (Washington, DC: Brookings Institution Press, 2015).

[46] See, e.g., Terry Smith, *What Is Contemporary Art?* (Chicago: University of Chicago Press, 2009); Alex Ross, *The Rest Is Noise: Listening to the Twentieth Century* (New York: Picador, 2009).

modern liberalism. In brief, the pragmatic re-articulation of the third thesis in liberal legal thought went something like the following. The old faith in naturalizing juridical science had gone out of fashion. It was no longer possible, in the wake of the readily available forms of ideology-critique, to argue with a straight face that the work of adjudication was at its best when it harmoniously (if not mathematically) resolved the dissonance of the theses of free competition and social control. The dissonance was as undeniable as it was unavoidable, especially if you were looking right at the antinomy. Pragmatic liberalism's *trompe l'oeil* focused right here. Rather than place faith in the resolution of antinomy – since that is impossible – just forget about it! Place your faith instead in Pragmatism itself, in its flat, eclectic, presentist, populist, consumerist, problem-solving platform. So long as some borrowing from among the ruins of formalism and functionalism gets the job done, solves our problems, so long as the borrowing *works*, we can place the antinomian threat in abeyance, perpetually.

If by the 1980s and 1990s American Pragmatism was unfolding everywhere in its plenitude, the best available approach for diagnosing the contemporary structure of pragmatic liberalism was already on the verge of desuetude.[47] That approach belonged to what I call the Harvard School of legal structuralism. In the 1970s, two junior professors joined the Harvard Law School faculty, Duncan Kennedy and Roberto Unger. Mentees of David Trubek, a stalwart of the law and society movement, Unger and Kennedy initiated a path-breaking approach to jurisprudence and legal history ready to interrogate legal thought in the United States.[48] Indebted to developments in French social theory and philosophy, it was an approach intended to understand the "structure" of lawyerly thinking.[49] But the Harvard School never had the chance. Besieged soon after it appeared, it collapsed in a wave of criticisms marching under the

[47] See, e.g., Duncan Kennedy, Form and Substance in Private Law Adjudication, 89 *Harvard Law Review* 1685, 1746 (1976) ("This pragmatic reasonableness on both sides conceals the fact that the disputants reached their similar positions by different routes.")

[48] Unger narrates a version of his early approach in *The Critical Legal Studies Movement: Another Time, A Greater Task* (London: Verso, 2015). One of Kennedy's origin stories is available in James R. Hackney, Jr., *Legal Intellectuals in Conversation: Reflections on the Construction of Contemporary American Legal Theory* (New York: New York University Press, 2012).

[49] Justin Desautels-Stein, Pragmatic Liberalism: The Outlook of the Dead, 55 *Boston College Law Review* 1041 (2014); Justin Desautels-Stein, The Judge and the Drone, 56 *Arizona Law Review* 117 (2014).

banners of poststructuralist[50] and deconstructionist[51] theory, condemned for having reproduced the naturalizing fallacies of liberal legalism it had meant to expose.[52] Accused of totalizing and universalizing the fundamental character of all law everywhere in a grand historical narrative, the Harvard School receded.[53] By the turn of the century, it was little more than an intellectual curiosity.[54]

The fall of the Harvard School was an unfortunate event in the jurisprudential life of the American law school. It was unfortunate for several reasons, but the most relevant reason here concerns the relatively invisible character of what it means to think like a lawyer today. As a structure of legal thought, pragmatic liberalism is built for hiding. Its constitutive features suggest the very impossibility of a structural explanation for what it might mean to think like a lawyer. If you want an answer, and you are a lawyer, a judge, or a legal academic in the sway of the pragmatist sensibility, your very training in how to think like a lawyer will mystify your inquiry, legitimating the experience as both intensely fragmentary and *just the way it is*. As this suggests, pragmatic liberalism

[50] See, e.g., Eve Taylor Bannet, *Structuralism and the Logic of Dissent* (Urbana: University of Illinois Press, 1989); Mark Poster, *Critical Theory and Poststructuralism: In Search of a Context* (Ithaca, NY: Cornell University Press,1989); Bjornar Olsen, "Roland Barthes: From Sign to Text," in *Reading Material Culture: Structuralism, Hermeneutics and Post-Structuralism* (Christophe Tilley, ed.) (Oxford: Blackwell, 1990); Jonathan Culler, *On Deconstruction: Theory and Criticism after Structuralism* (Ithaca, NY: Cornell University Press,1982).

[51] See, e.g., Harold Bloom et al., *Deconstruction and Criticism* (Continuum, 1979); J. Hillis Miller, Stevens' Rock and Criticism as Cure, II, 30 *Georgia Review* 5 (1976); Jacque Derrida, *Of Grammatology* (Gayatri Spivak, trans.) (Baltimore: The Johns Hopkins University Press, 1997); Paul de Man, *Blindness and Insight: Essays in the Rhetoric of Contemporary Criticism* (London: Routledge, 1983); Peter Dews, *Logics of Disintegration: Post-Structuralist Thought and the Claims of Critical Theory* (London: Verso, 1988).

[52] See, e.g., Joan Williams, Critical Legal Studies: The Death of Transcendence and the Rise of the New Langdells, 62 *New York University Law Review* 429 (1987).

[53] For a summary, see Gary Minda, *Postmodern Legal Movements: Law and Jurisprudence at Century's End* (New York: New York University Press, 1996).

[54] It needs clarifying that I treat "the Harvard School" and "the Critical Legal Studies Movement" as analytically separate entities. As I discuss in this book, the Harvard School represented a very particular association between structuralism and phenomenology. This intellectual alliance, to be sure, was an aspect of that larger conglomeration of critical legal studies. But CLS was much more than legal structuralism, and it enjoyed a very different history in the annals of American jurisprudence. On the passage of legal structuralism into history, see William Fisher III, Texts and Contexts: The Application to American Legal History of the Methodologies of Intellectual History, 49 *Stanford Law Review* 1065 (1997).

enacts its own, extremely sophisticated, piece of naturalizing. Perhaps we can no longer find harmony in law's immanence or in law's relation with society. Perhaps we cannot resolve the dissonance of the twin theses of free competition and social control. But these are a fool's errands. Harmony's law is a law that works, and working well is what pragmatism ensures.

I believe that for all its faults, the Harvard School continues to offer our best bet for coming to terms with what it means to think like a contemporary lawyer in the United States, and for understanding why it matters. Indeed, the account I have just summarized of liberal legal thought and its encounter with American Pragmatism is a result of my adoption and reconfiguration of the Harvard School's method, a reconfiguration requiring some explanation. In the foregoing pages I have used a number of terms of art, such as *structure*, *concept*, *jurist*, *style*, *practice*, and *context*. In the process of summarizing this book's substantial methodological intervention, I will explain each in turn. After, I answer the question of why we ought to care.

Legal Structure

The understanding of liberal legal thought presented throughout this book is *structuralist*.[55] When I say it is a presentation of liberal legal thought, I should emphasize that it is *only* about liberal legal thought. Thus, the following discussion, at least when I am talking about legal structures, legal styles, and so forth, relates exclusively to the legal language of liberalism. It is not that my discussion could not apply to other structures of legal thought. It is simply that I have conducted a study of only one, and not all.

[55] When Roman Jakobson coined the term structuralism in 1929, he wrote, "Were we to comprise the leading idea of present-day science in its most various manifestations, we could hardly find a more appropriate designation than *structuralism*. Any set of phenomena examined by contemporary science is treated not as a mechanical agglomeration but as a structural whole, and the basic task is to reveal the inner . . . laws of the system." Roman Jakobson, Romantic Panslavism – New Slavic Studies, in *Selected Writings*, II (The Hague: Mouton, 1971), p. 711. Others draw the field back to Freud, Marx, or Vico, but the typical source is Saussure. See generally, Terence Hawkes, *Structuralism and Semiotics* (London: Routledge, 2003); Peter Caws, *Structuralism: The Art of the Intelligible* 2 (Prometheus, 1988); Edith Kurzweil, *The Age of Structuralism: Levi-Strauss to Foucault* (New York: Columbia University Press, 1980). Probably the best collection of structuralist works is available in Jonathan Culler, *Structuralism: Critical Concepts in Literary and Cultural Studies*, Vols. I–IV (London: Routledge, 2006).

That caveat aside, let us turn very briefly to the structuralist method. Structuralism refers to those forms of social theory inspired by the linguist Ferdinand de Saussure and which describe social systems as language systems.[56] For the Harvard School, French structuralism counseled a semiotic approach to legal history, just as others had taken a semiotic approach to literature and so much else.[57] Kennedy and Unger suggested that we understand law as a language system, where the forms of lexical argument were governed by a deep syntax, or "grammatical understanding."[58] It is this deeper discourse, what Saussure called the *langue*, which is the structuralist's first target. As Kennedy explained, "it has been a premise of legal scholars for several generations that it is impossible to construct an autonomous logic of legal rules."[59] There is, in other words, nothing at all *logical* about a structure's underlying grammar. Nevertheless, Kennedy continued, "[legal structuralists] attempt to show an *orderliness* to the debates about policy with which we are left after the claim of neutrality."[60] Thus, legal structuralism posits from the beginning that we understand legal thought as an alogical or arational language rooted in a constraining grammar. This orderly but alogical grammar – the *langue* – is the fundamental and basic character of the structure. In addition to the structure's basic grammar is the way in which the language gets spoken. The utterance of the language is what Saussure called *parole*, and in the context of legal thought, we can take a judicial opinion as exemplary of *parole* in the linguistic structure. It is often through the study of the juridical opinion (*parole*) that the structuralist hopes to render her composition of the *langue*.

If we begin with the proposition that a legal language is constituted by a fixed and constraining grammar, we know that the speaker has to follow these grammatical rules, but we have yet to know anything of what he might say. This brings us to the *legal concept*.[61] Legal concepts are crucial, for they are the lifeblood of the fantasies we often call "bodies of

[56] Ferdinand de Saussure, *Course in General Linguistics* (Wade Baskin, trans.) (New York: Philosophical Library, 1959); Claude Levi-Strauss, *Structural Anthropology* (New York: Anchor, 1967).

[57] See, e.g., Jonathan Culler, *Structuralist Poetics: Structuralism, Linguistics and the Study of Literature* (New York: Routledge, 2002).

[58] Roberto Unger, *Knowledge and Politics* (New York: Free Press, 1975), p. 109; Duncan Kennedy, The Structure of Blackstone's Commentaries, 28 *Buffalo Law Review* 205 (1979).

[59] Kennedy, Form and Substance, supra note 47, at 1724. [60] Id.

[61] For a very different argument for the importance of the legal concept, see Henry Smith, On the Economy of Concepts in Property, 160 *University of Pennsylvania Law Review*

law." Most of us are familiar with the phrase: there is the body of property law, the body of constitutional law, the body of antitrust law, and so on. What makes up a body of law? In the structuralist view, the "body" is a red herring. The better target – the *structure* – is jerry-rigged out of a sea of legal concepts. But whereas in what we might call a conventional view that aspires to envision legal concepts as harmonious and settled, the structuralist encounters legal concepts as *open and indeterminate sites of technical knowledge*.[62] The fact that the legal concept is open and indeterminate implicates its unavoidably ideological aspect. When we confront a mature legal concept, such as the legal concept of servitudes in property law, we confront anything but a harmonious and settled "module" in the "body" of property law. Instead, we see nothing but conflicting choices among conflicting rules. The legal concept, in many ways, is itself a structure of antinomies. The fact that it is at the same time a site of technical knowledge implicates its linguistic specificity. To know how to speak the language of the legal concept, you must be more than a painter or a musician or a sociologist or a mathematician. You need to be a jurist, knowing the technical rules of the concept, sometimes obvious, sometimes arcane. The legal concept's technical knowledge is its doctrinal content. Putting the two facets together, we can say that a legal concept is an open and antinomian space for ideological conflict over certain fragments of technical knowledge.

The structural grammar of a legal language does not control which concepts are included in the "body of law," and more importantly, the grammar does not control how you should go about making your ideological choices for one rule or one interpretation as against another. What the grammar does instead is control the ways, forms, and techniques in which you go about making your choices. These "ways," as a result, are synonymous with neither *structure* nor *concept*. So far I have been referring to how "you" might navigate the grammar or the concept. That needs to end. From this point forward, I will refer instead to one of two figures: the *structuralist* and the *jurist*. The structuralist is the composer of the composition. It is she that creates both the presentation of the structure of legal thought, and the presentation of the jurist's performance in the structure. The jurist, in contrast, is the agent at work within the

2097 (2012); Henry Smith, The Language of Property: Form, Context, and Audience, 55 *Stanford Law Review* 1105 (2003).

[62] For a recent analysis waged in a similar spirit, if not in name, see David Kennedy, *World of Struggle: How Power, Law, and Expertise Shape Global Political Economy* (Princeton, NJ: Princeton University Press, 2016).

structure, the person performing from inside the language of a structure of legal thought. A jurist is any person trained in the know-how of legal thought.

The Jurisprudence of Style

What explains the jurist's navigation of grammar, concept, and conclusion in a given structure of legal thought? My answer is *style*.[63] A legal style is the rhetorical pathway linking grammar, rule, and conclusion in an argumentative justification. When the style is persuasive, the jurist experiences an effect of legal necessity. This means that the jurist has made a choice in the ideological terrain of the legal concept and felt that if he were to make any other choice, it could be condemned as activism. If we experience the effect of legal necessity, in other words, we feel that we could have made no other choice in good conscience. This is the task of legal style, to produce a justification for one choice of rule over another in the midst of antinomy.[64] Throughout the book, I refer to the domain of legal style as a *practice of legal argument*. Practices of legal argument give us an understanding and name for legal style. Unlike the open and indeterminate space of the legal concept, the practices of legal argument are closed. Indeed, in liberal legal thought the so-called bodies of law are filled out by an expansive list of open-ended legal concepts. In contrast, in liberal legal thought there are only three basic styles of argumentative practice. And these three basic styles, flowing as they do from the background grammar and into foregrounded analysis, dominate everything about the jurist's experience of the structure.

This reference to background and foreground suggests an important aspect of the jurisprudence of style, and it here that the Harvard School's

[63] For earlier discussions, see Horkheimer and Adorno, supra note 16, at 102–103; Jameson, Postmodern, supra note 40; Roland Barthes, *Writing Degree Zero* (New York: Hill and Wang, 1968); Stanley Fish, *Doing What Comes Naturally: Change, Rhetoric, and the Practice of Theory in Literary and Legal Studies* (Durham, NC: Duke University Press; 1990); Arthur Danto, *After the End of Art: Contemporary Art and the Pale of History* (Princeton, NJ: Princeton University Press); Stephen Ullman, *Language and Style: Collected Papers by Stephen Ullman* (Oxford: Oxford University Press, 1964); *Style, Society, and Person: Archaeological and Ethnological Perspectives* (Christopher Carr and Jill Neitzel, eds. (New York: Plenum Press, 1995). I suspect that the novelty of my use of style comes from the effort to bridge the phenomenological and semiotic elements of the legal structure. To that end, perhaps Maurice Merleau-Ponty is the best precedent. *Phenomenology of Perception* (London: Routledge, 1962), p. 327. This is my argument in Chapter 3.

[64] Kennedy, A Critique, supra note 8, at 134–136.

phenomenological influence is most noticeable.[65] A jurist's argumentative practice exists in a deep, prereflective understanding – this is background practice – as well as at a rational, conscious calculation of legal analysis. If the jurist is a master, a person with many years of experience and familiarity with his legal world, in his background practice the jurist operates in a way analogous to an expert soccer player "in the zone." The jurist is wholly absorbed in the legal materials, "flowing" from move to move in which "the equipmental contexture" of the legal structure is unobtrusive, unthematized, and unthought.[66] Indeed, in this condition of background mastery there is little sense in trying to distinguish between the jurist's consciousness and the legal material; they exist as a deep unity. Hubert Dreyfus describes background practice in the following way, usefully contrasting it with the practices of foreground analysis:

> From the perspective of the skilled coper absorbed in the solicitation of a familiar affordance, the affording object, as Heidegger puts it, "withdraws." We need not even be aware of the solicitations to go out *as* solicitations. Thanks to our background familiarity, when it is appropriate to leave [a room], we are simply drawn to go out. In general, the absorbed coper is directly drawn by each solicitation in an appropriate way: the chairs draw him to sit on them, the floorboards to walk on them, the walls may draw him to hang pictures on them, the windows to open them, and the door may draw him to go out. It might seem an argument for the pervasiveness of [foregrounded conceptual thinking] that we often have to use concepts to find our way about an unfamiliar situation. But, as in an unfamiliar city, we have to start to find our way by using concepts, but our situation gradually comes to make sense to us in a non-conceptual way as we learn our way around in it. Once our situation becomes familiar our skilled dispositions respond directly to the solicitations of the relevant affordances. Indeed, once a skill is acquired, concepts used in learning the skill need play no further role.[67]

I explore the relation between background and foreground further below,[68] but most of the necessary points are all loaded here in this passage. The master jurist is, as Dreyfus says, a skilled coper absorbed in the solicitation of familiar affordances.[69] The master jurist is skilled

[65] A clear example is Duncan Kennedy, Freedom and Constraint in Adjudication: A Critical Phenomenology, 36 *Journal of Legal Education* 518 (1986).

[66] Martin Heidegger, *Basic Problems of Phenomenology* (Bloomington: Indiana University Press, 1982), p. 163.

[67] Hubert Dreyfus, *The Myth of the Pervasiveness of the Mental, in Mind, Reason, and Being-in-the-World* (Joseph Schear, ed.) (London: Routledge, 2013), p. 18.

[68] A fun discussion of foreground and background is Douglas Hofstadter, *Gödel, Escher, Bach: An Eternal Golden Braid* (New York: Vintage Books, 1980), pp. 64–81. More on point, however, is the discussion in Kennedy, A Critique, supra note 8, at 247–263.

[69] Dreyfus here draws from the work of J. J. Gibson, *The Ecological Approach to Visual Perception* (Hillsdale, NJ: Laurence Erlbaum Associates, 1986).

and the affordances (i.e., the equipmental contexture of the legal materials) are familiar because he has been trained and has had many opportunities for practice. "Absorbed coping," as I discuss below, relates to the subject-object distinction and the phenomenological rejection of that distinction.[70] Rather than think of the jurist receiving a given set of rational concepts and assumptions from which to work, in the jurisprudence of style we think of the jurist's background practice as a unified and holistic absorption between legal consciousness and legal material. As the legal materials solicit the jurist to move in particular directions, the jurist "copes" with these solicitations in the same way that the soccer player copes with the equipmental contexture of the field, the players, the ball, the climate, and so on. It is a graceful flow. But the graceful flow of the background practice breaks down for the jurist once the affordances become unfamiliar. Thus, a jurist facing a takings problem for the first time, or with little experience in claims of anticompetitive behavior, shifts away from the prereflective background practice and into the foregrounded analysis of antinomy and ideological choice. It is legal style that contrapuntally ferries the jurist from deep background practice and into the foreground, and depending on how skillful and absorbed our jurist happens to be, the style will be better or worse at producing its *coup de grace*: the experience of legal necessity.

I should note here that among the criticisms leveled at the Harvard School was its tendency, most particularly in the work of Duncan Kennedy, to treat structuralism and phenomenology as complementary when they seemed much more likely to be not.[71] And while it is true that my own account of the relation between structure and style differs with Kennedy's, I am surely open to similar complaints. Thankfully, however, I have never found these complaints persuasive, at least in the context of legal thought. Rather than see structuralism as representing the object and phenomenology as representing the subject in a flimsy reproduction of the Cartesian model, I take the union of structure and style to present a univocal rejection of that model. What's more, whereas *structure* speaks to the linguistic architecture of the system, it says nothing about the ways in which the speaker navigates that system. And in legal thought,

[70] See also Hubert Dreyfus, *Skillful Coping: Essays on the Phenomenology of Every Day Perception and Action* (Oxford: Oxford University Press, 2014).

[71] See, e.g., Jacque Derrida, *Speech and Phenomena: And Other Essays on Husserl's Theory of Signs* (Chicago: Northwestern University Press, 1973); Theodor Adorno, *The Jargon of Authenticity* (London: Routledge Classics, 2003); David Rasmussen, Issues in Phenomenology and Critical Theory, in *Crosscurrents in Phenomenology* (Ronald Bruzina and Bruce Wilshire, eds.) (The Hague: Martinus Nijhoff, 1978).

this is a crucial issue: we have the jurist, and we must make sense of her.[72]

In this investigation of the concrete practices at play in that intermediate space between *langue* and *parole*, I heartily agree with the anthropologist Philippe Descola's recent recovery of the structuralist approach.[73] Descola rightly argues that a successful structuralism must do two things at once: explain the deep constitutive features at work in the system, as well as the more particular practices that spring from but fail to be determined by those constitutive features.[74] This involves the structuralist in both composing the linguistic regularities as well as those practices in the phenomenology of the target, which in this case is legal thought.[75] He goes on:

> It seems that what a structural analysis reveals, when well conducted, is a way of assessing an understanding of the schematization of experience carried out by the members of a collectivity and the manner in which this serves as a framework for the explicit codification systems to which its members adhere. What guarantees that the formal mechanism constructed by the analyst does indeed reveal certain underlying characteristics of the social system he is trying to understand is the fact that those characteristics express not so much universal properties of the human mind – or only do so at a very abstract level – but rather the tacit frameworks and procedures of objectivization by means of which the actors in the system themselves organize their relations to the world and Others. In between the model, or action, and the structure, the scheme constitutes an interface that is both concrete, since it is incorporated in individuals and put to work in their practices, and particularized, since it reflects some objective property of the relations to existing beings.[76]

This passage raises a final point worth emphasizing in this summary of the jurisprudence of style. This concerns the "concreteness" of practice.[77] As I have already suggested, a constant refrain in the pragmatist

[72] For discussion, see Pierre Schlag, The Problem of the Subject, 69 *Texas Law Review* 1627 (1991). See also Julia Kristeva, "The Speaking Subject," in *On Signs* (Marshall Blonsky, ed.) (Baltimore: The Johns Hopkins University Press, 1985).

[73] Philippe Descola, *Beyond Nature and Culture* (Chicago: University of Chicago Press, 2013). I should probably clarify: while I largely agree with much of Descola's perspective on structuralism, I am less convinced with respect to his application of it. For discussion, see Eduardo Viveiros de Castro, *Cannibal Metaphysics: For a Post-Structural Anthropology* (Minneapolis: Univocal Publishing, 2014); Peter Skafish, The Descola Variations: The Ontological Geography of Beyond Nature and Culture, 25 *Qui Parle* 65 (2016).

[74] Descola, supra note 73, at 93. [75] Id. at 99. [76] Id. at 110.

[77] An interesting collection primarily in the vein of analytic philosophy is *Theory and Practice (NOMOS XXXVIII)* (Ian Shapiro and Judith Wagner DeCew, eds.) (New York: New York University Press, 1995).

sensibility is a preference for the concrete, for the grounded, for the practical over the theoretical. Putting aside for now general questions about how to define "theory" in this dualism, or what a practical proposal or problem could even mean, bereft of "thought," I only want in this introductory space to refer to my own usage of thought and practice in the context of structure and style. Throughout this book I refer to the "structure" or "style" of liberal legal thought. Structure refers to the grammatical totality, whereas style refers to the jurist's operation of the grammar. Liberal legal *thought*, however, references both structure and style, encompassing the deep grammar of the *langue*, the lexical sea of technical and indeterminate legal concepts, and the rhetorical patterns of argumentative practice. The whole construct, in other words, is a composition of legal thought.

At the same time, that whole construct defines this composition of legal thought in terms of practice, from top to bottom. The deep grammar is not a set of principles; it is a set of prereflective background practices. They are prereflective, that is, if we are dealing with a master jurist, a person already skilled in coping with the affordances of the legal equipment. Depending on the jurist's familiarity with the language, these background practices extend right up and through the lexicon. For less skilled jurists, the background practices break down in the gaps and "hard cases," giving way to a foregrounded rational calculation of ideological influence. Either way, in the case of the master or the amateur, liberal legal *thought* is never experienced as anything other than a legal *practice*. And practices, even our pragmatist interlocutors will concede, are at least *prima facie* concrete.

The Legal Context

If in this methodological précis I have touched on its chief characteristics of structure and style, there is a third still to reckon with. This is the historical characteristic, and it concerns the historiographic dimension of legal structuralism. The question can be framed in the following way. Take as a given that we successfully establish a structure of liberal legal thought, with its recurring styles of legal argument. When did this structure come into being? What are its origins? In what contexts did the structure first emerge? Have those contexts changed since their inception, and if so, how have these changes caused the structure itself to change? These questions are familiar in the current conjuncture of legal history writing, and we might collect them under the heading of "contextualism."[78] The contextualist historian, as the name suggests, seeks a context in which to place her historical object. The context gives the object its best understanding, as well as the force for properly historicizing that object. The process of historicization is critical, for it supports the historian's claim that this object came into being at some point in time, but that it might have easily come about in some other way, given an alternate set of circumstances. Historicist contextualism, in other words, is the key ingredient in blessing historical narratives with contingency and accuracy.[79]

Among the complaints raised in the wake of the Harvard School's first round of works was that, as legal histories, they failed to provide the legal structure with sufficient context.[80] For example, we might like to see the socioeconomic context in which the legal structure emerged, or the socioeconomic factors that enable the structure to continue along. Or we might look instead at the forms of racial or gendered domination that brought the structure into being. Or we might ask of the relation between war and colonization and the origins of liberal legal thought. Or we might prefer less general contexts and explore the particulars, asking how particular people with particular projects wrought the foundations of a liberal legal language. Or we might continue in this vein, but find that in the pursuit of political power in its viral contexts, there was never any such thing as liberal legal thought in the first place. Of course, we could almost endlessly multiply the historical contexts in which we might place the legal structure, and, no doubt, often to great effect. My assumption is that there is no single context in which the history of liberal legal thought must be told, and that most historical contexts ought to be edifying – even those, maybe even especially those, that deny the very existence of liberal legal thought.

78 Christopher Tomlins, History in the American Juridical Field: Narrative, Justification, and Explanation, 16 *Yale Journal Law & Humanities* 323 (2004); Christopher Tomlins, The Strait Gate: The Past, History, and Legal Scholarship, 5 *Law, Culture, and the Humanities* 11 (2009).

79 For critiques of the view, see Peter Gordon, "Contextualism and Criticism in the History of Ideas," in *Rethinking Modern European Intellectual History* (Darrin McMahon and Samuel Moyn, eds.) (New York: Oxford University Press, 2014); Martin Jay, *Force Fields: Between Intellectual History and Cultural Critique* (New York: Routledge, 1993).

80 Although written much later, as a review of the 2006 publication of Kennedy's Rise and Fall, Barry Cushman's essay is a good example. Barry Cushman, The Structure of Classical Public Law, 75 *University of Chicago Law Review* 1917 (2008). See also Daniel Ernst, The Critical Tradition in the Writing of American History, 102 *Yale Law Journal* 1019 (1993).

What I find most intriguing about our historicist contextualism is, in its catholic celebration of every imaginable context in which to tell a legal history, its tendency to ignore the *legal context*.[81] No doubt, suggesting that the legal historian has somehow missed the legal context will, at first, come as something of a shock. Is not the legal historian focused *exactly* on the legal context, but working from the assumption that a focus on law on its own is insufficient for writing a legal history? My answer is yes, that is certainly the legal historian's basic assumption – that a narrow focus on law on its own makes for bad historiography.[82] This is, after all, the sort of legal history that makes legal historians cringe, seeing it everywhere from Part I of the conventional law review article to the legal brief to the newspaper article. This is the evolutionary story of legal rules changing over time. But my answer is also no, for as I hope my discussion has already made clear, a focus on doctrine or institutions or the legal process is *not* a focus on legal context.

To clarify, I need to suggest two ways in which the idea of "legal context" might be misunderstood. The first mistake equates legal context with legal doctrine, which tends to deal almost entirely with the shifting rules of the legal concept. But as I have already suggested, legal thought covers much more than the rule-indeterminacy of the concept; it also covers the deep grammar and the styles of argumentative practice, which, at least from the structuralist point of view, is where the action is. The second mistake equates the legal context with what we might call the entire universe of Law, a universe that extends beyond the structure of legal thought I am describing. This universe includes the strategies and obstacles facing the public defender, to the financial dynamics of deal lawyers working at giant firms, to the electoral college, to whatever institutional process you can imagine. When I speak of the legal context, I am not referring to this liquid sphere of legality, the bounds of which are neither known nor necessary.

Rather, when I say that historicist contextualism has missed the legal context, I mean the legal context of legal thought. And while it is understandable why the Harvard School was criticized for writing legal histories that were insufficiently contextualized, a reorientation toward the

[81] Though not in pursuit of legal history at all, the historian that has had the greatest influence on my thinking here is Hayden White. See, e.g., Hayden White, *Metahistory: The Historical Imagination in Nineteenth Century Europe* (Baltimore: Johns Hopkins University Press, 1975).

[82] See, e.g., Laura Kalman, Border Patrol: Reflections on the Turn to History in Legal Scholarship, 66 *Fordham Law Review* 87 (1997).

context of legal thought suggests why these criticisms were certainly right in their own terms, but off the mark in structuralist terms. Or to say that differently, if the idea is that in order to properly historicize a legal object, the history needs to put that object in a nonlegal context or a more expansive doctrinal context, then the critics were surely right. On the other hand, if we can say that we write a structuralist history when we take doctrine and put it in the context of legal thought, then this is surely a history that is as historicized and contextualist as any other. Well, almost. For while the structuralist historian works to put legal doctrine in the historical context of legal thought (its grammars and styles and lexicon, etc.), the structuralist historian rejects the intellectual historian's quest for origins or genealogies,[83] trading in explanations for *why* structures change for *how* structures change.[84]

The Problem with Pragmatism

Thus far I have described what it means to think like a lawyer in the context of liberal legal thought, and a methodological approach that supports that description. But why care? Of what practical use is a structuralist history of liberal legal thought? In what normative directions can it point? Unfortunately, if these are your reasons for caring, you will likely find my answers disappointing. For in each of these registers – the registers of practical use and normative direction – legal structuralism suffers from a vital disconnect. On the structuralist view, the register of practical use is so caught up in the pragmatist sensibility that it becomes tautological: we care about practical use because we care about practical use. American Pragmatism is not, in other words, a reason to care about structuralism; at least in this book, structuralism targets the problem-solving pastiche of American Pragmatism, and neither defends it nor seeks comfort in it. As for the register of normative direction, it too is a hostage in the

83 Foucault remains helpful in demonstrating the difference between a vertical, noncausal, structural history and a horizontal, genealogical history that disdains origins but is still after causes. See, e.g., his *Archaeology of Knowledge* and *The Order of Things* for the former, and his work on genealogy for the latter. For discussion, see Roger Chartier, *The Chimera of the Origin: Archeology, Cultural History, and the French Revolution, in Foucault and the Writing of History* (Jan Goldstein, ed. (Cambridge: Blackwell, 1994); Colin Koopman, *Genealogy as Critique: Foucault and the Problems of Modernity* (Bloomington: Indiana University Press, 2013).

84 A wonderful legal example is Martti Koskenniemi, *From Apology to Utopia: The Structure of International Legal Argument* (Cambridge: Cambridge University Press, 2006).

small-mindedness of American Pragmatism. American pragmatism assaults our creative and imaginative powers, cabining our abilities to think beyond liberalism's most deadened structures of thought.

The case for structuralism builds on a particular hope. That hope is that in coming to grips with the structure and style of pragmatic liberalism, we might finally face some hard choices, choices mystified for a generation. In his study of the naturalizing sensibility, Roland Barthes argued that structuralism "has taught us that myth has the task of giving a historical intention a natural justification, and making contingency appear eternal."[85] The principal figures in this process, Barthes continued, were inoculation, tautology, and the privation of history.[86] Pragmatic liberalism deploys these figures systematically, and the structuralist approach helps illuminate these processes. As I discuss at the book's end, I call these the structural, conceptual, and historical illusions. Each in their own way mystifies the jurist, legitimates faith in the pragmatist sensibility, and restricts those creative powers that might otherwise be placed in the service of social transformation. From the perspective of structuralism, we come to see that living with a practical, problem-solving faith is living on borrowed time.

The way forward is as follows. Part I details the structuralist method. It begins in Chapter 1 with a summary description of the Harvard School's initial elaboration of liberal legalism, and the Harvard School's fall in the wake of poststructuralist jurisprudence. Chapters 2 and 3 offer my reworking of the Harvard School's basic assumptions. The argument consolidates the structuralist view of liberal legal thought, from the constitutive antinomies of the background grammar to the style of the jurist in the practice of legal argument. Furthermore, I describe the structuralist approach to legal history, placing liberal legal thought in time. I suggest that while legal structuralism does in fact boast a contextualist historiography, it is a contextualism alien to most forms of contemporary practice. All in all, Part I's approach to structure, style, and history is an attempt to read Duncan Kennedy and Roberto Unger's project in the 1970s through the lens of Roland Barthes, Michel Foucault, and Maurice Merleau-Ponty, yielding a structuralist approach for today.

[85] Roland Barthes, *Mythologies: The Complete Edition, in a New Translation* (Richard Howard and Annette Lavers, trans.) (New York: Hill and Wang, 2013), p. 254.

[86] Id. at 267.

Part II turns from the book's method to its target, liberal legal thought, ranging from 1870 to 1970. Chapter 4 does double duty, reintroducing the discussion of the structure of liberal legalism from Chapter 1, as well as moving into an analysis of liberal legalism's classic style. What Chapter 4 does for the classic style, Chapter 5 does for the modern. In these two chapters the focus is entirely on the jurist's practice of legal argument in the context of the liberal theses of free competition and social control. Thus, while it is tempting to say that these chapters attempt a fragmentary coverage of "property law," "constitutional law," and "antitrust law," the better description is that they cover the juridical arguments about the market as a legal concept, as rendered in the language of liberal legalism. Chapter 6 reviews the structure and style of argument as detailed in the prior two chapters and historicizes the legal context.

Part III continues the book's analysis of liberal legalism, but shifts into a third and "contemporary" style of liberal practice, what I have been calling pragmatic liberalism. Chapter 7 begins the approach to pragmatic liberalism by way of an introduction to American Pragmatism. Chapter 7, as a result, is largely about developments taking place "outside" liberal legal thought: music, painting, and philosophy. American Pragmatism, in my telling, is a cultural sensibility that, in and around the 1970s, comes into contact with liberal legal thought. In order to understand this "contact" in the context of my argument, I describe American Pragmatism through a discussion of the naturalizing sensibility, the antinomian sensibility, and the pragmatist sensibility that followed. Chapter 8 turns to the union of the pragmatic sensibility and liberal legal thought: pragmatic liberalism. Following the analytical form of Chapters 4 and 5, Chapter 8 returns to the juridical practice of argument in the context of the market as a legal concept. Chapter 9 offers a criticism of pragmatic liberalism, focusing on the three illusions mentioned above: the structural, the conceptual, and the historical.

Finally, the book ends with a Coda in which Nietzsche's Madman returns only to encounter a Madman of another father, Soren Kierkegaard. This second Madman, much like the first, is defined in terms of an experience with the liberal view of "subjective truth," a willingness to transcend human subjectivity in order to see the world as God might see it, in its universal, eternal, timeless state. Nietzsche's Madman renounced this experience and in the process of doing so pronounced the death of God. The second Madman, Kierkegaard's Knight of Faith, finds himself in a similar position. Convinced of the emptiness of the liberal worldview, the Knight of Faith similarly renounces bourgeois belief. But Kierkegaard's crazy is not Nietzsche's crazy. For whereas Nietzsche madness leaves liberalism in silence, the Knight of Faith speaks.

PART I

LEGAL STRUCTURALISM

I

The Rise and Fall of the Harvard School

What was structuralism? Who were the structuralists? Why did they come, and what did they want? A generation after structuralism first took Paris by storm, there remains little agreement about whether structuralism was a movement or something else, who embraced the name and who recanted, and of what use the label "structuralism" might have after the apparent victories of a *post*structuralism.[1] In any case, the intellectual history of structuralism coalesces around a common starting point, and the naming of names: Claude Lévi-Strauss, Roman Jacobson, Roland Barthes, Michel Foucault, Jacque Lacan, Jean Piaget, Louis Althusser, and Paul Ricoeur fill the typical list.[2] These names signal a certain methodological posture with respect to the "the human sciences," and indeed, there is no single domain (save linguistics) in which structuralism might have been thought of as having an indigenous beginning. In its heyday, structuralism travelled far and wide, visiting the lands of anthropology, history, classics, religion, literature, philosophy, psychology, and sociology, to name a few. Nevertheless, canons are slippery. "Barthes might have once adhered to structuralism, but certainly not after *S/Z*!" "Foucault despised structuralism, he can't be on the list!" "Ricoeur was a phenomenologist!" And so on.

Thus, while I readily concede that the list of theorists and the list of disciplines are moving targets, there is a point on which virtually all sides

[1] See Phillip Lewis, "The Post-Structuralist Condition," in *Structuralism: Critical Concepts in Literary and Cultural Studies* (Johnathan Culler, ed.) (London: Routledge, 2006).

[2] François Dosse presents a helpful overview in *History of Structuralism*, Vols. I and II (Deborah Glassman, trans.) (Minneapolis: University of Minnesota Press, 1998).

agree. This is an agreement about what is not and has never been listed: Law. An effect of this chapter, I hope, is to expand those lists a bit, for as I argue below, Duncan Kennedy and Roberto Unger founded what I will call the Harvard School of legal structuralism.

The Harvard School of legal structuralism came into being between 1975 and 1984. Its principal agents were junior professors Duncan Kennedy and Roberto Unger, each hired in the early 1970s, though others like Gerald Frug and David Kennedy, and some not even based in the United States, such as Martti Koskenniemi, played important supporting roles.[3] My argument is that the Harvard School was a manifestation of the structuralist impulse originating in France and which eventually made its way to the United States, most famously at the Johns Hopkins Conference of 1966.[4] But before we arrive at the Harvard Law School of the 1970s and bear witness to the particular influence of Paris on Cambridge, I will recount just a bit of the relevant intellectual context. This bit of recounting is hardly exhaustive, and I have tailored it with the narrow purpose of introducing the Harvard School's approach to legal structuralism.

On the Road to Legal Structuralism

The French intellectual universe of the twentieth century is sometimes imagined as a series of stellar lights passing in the night sky. If it is a postwar story, the first light to illuminate the scene is the one called Jean-Paul Sartre. Sartre's existential philosophy is then eclipsed by the constellation of Claude Lévi-Strauss's structural anthropology, which is in turn swallowed up in the glare of Jacque Derrida's supernova that was deconstruction.[5] But hovering in and around all of this like so much dark matter was a reconceived idea of language,[6] and in particular, the influence of the Swiss linguist Ferdinand de Saussure's *Course on General*

[3] It is worth emphasizing once again that I am not listing those founding members of the critical legal studies movement. My focus is only on those scholars developing structuralist legal analysis.

[4] The papers are collected in *The Structuralist Controversy: The Languages of Criticism and the Sciences of Man* (Richard Macksey and Eugenio Donato, eds.) (Baltimore: The Johns Hopkins University Press, 2007).

[5] For a different chronology, see Peter Gordon, "Hammer without a Master: French Phenomenology and the Origins of Deconstruction (or, How Derrida Read Heidegger)," in *Histories of Postmodernism* (Mark Bevir et al., eds.) (London: Routledge, 2008).

[6] See, e.g., *The Linguistic Turn: Essays in Philosophical Method* (Richard Rorty, ed.) (Chicago: University of Chicago Press, 1967); Terry Eagleton, *Literary Theory: An Introduction* (Minneapolis: University of Minnesota Press, 2008).

Linguistics.[7] First put into print by Saussure's students in 1916, Saussure's *Course* offered a new platform for understanding the semiology of language systems, and it is here that structuralism is typically thought to begin.[8] Indeed, as the historian François Dosse has suggested, "In order to understand the structuralist paradigm ... we have to begin with the Saussurean break, since an entire generation read and considered [the *Course*] to be the founding moment."[9]

For present purposes, Saussure's two distinctions of *langue/parole* and synchronic/diachronic are the most relevant. *Langue* refers to the fundamental rules of syntax shaping the grammatical horizon of the linguistic structure. As Saussure explained, the *langue* represents "the whole set of linguistic habits which allow an individual to understand and be understood."[10] Denying it a natural or necessary character, Saussure situated the *langue* as a social construction with a determinate scope. Its contents were fixed and closed, and in the background context of the system, the *langue* governed the forms in which the language was uttered.[11] In contrast is *parole*, the open, arbitrary, and individually created speech-act.[12] Thus, where *langue* is prereflective, preconceptual, and often out of mind, *parole* is the surface manifestation. Where *langue* is unnoticed syntax, *parole* is deliberate utterance. Where *langue* represents a field of coercion, *parole* is free.[13]

[7] Ferdinand de Saussure, *Course in General Linguistics* (Wade Baskin, trans.) (New York: Philosophical Library, 1959), p. 77. See also, John Sturrock, *Structuralism* (Malden, UK: Wiley-Blackwell, 2003), pp. 6–10; *Critical Theory: A Reader* (Douglas Tallack, ed.) (New York: Harvester Wheatsheaf, 1995), p. 11. See also Eero Tarasti, *Existential Semiotics* (Bloomington: Indiana University Press, 2001).

[8] Jonathan Culler, *Ferdinand de Saussure* (Ithaca, NY: Cornell University Press, 1986); John Joseph, *Saussure* (Oxford: Oxford University Press, 2012); Anthony Giddens, *Central Problems in Social Theory: Action, Structure, and Contradiction in Social Analysis* (Berkeley, University of California Press, 1979), p. 10.

[9] Dosse, History of Structuralism, supra note 2, at 45.

[10] Saussure, Course in General Linguistics, supra note 7, at 77.

[11] Id. at 73. ("A language constitutes a system. In this one respect... language is not completely arbitrary but is ruled to some extent by logic; it is here also, however, that the inability of the masses to transform it becomes apparent. The system is a complex mechanism that can be grasped only through reflection; the very ones who use it daily are ignorant of it.")

[12] Id. at 76. ("Nothing could be more complex than [the way in which language evolves]. As it is a product of both the social force and time, no one can change anything in it, and on the other hand, the arbitrariness of its signs theoretically entails the freedom of establishing just any relationship between phonetic substance and ideas.")

[13] Rosalind Coward and John Ellis, *Language and Materialism: Developments in Semiology and the Theory of the Subject* (London: Routledge, 1977), p. 12.

If the *langue* is only discoverable through a study of *parole*, how do we conduct the study? Historically, looking at the development of English, or French, or whatever, in evolutionary time? How much time? How do we fix the limits of study? It is here that we encounter Saussure's second distinction, the distinction between synchronic and diachronic analysis.[14] For some, diachronic study was the only way to understand how languages formed, through historical, functionalist, and evolutionary treatments of the way in which language changed over time.[15] This is the diachronic search for historical origins, where it all started, and what happened from there.[16] Saussure contrasted this with the synchronic, in which the totality of the language was studied in series of frozen moments, snapshots in time.[17] To be sure, Saussure recognized that the agent's *parole* necessarily changes the *langue* over time. But the structuralist method, in its search for a total understanding of the system, bracketed out temporal links in a causal chain in favor of a static and relational analysis of the system. Thus, language was to be "explained" neither by the "real" world to which language seemed to be related, nor by the agent's operation of the language over time. Rather, linguistic explanation followed purely through reference to relations in the interspace between a background system of norms and the uttered manifestations made possible by that background. As Jonathan Culler put it, "despite pretensions to causal analysis, one might say that what is being offered is a structural rather than a causal explanation: one attempts to show why a particular action has a significance by relating it to the system of underlying functions, norms, and categories which make it possible."[18]

In the starry night of the French 1960s, it was increasingly common to analyze social practices in the light of Saussure's linguistic devices. This socio-linguistic posture had been a work in progress since World War II, with Lévi-Strauss at the helm.[19] In his wake, Saussure's semiology was taken beyond linguistics and applied to much of the social world, including the rituals of familial relations, myth-making, cuisine, and poetry, among other things.[20] That is, the structuralist took a given field, say

[14] Saussure, General Course in Linguistics, supra note 7, at 79–100.

[15] Id. [16] Id. [17] Id. at 82.

[18] Culler, Ferdinand de Saussure, supra note 8, at 88.

[19] See, e.g., Claude Lévi-Strauss, *Structural Anthropology* (New York: Anchor Books, 1967); Claude Lévi-Strauss, *The Savage Mind* (Chicago: University of Chicago Press, 1966). For discussion, see Edmund Leach, "Structuralism in Social Anthropology," in *Structuralism: An Introduction* (David Robey, ed.) (Oxford: Clarendon Press, 1973).

[20] See, e.g., *The Structuralists: From Marx to Lévi-Strauss* (Richard T. De George and Fernande M. De George, eds.) (New York: Anchor Books, 1972), p. ix.

fashion, and suggested that the style of dress in a particular community could be explained by way of Saussure's view of the language system.[21] Just as French is governed by a deep totality of coding means (*langue*), Barthes suggested that there was a language of fashion – fashion was *uttered* through the medium of dress.[22] And just as there are a virtually unlimited number of French utterances, so too are there many ways to dress.

But structuralism was not simply a proxy for the obvious sense of open-endedness apparent in our choices to say certain things or wear certain outfits. More importantly, structuralism was also an argument about the background *constraints* on what we say, or what we wear. These limits are found in the structure's *langue*, governing and shaping the surface-level forms in ways that were almost always invisible to the user of the grammar, at least when everything was working normally. And so, to repeat, structuralists sought to explain what appeared to be random social practices as constituted and controlled by these backgrounded grammars. As Culler explained, "structuralism thus involves the attempt to spell out, explicitly, what members of a culture know without knowing it: the structures that underlie cultural practice, and make possible, for instance, people's judgments about what is ordinary, strange, meaningful, or meaningless."[23]

What the structuralists were *not* generally interested in explaining, however, was the role of individual agency, the moment of existential decision that might operate from within the structure.[24] And it is here that the conflict between structuralism and existential phenomenology seemed its most severe. For whereas structuralist analysis seemed decisively in favor of dehumanizing the analysis of structure and agent,

[21] For the broad strokes, see Gilles Deleuze, "How Do We Recognize Structuralism?" in *The Two-Fold Thought of Deleuze and Guattari: Intersections and Animations* (Charles J. Stivale, ed.) (New York: Guilford Press, 1998), p. 254.

[22] Jonathan Culler, "Introduction," in *Structuralism: Critical Concepts in Literary and Cultural Studies* (Johnathan Culler, ed.) (London: Routledge, 2006), p. 3 ("To investigate neckties, for instance, structuralism would attempt to reconstruct (a) the structure of neckties themselves (the oppositions – wide/narrow, loud/subdued – that enable different sorts of neckties to bear different meanings for members of a culture) and (b) the underlying 'vestimentary' structures or system of a given culture (how do neckties relate to other items of clothing and the wearing of neckties to other socially-coded actions?)"). See also Roland Barthes, *The Fashion System* (Matthew Ward and Richard Howard, trans.) (Berkeley: University of California Press, 1990).

[23] Culler, supra note 22, at 3.

[24] Philippe Descola, *Beyond Nature and Culture* (Chicago: University of Chicago Press, 2013), pp. 110–111.

existential phenomenology was entirely committed to the reverse. Or, at least, so the story went.[25]

Before moving forward, however, I should emphasize that none of the Harvard structuralists worked under a single set of influences. Duncan Kennedy, for example, was very much indebted to both Sartre's phenomenology and Lévi-Strauss's structuralism, whereas Unger's relation to those thinkers was more ambiguous.[26] But the question of influence is, in some important ways, not about what *caused* the Harvard School to turn out as it did. The question of influence, rather, is about the general intellectual milieu in which the Harvard School ought to be situated. If structuralism is a family of thinkers and disciplines, the Harvard School was certainly a part of it.

The Rise of Legal Structuralism (1975–1984)

Duncan Kennedy circulated the first of the Harvard School's works – *The Rise and Fall of Classical Legal Thought* – in 1975. The first proper publication, however, belonged to Roberto Unger, with his *Knowledge and Politics* (1975), which was promptly followed by his *Law in Modern Society* (1976). Kennedy's two subsequent and lengthy articles, "Form and Substance in Private Law Adjudication" (1976) and "The Structure of Blackstone's Commentaries" (1979), round out the Harvard School's basic platform. Other Harvard Law Professors, such as Gerald Frug and David Kennedy, would very soon apply that platform to particular semiotic subsystems, beginning in 1980.[27] Eventually, legal fields as diverse as international law, labor law, antitrust law, local government law, and property and contract, would all serve as vehicles for structuralist analysis.[28]

25 For discussion, see Hugh Silverman, *Textualities: Between Hermeneutics and Deconstruction* (New York: Routledge, 1994). I return to this issue in Chapter 2.

26 Duncan Kennedy, *The Rise and Fall of Classical Legal Thought* (Washington, DC: Beard Books, 2006); Roberto Unger, *Knowledge and Politics* (New York: Free Press, 1975), pp. 127–130. In Unger's case, I should clarify that while he is ambiguous on his precise intellectual relations with the structuralists – sometimes very critical, sometimes very friendly – his views are available at length in his nonlegal works. See Roberto Unger, *Social Theory: Its Situation and Its Task* (Cambridge: Cambridge University Press, 1987).

27 Gerald E. Frug, The City as a Legal Concept, 93 *Harvard Law Review* 1057 (1980); David Kennedy, Theses about International Law Discourse, 23 *German Yearbook International Law* 353 (1980).

28 Duncan Kennedy provides a list of exemplary works in The Rise and Fall of Classical Legal Thought, supra note 26, at xliii.

I explain Harvard School structuralism in three parts. The first concerns the interaction between existential phenomenology and legal structuralism in the construction of the legal subject: the *jurist*. The second turns to the legal language of liberal legalism with a focus on that language's constitutive antinomies. The third continues the discussion of liberal legalism, but shifts from *langue* to *parole*, and the implications of lexical indeterminacy.

1 The Author Isn't Dead; He's a Jurist

I begin with some conventional Cartesian talk, with a view toward quickly complicating it. The legal subject is an agent we can call the *jurist*. The jurist is anyone trained to "think like a lawyer," whether a judge, professor, attorney, or some other legal sophisticate. In contrast is the legal object, law's language system.[29] In the analytic philosophy of language, we might then go about understanding the various elements in the subject-object interface.[30] But the Harvard School's approach to this subject-object problem is phenomenological and semiotic rather than analytic.[31] The legal language never has a positive essence or any ontologically uniform objectivity that might be conceived or articulated independent of the jurist's consciousness. The reality of the language englobes the jurist, and only manifests once it is already in the interactive space of juridical speech. This embeddedness, in which legal subject and legal object are now really two words for what is practically the same thing, is what Kennedy called "legal consciousness."[32] And legal consciousness is "legal thought," "the conceptual apparatus, the reasoning techniques, the legal ideals and the key images that the elite bar, including judges, treatise writers and important lawyers, deploy when they make legal arguments or give opinions or declarations about what the law 'is' or ought to be."[33] Consequently, the Harvard School's jurist is not some autonomous subject rationally contemplating an independent world in the warmth of his man-cave. For even as I began by noting the existence of a legal subject (the jurist) and a legal object (the language), these two elements become indistinguishable in the milieu of legal thought, manifested in what I will later define as a "style of argumentative practice."

29 Unger, Knowledge and Politics, supra note 26, at 80.

30 See, e.g., J. L. Austin, *How to Do Things with Words* (J. O. Urmson and Mariana Sbisa, eds.) (Cambridge, MA: Harvard University Press, 1975); John R. Searle, *Speech Acts: An Essay in the Philosophy of Language* (Cambridge: Cambridge University Press, 1969).

31 Duncan Kennedy, The Structure of Blackstone's Commentaries, 28 *Buffalo Law Review* 205 (1979), p. 209.

32 Id. at 2. 33 Id. at ix.

Drawing on Sartre's reworking of Husserl in *Being and Nothingness*, Kennedy suggested that the legal language had an existence-as-appearance made real in the encounter with the jurist's legal consciousness. That is, while it could be that a universe of law existed outside of or beyond its solicitations to legal consciousness, there was no way to understand that "object" in any meaningful way. The Harvard School's approach, in other words, was not empiricist. The meaningful existence of the legal language could only be found in its "adumbrations" for and "solicitations" of the jurist's consciousness. To further underline the point, there was nothing ontologically independent about the legal language – the language of law never comes *to* the jurist's consciousness. The structure of the legal language was always already the very stuff of legal consciousness. Legal consciousness does not exist in the absence of the legal language.

The Sartrean variety of phenomenological existentialism counsels an absolute view of freedom through consciousness – consciousness *decides*, intends to encounter an object, always. But a Sartrean freedom of decision immanent in consciousness, in the work of both Kennedy and Unger, was always realized only in the constraints of the legal language and its backgrounded interactions *with* legal consciousness. Legal consciousness, in other words, always exists in a unity of freedom and constraint. This is a version of what Sartre called the "paradox of freedom," in which consciousness is at once totally determined and totally free. The situation of the legal object may be totally determined – the jurist has no control over the existence of the legal materials that appear to her. Those materials are sourced in the decisions of other people, often ranging over the course of several centuries, and it would be silly to suggest that the jurist is "free" to conceptualize those materials any way she might like. Nevertheless, while the situation of the legal object is determined, the meaning of the object is open: the jurist *always* has a decision to make about what to do with the situated materials, which materials to read, which materials to ignore, which materials to read closely, and so on. It is because the jurist *always* faces such decisions that we sense the resonance of Sartre's remark: "We are condemned to be free."

For Kennedy and Unger, this attachment to an existential conception of freedom and constraint was consistently fastened to the structuralist view of law.[34] Like Kennedy, Unger believed that legal consciousness was

[34] Roberto Unger, *Law in Modern Society: Toward a Criticism of Social Theory* (New York: Free Press, 1976), p. 136; Unger, Knowledge and Politics, supra note 26, at 124;

a structure of argumentative practice, a practice that was neither logical nor causal,[35] but manifested as a juridical experience.[36] As Unger explained, "To grasp a way of thinking we have to understand the problems with which it is concerned and the methods it uses to solve them. The problems and methods become in turn intelligible in the context of an experience of the world. Problems, methods, and experience constitute the 'deep structure' of the thought."[37] For Kennedy, ground zero involved the "experience of unresolvable conflict among our own values and ways of the understanding the world ... "[38] It is easy to see why. Although it is certainly true that Sartre's phenomenology and Lévi-Strauss's structuralism came to be seen as incompatible in their central commitments, it is also easy to see why Kennedy and Unger were so interested in bringing together these phenomenological and structuralist ideas in the terrain of a stylized and structured form of legal consciousness: In the context of the object of legal language, the semiotic *langue* and *parole* bore an undeniable resemblance with the "situation" and "decision" of phenomenological existentialism. But before pressing that issue further, we must turn to the jurist's know-how, the terrain of the legal language.

2 *The Legal Language: Constitutive Antinomies*

In these early works from the 1970s, the target of the Harvard School was "liberal legalism."[39] More specifically, the target was the language system of liberal legalism, or what we can call liberal legal thought. What was liberal legal thought? First, here is what it was not. It was not the universe of Law, a legal reality encompassing pretty much whatever one might want to define as having a legal aspect. "Law," in this extremely broad sense of actors, institutions, processes and the like, *could be* synonymous with liberal legalism. But it is not necessary to make such a leap, and my suggestion is that we don't. Second, even in the more particular territory of legal language, we should not make the mistake of conflating liberal legalism with all forms of legal thought. Liberalism is merely a subset in the larger category of legal language, whereas "Republicanism"

Duncan Kennedy, Form and Substance in Private Law Adjudication, 89 *Harvard Law Review* 1685 (1976), p. 1775; Kennedy, The Structure of Blackstone's Commentaries, supra note 31, at 213.

35 Unger, Knowledge and Politics, supra note 26, at 118.

36 Id. at 108–109. 37 Id. at 8.

38 Kennedy, Form and Substance in Private Law Adjudication, supra note 34, at 1712.

39 Kennedy, The Structure of Blackstone's Commentaries, supra note 31, at 211; Unger, Knowledge and Politics, supra note 26.

or "Buddhism" might be contenders for other structures of legal thought. Thus, while it might be tempting to mistake the Harvard School's target to have been *American* Legal Thought, the actual target was more discrete: what Unger called a "*style* of thought," the style(s) of liberal legalism.[40] As Unger explained, "Much in modern thought is irreconcilable with liberal principles; the polemic against them dates back to the time of their original formulation."[41] Liberal legalism, to underline the point, should be confused as a proxy for neither the entirety of American Legal Thought nor the entire universe of legality.[42]

What then *was* liberal legal thought? At the level of deep grammar – the *langue* – liberal legalism was constituted by an antinomy between two general theses. The first thesis was that human beings are and ought to be motivated by Thomas Hobbes' theory of social conflict, rooted in equal rights of self-preservation.[43] I call this the first thesis of free competition. The second thesis was that in order for society to enjoy the benefits of the new individualism, the freedom of the individual could never be free.[44] I call this the thesis of social control. The antinomy between these two theses, Kennedy and Unger agreed, was pervasive in its constitution of an entire legal language.[45] Kennedy wrote that there existed a "fundamental contradiction" between the theses of free competition and social control, and that it formed the very "essence of every problem" and that "there are simply no legal issues that do not involve directly the problem of the legitimate content of collective action."[46] And Unger, in his exploration

[40] Unger, Knowledge and Politics, supra note 26, at 8. [41] Id.

[42] To be sure, Kennedy and Unger both spoke at times as if the antinomies of liberal legalism were universal, features of an inescapable human condition. And Unger, especially, continues to talk that way today. Both Kennedy and Unger were criticized in this respect by the poststructuralists, as I discuss further below.

[43] Unger, Knowledge and Politics, supra note 26, at 63–83.

[44] Kennedy, Form and Substance in Private Law Adjudication, supra note 34, at 1719.

[45] Foucault described the antinomy in the following terms: "If man is indeed, in the world, the locus of an empirico-transcendental doublet, if he is that paradoxical figure in which the empirical contents of knowledge necessarily release, of themselves, the conditions that have made them possible, then man cannot posit himself in the immediate and sovereign transparency of a *cogito*; nor, on the other hand, can he inhabit the objective inertia of something that, by rights, does not and can never lead to self-consciousness." Michel Foucault, *The Order of Things: An Archaeology of the Human Sciences* (London: Psychology Press, 2002), p. 322.

[46] Kennedy, The Structure of Blackstone's Commentaries, supra note 31, at 213. Granted, this certainly sounded like liberal legalism was *everything*. Kennedy wrote that "Most participants in American culture believe that the goal of individual freedom is at the same time dependent on and incompatible with the communal coercive action that is necessary to achieve it." Id. at 211. Kennedy's future explanations of the modern/postmodern prove

of "modern society" explained that "the opportunities for thought available to us within a given vision of the world are laid bare, and their limits, premises, and interconnections become transparent... Without that discovery, the critique of the metaphysical framework of our ideas about knowledge and politics would be reduced to an endless game of hide-and-seek."[47]

We should be careful to see, however, that this antinomy constitutes *liberal legal thought*, and is not a positive statement about the human condition or natural society or Law, writ large. Kennedy clarified that the structure ought to be seen as a set of "contradictory utopian visions,"[48] visions which were "neither falsifiable empirical statements about a determinate mass of data, nor logically pure 'models' totally abstracted from reality."[49] And Unger explained that "the fundamental incoherencies of liberal thought are not quite contradictions. [Liberalism's] unity evokes a meaningful whole rather than a logical system, and its tensions represent conflicting trends in society and culture rather than logical contradictions."[50] The antinomies of liberal legalism were best rendered in the language of style, rather than logic, a way of thinking rather than a natural condition of thought.[51] As Kennedy put it, "liberalism is a way of thinking about [antinomies], a way of thinking that begins with rights and constructs the state and its powers as a means to their protection."[52] But these antinomies are involved only in a "way of thinking,"[53] albeit a way of thinking with a structure "strikingly analogous to the basic issues

a helpful antidote for those worried about a stealth universalism. See Duncan Kennedy, A Semiotics of Critique, 22 *Cardozo Law Review* 1147 (2001), pp. 264–296.

47 Unger, Knowledge and Politics, supra note 26, at 9. Again, passages like these need to be read in the context of Unger's views about "structure as hypothesis" rather than "structure as science." Consider Unger's statement on how the universal and the particular come together in the context of art: "In the plastic or narrative work of art, universality of meaning is often achieved not through abstraction from the particularity of individual things but by the very richness with which this particularity is represented. The work fails wither when it lacks a general significance or when it stands for general ideas and ideals not fully expressed in the work itself but left in a formal, abstract state. In the first case, art becomes frivolous; in the second, didactic. But in the great work of art men are able to recognize that something is being shown that has a broad and therefore lasting significance and illuminates hidden features of many situations. This something, the universal, cannot be reduced to abstract propositions. It is embodied in expressions; it can be rediscovered elsewhere." Id. at 144.

48 Kennedy, Form and Substance in Private Law Adjudication, supra note 34, at 1722.

49 Id. at 1722–1723.

50 Unger, Knowledge and Politics, supra note 26, at 118.

51 Kennedy, Form and Substance in Private Law Adjudication, supra note 34, at 1723.

52 Kennedy, The Structure of Blackstone's Commentaries, supra note 31, at 294.

53 Id.

in many other disciplines,"[54] a structure of ideas "powerful in their hold over the mind as they are unacknowledged and forgotten."[55]

Much of Unger's first book, *Knowledge and Politics*, is dedicated to the explication of the master grammar of liberal legalism, the antinomy of freedom and order. Kennedy's first two articles, "Form and Substance" and "The Structure of Blackstone's Commentaries," are similarly directed to the same task. In what follows I blend Unger and Kennedy's accounts in the effort to construct a single vision of the background typically submerged in the language of liberal legal thought.[56] Some violence is necessarily done in the process, but I think the benefits worth the cost, particularly as this summary forms the basis of this book's application.

Harvard School texts often gave the appearance of doing intellectual history,[57] treating liberalism as the political theory of Hobbes, Locke, Blackstone, Bentham, Mill and others – a political theory waged in a war against the "medieval Aristotle."[58] This liberal story began with the invention of the *Individual*.[59] Not the human being, of course, but the individual qua "rights-bearing subject." No longer predefined in terms of good and virtue and teleology, the newly minted liberal individual determined for himself what it meant to lead a good life.[60] This liberal individual enjoyed "total arbitrary discretion (often referred to as total freedom) to pursue their ends (purposes, values, goals, interests) without regard to the impact of their actions on others."[61] At the heart of individual *right* was the notion of self-preservation.[62] For in this new liberal world, all individuals possessed this ultimate entitlement, and each could decide just what the right of self-preservation entailed.[63] For theorists like Hobbes, this led to a war of all against all, as there no longer existed an objective standard of justice determining when one individual had wronged another. There was, in other words, no meaningful idea of right and wrong that could exist independently of the individual's subjective perception of it. Freedom, in this liberal view, "has no moral content whatever."[64] Of course, the precise context of individualism varies in this respect, depending on

[54] Unger, Knowledge and Politics, supra note 26, at 8. [55] Id. [56] Id. at 80, 84.

[57] See, e.g., Alan Watson, The Structure of Blackstone's Commentaries, 97 *Yale Law Journal* 795 (1988).

[58] Unger, Knowledge and Politics, supra note 26, at 5.

[59] For useful discussion, see Barbara Young Welke, *Law and the Borders of Belonging in the Long Nineteenth Century United States* (New York: Cambridge University Press, 2010).

[60] Id. at 63–103.

[61] Kennedy, Form and Substance in Private Law Adjudication, supra note 34, at 1767–1768.

[62] Unger, Knowledge and Politics, supra note 26, at 64–67. [63] Id.

[64] Kennedy, Form and Substance in Private Law Adjudication, supra note 34, at 1774.

which liberal theorist is serving the gospel. In Locke's mercantilist version, for example, the situation led to the creation of a market society in which people happily became property owners, buying, selling, and elaborating ever more sophisticated forms of economic transaction.[65]

In either the images of a Hobbes or a Locke, the world of liberal individualism was unsustainable on its own terms. To assist us in seeing why that would be, and again with shades of an anemic intellectual history, Harvard School texts sketched the coming conflict in the context of what liberalism had been meant to replace: a pre-liberal Aristotelianism.[66] In this worldview, everything had some purpose – an essence – including human beings, and particular people were destined for particular purposes: perhaps a slave or a farmer or a philosopher.[67] Failing to achieve one's purpose was not an option. To not fulfill one's *telos* was to become a moral defect.[68] Order was established through a natural will, and that will was readily discernible through the habitual practice of reason.[69] As Unger explained, liberalism represented a "total critique" of these Scholastic ideas, and in particular, the "theory of intelligible essences."[70] For the new liberals, human beings were no longer to be objectified as acorns.[71] Liberal individuals had no essence at all, for it was their right to choose the story of their life, and what they would become.[72]

But, and it was a big but, the problem was that liberal individualism required a degree of political *order* in order to do what it was meant to do, to realize individualism in a functioning *society*. To be sure, for liberalism the individual was natural, society artificial. But the artifice of order and the reality of the police power, on liberalism's own terms, was a necessity.[73] For as much as liberalism touted the primacy of self-reliance, liberalism also countenanced its *natural* limits and the necessity of social cooperation. Here was the problem, and the problem that continues today in the grammar of liberal legal thought: how can we have political hierarchy after the abolition of teleological hierarchy? How might liberalism produce a political order that at once facilitated the equal rights of

[65] See, e.g., C. B. MacPherson, *The Political Theory of Possessive Individualism: Hobbes to Locke* (Oxford: Oxford University Press, 2011). For the other view, see John Dunn, *The Political Thought of John Locke: An Historical Account of the Argument of the 'Two Treatises of Government'* (Cambridge: Cambridge University Press, 1982).

[66] Unger, Knowledge and Politics, supra note 26, at 80.

[67] Aristotle, *Nicomachean Ethics* (Terence Irwin, trans.) (Indianapolis: Hackett, 1999).

[68] Unger, Knowledge and Politics, supra note 26, at 80. [69] Id. at 76. [70] Id. at 80.

[71] Id. [72] Id. at 81–83. [73] Id. at 80.

autonomous beings and instituted a degree of coercion that was uniform, general, and comprehensive? As the variations of social contract and democratic theory would eventually suggest, the answer began with the realization that if order was to be achieved, certain natural rights would have to be renounced.[74] In exchange for the renunciation of an individual's monopoly over the definition of justice, political society would form, and a sovereign would come into being as the guarantor of order and wielder of the police power.[75] Here emerges the characteristic split in liberal theory between civil society on one side and political society on the other.[76] Liberal theory presents a way of styling the relation between the new liberal being and the secular state that would come to facilitate the possibility of a functioning society of "rights-bearing individuals."[77] In order for individuals to enjoy their natural rights in civil society – the rights they still retained after the renunciation – the artifice of government was defined as something *other* than civil society.[78]

It is here that the master grammar of liberal legalism emerges in the form of antinomy, a basic antinomy between the problems of individualism and political order. The renunciation of the full cache of natural rights and the formation of political society, in other words, was only a start and not a solution; this compromise did not yet help us know how to fashion a government in the absence of the Aristotelian theory of intelligible essences. If it were a solution, we would have known how to resolve the following tasks: respect the thesis of individualism and its demand that we honor the individual as a source of subjective value, and respect the thesis of political order that necessarily limits the freedoms of certain individuals at the expense of others. In the absence of a theory of objective value (intelligible essences), the only "good" is the satisfaction of personal desire.[79] But the very purpose of law is to empower some desires and restrict others, to assert a view of "justice consisting of an order according to shared ends."[80] On what basis can we make this distinction between those desires worth protecting, and those deserving

[74] Id. at 64–67. For discussion, see Will Kymlicka, *Contemporary Political Philosophy: An Introduction* (Oxford: Oxford University Press, 2001). For another view, see Richard Tuck, *Natural Rights Theories: Their Origin and Development* (Cambridge: Cambridge University Press, 1979).

[75] Unger, Knowledge and Politics, supra note 26, at 64–67.

[76] Kennedy, The Structure of Blackstone's Commentaries, supra note 31, at 217.

[77] Id. at 234. [78] Unger, Knowledge and Politics, supra note 26, at 88–100. [79] Id.

[80] Kennedy, Form and Substance in Private Law Adjudication, supra note 34, at 1771.

punishment? This is what Unger called the problem of freedom: "How then can order be instituted in such a way that no one's liberty is unjustifiably preferred or downgraded and that everyone has the largest amount of liberty compatible with the absence of such arbitrariness?"[81] It is in this way, as Kennedy explained, that "mechanisms of social order dependent on consensus about ends will run into terrible trouble."[82]

"The creation of an order within which there are no occasions on which it is necessary for group members to achieve a consensus about the ends they are to pursue, or indeed for group members to make the slightest effort toward the achievement of other ends than their own, makes perfect sense" once one begins with the principle of individualism.[83] But once we advantage certain values as against others, we violate the standard of equal rights. And then, when we resuscitate the thesis with a return to ideas of subjective value, self-reliance, etc., we violate the thesis of political order, which demands we place limits on what individuals ought to be able to decide. Caught himself, Unger wrote, "the house of reason in which I was working proved to be a prison-house of paradox whose rooms did not connect and whose passageways led nowhere."[84]

The traditional way in which liberal theory sought to escape this fundamental antinomy was through the elaboration of a third thesis. I call this the third thesis of naturalizing juridical science.[85] Why turn to law for the remedy? In a world without objective value, a concept of order can only be sustained through the creation of something that might perform in the guise of objective rule.[86] This "something" needed to be impersonal, general, and defined in opposition against the notion of subjective value.[87] If law could be a device for placing objective limits on individual freedoms, the liberal effort to succeed its Aristotelian predecessor might take flight. Could it?

In the work of the Harvard School, the answer was, decidedly, no. The third thesis of naturalizing juridical science functions to *mediate* the antinomy, to place its tensions at such a distance from the immediate experience of jurists that they never come to consciousness. This mediation of the basic antinomy between the theses of free competition and social control took a doubled form. The third thesis first attempts

[81] Unger, Knowledge and Politics, supra note 26, at 67.
[82] Kennedy, Form and Substance in Private Law Adjudication, supra note 34, at 1769.
[83] Id. at 1769. [84] Unger, Knowledge and Politics, supra note 26, at 8.
[85] Id. at 72–76. [86] Id. at 72. [87] Id. at 88–100.

to mediate the antinomy in the context of theories of law creation, or legislation.[88] It next attempts the mediation in the context of law application, or adjudication.[89] Together, these four modes represent the double task of mediating the antinomy between the demands of order and freedom, rule and value.[90] As Kennedy argued, "One of the functions of systems of legal thought – one of the reasons for their existence – is the reconciliation of what appear to be conflicts between institutions and contradictions among ideas. In other words, system is necessary not just to permit us to deal in a cognitively effective way with the chaotic mass of rules. It is also necessary because the theorist wishes to show that where many perceive confusion, danger, insecurity, rivalry, and aggressive action, there exists a latent order that has a legitimate claim to our respect."[91]

The first way in which liberal legalism attempts to reconcile the problem is through a focus on the *source* of its ostensibly "impersonal" rules. If the introduction of impersonal rules is expected to simultaneously solve the problems of order and freedom, liberalism suggests that the solution will be found in the rule's pedigree, or in other words, in a theory of legislation. Another way of understanding this attempt to ground the "impersonal" nature of rules in a theory of legislation is to introduce the notion of legal *right*. On this view, coercive power is a good thing, and useful in its maintenance of social order, but only to the extent that official coercion respects the sanctity of individual right. The existence of a meaningful and definable category of right therefore answers the problem of order and freedom by drawing a bright line between what the state can and cannot do.[92] "Rights mediate the fundamental contradiction because they allow their bearers to fuse with others without being annihilated by them."[93] The rub, as Kennedy continued, was precisely the problem of determining the meaning and identity of such rights, of distinguishing "good fusion" from "annihilation." Unless one could secure an objective and intelligible understanding of reasoning about rights, any theory of rights would dissolve on the grounds of subjective value. In order to keep

[88] Id. at 83–88. [89] Id. at 88–100.

[90] In later chapters, my discussion of the third thesis of naturalizing juridical science is entirely directed at adjudication. On legislation, see Unger, Knowledge and Politics, supra note 26, at 83–88.

[91] Kennedy, The Rise and Fall of Classical Legal Thought, supra note 26, at 8; Kennedy, The Structure of Blackstone's Commentaries, supra note 31, at 214.

[92] Kennedy, The Structure of Blackstone's Commentaries, supra note 31, at 259, 265, 279.

[93] Id. at 295.

this from happening, juridical work in the light of the third thesis often enacts a form of reification, treating rights as things:

> Liberal political/legal theory is characterized by a deep consensus that rights exist, that we have them, and that their content is knowable. All the modes of mediating the fundamental contradiction that I will call liberal share this common trait: the sense of the reality of rights is close to the sense of the physical reality of objects in the world.[94]

The second way liberalism mediates the contradiction is in its attitude toward the application of rules to disputes between rights-bearing subjects. Thus, in contrast to questions about the rule's provenance, liberal legal thought here attacks the antinomy of rule and value through faith in adjudication. In either its formalist or functionalist mode of naturalizing juridical science, explored further in Chapters 4, 5, and 6, liberal legal thought believes in the real possibility of countering political value with the settled weight of legal rule.

To sum up this discussion of the basic antinomies of liberal legal thought: First, the Harvard School urged us to step away from the tendency to think about questions of epistemology and politics as separate fields with separate problems. Instead of compartmentalizing the various segments of society, the structuralist encourages a view of social practice as language, a language that resists segmentation along social vectors. The language's borderlines are semiotic rather than political or legal or cultural or whatever. Second, the Harvard School identified liberal legalism as itself a kind of language system, with a grammar and lexicon and rhetorical pathways, rather than a philosophy or a politics or an epistemology. Third, the grammar of liberal legal thought is shaped out of an antinomy between the theses of free competition and social control, and the mediating effects of a third thesis: faith in the power of a naturalizing juridical science to resolve the antinomy. These three theses constitute the master *langue* of liberal legal thought, the governing mechanism for the conceptual lexicon, and the styles of argumentative practice.

3 The Legal Language: Lexical Indeterminacy

I have so far focused on the master *langue* in liberal legal thought. Now I want to turn to the Harvard School's approach to liberal legalism's lexicon, the level of the legal concept. As discussed above, whereas the deeper grammatical level provides hard constraints on juridical speech,

94 Id. at 261.

the lexical level is far more discretionary, or to use a term that became increasingly popular at the time, "indeterminate."[95] It is important to see how the Harvard School managed this distinction between a hard system of constraints and a loose and indeterminate sea of legal concepts. The distinction is important in itself, for understanding just what the structuralist approach involved. It is also important in order to distinguish structuralism from what it was *not*. Throughout the 1980s and '90s, it was sometimes believed that the "fundamental contradiction" condemned the entire legal system, forever and always, to an anything-goes morass. This focus on indeterminacy tended to forget the hard constraints of the *langue*, yielding to a somewhat nihilistic takeaway: forget law and learn the *politics* of law, because law was nothing more than a smokescreen blinding us to what was really going on behind the scenes.

The "politics of law" was a phrase at times connected with another: "trashing."[96] The caricature of the trashing jurist suggested the limitless ways in which legal concepts and legal reasoning might contort to justify any imaginable conclusion.[97] Suggest a natural, neutral, or necessary construction of a legal concept, you'll get trashed. The growing obsession with trashing and indeterminacy, as I have already suggested, increasingly misunderstood what the structuralist project was all about. As a result, the Harvard School was mistakenly identified as simply the rehash of an older moment in legal thought, legal realism.[98] The idea that a given set of legal materials might fail to produce logically necessitated legal conclusions had been thoroughly debated since at least the work of Rudolph von Jhering, and in the United States, since at least the earliest writings of Oliver Wendell Holmes.[99] For some realists, indeterminacy was an inevitable result of an open-ended set of legal

[95] A helpful example is Duncan Kennedy, A Semiotics of Legal Argument, 42 *Syracuse Law Review* 75 (1991). For another view, see Jack Balkin, The Crystalline Structure of Legal Thought, 39 *Rutgers Law Review* 1 (1986).

[96] See Mark Kelman, Trashing, 36 *Stanford Law Review* 293 (1984); *The Politics of Law: A Progressive Critique* (David Kairys, ed.) (New York: Basic Books, 1998).

[97] See, e.g., Alan David Freeman and John Henry Schlegel, Sex, Power, and Silliness: An Essay on Ackerman's Reconstructing American Law, 6 *Cardozo Law Review* 847 (1985).

[98] On legal realism, see Joseph William Singer, Legal Realism Now, 76 *California Law Review* 465 (1988). For a recent symposium, see Volume 163, Issue 7 of The Pennsylvania Law Review (2015).

[99] See, e.g., Rudolph von Jhering, *Law as a Means to an End* (London: Forgotten Books, 2015); Oliver Wendell Holmes, Jr., Privilege, Malice, and Intent, 8 *Harvard Law Review* 1 (1894).

materials.[100] Often called formalism, realists assaulted a mode of reasoning in which the jurist believed in the objective capacity to deduce logically necessitated legal answers from a given set of legal materials. The realists showed how the supposed logic of formalist reasoning very rarely if ever achieved the status of objectivity, but rather served to hide the subjective values of the judge.[101] Law, in this view, was a mere plaything.[102]

Of course, it is true that Harvard School thinkers identified a substantial degree of ideological content at the level of the legal concept and suggested that the affordances of argumentative practice were undeniably political. The structuralist does have, at least in the language of liberal legalism, an interest in pointing to the "politics of law." And this is very largely what I do in this book's concluding chapter, with its critique of mystification, legitimation, and myth. But the structuralist view of conceptual indeterminacy is something quite different from both the "realist" version of the idea that had surfaced earlier[103] and the popular notion of trashing that was in the air of the 1980s and '90s.

For the structuralists, there was a lot more going on. Law *was not* just politics, it was not simply a cue for social science, and it was not about what you'd had for breakfast. It was an entire language system, with its grammar, concepts, and styles of argumentative practice.[104] The Harvard School's take on legal indeterminacy was categorically different from and far more specific than the idea that all legal rules were vulnerable to political hijacking. From the structuralist perspective, yes, jurists encounter open-ended legal concepts and must make ideological choices. But they can't flip *any* rule, *any* time, to justify *any* conclusion.[105] There are, at least in liberal legal thought, structural constraints. The extent to

[100] See, e.g., Walter Wheeler Cook, *The Logical and Legal Bases of the Conflict of Laws* (Cambridge, MA: Harvard University Press, 1949). For general discussion, see Neil Duxbury, *Patterns of Jurisprudence* (Oxford: Clarendon Press, 1997); *American Legal Realism* (William Fisher et al., eds.) (Oxford: Oxford University Press, 1993).

[101] Unger, Knowledge and Politics, *supra* note 26, at 88–100; Kennedy, Form and Substance in Private Law Adjudication, supra note 34, at 1770.

[102] Rightfully or not, this sort of view is often attributed to Jerome Frank, *Law and the Modern Mind* (New York: Doubleday, 1963).

[103] See, e.g., Karl Llewellyn, Remarks on the Theory of Appellate Decision and the Rules or Canons about How Statutes Are to Be Constructed, 3 *Vanderbilt Law Review* 395 (1950).

[104] Kennedy, The Rise and Fall of Classical Legal Thought, supra note 26, at xiv–xv.

[105] See, e.g., Lawrence Solum, *Indeterminacy and Equity, in Radical Critiques of the Law* (Stephen Griffin & Robert Moffat, eds.) (Lawrence: University Press of Kansas, 1997); Alan Madry, Analytical Deconstructionism? The Intellectual Voyeurism of Anthony D'Amato, 63 *Fordham Law Review* 1033 (1995).

which a jurist is capable of generating arguments and counterarguments is ultimately a question about the bounds of the structure in question and the frontiers of the subsystem the jurist happens to be operating. This is why there are so many cases with right answers (or at least, why there are so many cases in which the effect of legal necessity is overpowering): the subsystem in which the jurist is arguing is subject to such strict grammatical constraints that there really are only a few ways, maybe even just one way, to come out. In other subsystems governed by a broader practice, however, the jurist will have more styles of decision to choose from, more affordances to accept. Thus, from the structuralist's point of view, the reason for the jurist's discretion has little to do with cores and penumbras, or law as integrity, or any such thing.[106] It has to with the idea that jurists are immersed in legal languages, and that if a jurist wants to be recognized as speaking the language – which all jurists do – then they have to follow its rules.

The reason for belaboring the point is to disassociate the Harvard School from the tired idea of trashing and the unhelpful conclusion that law is merely a smokescreen for politics. I want to press this separation for two reasons. The first concerns the intellectual development of the claim that "law is just politics." On one side, the phrase now belongs to the arsenal of pragmatic liberalism, discussed in Chapter 8. On the other side, the phrase is charged with parading a "warmed-over legal realism."[107] The strategy here, in the context of analytical philosophers keen to rebuke what they saw as the threat of legal nihilism, was to show how indeterminacy was an old problem that had largely been solved.[108] As I have already suggested, the tendency to respond to the structuralists as if they were merely rehashing an old problem was a mistake. The structuralist view of legal indeterminacy was simply of a very different sort than the kind usually addressed by analytic philosophers.[109]

In addition to pressing this distinction between the manner in which the "politics of law" was understood by the Harvard School and how it was

106 For a recent summary, see Scott Shapiro, *Legality* (Cambridge, MA: Harvard University Press, 2013).

107 See, e.g., Richard Nunan, "Critical Legal Parricide, or: What's So Bad About Warmed-Over Legal Realism?" in *Indeterminacy and Equity, in Radical Critiques of the Law* (Stephen Griffin & Robert Moffat, eds.) (Lawrence: University Press of Kansas, 1997), p. 21.

108 See, e.g., Andrew Altman, *Critical Legal Studies: A Liberal Critique* (Princeton, NJ: Princeton University Press, 1993).

109 See, e.g., Jules Coleman and Brian Leiter, Determinacy, Objectivity, and Authority, 142 *University of Pennsylvania Law Review* 549 (1993).

understood in the legal mainstream, a second and more important reason for underscoring the issue is this: the intense focus on the argument that "law is politics" obscured the Harvard School's view that *politics is law*. In liberal legal thought, we might say that the designation *law is politics* is doing considerable work at the level of the conceptual lexicon, the level at which jurists encounter so many conflicting choices immanent in the legal concept. At the level of its grammar, and at the level of argumentative practice (which I describe in Chapters 2 and 3), it is the more curious designation *politics is law* that is the more relevant. Law, in other words, constitutes politics, but only in the way that a grammar controls the forms a lexicon manifests in its argumentative practice. It is not an empirical argument about how law and society interact.[110]

Confusion about the meaning of *law is politics* was present even among the friendliest of audiences. In their contributions to the 1984 Symposium on Critical Legal Studies in the Stanford Law Review, David Trubek and Robert Gordon both fastened on the point.[111] For Trubek, the idea of legal consciousness was a valuable addition to the theoretical toolkit, but what was largely lacking in it was work on the social dynamic of legal practice.[112] Studying legal doctrine was important, because it provided the scholar with a better understanding of the structures of legal thought. But where, Trubek asked, did these structures come from? What put them in place? Why did they change? And what were the effects of the structures gleaned from doctrine on actual experience? What of the law in action? Five years earlier, Kennedy had explained that "what I have to say is descriptive, and descriptive only of thought. It means ignoring the question of what brings a legal consciousness into being, what causes it to change, and what effect it has on the actions of those who live in it."[113] Trubek's reaction in 1984: "If Kennedy omits any discussion of the effects of legal consciousness in a 173-page article on Blackstone's legal thought, how confident can he be that his method bears any relationship

110 More recently, Unger has moved in this direction. Roberto Unger, *The Critical Legal Studies Movement: Another Time, A Greater Task* (Cambridge, MA: Harvard University Press, 1986), p. 47.

111 For further discussion along these lines, see John Schlegel, Does Duncan Kennedy Wear Briefs or Boxers? Does Richard Posner Ever Sleep? Writing about Jurisprudence, High Culture, and the History of Intellectuals, 45 *Buffalo Law Review* 277, 297 (1997); John Schlegel, CLS Wasn't Killed By a Question, 58 *Alabama Law Review* 967 (2007).

112 David Trubek, Where the Action Is: Critical Legal Studies and Empiricism, 36 *Stanford Law Review* 575 (1984).

113 Kennedy, The Structure of Blackstone's Commentaries, supra note 31, at 220.

to his political intent?"[114] The problem was that the *politics is law* idea simply had no meaning unless it was grounded in empirical analysis, and as Trubek concluded, "This is a challenge that CLS must meet. Until we can produce convincing maps of the relationships between elite ideological production, the social definition of meaning, and the history of social relations, we will not be able to sustain the claims made for Critical studies."[115]

As I have already suggested, Trubek's law-and-society critique misses an essential point about the structuralist understanding of the relation between legal thought and legal practice. What Trubek is concerned about is the place of the social, and the lack of concern in legal structuralism for "the law in action," as opposed to its stale life in the law of the books. While it is certainly true that legal structuralism makes no claims for causal explanation, and that it remains agnostic on the empirical analysis of law in society, this critique of legal consciousness is off the mark. In contrast with a conception of legal consciousness as distant and detached from legal practice, the Harvard School argued that adjudication manifested as a *practice* of legal argument. Legal thought only happens – *can* only happen – in the embodied practice of legal argument, in some actualized structure of legal language. A study of legal consciousness is, as a result, nothing other than a study of the jurist's experience, of the law in action. To think otherwise is to indulge in the Cartesian split.[116]

To some extent, Trubek's complaint found an answer in Gordon's *Critical Legal Histories*,[117] published in the same issue. In that justifiably well-known article, Gordon addressed the use of functionalism in legal history, so widely applied by law-and-society scholars like Trubek. Legal functionalism, which I explore further in Chapter 5, is the modern manifestation of the third thesis in liberal legal thought's constitutive grammar. It requires a belief that law changes over time as a function of changing social needs and interests. Famously, Gordon demolished this functionalist view of legal history, both as it manifests in the classic and modern styles of liberal legal thought.[118] Gordon then suggested a *post*functionalist perspective, a perspective he elaborated in three moves. The first blurred the distinction

[114] Trubek, supra note 112, at 612. [115] Id.

[116] For further discussion from the symposium on this issue, see William Simon, Visions of Practice in Legal Thought, 36 *Stanford Law Review* 469 (1984).

[117] Robert Gordon, Critical Legal Histories, 36 *Stanford Law Review* 57 (1984). See also, Robert Gordon, "Critical Legal Histories Revisited": A Response, 37 *Law and Social Inquiry* 200 (2012).

[118] Gordon, Critical Legal Histories, supra note 117, at 71.

between law and society so fundamental for legal functionalists. Functionalist historians sought to understand how law had changed over time in response to the basic conditions of material life by identifying the essential "needs" of society and the powerful interests that had a hand in shaping those needs.[119] They then sought to locate the many ways in which these social threads unpacked in any given legal system, though without reference to a necessary progress narrative: how had legal rules emerged in response to social needs and practices, however unfair? For Gordon, the new critical historiography rejected this distinction between a prelegal social realm and a legal order somehow directed by these more "fundamental" social forces. For Gordon's new legal historians, society was as legally constructed as the other way around.[120] The point, from here on out, would be to reject stale, functionalist depictions of law as society's everlasting lady-in-waiting, and to do this one needed to recognize that "law and society are inextricably mixed."[121]

The second move pushed this idea further. Gordon explained that legal historians needed to accept not only the mutually constitutive nature of law-in-society but also a prioritization of law's role in the construction of society.[122] Gordon's critique of functionalism turned in part on the argument that the distinction between a social world and a law that took its shape from the social failed to acknowledge the fact that the social world is already legally constituted.[123] Here, Gordon seemed to be in the posture of defending Kennedy against the likes of Trubek's friendly critique, for Gordon was arguing that *politics is law*: "it is just about impossible to describe any set of 'basic' social practices without describing the legal relations among the people involved – legal relations that don't simply condition how the people relate to each other but to an important extent define the constitutive terms of the relationship, relations such as lord and peasant, master and slave, employer and employee, ratepayer and utility, and taxpayer and municipality."[124]

119 Id. 120 Id. at 103. 121 Id. at 107.

122 Id. at 111. But as Gordon explained recently, his focus here was mostly on legal structuralism, and he had not intended to suggest that all forms of critical historiography would include these three elements. Gordon, Critical Legal Histories Revisited, supra note 117, at 205 ("All I was trying to do was to explain what a particular kind of critical legal history – the work pioneered by Duncan Kennedy and his circle on the history of contradictions in liberal legal thought – was all about and why it was worth doing. Kennedy's work had struck me and many others reading it for the first time as shockingly, brilliantly enlightening, and it made me at least reevaluate my prejudice going in that doctrine was mostly a sideshow.")

123 Gordon, Critical Legal Histories, supra note 117, at 103. 124 Id.

But this is precisely where thinkers like Trubek were left scratching their heads.[125] Why prioritize *politics is law*? In Gordon's article, the answer was never very clear; it wasn't obvious why Gordon privileged law's role in this way, particularly as it followed the seeming counterpoint that law and society were "inextricably mixed." Probably as a result, this emphasis on law's constitutive role in the social, which necessarily came at the expense of the social role in constituting law, was somewhat ill-formed.[126] Gordon seemed anxious about the point, explaining that the critic "takes each event as situated not on a single developmental path but on multiple trajectories of possibility, the path actually chosen being chosen not because it had to be but because the people pushing for alternatives were weaker and lost out in the struggle . . . "[127]

But this shaky emphasis on law's constitutive role in the social slid quickly toward a more reliable and trendier third move: "indeterminacy located in contradiction."[128] This, as is hopefully clear, is not *politics is law*, but rather, *law is politics*. That is, while the new critical historian might focus on law's role in determining social needs, rather than the other way around, one must be reminded that "law" never means any one thing. Borrowing from Kennedy's analysis of *Blackstone's Commentaries*, Gordon explained that this deep sense of law's indeterminacy was grounded in a fundamental contradiction between "our need for others and our fear of them."[129] Thus, the new critical historiography was committed to exploring reality's astonishingly complex blending of law in the political, emphasizing law's role in what was nevertheless conceded to be a state of mutual constitution, and elaborating law's endlessly indeterminate, albeit constitutive, social life.

The best example of an approach embodied in these three moves, Gordon concluded, was legal structuralism.[130] But while it is clear that Gordon had little interest in debunking legal structuralism and rather wanted to celebrate it, his account of the Harvard School's approach to the *politics is law/law is politics* problem actually coalesced with Trubek's critique. The crux of the problem was the confusing relation between law's

[125] For more recent head-scratching, see Susan Silbey, After Legal Consciousness, 1 *Annual Review of Law and Social Science* 323 (2005). Much of this work relies on Clifford Geertz, *The Interpretation of Cultures* (New York: Basic Books, 1973).

[126] See Christopher Tomlins, What Is Left of the Law and Society Paradigm after Critique? Revisiting Gordon's "Critical Legal Histories," 37 *Law and Social Inquiry* 155, 160 (2012).

[127] Gordon, Critical Legal Histories, supra note 117, at 112.

[128] Id. at 114. [129] Id. [130] Id. at 116–117.

constitutive role in society and the apparent inability of law to constitute anything if it was really so indeterminate. Once again, what was intended as a semiotic analysis of liberal legalism was being mistaken for an empirical account of legality, writ large. "Indeterminacy rooted in contradiction," while accurate enough, was not the right way to present the idea; "structured indeterminacy," with its double nod in the directions of grammatical constraint and lexical ideology, would have helped prevent much of what was to come.

In any case, this holism – the unity threading lexical and grammatical practice together in a "structured indeterminacy" – was missed entirely. To be sure, the content was there. But over the course of the discussion, the three moves were articulated in the form of a checklist rather than a more organic structure of argumentative practice. What's more, the important emphasis on the grammar constraining indeterminacy in legal structuralism was articulated instead as "law's constitutive role *in society*." In a way, Gordon's choice to frame the point in this way made a lot of sense;[131] but without also hammering the way in which law itself was deeply structured, and how legal consciousness itself was only knowable as a practice of legal argument, the reader was left without much understanding of how that phrase could have any real meaning, since law itself was – apparently – endlessly indeterminate.

The consequence of framing the elements in this way was dramatic. In the years that followed, Gordon's stress on law's constitutive role in politics rang hollow and came to be seen as out of step with the general sway of what was becoming known as *post*structuralist thinking. At the same time, the first and third steps merged, making room for the view of critical legal history that would follow.[132] The first move – Gordon's critique of evolutionary historicism, along with the attendant blurring of law and society and the complex and contingent dynamics inherent in that

131 See, e.g., Karl Klare, Law-Making as Praxis, 40 *Telos* 123 (1979).

132 It is easy to miss the point here. It is not that legal historians and law-and-society people did not care about law's role in constituting the social. They cared about it a great deal. Thus, by saying it was the first and third moves that took off, leaving the second behind, I do not meant to suggest that the new approach entailed a privileging of the social over the legal. That, after all, was the modus operandi of the functionalist historicist. Rather, the point to focus on is that the whole idea of *privileging* was rendered suspect after post-structuralist historicism took hold. Law and society were mutually constitutive, and so it made sense to spend time looking at both sides, but it did not make sense to prioritize one side over the other. To do so would miss the true complexity of the real. See, e.g., *History, Memory, and the Law* (Austin Sarat and Thomas Kearns, eds.) (Ann Arbor: University of Michigan Press, 2002).

relationship – lined up nicely with the argument for legal indeterminacy. "Indeterminacy," after all, seemed to bear a family resemblance to concepts like "complexity" and "contingency." In this posture, critical legal history was primed for its new mission: finding the traces of the ebb and flow of a rootless, unstructured discursivity.[133] The cumbersome notion of law's constitutive role in society, along with talk of the "fundamental contradiction," was easily detached from the broader program.[134] Not only was it unclear why these "tin cans"[135] had been there in the first place, but it was also becoming evident that such positions were deeply problematic for their "totalizing" view of law's discursive origins.[136] The idea of structuralist legal history, lashed at the waist to those tin cans, sunk out of sight. The result: an invitation to abandon the Harvard School for a *poststructuralist* view of law.

The Stanford Symposium marks something of a trigger-moment in the Harvard School's coming desuetude. As Peter Goodrich suggested in a

[133] See, e.g., Marianne Constable, *Just Silences: The Limits and Possibilities of Modern Law* (Princeton, NJ: Princeton University Press, 2005); Guyora Binder and Robert Weisberg, *Literary Criticisms of Law* (Princeton, NJ: Princeton University Press, 2000).

[134] See, e.g., Pierre Schlag, Cannibal Moves: An Essay on the Metamorphoses of the Legal Distinction, 40 *Stanford Law Review* 929, 935 (1988).

[135] In a frequently cited passage from *Roll Over Beethoven*, co-authored with Peter Gabel, Kennedy distanced himself from the discussion of a fundamental contradiction in *Blackstone's Commentaries*, calling it the tin can hanging around the neck of critical legal studies. Peter Gabel and Duncan Kennedy, Roll Over Beethoven, 36 *Stanford Law Review* 1, 15 (1984).

[136] See Hendrik Hartog, Introduction to Symposium on 'Critical Legal Histories': Robert W. Gordon. 1984. Critical Legal Histories. Stanford Law Review 36:57-125, 37 *Law & Social Inquiry* 147, 153 (2012) ("To insist on the constitutive power of law, its capacity to shape lives and understandings outside of law, was, in that context, to issue a bold challenge to prevailing scholarly fashions. To think of law as a producer of consciousness was to give law a power to challenge most of the mainstream discourses about law. Now, a full interrogation of what constitutive means in legal history is a subject for another occasion. Today, I am less confident than I was in 1984 that I understand it. How to distinguish legal values from religious or political values – what turns, for example, on calling a faith or belief in promise keeping a legal value – is a question that concerns me today. I know that many of the nineteenth-century lay people I study were immensely sophisticated in their mobilization and use of legal institutions. They understood testator's freedom; many, even when semiliterate, seemed to have understood the effects of the Statute of Frauds on their transactions. But were they constituted by law in any significant degree? Or, on the other hand, is it better to describe their consciousness through the lens of existential or economic or psychic conflicts (all of which, of course, have some legal features)? And when I read legal history that mobilizes the term (usually inspired consciously or unconsciously by Gordon), it sometimes seems to me that the word 'constitutive' is mobilized most often by those who wish to justify the significance of what they do without looking far beyond the confines of the law library or the Westlaw or Lexis databases. 'Constitutive' then becomes a way to foreclose deeper study and exploration.")

review of Kennedy and Gabel's contribution to that issue: "In style and content, lacking footnotes and citations, itself another instance of textual event, the new moment in critical legal studies that the Stanford conference most visibly represented owed its novelty and playfulness, its irreverence, and its sense of a future more to Derrida or to the deconstructive mood of the linguistic turn than to the weightier names in structuralist theory or historical fact that circulated in other contributions."[137] But it was certainly more than the collection of dissents assembled in that particular volume that signaled a turn in the intellectual climate. A more general transatlantic movement was afoot, a movement we can call poststructuralist jurisprudence.

The Rise of the Poststructuralist Jurist

Poststructuralism, of course, was hardly limited to the law school. As Perry Anderson described the situation in 1984, "where structuralism had been, now poststructuralism was. The exact relationship between the two, the family resemblance or common descent that unites them across the slim temporal marker, remains to be established. It may prove to be the most revealing feature of both."[138] While the "exact relationship" between structuralism and poststructuralism is surely chimerical, there are a few points of solid ground. Rather than looking to Saussure or Lévi-Strauss, for instance, the new poststructuralism took Derrida and the "deconstruction"[139] of structuralist analysis as its point of departure.[140]

137 *Derrida and Legal Philosophy* (Peter Goodrich et al., eds.) (New York: Palgrave Macmillan, 2008), p. 5.

138 Perry Anderson, *In the Tracks of Historical Materialism* (London: Verso, 1983), p. 39.

139 The common marker here is Jacque Derrida, Structure, Sign, and Play in the Discourse of the Human Sciences, in Macksey and Donato, supra note 41. See also Paul de Man, Semiology and Rhetoric 3 *Diacritics* 27 (1973). In this early illustration, de Man criticized structuralists for their use of grammatical (especially syntactical) structures conjointly with rhetorical structures, without apparent awareness of possible discrepancies between them. "In their literary analyses, Barthes, Genette, Todorov, Greimas and their disciples all simplify and regress from Jacobson in letting grammar and rhetoric function in perfect continuity, and in passing from grammatical to rhetorical structures without difficulty or interruption. Indeed, as the study of grammatical structures is refined in contemporary theories of generative, transformational, and distributive grammar, the study of tropes and figures ... becomes a mere extension of grammatical models, a particular subset of syntactical relations." Id. at 28.

140 In law, examples of the deconstructionist turn include David Kennedy, Spring Break, 63 *Texas Law Review* 1377 (1985); Clare Dalton, An Essay in the Deconstruction of Contract Doctrine, 94 *Yale Law Journal* 997 (1985); Costas Douzinas, A Short History of the British Critical Legal Conference or, The Responsibility of the Critic, 25 *Law and Critique* 187 (2014); Symposia: Deconstruction and the Possibility of Justice,

And while debate continues about whether deconstruction actually preceded structuralism, rather than having emerged as a response to it, as Peter Gordon has suggested,[141] in the case of legal thought the chronology is clear. Deconstruction in legal thought came after and in many cases as a response to the Harvard School.[142]

Even Unger and Kennedy joined in. In a frequently cited passage from *Roll Over Beethoven*, Kennedy distanced himself from the discussion of a fundamental contradiction in *Blackstone's Commentaries*.[143] Whatever purpose it might have once served in 1978, Kennedy explained, by 1984 it had been used up.[144] Similarly, Unger cautioned in a 1983 postscript to *Knowledge and Politics* against an essentialist reading of his book.[145] Perhaps in retrospect, Unger seemed to worry, the book had veered too close to precisely the sort of "totalizing" account he had criticized in the works of Chomsky and Lévi-Strauss.[146]

In the remainder of this chapter I quickly canvass some of the standout articles published right around the time of the Stanford Symposium, in an effort to give the flavor of this new anti-structuralism.[147] A first bone to pick was with the tendency in the work of the Harvard School to couple legal structuralism with a phenomenology of legal consciousness. Pierre Schlag, for example, was having none of

11 *Cardozo Law Review* (1990); Symposium: Derrida/America: The Present State of America's Europe, 27 *Cardozo Law Review* (2005); *Derrida and Law* (Pierre LeGrand, ed.) (London: Routledge, 2009).

141 Gordon, Hammer without a Master, supra note 5.

142 See, e.g., Gary Minda, *Postmodern Legal Movements: Law and Jurisprudence at Century's End* (New York: New York University Press, 1996), p. 116.

143 Gabel and Kennedy, supra note 135, at 15.

144 Even Foucault seemed relieved at Kennedy's recantation, taking his leave of materiality that same year. Michel Foucault, *The Archaeology of Knowledge: And the Discourse on Language* (New York: Pantheon Books, 1972), pp. 150–153.

145 Unger, Knowledge and Politics, supra note 26, at 337–341. Nevertheless, Unger's hunt for "deep structure" wouldn't perish. In addition to much of his recent writing, Unger explains on his website that "Although 'Knowledge and Politics' is distant, in form as well as in content, from my present work, it explores intellectual and political concerns that have continued to hold me in their grip." (available at http://www.law.harvard.edu/faculty/unger/social.php).

146 Id. See also id. at 126.

147 This trend is sometimes referred to as "second-wave" scholarship associated with the critical legal studies movement. *See* David Kennedy, "A Rotation in Contemporary Legal Scholarship," in *Critical Legal Thought: An American-German Debate* (Nomos, 1989), p. 356; James Boyle, "Introduction," in *Critical Legal Studies* (James Boyle, ed.) (New York: New York University Press, 1992). See also Duncan Kennedy, Psycho-Social CLS: A Comment on the Cardozo Symposium, 6 *Cardozo Law Review* 1013 (1985).

it.[148] For Schlag, phenomenological existentialism and structuralism were each beset by the same old Cartesian mystifications of subject and object, inside and out. And then, to marry the two was simply to make a Frankenstein's monster: "[S]tructuralism and existentialist phenomenology lead to each other precisely because they are complementary parts of the same subject-object map – that which has channeled virtually all thinking in the American legal academy since its inception. According to this view, cls thought is the most advanced expression of a flawed conception of subject-object relations."[149] James Boyle was of a similar mind, attacking the union of experience and structure:

> Duncan Kennedy's account of the fundamental contradiction [offers] a picture of 'what went on' that draws on the participant's awareness and yet transcends it. By uncovering 'what is really going on,' the structuralist strand in critical legal studies tries to expose the constraining quality of the structures of everyday life, which are embedded in legal decisions, standard arguments, or in the unproblematic assumptions on which a discussion is based . . . By offering a convincing account of knowledge, power, and life that is largely independent of the 'intentionally acting subject,' [Kennedy's structuralism] seems to undermine the central role that the subjectivist strand has held in the Western epistemological and political tradition. Each strand, in other words, both contradicts and relies on the other. Each contains the dangerous supplement, the trace, of its opposite.[150]

Gary Peller's "The Metaphysics of American Law"[151] from 1985 was somewhat more sympathetic to the Harvard School approach, yet at the same time consistent with the different, Derridean path being forged in Boyle's and (later) Schlag's work. In the introduction, Peller suggested that

148 Pierre Schlag, The Problem of the Subject, 69 *Texas Law Review*, 1627, 1700 (1991) ("What is wrong is that this division among the structuralist (appellate doctrine in itself) strand and the phenomenological subjectivist (value choices) strand has become, consciously or not, the master rule, the totalizing framework. Not only is this totalizing, structured practice intellectually limiting, it is politically disabling and oppressive."); Pierre Schlag, Rules and Standards, 33 *University of California Los Angeles Law Review* 379 (1985) ("It does no good to explain the dialectic in terms of consciousness – political or otherwise. Once we privilege consciousness, there is as good a reason to find there any one thing as another. And the question of what gets privileged is merely replicated within the language used to describe consciousness.")

149 Pierre Schlag, Normativity and the Politics of Form, 139 *University of Pennsylvania Law Review* 801, 913 (1991).

150 James Boyle, The Politics of Reason: Critical Legal Theory and Local Social Thought, 133 *University of Pennsylvania Law Review* 685, 744 (1985). For a recent suggestion that Kennedy was trying to explain what "was really going on," see John C. P. Goldberg, Introduction: Pragmatism and Private Law, 125 *Harvard Law Review* 1640, 1645 (2012). Curiously, Goldberg describes Kennedy as a "brass-tacks pragmatist." Id.

151 Gary Peller, The Metaphysics of American Law, 73 *California Law Review* 1151 (1985).

American law was conditioned by a "deep metaphoric structure for interpreting the social world."[152] This structure sat "beneath" what appeared to be very different ways of thinking about law, ranging from the legal formalism of the Nineteenth Century to the legal functionalism of the Twentieth. Peller described this metaphoric structure as "the subject/object dichotomy, the notion that the social world can meaningfully be described by separating subjective and objective realms of social life."[153] Peller suggested that this "background structure" served as a "language" in which the subject/object dichotomy was repeatedly reordered at different moments in the history of American legal thought.[154] Peller's project was to "explicate the various historical modes of legal thought by attempting to reconstruct the background metaphors of each approach in order to understand why each approach seems plausible to its adherents."[155]

In these first few pages, it is tempting to see this as an artifact of Harvard School structuralism. But it's not, or not quite. While legal discourse attempts to characterize itself as a particular language, Peller argued, the *truth* was that there was really nothing distinguishing legal discourse from any other kind of discourse.[156] There was no special legal *langue* at all, liberal or otherwise. The experience of law as a distinct mode of communication with knowable frontiers – distinct from poetry or colloquial coffee-shop talk – was an illusion produced by the background metaphors of law. All discourse is, *in the real world*, political, fluid, endlessly entangled. It was a mistake to think about a *thing* called liberalism that might exist in that real world, producing or governing law through a fundamentally contradictory structure.[157] As Peller explained, "the point here is not that there is no world separate from consciousness; of course there is. But there is no determinative way to *know* this world separate from the socially created representational systems through which we approach the world. Knowledge and social power are inseparable."[158]

Obviously, this was problematic for anyone interested in showing that all law everywhere was pervaded by a fundamental contradiction of some kind.[159] What you might have interpreted as a reflection of liberalism could be interpreted otherwise – the difference between liberal argument

[152] Id. at 1154. [153] Id [154] Id. [155] Id. at 1155. [156] Id.

[157] Boyle, The Politics of Reason, supra note 150, at 715 ("If we are rejecting essences, we cannot claim to have discovered the canonical, essential structure of thought from which liberal theorists depart at their peril.")

[158] Peller, supra note 151, at 1170.

[159] Boyle, for example, said that Kennedy and Unger fell prey to precisely the same critiques they were making of liberal legalism: essentialist analyses of totalities. Boyle, The Politics

and illiberal argument was precisely that, a matter of interpretation. Liberalism was merely in the eye of the beholder, as was the assessment of any possible totalization of law. After a lengthy treatment of Derrida's *differance*, Peller moved into the heart of the article and a discussion of the "metaphoric root system" common to the "liberty of contract" and "legal realist" periods of law.[160] As Peller was well aware, the discussion bore a heavy resemblance to Harvard School treatments of liberal legalism. The difference for Peller was that these metaphysical assumptions had no source in liberal political theory, or in anything else for that matter. There was no liberal "center" from which to suggest a language of law, despite the sense that what Peller was describing had much in common with liberalism. The worry was that in attributing his analysis to "liberalism," Peller wanted to avoid the mistake of suggesting that something like the "public-private distinction" was *real*.[161] The distinction might very well unpack in any number of ways: "the distinction between public and private was a legal construction, not a reflection of some code pre-existing the legal practice. Rather than explicate a determinate structure which animated the discourse, I have offered what may be best described as a table of contents or indexing system."[162] Indeed, this is a telling qualification, since the "indices of discourse" indicated precisely the shift away from the systems of *langue* and toward the discourse of *parole* in critical legal scholarship.

This turn away from the Harvard School, initiated in articles like Peller's, was further advanced in works like Thomas Heller's *Structuralism and Critique* (1985).[163] Heller argued at the outset that structuralism

of Reason, supra note 150, at 712–729. The critique of legal structuralism by "progressive" scholars didn't always lead into deconstruction, however, as it did in the case of Boyle, Schlag, and Peller, and in some cases they were equally critical of these "second-wave" efforts. See Drucilla Cornell, Toward a Modern/Postmodern Reconstruction of Ethics, 133 *University of Pennsylvania Law Review* 291 (1985); Joan Williams, Critical Legal Studies: The Death of Transcendence and the Rise of the New Langdells, 62 *New York University Law Review* 429, 442 (1987).

160 Peller, supra note 151, at 1215.

161 Peller concluded: "Thus, while the metaphoric representation of the social world was consistent with the broad outlines of the political theory of Lockean liberalism, it would completely miss the mark to simply describe the period as an attempt to institute classical liberal political theory. It is more accurate to say that classical social contract theory itself depended on the metaphoric root system . . . The liberty of contract approach was not a deduction from the premises of a political theory, but rather was an embedded representational structure for perceiving and communicating about the world." Id. at 1219.

162 Id.

163 Thomas Heller, Structuralism and Critique, 36 *Stanford Law Review* 127 (1984).

was already a "now-dissolved intellectual movement" and "passé" in France, and had never caught on at all in the United States.[164] Without a doubt, Heller assured the reader, the critical legal studies movement was certainly not synonymous with legal structuralism: the former was raging, the latter was dead.[165] And yet, despite the gloomy prognosis, Heller began the article by explaining that while he felt committed to providing a "structuralist" account of structuralism itself, the account would proceed in a "self-reflectively critical" way – a self-reflectivity apparently absent in prior works of legal structuralism.[166] This self-awareness involved a sense that the production of a legal structure should be "contingent" and "constructed."[167] This was the idea that the legal structuralists had been out to identify totalizing accounts of the legal universe, and that they had failed to be critical enough of their own work to see this. Poststructuralists, Heller explained, already understood that it was impossible to identify true and universal social structures.[168]

Heller covered the typical critiques of structuralism of the time. First, the multiplicity of structuralist accounts was often over-determinative of the object in question.[169] If there were so many competing structures apparently responsibly for the same phenomenon, how was anyone to know which one was right?[170] The number of apparently available structures, Heller explained, threatened to liken structuralism to fiction, where "each structuralism is reduced to an artifact of volitional or subjective spirit."[171] Second, structuralism was persistently under-determinative in its specification of the relation between the fixed structure, and the apparently random way in which specific practices develop within the structure.[172] Why did this culture create that particular myth, why did this judge follow that particular pattern? Why not another? Structuralists seemed doomed either to suggest a kind of biological necessity determining all outcomes completely, or to throw up their hands in exasperation, claiming particular practices as entirely arbitrary.[173] A related third objection turned on the structuralist's inability to explain the subject's role in the structure, thus resorting to the analytically suspect notion of "relative autonomy."[174] If the structure had a relative autonomy from the society

[164] Id. at 127–128. [165] Id. at 128. [166] Id. at 129. [167] Id.
[168] Id. at 133. [169] Id. at 157.
[170] See also, Boyle, The Politics of Reason, supra note 150, at 749; James Boyle, Is Subjectivity Possible – The Postmodern Subject in Legal Theory, 62 *University of Colorado Law Review* 489, 499 (1991).
[171] Heller, supra note 163, at 157. [172] Id. at 158. [173] Id. at 159.
[174] Id. at 146.

which it was understood to be structuring, where were the lines to be drawn? How could the difference between structure and the structured be maintained, even at a "relative" distance? A fourth complaint was directed at the preference for synchronic analysis, and the disturbing lack of attention to questions about the provenance of particular structures.[175] Like most other poststructuralists, Heller expected these to be questions that hadn't yet occurred to the legal structuralists.

A year later David Kennedy joined his voice to the nay-sayers in *Critical Theory, Structuralism, and Contemporary Legal Scholarship* (1986),[176] apparently reversing course from his own work with the Harvard School. In Derridean language, Kennedy explained at the outset how structuralists bracketed out the question of historical origins, but at the cost of producing a desiccated analysis of rigid form.[177] Deconstruction of structuralist texts tended to show that such analyses were "always supplemented by shadow theories of the origin of the social relations or structures which they analyzed."[178] In one sense, Kennedy was referring here to what I described above as the tendency to connect legal structuralism with legal realism. The indeterminacy critique, it will be recalled, followed from the posited analogy between legal argument and *parole*. If the structuralist wants to go further, however, and say something about an ideological basis for patterning *parole* in a certain way, or relating a *langue* to capitalism, or making a claim about the legal structure's role in social development, this seemed to represent a departure from structuralist method.[179] Structuralism, even if it was possible to conduct at all (can the analyst really get out from under the constraints of the relevant *langue* in her attempt to describe it?), seemed unable to do anything but offer formal and sterile accounts of legal structure, even when the structuralist's intention was precisely to provide a critical account. Synchronic analysis seemed forced to dissolve into diachrony; structuralism seemed forced elsewhere, always.

For Kennedy (following Derrida), it was not possible to locate a legal structure at a present moment, and despite the structuralist's attempt to

[175] Id. at 159.

[176] David Kennedy, Critical Theory, Structuralism, and Contemporary Legal Scholarship, 21 *New England Law Review* 209 (1985).

[177] Id. at 214. [178] Id.

[179] Kennedy, Critical Theory, Structuralism, and Contemporary Legal Scholarship, supra note 176, at 269. ("Typically, after exposing a contradiction resolved within a legal text, the structuralist legal scholar will turn to critical theory for assistance in interpreting this 'deception.' In this, like structuralists in other disciplines, they seem unable to resist the temptation to reintroduce diachrony into their analysis.")

hide this "dangerous supplement" by placing it indefinitely in abeyance, it is this knowing that ultimately undermines the notion that there is a structure to be explained.[180] For the poststructuralist, structuralists were obsessed with totalities and universals.[181] Echoing a now-familiar theme, Kennedy explained, "the structuralist tried to figure out what was *really going on* in myth or literature or language. The post-structuralist is more interested in the construction and reproduction of these projects than in their resolution. To the post-structuralist, it was precisely the determination to 'get it right' that led . . . the structuralist to invent an authoritative 'deeper' level which could account for the diversity of myth or language."[182]

Over in the United Kingdom, similar discontents were on the rise.[183] In their book *Postmodern Jurisprudence*, for example, Costas Douzinas, Ronnie Worthington, and Shaun McVeigh opened with a chapter on the same liberal foundations explored in the Harvard School texts, but rather than treat these "foundations" as structured in any particular way, Douzinas instead emphasized their openness and ultimate indeterminacy. Pointing to liberal legalism and its charge to "ground its own discourse and to justify rationally its claims to act as the secular God,"[184] Douzinas recognized the antinomy already articulated by Unger and Kennedy. Liberal legalism, Douzinas explained, was "entrusted with the task of

[180] Kennedy cites Sartre and Foucault for the notion that structuralists sought access to "social totality." Id. at 275.

[181] For Duncan Kennedy's accommodation of the Derridean critique, see Kennedy, A Semiotics of Critique, supra note 46, at 1183–1184 ("Play is *bricolage* is *parole*.")

[182] Kennedy, Critical Theory, Structuralism, and Contemporary Legal Scholarship, supra note 176, at 278–279. Conceivably the most damning of all was the argument that in seeking out patterns and structures, the structuralist was inevitably already engaging in an interpretive activity. As Stanley Fish put it, the structuralist exercise was arbitrary, "ruled by the determination to have a relation rather than by a procedure which demonstrates it . . . That is, the pattern emerges under the pressure of an interpretation and does not exist as independent evidence of it. In the event of a different interpretation, the pattern would be seen differently and be evidence in another direction." Stanley Fish, *Is There a Text in This Class? The Authority of Interpretive Communities* (Cambridge, MA: Harvard University Press, 1980), p. 253.

[183] Though not "in" the UK exactly, Peter Goodrich is a great representative. See, e.g., Peter Goodrich *Legal Discourse: Studies in Linguistics, Rhetoric, and Legal Analysis* (New York: St Martin's Press, 1987); Peter Goodrich, *Oedipus Lex: Psychoanalysis, History, Law* (Berkeley: University of California Press, 1995). See also Costas Douzinas, A Short History of the British Critical Legal Conference or, The Responsibility of the Critic, 25 *Law and Critique* 187 (2014).

[184] Costas Douzinas et al., *Postmodern Jurisprudence: The Law of Texts in the Texts of Law* (New York: Routledge, 1993), p 14.

constraining individual egoism while enforcing personal and contractual autonomy."[185] But rather than focus on the mediations through which the structure of liberal legalism attempts to avoid this basic antinomy, Douzinas emphasized liberalism's outright failure. "Theories of adjudication . . . keep claiming that they can ground value-free interpretations and applications of pre-existing general and abstract rules."[186]

> But the instantiation of rules always involves discretion, in this instance, the description and assessment of individual particularities and the choice amongst the customers of bureaucratic largesse. Discretion openly reintroduces value choice. [Liberal legalism] was conceived as an answer to the degeneracy of moral consensus. The conditions that led it its genesis, however, further exacerbated by the onset of full-fledged modernity, prevent it from ever delivering what it claims; a neutral non-subjectivist resolution of value disagreement and social conflict.[187]

This is, of course, only a tiny sample of the critical works emerging between the mid-1980s and early 1990s. But it is enough to get a sense of the problems quickly being associated with the Harvard School. In summary, they were the following: First, the union of existential phenomenology and legal structuralism simply reproduced the already very troubled subject-object relation. Second, the Harvard School failed to understand that its posited differences between an autonomous, or relatively autonomous, legal mode of discourse and all other discourse – the idea that *politics is law* – were endlessly susceptible to deconstruction. Third, legal structuralism was ahistorical, with no apparent sense for where these structures came from or for their situatedness in time. Fourth, Harvard School thinking tended to reify liberalism, treating it as a thing in the world with properties that might be scientifically rendered. And fifth, and most broadly, Harvard School thinking sought to discover the world as it really was, to explain was truly going on, totalizing, universalizing, in the hopes of providing an objective science of law.

With this last criticism, the Harvard School was painted as simply a reinvented version of what it had been ostensibly fashioned to interrogate: an Enlightenment vision of law and politics. After all, Schlag, Boyle, Heller, Peller, Kennedy, and Douzinas all seemed to suggest that the Harvard School had, however unintentionally, dressed an old analytic in some fancy French clothes. As Martin Jay describes, "Even when Bacon castigated normal vision for staying on the surface of things and failing to

[185] Id. [186] Id. at 13. [187] Id. at 14.

pay attention to the invisible world beneath, he hoped that ultimately its secrets would be 'brought to light.'"[188] Is this what Unger and Kennedy had been up to? Had they been duped, only now unmasked as the unwitting playthings of an Enlightenment project?

[188] Martin Jay, *Songs of Experience: Modern American and European Variations on a Universal Theme* (Berkeley: University of California Press, 2005), p. 37.

2

Toward a Jurisprudence of Style

Was Harvard School structuralism an unintended Enlightenment project, a positivism in disguise? I don't think so. Be that as it may, this chapter does not provide apologetic intellectual history for legal structuralism as it stood in 1980. I have little doubt that such a history could be written, and that as an apology, it would succeed. In this and the following chapter, however, I prefer to offer a view of legal structuralism as it might operate today. It is a view heavily indebted to the founding Harvard School thinkers, but it is also a view renewed. The result is what I call a jurisprudence of style, and what I believe to be the Harvard School's contemporary heir.

A basic assumption in the Harvard School wheelhouse was the necessity of incorporating the jurist's phenomenology of experience into a structuralist understanding of legal thought.[1] Despite the pushback engendered over the years, I think that this basic assumption remains sound. In the following pages, I press this assumption forward with the assistance of a trio of thinkers who lent little support in the initial construction of the Harvard School's intellectual platform: Maurice Merleau-Ponty, Michel Foucault, and Roland Barthes. In the jurisprudence of style, these thinkers help establish a series of footholds.

Summarily, those footholds are these. First, we reject the *cogito*. Legal consciousness is not a Cartesian "inside" ontologically distinct from

[1] In his characteristic prose, Terry Eagleton put the conflict between the two like this: "Instead of poems as plump as an apple, we now have texts as material as an armpit. This turn to the body sprang partly from a structuralist hostility to consciousness, and represents the final expulsion of the ghost from the machine." Terry Eagleton, *The Illusions of Postmodernism* (Oxford: Oxford University Press, 1996), p. 70.

an objectified "outside."[2] Rather, consciousness is thoroughly integrated with what comes to hand, manifesting at a prereflective and preconceptual level a kind of coping or dealing with the solicitations and affordances of the material that constitutes us in this backgrounded "interspace." Second, in a traditionally antirealist posture, we mark off the attempt of "Objective Thought" to understand "true reality" as having little use for the structuralist. We provisionally accept the myth of the given that "true reality" is radically indeterminate and only knowable through interpretation. Third, we similarly avoid attempts to interpret "true reality" and focus instead on the *style* in which consciousness manifests its world of coping and dealing. To be sure, style is not code for freedom of choice. Rather, style is code for a structured pattern of argumentative practice. As Merleau-Ponty would put it, the jurist's "speech *is* his thought."[3] That is, style at once denotes the existence of multiple *structures*, since each structure is itself stylized, as well as the capacity for consciousness to navigate the structure at a conceptual level, foregrounded at a level "above" the deeper level of preconceptual coping. In other words, there are styles in which one can render a structure, and there are the styles in which the jurist operates within a given structure. Fourth, this view of a style of consciousness rendered as argumentative practice is thoroughly chiastic. It is a mistake to think about the relation between consciousness and structure either as a Cartesian inside/outside or as a singular entity. It is neither and both, a repeating set of reversals. The jurisprudence of style is, in the Kierkegaardian sense further explored at the book's end, a kind of madness.

I articulate these propositions more fully in the context of a sample of writings from Merleau-Ponty, Foucault, and Barthes. In Chapter 3, I push these propositions into the jurisprudence of style, encapsulating what I call a legal structuralism of today, or if you like, a second generation of the Harvard School. But before moving to those texts, a preliminary point.[4] The criticisms of the Harvard School surveyed at the end of the

[2] For a helpful overview, see Anil Gupta, *Empiricism and Experience* (New York: Oxford University Press, 2006).

[3] Maurice Merleau-Ponty, *Phenomenology of Perception* (London: Routledge, 1962), p. 209.

[4] And another preliminary: I resist canonical understandings of a given author's oeuvre. I resist it for the same reason that I resist canonical understandings of phenomenology and structuralism, writ large. Was Merleau-Ponty *really* a phenomenologist? Wasn't the body, in which Merleau-Ponty had so much interest, entirely different from and incompatible

last chapter are in many (but not all) ways consistent with the jurisprudence of style; it is not, in other words a jurisprudence built for hiding (this is what pragmatic liberalism is built for, as I suggest in Chapter 9). If we take scientism to refer to or depend upon the availability of an apodictic conceptualization of the subject-object relation, scientism is a topos simply out of place in the discussion that follows. Roland Barthes' depiction of the structuralist enterprise is characteristic of the view I will be developing: "The semiology proposed here is therefore negative . . . not in that it repudiates the sign, but in that it denies that it is possible to attribute to the sign traits that are positive, fixed, ahistoric, acorporeal, in short scientific."[5] Or, to put the point differently, I agree with Hubert Dreyfus and Charles Taylor when they write that "almost everyone seems to agree that the great enterprise of Descartes, to build up certain knowledge from undeniable building blocks, is misconceived."[6] The effort to establish an unproblematic correspondence between reality and our language and ideas about reality is simply out of fashion. And yet – and I think this is crucial – I also agree with Dreyfus and Taylor when they suggest that this powerful antirealism is not the end of the story. Antirealism, in the sense that an individual's subjective understanding of reality will never capture an objective rendering of the real, obviously depends on a distinction between subject and object, inside and outside. If the claim is that one can never get out of her own insides to *really know* the outsides, well, we are clearly already working within the ambits of an inside/outside distinction. Antirealism is, as a result, in some sense the progeny of the worldview it is intended to problematize.[7] This lack of sympathy for antirealism cashes out, as I will later explain, in the view of legal thought *as* the practice of legal argument.

with the "body" scrutinized by Barthes and Foucault? Didn't the later Barthes reject his earlier, more "militant" structuralism? Didn't Foucault, in the foreword to his *The Order of Things*, beg his readers to stop calling him a structuralist, and heed his rejection of the "phenomenological approach"? Michel Foucault, *The Order of Things: An Archaeology of Human Sciences* (New York.: Vintage Books, 1994), p. xiv. Sure he did, some paragraphs after having asked, "What right have I, then, to suggest that [my work] should be used in one way rather than another?" Id. at ix. These questions presume a degree of continuity and stability both with respect to phenomenology and structuralism, as well as with the "work" of the three authors in question, that I am simply not willing to grant.

5 Roland Barthes, *A Barthes Reader* (Susan Sontag, ed.) (New York: Vintage, 2000), p. 473.

6 Hubert Dreyfus and Charles Taylor, *Retrieving Realism* (Cambridge, MA: Harvard University Press, 2015), p. 41.

7 Id. at 56.

Maurice Merleau-Ponty: Thought as Practice

The englobing site of consciousness and the phenomenal world, and for our purposes we can anticipate a *legal* consciousness of a *legal* world,[8] was for Merleau-Ponty neither a sum of objects nor a list of analytic propositions.[9] It did not involve the *cogito*. To think about a "reality" of subject-object relations in these familiar Cartesian terms was counterproductive, since the effort to pull the thinking mind apart from the world in which it does its thinking is mistaken: "[e]very analysis which disentangles renders unintelligible."[10] In Merleau-Ponty's phenomenology, drawn in part from Heidegger's, the aim is embodiment, entanglement, imbrication; this allows us to see how our "structure of consciousness"[11] is essentially that of a material embeddedness. The world is not, on his view, rendered as a representation in an inside mind of an outside universe, but rather as a constant and continuing intermingling of lifeworld. As we move through our worlds, *things* solicit our attention, arise to use as *equipment*, afford us opportunities, draw certain responses. And as we accept these solicitations and invitations, embrace these affordances, cope with these "lines of force," go with the flow, fall into our work, and so on, consciousness manifests as a backgrounded being in the world. This is not determinism, but instead a deep familiarity of practice. Consider soccer.

> For the player in action the football field is not an "object," that is, the ideal term which can give rise to an indefinite multiplicity of perspectival views and remain equivalent under its apparent transformations. It is pervaded with lines

[8] A very interesting anticipation is Peter Gabel, Intention and Structure in Contractual Conditions: Outline of a Method for Critical Legal Theory, 61 *Minnesota Law Review* 601 (1977).

[9] Maurice Merleau-Ponty, *The Primacy of Perception* (William Cobb, trans.) (James Edie, ed.) (Chicago: Northwestern University Press, 1989), p. 25. For further discussion of Merleau-Ponty's phenomenology, see James Schmidt, *Maurice Merleau-Ponty: Between Phenomenology and Structuralism* (New York: Saint Martin's Press, 1985); Hugh Silverman, *Inscriptions: Between Phenomenology and Structuralism* (New York: Routledge, 1987); Christopher Macann, *Four Phenomenological Philosophers: Husserl, Heidegger, Sartre, Merleau-Ponty* (New York: Routledge, 1993). See also Paul Ricoeur, *Freud and Philosophy: An Essay on Interpretation* (Denis Savage, trans.) (New Haven, CT: Yale University Press, 1970); Jean-Francois Lyotard, *Phenomenology* (Brian Beakley, trans.) (Albany: State University of New York Press, 1991).

[10] Maurice Merleau-Ponty, *The Visible and the Invisible* (Claude Lefort, ed.) (Alphonso Lingis, trans.) (Chicago: Northwestern University Press, 1968), p. 268.

[11] Maurice Merleau-Ponty, *The Structure of Behavior* (Alden Fisher, trans.) (Boston: Beacon Press, 1963), p. 166.

of force (the "yard lines"; those which demarcate the "penalty area") and articulated in sectors (for example, the "openings" between the adversaries) which call for a certain mode of action and which initiate and guide the action as if the player were unaware of it. The field itself is not given to him, but present as the immanent term of his practical intentions; the player becomes one with it and feels the direction of the "goal," for example, just as immediately as the vertical and the horizontal planes of his own body. It would not be sufficient to say that consciousness inhabits this milieu. *At this moment consciousness is nothing other than the dialectic of milieu and action.* Each maneuver undertaken by the player modifies the character of the field and establishes in it new lines of force in which the action in turn unfolds and is accomplished, again altering the phenomenal field.[12]

As Merleau-Ponty says here, what seems to be happening is a dialectic of environment and mind, milieu and agency. But even this talk of a dialectic might be too suggestive of distance, a Cartesian separation. Merleau-Ponty offered in his last writings another way to talk about the deep practice of skilled coping, as Hubert Dreyfus calls it, and this was the embodiment of consciousness and world in the figure of the chiasm.[13] Conventionally deployed in the study of religious texts and literature, the chiasm is a rhetorical figure denoting a repetition of paradoxical reversals and returns.[14] From within the Cartesian outlook that so dominates the Western tradition, this chiastic approach comes off as a paradoxical view of consciousness and world, where "reality" is described in its essence, but essences that are necessarily dependent on consciousness. For

[12] Id. at 168–169.

[13] Merleau-Ponty, Visible, supra note 10, at 264. For discussion, see Ted Toadvine, "The Chiasm," in *The Routledge Companion to Phenomenology* (Sebastian Luft and Soren Overgaard, eds.) (New York: Routledge, 2012), p. 336; Schmidt, supra note 9, at 91. See also Justin Desautels-Stein, Chiastic Law in the Crystal Ball: Exploring Legal Formalism and Its Alternative Futures, 2 *London Review International Law* 263 (2014).

[14] Eve Kosefsky Sedgwick provides a typical definition of chiasmus in the context of rhetoric: "chiasmus: ki-AZ-mus. Gr. 'a placing crosswise, a diagonal arrangement.' Repetition of ideas or grammatical structures in inverted order (AB-BA). 'It is boring to eat; to sleep is fulfilling'; 'Ask not what your country can do for you; ask rather what you can do for your country.' Like anacoluthon, it generally presumes a context of parallel structure. Because of its criss-cross relation to temporality, a looser, narrative notion of chiasmus is often associated with the psychoanalytic notion of Nachträglichkeit or deferred action (what Silvan Tomkins calls posticipation), in which experiences, impressions, and memory traces may be revised at a later date to fit in with fresh experiences or with the attainment of a new stage of development." Eve Kosefsky Sedgwick, *Rhetorical Devices* (2001), available at http://evekosofskysedgwick.net/teaching/rhetorical-devices.html (last visited November 16, 2017). See also Anthony Paul and Boris Wiseman, "Chiasmus in the Drama of Life," in *Chiasmus and Culture* (Boris Wiseman and Anthony Paul, eds.) (New York: Berghahn, 2014).

Merleau-Ponty, in contrast, it is a field of reflection regarded as a "creative operation which itself participates in the facticity of the experience."[15] The chiastic vision of consciousness and world is consequently neither dialectical nor about mutual constitution; it is about an interaction that is both at the same time.[16] As Merleau-Ponty put it,

> It is true that I do not feel that I am the constituting agent either of the natural or the cultural world: into each perception and into each judgement I bring either sensory functions or cultural settings which are not actually mine. Yet although I am outrun on all sides by my own acts, and submerged in generality, the fact remains that I am the one by whom they are experienced, and with my first perception there was launched an insatiable being who appropriates everything that he meets, to whom nothing can be purely and simply given because he has inherited his share of the world, and hence carries within him the project of all possible being, because it has once and for all been imprinted in his field of experiences.[17]

There is a repeating set of reversals here, where the "object" and its "essence" are neither located in pure consciousness as mental facts, nor contrasted with subjects in an objectified "true reality,"[18] but instead manifest in a chiastic and bodily interspace of consciousness.[19] As Merleau-Ponty suggested, "The relations between things or aspects of things having always our body as their vehicle, the whole of nature is the setting of our own life, or our interlocutor in a sort of dialogue."[20] And more to the point of the particularly chiastic nature of an englobed consciousness, Merleau-Ponty wrote, "Whether we are concerned with my body, the natural world, the past, birth or death, the question is always how I can be open to phenomena which transcend me, and which nevertheless exist only to the extent that I take them up and live them."[21]

A second point from Merleau-Ponty, beyond the need to demonstrate the illusory status of the subject-object dualism, was the thoroughly *indeterminate* nature of the universe that exists outside and beyond the process of an individual consciousness coping with an environment

[15] Merleau-Ponty, Phenomenology, supra note 3, at 61.

[16] See Paul de Man, *Allegories of Reading: Figural Language in Rousseau, Nietzsche, Rilke, and Proust* (New Haven, CT: Yale University Press, 1979), p. 38. As de Man explained, with chiasmus, "you have it all: you have the critical perception, you have the possibility of carrying on in apocalyptic tones, you have the particular eloquence that comes with that (because one can only really get excited if one writes in an apocalyptic mode); but you can still talk in terms of hope, and Benjamin would be an example of this combination of nihilistic rigor with sacred revelation." Paul de Man, "Conclusions" in Walter Benjamin's "The Task of the Translator" Messenger Lecture, Cornell University, March 4, 1983, 69 *Yale French Studies* 10 (1985), p. 18.

[17] Merleau-Ponty, Phenomenology, supra note 3, at 358. [18] Id. at 58.

[19] Id. at xiv–xv. [20] Id. at 320. [21] Id. at 363.

of affordances. In step with the Cartesian tradition was the fantasy of "Objective Thought," which in its various ways "build[s] up all knowledge out of determinate qualities, offers us objects purged of all ambiguity, pure and absolute, the ideal rather than the real themes of knowledge."[22] This purging and the belief in the freestanding object was "based on the foreshadowing of an imminent order which is about to spring upon us a reply to questions merely latent in the landscape."[23] But Objective Thought was mistaken in its presentation of a world awaiting rational analysis, a world kept distant from the perceiving subject. To move away from this representational view of knowledge, and enter the chiasm of consciousness in world and world in consciousness, was therefore to accept "the indeterminate as a positive phenomenon."[24] Coming to recognize the radical indeterminacy of things, Merleau-Ponty believed, opens us to a proper phenomenological inquiry into the "pre-objective realm"[25] of experience I have already alluded to.[26] This pre-objective, or better, pre-conceptual field remains hidden, "as long as the attempt is made to build up the shape of the world (life, perception, mind) instead of recognizing, as the source which stares us in the face and as the ultimate court of appeal in our knowledge of these things, our *experience* of them."[27] Standing against this understanding of an empirical pursuit of an objective world was therefore a prioritization of experience with radical indeterminacy. "The world," Merleau-Ponty explained, "does not hold for us a set of outlines which some consciousness within us binds together into a unity."[28]

The third point I take from Merleau-Ponty in this setup of the jurisprudence of style, and the point that coalesces in the prior two, is Merleau-Ponty's own notion of style. Given the state of global indeterminacy in which we find ourselves, Merleau-Ponty's chiastic repositioning of consciousness and world suggested the importance of orientation, the posture in which the entanglement of consciousness and world is experienced and rendered intelligible. This figured *orientation*, this *posture*, something quite other than pat subjectivity, is "style."[29] That is, while Merleau-Ponty believed in the unavailability of giving unified expression to a natural reality, he did believe that we could describe a unified lifeworld, a unity in which "the antinomies of objective thought

[22] Id. at 11. [23] Id. at 17. [24] Id. at 6, 320. [25] Id. at 12. [26] Id. at 304.
[27] Id. at 23. [28] Id. at 328–329.
[29] Id. at 327. See also Robert Denoon Cumming, *Phenomenology and Deconstruction* (Chicago: University of Chicago Press, 1991), p. 166.

vanish."[30] This intelligible unity, he explained, could be experienced in the same way in which we recognize a unity in individual persons.

> The world has its unity, although the mind may not have succeeded in interrelating its facets and in integrating them into the conception of a flat projection. This unity is comparable with that of an individual whom I recognize because he is recognizable in an unchallengeably self-evident way, before I ever succeed in stating the formula governing his character, because he retains the same style in everything he says and does, even though he may change his place or opinions. A style is a certain manner of dealing with situations, which I identify or understand in an individual or in a writer, by taking over that manner myself in a sort of imitative way, even though I may be quite unable to define it . . . I experience the unity of the world as I recognize style.[31]

Merleau-Ponty's idea of style is complicated. On the one hand, and with reference to older usages in stylistics, *style* suggests subjectivity, individual discretion, choice.[32] If I appear to you in a particular manner, with a discrete style, if I write in a *stylized* manner or sing or dress or cook or dance with a particular style, what seems evident above all else is that I might have chosen some other style, had I been in a different mood.[33] It is mere *technique*. On the other hand, I recognize style in an "unchallengeably self-evident way, before I ever succeed in stating the formula governing [its] character." This suggests the existence of *certain* styles, styles that preexist and even shape the individual's freedom to choose, and the possibility that we may not choose style so much as a given set of styles choose us. Style, in this sense, emerge as the "lines of force" themselves rather than as a modes of knowledge production. Once we begin to consider style in this second way, however, we seem on the path toward a de-individualizing tendency in French thought, a tendency with which Merleau-Ponty was uncomfortable, to say the least. Style, for Merleau-Ponty, was a chiasm, reversing the subject-object duality into a singular – and paradoxical – unity.

> The central phenomenon, at the root of both my subjectivity and my transcendence towards others, consists in my being given to myself. *I am given*, that is, I find myself already situated and involved in a physical and social world – *I am given to myself*, which means that this situation is never hidden from me . . . I am

[30] Merleau-Ponty, Phenomenology, supra note 3, at 351. [31] Id. at 327.

[32] For discussion, see Lesley Jeffries and Dan McIntyre, *Stylistics* (Cambridge: Cambridge University Press, 2010).

[33] An interesting discussion on the phenomenology of mood is Hubert Dreyfus and Sean Kelly, *All Things Shining: Reading the Western Classics to find Meaning in a Secular Age* (New York: Free Press, 2011).

never in effect enclosed in it like an object in a box. My freedom, the fundamental power which I enjoy of being the subject of all my experiences, is not distinct from my insertion into the world. It is a fate for me to be free, to be unable to reduce myself to anything that I experience, to maintain in relation to any factual situation a faculty of withdrawal, and this fate was sealed the moment my transcendental field was thrown open, when I was born as vision and knowledge, when I was thrown into the world.[34]

In this initial foray, Merleau-Ponty helps launch the jurisprudence of style in the following way. First, we introduce a view of consciousness in which we bypass the Cartesian distinction between an inside making representations of an outside, and instead accept a view in which consciousness is constituted through a constant coping with our equipmental context, copings and dealings that only sometimes rise to the level of rational and conceptual awareness. Second, this background space of consciousness takes place against a backdrop of thorough indeterminacy. This is a basic antirealism, in which we deny, at least for the sake of argument, the demands of scientism and "objective thought." But remember, at least for someone like Merleau-Ponty, the antirealist moment is quick – its work is important only in its contest with the champions of "objective thought." It is quick because the third point, Merleau-Ponty's suggestion that we can think about the movement of being (i.e., consciousness *as* a spiraling world of affordances) taking recognizable styles in the milieu of radical indeterminacy, returns us, however paradoxically, to a feel for the *real*.

Michel Foucault: Practice as Structure

I will soon return to Merleau-Ponty's chiastic consciousness, but first, we need more structure. Now, as I have already mentioned, phenomenology and structuralism have never been natural allies, and Michel Foucault claimed to be an ally of neither.[35] Foucault believed that it was precisely this coming back to the fundaments of the *I* that defined the essence of a deeply problematic philosophy: "If phenomenology has any allegiance, it is to . . . the new figure which, under the old name of man, first appeared

34 Merleau-Ponty, Phenomenology, supra note 3, at 360.

35 See, e.g., Tilottama Rajan, *Deconstruction and the Remainders of Phenomenology: Sartre, Derrida, Foucault, Baudrillard* (Redwood City, CA: Stanford University Press, 2002); *Foucault and Heidegger: Critical Encounters* (Alan Milchman and Alan Rosenberg, eds.) (Minneapolis: University of Minnesota Press, 2003).

less than two centuries ago."[36] And even while Merleau-Ponty problematized that figure, Foucault complained that all of the situating just made things worse, as "the phenomenological project continually resolves itself, before our eyes, into a description – empirical despite itself – of actual experience."[37] Indeed, this is precisely the complaint we heard in the last chapter from the poststructuralist jurists, that phenomenology engaged the "search for the origin, for formal a prioris, for founding acts, in short, [everything Foucault's own method was meant to undermine]."[38]

At first blush then, it is well to ask, why include Foucault in the case of characters intended to help compose the jurisprudence of style? Merleau-Ponty was trying to solve the problem of the subject, while Foucault sought to abandon it. But it gets worse. For as much venom Foucault might have reserved for phenomenology, he was equally hostile to structuralism.[39] In sounds entirely reminiscent of the poststructuralist jurists, in *The Order of Things* and *The Archaeology of Knowledge*[40] Foucault repeatedly rejected structuralism. Structuralism was *totalizing, universalizing, scientistic*: "A [structuralist] description draws all phenomena around a single center – a principle, a meaning, a spirit, a world-view, an overall shape."[41] In their well-known work on Foucault, Hubert Dreyfus and Paul Rabinow came down with the familiar verdict: "The structuralist approach attempts to dispense with both meaning and the subject by finding objective laws which govern all human activity."[42]

So, again, why Foucault, a thinker so obviously set against the intellectual foundations of the Harvard School?[43] We know Foucault for his

36 Foucault, Order of Things, supra note 4, at 325.

37 Id. at 326.

38 Michel Foucault, *The Archaeology of Knowledge: And the Discourse on Language* (New York: Pantheon Books, 1972), p. 203.

39 Michel Foucault, Order of Things, supra note 4, at xiv. ("In France, certain half-witted 'commentators' persist in labeling me a 'structuralist.' I have been unable to get it into their tiny minds that I have used none of the methods, concepts, or key terms that characterize structural analysis.")

40 For the suggestion that Foucault later rejects much of the theory worked out in *Archaeology*, see Hubert Dreyfus and Paul Rabinow, *Michel Foucault: Beyond Structuralism and Hermeneutics* (Chicago: University of Chicago Press, 1983), p. 86.

41 Foucault, Archaeology, supra note 38, at 10.

42 Dreyfus and Rabinow, supra note 40, at xv. See also Eve Taylor Bannet, *Structuralism and the Logic of Dissent* (Urbana: University of Illinois Press, 1989); Mark Poster, *Critical Theory and Poststructuralism: In Search of a Context* (Ithaca, NY: Cornell University Press, 1989).

43 For discussion of Foucault in the context of law, see Ben Golder, *Foucault and the Politics of Rights* (Redwood City, CA: Stanford University Press, 2015); Ben Golder and Peter

interest in taking preestablished unities and wholes and asking, what might nevertheless establish the unity of this object, after we have first abandoned the conventional modes in which the unity has been traditionally established? We can take this same approach to Foucault himself. Must we accept his condemnations of phenomenology and structuralism at face value? Or rather, might he actually be of assistance in producing an intelligible unity? I believe that, with Foucault's disclaimers duly noted, elements of Foucault's approach to the world of objects, particularly as articulated it in these two books from the late 1960s, harmonizes well with Merleau-Ponty's rich textures. And more specifically, these harmonies go some way toward dispelling the bad dissonance of the post-structuralist reaction with which I ended the last chapter. To be sure, there are many areas in which Merleau-Ponty and Foucault's music clash – but as I have said, my aim is neither to exhaust nor to reconcile the oeuvres of the respective authors. It is instead to cherry-pick, ruthlessly, in the effort to compose a jurisprudence of style.

First, Foucault's understanding of the subject is deeply complementary with that of Merleau-Ponty.[44] Most fundamentally, both thinkers fault those efforts at bringing coherence and mediation to the contradictions of the subject's experience in the world, and are concerned instead with what Foucault called "the effective field of appearance."[45] We have seen Merleau-Ponty's willingness to suspend the image of the coherent individual; Foucault goes further. In much the same way that Kennedy and Unger would soon criticize the liberal individual, Foucault described that being as a modern creation, inflicted at its core with a basic and undeniable contradiction: "the threshold of our modernity is situated . . . by the constitution of an empirico-transcendental doublet."[46] The individual subject, Foucault suggested, is this doubled relation of empiricism and transcendentalism, a relation that perpetually plays, in Unger's (and Barthes') words, a game of hide-and-seek.[47] It is a game in which the human sciences, the sciences circumambulating the modern subject, "find

Fitzpatrick, *Foucault's Law* (New York: Routledge, 2009); *Re-reading Foucault: On Law, Power, and Rights* (Ben Golder, ed.) (New York: Routledge, 2013); Duncan Kennedy, *Sexy Dressing, Etc.* (Cambridge, MA: Harvard University Press, 1993).

44 Foucault, Order of Things, supra note 4, at xiv, 244, 248–249.

45 Foucault, Archaeology, supra note 38, at 144.

46 Foucault, Order of Things, supra note 4, at 319.

47 Roland Barthes, *Mythologies: The Complete Edition, in a New Translation* (Richard Howard and Annette Lavers, trans.) (New York: Hill and Wang, 2013), p. 227.

themselves treating as their object what is in fact their condition of possibility."[48] As Foucault explained,

> [The discourse of the modern subject either] finds its foundation and model in the empirical truth whose genesis in nature and in history it retraces, so that one has an analysis of the positivist type (the truth of the object determines the truth of the discourse that describes its formation); or [it] anticipates the truth whose nature and history it defines; it sketches it out in advance and foments it from a distance, so that one has a discourse of the eschatological type (the truth of the philosophical discourse constitutes the truth in formation). In fact, it is not so much an alternative as a fluctuation inherent in all analysis, which brings out the value of the empirical at the transcendental level... This is why modern thought has been unable to avoid... searching for the locus of a discourse that would be neither of the order of reduction nor of the order of promise: a discourse whose tension would keep separate the empirical and the transcendental, while being directed at both; a discourse that would make it possible to analyse man as a subject, that is, as a locus of knowledge which has been empirically acquired but referred back as closely as possible to what makes it possible, and as a pure form immediately present to those contents.[49]

This "inherent fluctuation" between the effort to stabilize the individual as at once a being that can stand *outside* of time and knowledge in order to also diagnose the individual moving *through* time and knowledge was thoroughly and constantly mediated in order to vacate the sense of paradox permeating the effort.[50] But like Merleau-Ponty, Foucault had little interest in these mediating devices, other than in their identification and explication. Rather, Foucault had nothing but affection for the paradoxical. As Foucault explained of his "archaeological" approach, of which I will have more to say in a moment, it "describes what might be called *intrinsic* contradictions: those that are deployed in the discursive formation itself, and which, originating at one point in the system of formations, reveal sub-systems... It is these intrinsic oppositions that are relevant to archaeological analysis."[51]

In what could very well be termed a chiastic reversal with respect to the human relation and the object, Foucault explained that on the one hand, the most powerful mediating device in the modern arsenal was that of empiricism and its affiliation with "actual experience": "The analysis of actual experience... seeks to articulate the possible objectivity of a knowledge of nature upon the original experience of which the body

[48] Foucault, Order of Things, supra note 4, at 364. [49] Id. at 320–321.
[50] Id. at 321. See also Michel Foucault, What Is Enlightenment? in *The Foucault Reader* (Paul Rabinow, ed.) (New York: Pantheon Books, 1984).
[51] Foucault, Archaeology, supra note 38, at 153–154.

provides an outline; and to articulate the possible history of a culture upon the semantic diversity which is both hidden and revealed in actual experience. It is doing no more, then, than fulfilling with greater care the hasty demands laid down when the attempt was made to make the empirical, in man, stand for the transcendental."[52] "Actual experience," as a result, is a way of justifying the modern subject, reconciling its doubled nature in a unified and coherent vision. And yet, Foucault explained that in this attempt to lay bare the conditions of possibility for this modern subject, his inquiry aimed at the "the *pure experience* of order and of its modes of being."[53] Foucault was not interested in describing the empirical flow of trace events – Merleau-Ponty's universe of radical indeterminacy – though he was, like Merleau-Ponty, deeply invested in the pure experience of order. Foucault's orientation therefore sought to "*uncover* the principles,"[54] "*fix* its boundaries," "*reveal* its own specific type of relations," "*formulate* its laws . . . "[55] This notion of pure experience, a kind of experience constituted through an encounter with an *intelligible unity* that neither precedes consciousness nor is a matter of proceeding from consciousness, reminds us of the phenomenology Foucault so wanted to abandon.

Second, there is the world of objects. Like Merleau-Ponty, and as I have just intimated, Foucault was at war with Objective Thought. This opposition has a negative orientation, for in order to properly articulate the object of analysis, Foucault, like Merleau-Ponty, explained that "we must rid ourselves of a whole mass of notions," notions like "tradition," "influence," "development," "evolution," and "spirit."[56] These notions all have in common the search for genesis, for totality, for continuity – notions Foucault associated with phenomenology and structuralism.[57] "We must question those ready-made syntheses, those groupings that we normally accept before any examination, those links whose validity is recognized from the outset; we must oust those forms and obscure forces by which we usually link the discourse of one man with of another; they must be driven out from the darkness in which they reign."[58] This interest in exploding our received conceptions is not manifested, however, in a total about-face. Like Unger's permanently provisional encounter with liberalism, Foucault lobs the object in the air, suspended just long enough to connect that preconceived unity with the end of a bat. It is in this process of demolition

[52] Foucault, Order of Things, supra note 4, at 321. [53] Id. at xxi.
[54] Foucault, Archaeology, supra note 38, at 15. [55] Id. at 7–8. [56] Id. at 21–22.
[57] Id. at 138. [58] Id. at 22.

that new possibilities for the re-presentation of the object unfold, that "an entire field is set free."[59] "If there really is a unity, it does not lie in the visible, horizontal coherence of the elements formed; it resides, well anterior to their formation, in the system that governs and makes possible that formation."[60]

> I shall take as my starting-point whatever unities are already given (such as psychopathology, medicine, or political economy); but I shall not place myself inside these dubious unities in order to study their internal configurations or their secret contradictions. I shall make use of them just long enough to ask myself what unities they form; by what right they can claim a field that specifies them in space and a continuity that individualizes them in time ... I shall accept the groupings that history suggests only to subject them at once to interrogation; to break them up and see if they can be legitimately reformed.[61]

To put the point in a way that draws an obvious connection with Merleau-Ponty's antirealism: the real world is radically indeterminate. If it holds unities of its own, we will never know them. "Actual experience" will go nowhere in establishing its orders and forms. To do that, a new way of fashioning an encounter would be required.

A third point speaks to that fashion. Merleau-Ponty and Foucault shared an interest in reconstituting the formerly demolished object in light of what they both called the "Prose of the World."[62] Whereas this interest was only hinted at in Merleau-Ponty's later writings, it takes center stage in Foucault's *Archaeology of Knowledge*. Of course, Foucault was at pains to show how his understanding of the governing and constituting rules of a given discipline were something other than semiotic. And while the difference between Foucault's approach and, say, that of a Chomsky or Hjelmslev[63] might have been significant, the difference between what Foucault is here offering and what I am suggesting for a jurisprudence of style is not.[64] The difference, once again, turns on whether you take

[59] Id. at 26. [60] Id. at 80. [61] Id.

[62] Maurice Merleau-Ponty, *The Prose of the World* (Claude Lefort, ed.) (John O'Neill, trans.) (Evanston, IL: Northwestern University Press, 1973); Foucault, Order of Things, supra note 4, at 17. To be sure, they used the phrase differently. I note it here simply to indicate how they both sought to illuminate the object through discursive practice.

[63] See, e.g., Noam Chomsky, *Aspects of the Theory of Syntax* (Cambridge, MA: MIT Press, 2014); Louis Hjelmslev, *Prolegomena to a Theory of Language* (Francis Whitfield, trans.) (Madison: University of Wisconsin Press, 1961). See also Noam Chomsky and Michel Foucault, *The Chomsky-Foucault Debate* (New York: The New Press, 2006).

[64] For Foucault's critique of "style," aimed as it is at a mid-twentieth century fixture, see Foucault, Archaeology, supra note 38, at 33–34.

structuralism as offering an *objective* explanation of what is "really going on" – as Foucault and the poststructuralist jurists took it to be.

Having taken the pre-given unity of a discipline as a provisional starting point, what happens once we divest the object of its "natural totality"?[65] Say that the object in question is a so-called body, that of political economy. Foucault explained that in performing an archaeological interrogation of that object-discipline, one must characterize in political economy "the coexistence of these dispersed and heterogeneous statements; the system that governs their division, the degree to which they depend upon one another, the way in which they interlock or exclude one another, the transformation they undergo, and the play of their location, arrangement, and replacement."[66] In the encounter with these dispersed statements, we then look for regularities, and if we succeed,[67] we have identified what Foucault called a "discursive formation,"[68] which were themselves conditioned by deep rules found in a "preconceptual field."[69] "A discursive formation will be individualized if one can define the system of formation of the different strategies that are deployed in it; in other words, if one can show how they all derive (in spite of their sometimes extreme diversity, and in spite of their dispersion in time) from the same set of relations."[70] And how will these statements and strategies *derive*?

> Certain groups of statements put these rules into operation in their most general and most widely applicable form; using them as a starting point, one can see how other objects, other concepts, other enunciative modalities, or other strategic choices may be formed on the basis of rules that are less general and whose domain of application is more specified. One can thus describe a tree of enunciative derivation: at its base are the statements that put into operation rules of formation in their most extended form; at its summit, and after a number of branchings, are the statements that put into operation the same regularity, but one more delicately articulated, more clearly delimited and localized in its extension. Archaeology – and this is one of its principal themes – may thus constitute the tree of derivation of a discourse.[71]

Further, "[t]he conditions to which the elements of this division are subjected we shall call the rules of formation. The rules of formation are

[65] Foucault, Order of Things, supra note 4, at xx.
[66] Foucault, Archaeology 38, supra note, at 34.
[67] Of which Foucault conceded there was never any guarantee. "For an initial probe, I made use of certain fairly loose, but familiar groups of statement: I have no proof that I shall find them again at the end of the analysis." Id. at 38.
[68] Id. [69] Id. at 63. [70] Id. at 68. [71] Id. at 147–148.

conditions of existence...in a given discursive division."[72] Again, the point was not to demolish the "body" of "political economy" merely in order to see if it could be replicated, in order to vindicate empiricism; the question was whether a given unity might be destroyed and then reassembled in order to discover whether there were rules governing what *could* be said in that discipline, and whether and when these rules had been operative.[73] These linguistic rules were hiding in the spaces between statements, the "what has been said," in the relations that thread them together.[74] "It is these rules of formation, which were never formulated in their own right, but are to be found only in widely differing theories, concepts, and objects of study, that I have tried to reveal, by isolating, as their specific locus, a level that I have called, somewhat arbitrarily perhaps, archaeological."[75]

It is these rules of formation, these linguistic patterns and regularities, that "make possible the formation of a whole group of various objects... One might say, then, that a discursive formation is defined... if one can establish such a group; if one can show how any particular object of discourse finds in it its place and law of emergence."[76] The object, Foucault instructs, is instituted through linguistic practices, though not in such a way that they construct the object from the inside out, but rather in such a way that the rules *enable the object to appear*: "The object does not await in limbo the order that will free it and enable it to become embodied in a visible and prolix objectivity; it does not preexist itself, held back by some obstacle at the first edges of light. It exists under the positive conditions of a complex group of relations."[77] "The dispersion itself... can be described in its uniqueness if one is able to determine the specific rules in accordance with which its objects, statements, concepts and theoretical options have been formed: if there really is a unity, it does not lie in the visible, horizontal coherence of the elements formed; it resides, well anterior to their formation, in the system that makes possible and governs that formation."[78]

This brings me to the fourth Foucauldian point, that of the coalescing relation between *practice* and *style*. As with the poststructuralist reaction to the Harvard School, Foucault was eager to banish the structuralist

[72] Id. at 38. [73] Id. at 48. [74] Id. at 68–69.
[75] Foucault, Order of Things, supra note 4, at xi.
[76] Foucault, Archaeology, supra note 38, at 44. [77] Id. at 45.
[78] Id. at 72. Above and beyond, or way down below, or off to the side, depending on how you want to envision it, was the *episteme*: "the total set of relations that unite, at a given period, the discursive practices." Id. at 191.

langue to the margins of his texts. In a typical phrase, Foucault emphasized how the linguistic rules constituting his discursive formations were not *langue*, but were rather "immanent in a practice."[79] And "to define a system of formation in its specific individuality is therefore to characterize a discourse or a group statements by the regularity of a practice."[80] The practices that form disciplinary objects, and the rules immanent in those practices, were not reducible to a basic grammar, but were instead tangled pluralities groping through liminal spaces.[81] In this tangled plurality of practice, Foucault explained, exists an open space of discretion, "the principle of the possibility of choices."[82]

> My aim was to show what the differences consisted of, how it was possible for men, within the same discursive practice, to speak of different objects, to have contrary opinions, and to make contradictory choices; my aim was also to show in what ways discursive practices were distinguished from one another; in short, I wanted not to exclude the problem of the subject, but to define the positions and functions that the subject could occupy in the diversity of discourse.[83]

> A discursive formation does not occupy therefore all the possible volume that is opened up to it of right by the systems of formation of its objects, its enunciations, and its concepts; it is essentially incomplete, owing to the system of formation of its strategic choices. Hence the fact that, taken up again, placed, and interpreted in a new constellation, a given discursive formation may reveal new possibilities.[84]

Thus, to force Foucault where he said he did not want to go, while there may exist deep constraints at the level of the *langue*, and relative freedom at the level of lexical indeterminacy, there is a more textured pathway of practice, a question of how an actor *at once* falls to work in those lines of force operating from deep background into conceptual foreground.[85] And Foucault reinforces the idea of a structure of practice: "I have shown that the strategic choices do not emerge directly from a world-view or from a predominance of interests peculiar to the speaking subject; but this very possibility is determined by points of divergence in the group of concepts."[86] It is precisely in this vast and crucial liminal space of Foucault's structure of discursive *practice* that we also find Merleau-Ponty's notion of *style*.[87]

[79] Id. at 46. [80] Id. at 74. [81] Id. at 48–49. [82] Id. at 67, 208–209.
[83] Id. at 200. [84] Id. at 67. [85] Id. at 129. [86] Id. at 72, 122.
[87] As Merleau-Ponty says of the field not being given to consciousness, Foucault wrote that the background practices "are not imposed from the outside of the elements that they relate together; they are caught up in the very things that they connect; and if they are not modified with the least of them, they modify them, and are transformed with them into certain decisive thresholds." Id. at 127.

Roland Barthes: Structure as Ideology

What we are settling into here, in this blend of Foucault's archaeology and Merleau-Ponty's chiastic consciousness, is the situating of a phenomenology of practice in a linguistic structure.[88] It is here that I want to bring Roland Barthes's voice into the mix. Once again, however, we ought to ask, of what sense is there in using Barthes to help establish a jurisprudence of style? Did not Barthes repudiate his earlier, "scientific" structuralism in favor of a more poststructuralist predilection?[89] Perhaps, but what matters here are the creative possibilities we can squeeze from their texts.[90] What matters least is paying dutiful homage to a progressive current supposedly reaching from a militant structuralism into a more playful poststructuralism.

Like Foucault and Merleau-Ponty, Barthes saw language as the primal material. And like Foucault and Merleau-Ponty, Barthes did not see the primal materiality of language in an analytical grid. Language "is not so much a stock of materials as a horizon, which implies both a boundary and a perspective... *it is a field of action*... a distant setting of *familiarity*."[91] Here we can imagine Barthes preparing a structuralist reading of soccer, its background practices, its pre-conceptual and embodied lines of force: soccer's *langue*, a field of action. In addition to this background horizon, Barthes also described the relation between language and style. Style, Barthes explained, is

> a form with no clear destination, the product of a thrust, not an intention, and, as it were, a vertical and lonely dimension of thought... A closed personal process, it is in no way the product of a choice or of a reflection on Literature. It is the private portion of the ritual, it rises up from the writer's myth-laden depths and unfolds beyond the area of control. It is the decorative voice of a hidden, secret flesh.[92]

[88] See Jonathan Culler, Phenomenology and Structuralism, 5 *Human Context* 35, 36 (1973).

[89] See John Sturrock, *Structuralism* (Malden, UK: Wiley-Blackwell, 2003), pp. 73–77; Rosalind Coward and John Ellis, *Language and Materialism: Developments in Semiology and the Theory of the Subject* (London: Routledge, 1977), p. 6; Bjornar Olsen, "Roland Barthes: From Sign to Text," in *Reading Material Culture: Structuralism, Hermeneutics and Post-Structuralism* (Christophe Tilley, ed.) (Oxford: Blackwell, 1990); p. 165. For further discussion, see Fredric Jameson, *The Prison-House of Language: A Critical Account of Structuralism and Russian Formalism* (Princeton, NJ: Princeton University Press, 1972).

[90] In this, I am likely a product of Duncan Kennedy's approach to intellectual consumption.

[91] Barthes, Reader, supra note 5, at 31–32.

[92] Id. at 32–33.

Again, style is something other than either a deep grammar or a subjective decision; it exists in vertical space reaching from the depths of the one up into the surface of the other. Barthes continues,

> A language is therefore a horizon, and style a vertical dimension, which together map out for the writer a Nature, since he does not choose either. The language functions negatively, as the initial limit of the possible, style is a Necessity which binds the writer's humor to his form of expression. In the former he finds a familiar history, in the latter a familiar personal past. In both cases he deals with a Nature, that is, a familiar repertory of gestures, a gestuary, as it were, in which the energy expended is purely operative, serving here to enumerate, there to transform, but never to appraise or signify a choice.[93]

While Foucault and Merleau-Ponty might very well harmonize with much of what Barthes was saying here in *Writing Degree Zero*, in *The Structuralist Activity*, Barthes clashed with Foucault on at least one key point: for Barthes, structuralism was not structuralism if it lacked the organizing architecture of Suassurean semiotics, of *langue* and *parole*. But from there, consider the consonance. Like Merleau-Ponty and Foucault, Barthes' rejected the poststructuralist jurists' view of structure: they were *not* objective, empirically determinable, preexisting universals, meant to explain *what had really happened*. "[S]tructuralism is essentially an *activity*, i.e., the controlled succession of a certain number of mental operations: we might speak of structuralist activity as we once spoke of surrealist activity."[94] What is this activity, this structuralist *engagement*? It is, once again, a chiastic imbrication of consciousness and world, a "distinctive experience for *structural man*, defined not by his ideas or his languages, but by his imagination – in other words, by the way in which he mentally experiences structure."[95] Here, perhaps, we have a problem: Is Barthes saying that the structure *precedes* this structural man, that it awaits his *cogito* in a mind-independent condition? It does not. For Barthes, the structuralist activity bears strong resemblance to Foucault's archaeology:

> The goal of all structuralist activity, whether reflexive or poetic, is to reconstruct an 'object' in such a way as to manifest thereby the rules of functioning ('the functions') of this object. Structure is therefore actually a *simulacrum* of the object... Structural man takes the real, decomposes it, then recomposes it; this

[93] Id. at 34.
[94] Roland Barthes, *Critical Essays* (Richard Howard, trans.) (Evanston, IL: Northwestern University Press, 1972), p. 214.
[95] Id.

appears to be little enough ... Yet from another point of view this 'little enough' is decisive: for between the two objects, or the two tenses, of structuralist activity, there occurs something new, and what is new is nothing less than the generally intelligible.[96]

As with Foucault, Barthes suggests that the structuralist takes the object as given. But the object – the discipline – is not given to the structuralist for understanding, as the Cartesian object is given to consciousness – it is given for cutting.[97] The unity of the discipline is immediately dissected and decomposed, to see dispersions and to follow them. It is in these dispersions explored in the structuralist activity that we find "certain mobile fragments whose differential situation engenders a certain meaning;" but the fragments in themselves are meaningless for the structuralist – they "have no significant existence except by their frontiers."[98] A few paragraphs on, Barthes explained, "the simulacrum, thus constructed, does not render the world as it has found it."[99] It would be impossible to render the real world on *its own terms* – "the real is not representable, but only demonstrable."[100] The structure "is neither the real nor the rational,"[101] but rather, as Barthes would explain later, is never anything more than an *eliciting* of the real.

In other words, semiology is not a grid; it does not permit a direct apprehension of the real through the imposition of a general transparency which would render it intelligible. It seeks instead to *elicit* the real, in place and by moments, and it says that these efforts to elicit the real are possible without a grid. It is in fact precisely when semiology comes to be a grid that it elicits nothing at all.[102]

The structure thus achieves its intelligibility through relations of *langue* and *parole*, attention paid to the functional difference between utterances in their formations (or styles). Broken down, dissected, and smashed into its differentiated pieces (all the while knowing full well that *de*differentiation has been marginalized, waiting, along the edges),[103] the

96 Id. at 214–215.
97 Michel Foucault, Nietzsche, Genealogy, History, in Foucault Reader, supra note 50, at 88.
98 Barthes, Critical Essays, supra note 95, at 216.
99 Id. at 218.
100 Barthes, Reader, supra note 5, at 465.
101 Barthes, Critical Essays, supra note 95, at 218.
102 Barthes, Reader, supra note 5, at 474.
103 As Barthes explained in his inaugural lecture at the *College de France*, the distinction between *langue* and *parole* is a device and shouldn't be understood as a verity. If it is useful, then use it. But we can use it even while understanding fully the ways in which *langue* and *parole*, or "language" and "discourse," ceaselessly blend. Id. at 470.

discipline is composed as if for the first time. It is a new unity, or what Foucault called a discursive practice and what Barthes called semiology, a difference without much distinction given the hard constraints at work in both. For Foucault and Barthes, the intelligible unity produced through this archeological semiology, if you will, only and ever occurs at the level of formal rules of association, and not content, and rather than assign meanings to objects, the structure is a syntax governing how meanings are made possible.[104]

My trio agree on another point as well. As Foucault would make explicit in essays such as "Nietzsche, Genealogy, History," the elucidation of discursive practices had a critical edge. All efforts at totalization, the acceptance of pre-given continuities, beliefs in the universal progress of an idea – all such efforts were suspect. "Humanity does not gradually progress from combat to combat until it arrives at universal reciprocity, where the rule of law finally replaces warfare; humanity installs each of its violences in a system of rules and thus proceeds from domination to domination."[105] Barthes was of a similar view. In the process of composing a semiotic structure, a critical operation takes place through the structuralist activity, an operation that cancels out, or at least seeks to cancel out, an analogous operation conducted by ideology. For Barthes, historical reality was unknowable in the absence of a mediator. One very powerful mediator is that of the ideological, which takes historical reality and gives it a natural justification, replacing contingency with necessity.[106] Ideology, in this sense, depoliticizes the political in the service of rendering some discipline, some object, some story, natural, neutral, and necessary, "a harmonious display of essences."[107]

Semiology has taught us that myth has the task of giving a historical intention a natural justification, and making contingency appear eternal. Now this process is exactly that of bourgeois ideology . . . just as bourgeois ideology is defined by the abandonment of the name *bourgeois*, so myth is constituted by the loss of the historical quality of things: in it, things lose the memory that one they were made . . . A conjuring trick has taken place; [bourgeois ideology] has turned reality inside out, it has emptied it of history and filled it with nature, it has removed from things their human meaning so as to make them signify a human insignificance. The function of a myth is to empty reality: it is literally, a ceaseless flowing out, a hemorrhage, or perhaps an evaporation, in short, a perceptible absence.[108]

[104] Barthes, Mythologies, supra note 47, at 223.
[105] Foucault, Reader, supra note 50, at 236.
[106] Barthes, Mythologies, supra note 47, at 254. [107] Id. at 255.
[108] Id. at 254–255.

Barthes' structuralism combats the ideological depoliticization of "hemorrhage" in the process of *naming* what bourgeois ideology insisted on remaining unnamed. Take the mythology of the bourgeois, demolish it, dissect it, cast it in its most dispersed light. And then ask, what discursive practices provide the conditions of possibility for this mythology, what rules of association govern its statements, what formal unities render it intelligible? If the structuralist finds answers in her composition, the depoliticizing, naturalizing, hemorrhaging work of the myth is, perhaps, stanched.

Question: What happens when the structuralist fails in the effort to compose a structure of background practices and style? Is there some guarantee? Barthes explained that in the effort to identify forms in the rubble, the structuralist is in a "kind of battle against chance."[109] If patterns emerge, perhaps we are on the way to a structuralist composition, a work of art, and "the work of art is what man wrests from chance."[110] Foucault said much the same thing. In this I find a helpful analogy in the early work of the composer Steve Reich. A pioneer in musical minimalism, Reich did for sounds what Barthes was hoping to do for words.[111] Describing his *Violin Phase*, Reich explained, "As one listens to the repetition of several violins, one may hear first the lower tones forming one of several patterns, then the higher notes are noticed forming another, then the notes in the middle may attach themselves to the lower notes to form still another. All these patterns are really there; they are created by the interlocking of two, three, or four violins all playing the same repeating pattern out of phase with each other. Since it is the attention of the listener that will largely determine which particular resulting pattern he or she will hear at any one moment, these patterns can be understood as psychoacoustic by-products of the repetition and phase-shifting."[112] Of course, Reich, unlike Barthes or Foucault, believes his structures and patterns are due to a "reality of cadence ... basic in all the music of the world (Western *and* non-Western) ... Any theory of music that eliminates these realities is doomed to a *marginal* role in the music of the world."[113]

[109] Barthes, Critical Essays, supra note 95, at 152.

[110] Id.

[111] Steve Reich, *Writings on Music, 1965–2000* (Paul Hillier, ed.) (New York: Oxford University Press, 2002), p. 199.

[112] Id. at 26.

[113] Id. at 186–187. In this sense, it may be worth being mindful of Duncan Kennedy's warning about assuming an equivalence between a musician's musical sophistication and ability to express that sophistication in the written word. Kennedy, Critique, supra note 8, at 347.

But the point remains: if in the fragments of a demolished discipline we encounter the surprising lights of a constellation, the nascent work of a structural composition is under way.[114]

In marshaling this roundup, I understand structuralism as incorporating rather than rejecting much of what the poststructuralist jurists were complaining about in their rebukes of the Harvard School. That is, in my view, legal structuralism is decisively *post*-poststructuralist (and in the case of the Harvard School, it has always been so). The next step is to illustrate the point, transposing these ideas from Merleau-Ponty, Foucault, and Barthes into a *jurisprudence* of style. On the one side is a series of rejections. These ideas reject a belief in the structure's "natural reality," the idea that an elucidation of the structure might tell us, in the register of a positivist science, *what really happened*; they reject the idea that the real world of actual experience might be totalized, universalized, rendered continuous through history; they reject the idea that structuralism is incompatible with critique, but rather, that structuralism is at its best when it denaturalizes mythical structures of thought. On the other side, Merleau-Ponty, Foucault, and Barthes provide us with affirmative significations: it is a sensibility embracing the chiastic and refusing mediation in the acceptation of a phenomenology of structuralism; it is a sensibility embracing the chiastic, composing a simulation of that which cannot be simulated, or as Barthes put it, considering "sane its desire for the impossible";[115] it is a sensibility embracing the chiastic in an effective field of consciousness and world, without affirming either the transcendental subject or the dehumanizing structure; it is a sensibility embracing the chiastic in a confluence of thought as practice and practice as thought, practice as structure and structure as practice.[116]

[114] For discussion, see Christopher Tomlins, "Toward a Materialist Jurisprudence," in *Transformations in American Legal History: Essays in Honor of Professor Morton J. Horwitz* (Daniel Hamilton and Alfred Brophy, eds.) (Cambridge, MA: Harvard University Press, 2010).

[115] Barthes, Reader, supra note 5, at 466.

[116] Barthes, Mythologies, supra note 47, at 238 ("The freedom in choosing what one focuses on is a problem which does not belong to the province of semiology; it depends on the concrete situation of the subject.")

3

The Context of Legal Thought

Structure and Style in Time

This chapter ferries the ideas surveyed throughout the last two chapters toward the animating themes of a structuralist jurisprudence of style. The itinerary is as follows. First, I return to the question of the legal subject. This entails the *who* of legal structuralism, the persona of the *jurist*. Second is the question of place, or more specifically, the question of *where* we find the jurist. The easy answer to this question is the United States, since this study limits itself to the juridical work of that country. The better answer is disciplinary, since this is not a claim about a structure of legal thought that has its origins in the United States, migrates from the Unites States, or is somehow distinctively American. The question of place receives an answer *wherever* we find jurists trained in what I will call the Office of Liberal Legalism. Third and fourth is the *what* and *when* of legal structuralism. Just as the choice to limit the analysis to the United States is arbitrary, so too is the choice to limit the target to only one legal language, that of liberal legal thought. My choice to pursue this language and not another is in large measure about picking up where the Harvard School left off. Although a study of liberalism might be the best route to legal thought in the United States, it is certainly not the only one. This last point implicates the related question of time, for if the project is concerned with a juridical person (the *who*) trained in the Office (the *where*) of Liberal Legalism (the *what*), we still need a historical context, which I supply with a structuralist understanding of legal thought (the *when*). Legal thought, as I explain below, is a grammatical context in which the rules of law gain meaning, a grammatical context that shifts over time, much like Foucault's discursive formations. And finally, as to *how* legal thought shifts over time, it is possible to see how patterns in the practice of legal argument morph and displace, as when, for instance, legal formalism shifts into legal functionalism, or in the way that formalism and functionalism together coalesce in what I will call pragmatic liberalism. Nevertheless, while this vision of legal structuralism addresses the question of how liberal legalism transforms in its various styles, it brackets the question of why these changes occur.

Persona: Structuralists and Jurists

A jurisprudence of style implicates two personas: these are the *structuralist* and the *jurist*. I have already mentioned the Harvard School's preference for the term "jurist," which we can take to signify any person trained in the use of a legal language and with skilled familiarity in the background practices of legal thought.[1] The jurist is fluent, or at least on the way to fluency, in the generic practices of legal argument, the techniques, forms, rituals, and so forth that carry a jurist on the way from a set of facts to a legally necessitated legal conclusion. In the case of a structuralist analysis of law, it is very likely that the person engaged in the structuralist activity – the *structuralist* – is also a jurist. Is it possible for the legal structuralist not to be a jurist? I imagine so, but the structuralist composition will likely suffer for it. What about moving in the other direction? Can one adopt the persona of the jurist, but not of the structuralist? Certainly. And in fact, of the many jurists at work in the United States, only a small handful are also structuralists.

In describing the structuralist activity there are therefore two layers of inquiry: (1) the structuralist sensibility, in which the structuralist encounters the practices of legal argument in a jurist's work, and (2) the jurist's style of practice. The jurists, and the world in which they live, are the targets of the structuralist activity, but this just begs more: If the structuralist assumes that the target discipline is a language system, why or

[1] Duncan Kennedy and Roberto Unger have regularly used the term in this way. See, e.g., Duncan Kennedy, *Legal Reasoning: Collected Essays* (Aurora, CO: Davies Group, 2008); Roberto Unger, *What Should Legal Analysis Become?* (London: Verso, 1996). Recently, Unger wrote: "By jurist I mean a lawyer with higher pretensions and ambitions: he claims to deploy a method that authoritatively interprets the law or develops it in the service of ideals as well as interests . . . He may be an academic lawyer, a judge, a critic of established law, or what in the tradition of Roman law was called a jurisconsult." Roberto Unger, *The Critical Legal Studies Movement: Another Time, A Greater Task* (London: Verso, 2015), p. 5.

how can the structuralist construct a language system in which she, as a jurist, is always already a part? As Barthes put it, "I cannot function outside language, treating it as a target, and within language, treating it as a weapon."[2] And Frederic Jameson seems to have a similar idea in mind, when he said in advance of his well-known structuralist critique, "There is a profound consonance between linguistics as a method and that systematized and disembodied nightmare which is our culture today."[3] Foucault said as well, "I shall try to reveal, in its own regularity – a regularity that I have not yet succeeded in mastering – what made it possible to say what I did."[4] If the structuralist assumes that its target discipline is a structure of language, and if the structuralist is already constituted by that language, is the structuralist a player in a game in which she is always already entangled? Is not the structuralist forced to concede that, since "everything" is amenable to linguistic analysis,[5] her composition of the jurist's practice is necessarily compromised?

In the jurisprudence of style I am here articulating, the answer is: not really. It is dogma and power worship and little else that might force the structuralist to concede that *everything* in human experience is free-floating discourse, a text among texts, and that as a result, the structuralist must, like Foucault, seek out the regularities, patterns, and structures that may determine the structuralist's relation to the jurist. No doubt, such inquiries may be fruitful and edifying; but what I want to make clear is that nothing in the structuralist vision requires the structuralist to place faith in the idea that our entire universe of experience is linguistic and that the *real* is *truly* ever and only a series of discursive turtles, going all the way down. Legal structuralism, in the style I am articulating here at any rate, harbors no such totalizing beliefs. The default position for the structuralist is therefore one of agnosticism on the question of whether the very use of structuralism in itself is structured by some set of discursive formations. Perhaps it is, but once again, there is simply nothing in the structuralist style requiring faith in such a belief.

2 Roland Barthes, *A Barthes Reader* (Susan Sontag, ed.) (New York: Vintage, 2000), p. 473; See also Terry Eagleton, *The Illusions of Postmodernism* (Oxford: Oxford University Press, 1996), p. 36.

3 Fredric Jameson, *The Prison-House of Language: A Critical Account of Structuralism and Russian Formalism* (Princeton, NJ: Princeton University Press, 1972), p. ix.

4 Michel Foucault, *The Archaeology of Knowledge: And the Discourse on Language* (New York: Pantheon Books, 1972), p. 114.

5 Jameson, The Prison-House of Language, supra note 3, at viii.

Office: Training Jurists in the Language of Liberal Legalism

In order to adopt one of these persona, one must be trained. With respect to the persona of either the structuralist or the jurist, this training takes several forms. The form of structuralist persona I have been elaborating is that of the Harvard School. What of the jurist? The world of law is both large and diverse; which jurists and where? The activity might begin in the search for "American" jurists, but such a designation would take us to "American Law," or "Anglo-American Law," or "Property Law," or "Antitrust Law" or some such thing. But even if we bracket out the supposition that we might give a "structure" to all "Law," the *legality of the contingent* is perplexing,[6] thoroughly indeterminate, as Merleau-Ponty, Foucault, and Barthes have advised. Instead, the structuralist seeks out juridical practices that cut across the bodies of law, and while she can never be sure that anything really cuts anywhere, or whether these activities will have any coherence or unity, she posits at the outset a particular mode of training for the jurist, a particular style in which the jurist operates, without regard to the boundaries we have come to expect between legal bodies, disciplinary or national.

As I have already recounted, the Harvard School thinkers identified these juridical practices with liberal legal thought, and poststructuralist jurists attacked them for it. Among other things, the poststructuralist jurists argued that the Harvard School thinkers failed to see that the indeterminacy of *parole* went all the way down, and that because Unger and Kennedy misunderstood the liberal *langue*, they indulged in the fantasy of an autonomous liberal legalism, somehow distinct from some other, *non-liberalism*.[7] As Costas Douzinas argued,

> The principle of systemic unity is central to both naturalism and positivism ... [as well as] the structuralist linguistics of Saussure and his followers ... An entity, work, or field can claim unity only if it can be clearly delineated from its outside. As we saw, this is the first law of jurisprudence, and of legal dogmatics. However, a field is self-sufficient only if its outside is marked as distinct from its own beginning and end so as to frame and constitute what is inside ... In other words, what is non-legal is always necessary to make law properly legal. The frame

[6] Peter Goodrich, *Oedipus Lex: Psychoanalysis, History, Law* (Berkeley: University of California Press, 1995), p. 223.

[7] Costas Douzinas et al., *Postmodern Jurisprudence: The Law of Texts in the Texts of Law* (New York: Routledge, 1993), p. 26. See also Pierre Schlag, The Problem of the Subject, 69 *Texas Law Review*, 1627 (1991), pp. 1696–1697.

between the two, rather than being a wall, is a point of passage. Law's empire, as proper, united, and coherent, depends on what is legally improper and denies law's imperialism.[8]

As we settle into the structuralist posture, a posture drummed up out of the discussion of Merleau-Ponty, Foucault, and Barthes, it is clear that there is an illusory distinction between liberalism and its others, there are very real slippages between *langue* and *parole*, as well as dubious claims from the like of Louis Hartz that liberalism *was* the real world.[9] Speaking of naturalism and positivism, Douzinas explained that "An entity, work, or field can claim unity only if it can be clearly delineated from its outside." That seems right, and recalls Barthes' claim about the inability of simultaneously being able to treat language as a target and a weapon. But these problems are not the structuralist's problems. The structural unity of liberal legal thought has nothing to do with a rendition of *the real*, independent of consciousness; it is a structure of argumentative practices, no more, no less.[10] Duncan Kennedy made the point in similar terms, suggesting "[l]egal semiotic discourse seems (at every moment, and why not?) to replace its object of study with a pseudo-object more amenable to its internal requirements."[11] And further,

I have chosen [structuralism] in part out of the conviction that each method that I know at all how to use, and methodology in general, have been subjected to a critique that undermines any claim their practitioners might have to get at the truth of the objects they represent. So I don't believe that my object (adjudication) corresponds, in fact, only and truly, to a representation made in the 'correct' medium. It will transcend or surpass my representation, and indeed my understanding, no matter what method(s) I adopt, and that's fine with me.[12]

Foucault suggests the same:

What has emerged is a unity of another type, which does not appear to have the same dates, or the same surface, or the same articulations, but which may

[8] Douzinas, Postmodern Jurisprudence, supra note 7, at 26.

[9] In his famous study of liberalism in US history, Hartz asked questions like, "Did these men grasp the America in which they lived?" Louis Hartz, *The Liberal Tradition in America: An Interpretation of American Political Thought Since the Revolution* (New York: Harcourt, 1955), p. 236.

[10] For discussion, see Goodrich, Oedipus Lex, supra note 6, at 23–30.

[11] Duncan Kennedy, A Semiotics of Legal Argument, 42 *Syracuse Law Review* 75 (1991), p. 90.

[12] Duncan Kennedy, *A Critique of Adjudication* (Cambridge, MA: Harvard University Press, 1999), p. 15.

take account of a group of objects for which the term [Liberalism] was merely a reflexive, secondary, classificatory rubric. [Liberalism] finally emerged as a discipline in a constant state of renewal, subject to constant discoveries, criticisms, and corrected errors; the system of formation that we have defined remains stable. But let there be no misunderstanding: it is not the objects that remain constant, nor the domain that they form; it is not even their point of emergence or their mode of characterization; but the relation between the surfaces on which they appear, on which they can be delimited, on which they can be analyzed and specified.[13]

And while taking liberal legal thought as the target discipline for the structuralist activity suggests nothing about the truth of Law or the way it really happened, it similarly says nothing about the "truth" of liberalism. Taking the name of liberal legalism as a marker for a family of argumentative practices is, as Barthes explained and as I discuss further in Chapter 9, a necessary tactic in the work of deciphering myths,[14] or as Foucault put it, merely a "finger to point with."

These proper names would form useful landmarks and avoid ambiguous designations; they would tell us in any case what the painter is looking at, and the majority of the characters in the picture along with him. But the relation of language to painting is an infinite relation. It is not that words are imperfect, or that, when confronted with the visible, they prove insuperably inadequate. Neither can be reduced to the other's terms: it is in vain that we say what we see; what we see never resides in what we say. And it is in vain to that we attempt to show, by the use of images, metaphors, or similes, what we are saying; the space where they achieve their splendor is not that deployed by our eyes but that defined by the sequential elements of syntax. And the proper name, in this particular context, is merely an artifice: it gives us a finger to point with ...[15]

In approaching the language of liberal legal thought, the structuralist activity seeks unities and coherences, but these are not universal, continuous, or natural unities and coherences. They are unities that instead speak to a style of performance helpfully linked with Shaun McVeigh's conception of the legal Office.[16] The concept of Office tends to

[13] Foucault, Archaeology, supra note 4, at 47. Note that I have replaced Foucault's own terms with "Liberalism," merely to indicate a clarity of exposition, not Foucault's intention to speak of "liberalism."

[14] Roland Barthes, *Mythologies: The Complete Edition, in a New Translation* (Richard Howard and Annette Lavers, trans.) (New York: Hill and Wang, 2013), p. 228.

[15] Michel Foucault, *The Order of Things: An Archaeology of Human Sciences* (New York.: Vintage Books, 1994), p. 9.

[16] Shaun McVeigh, Afterword: Office and Conduct of the Minor Jurisprudent, 5 *University of California Irvine Law Review* 499 (2015).

have an administrative or institutional meaning, referring to the *status* of the jurist, in the capacity of (say) king, judge, professor, or lawyer.[17] As Dorsett and McVeigh have explained, "For judges, the limits and bounds of the office is the administration of the law equally and impartially to all."[18] But if we take Office as indicating something beyond status and more of a mode of *training* in the dispensation of an equal and impartial law, "as a social or intellectual office [requiring] some historical reconstruction," then the site of Office becomes much more suggestive as a space beyond institutional form and as a possible location for liberal legal thought.[19] It is therefore in this sense of Office as training for practice that I will suggest the jurist experiences unities and coherence.[20]

If liberal legalism is an Office for training the jurist, where is this Office? Downtown? We can find the Office of liberal legal thought anywhere in which its techniques, styles, and so forth are offered for study and replication. As practical constraints go, this book mostly limits itself to a composition of argumentative practices as personified in the United States. The Office of liberal legal thought almost certainly transcends such national frontiers; does the practice of Liberal Legalism differ in different sociocultural settings? Very likely, but once again, I make no such geographical studies here. The training dispensed in the Office of liberal legal thought might be practiced anywhere, from the law school to the law office to the court house and so on, so long as the jurist is trained in the regularities of its argumentative practice.

Finally, what is the difference between the *office* and *structure* of liberal legal thought? Office, as I have said, relates to a site of training. Structure, in contrast, relates to the substance of the language being learned. Thus, we can speak of the office of liberal legal thought as a reference to spatiality, and structure as a reference to the semiotics and style of argumentative practice. While I leave the concept of office behind as this book's claim progresses, I turn to the structure of liberal legal thought beginning in Chapter 4.

[17] Shaunnagh Dorsett and Shaun McVeigh, The Persona of the Jurist in Salmond's Jurisprudence: On the Exposition of 'What Law Is . . . ' 38 *Victoria University Wellington Law Review* 771 (2007), p. 773.

[18] Id.

[19] And to press the point further, I take Dorsett and McVeigh's explication of the office of the jurist as expressed in Salmond's work to be a very strong illustration of what I will call "Classic Liberalism" in Chapter 4.

[20] Unger, The Critical Legal Studies Movement, supra note 1, at 5.

Speaking of History

So far in this explication of the jurisprudence of style, we have two personas and one office. The first persona is that of the structuralist, the person engaged in the structuralist activity. The second is the jurist, the person engaged in a style of argumentative practice. The concept of office refers to a physical site of training, a place in which jurists become jurists, a place in which jurists learn the skilled familiarity of the language of liberal legalism. The office of liberal legal thought may have particular national origins, and it may predominate in some particular geographical space. But the structuralist is agnostic on these questions, leaving them for others.[21] It is here that we reach a new passageway. For while we may feel comfortable with jurisprudential notions like the juridical persona and the office of liberal legal thought, if we want to know something of the jurist's style of argumentative practice as it operates in the context of liberal legalism, we must now ask the historical question of *when?* It may be that the offices of liberal legalism care little for national frontiers, but this says nothing about the time in which liberal practice is taking place. In other words, we need to know something of the structuralist approach to legal history. As I will suggest, this approach shares certain features with intellectual history, but is dissimilar as well, in particular with respect to the intellectual historian's typical interest in origins and causal explanations.[22] Analogously, the structuralist approach to legal history has something in common with its poststructuralist sibling, though they ought not to be confused. In clarifying these contrasting positions, I begin with a brief exposition on intellectual history, move to the poststructuralist view of genealogy, and then turn to the heart of the matter: structuralist legal history.

The twentieth century's historiographical terrain is not flat. It's bumpy, with its many hills and divots, rivulets and reaches.[23] The particular foothold I'm looking for here is that of *context*, for what unites so many of today's modes of historiography is a sort of postmodern historicism: a

[21] For an example of the complementary nature of these tasks, see Arnulf Becker Lorca, *Mestizo International Law* (Cambridge: Cambridge University Press, 2015).

[22] See, e.g., Gordon Wood, "Intellectual History and the Social Sciences," in *New Directions in American Intellectual History* (John Digham and Paul Conkin, eds.) (Baltimore: Johns Hopkins University Press, 1980).

[23] See generally, Michel de Certeau, *The Writing of History* (Tom Conley, trans.) (New York: Columbia University Press, 1988); Donald Kelley, *Fortunes of History* (New Haven, CT: Yale University Press, 2003); Donald Kelley, *Frontiers of History* (New Haven, CT: Yale University Press, 2006).

view of history in which past events, if they are to be understood and given meaning, must be placed in their "proper" contexts.[24] But what makes this a postmodern historicism is the added feature of knowing that the search for a proper context is never objective, and that what seems like the proper context has everything to do with the historian's very contextualized perspective.[25] As Quentin Skinner put it in 2002, "Scarcely anyone nowadays believes in the possibility of building up structures of factual knowledge on foundations purporting to be wholly independent of our judgements."[26] To think otherwise is to make the mistake of a vulgar empiricist presentism, the tendency to see the past as objectively knowable through the problematics of the present. And yet, we cannot forget the sound of the other shoe, for as Skinner stated back in 1969, "a further feature of historical studies is that they are at least supposed to be true."[27]

Let us begin with the *Annales* School and the long-term history of systems of beliefs specific to some group in space and time.[28] Early on, the *Annales* historians seemed eager to hook the history of ideas into "social reality."[29] This is a rebuke of the "thin" philosophical history of what in the United States was known as the History of Ideas, often associated with Arthur Lovejoy.[30] Rather than pursue an arid and abstract disquisition on the ideas of Aristotle floating through time and space, the *Annales* School sought out those daily habits of social life and "socio-economic evolutions" ultimately responsible for the production of elites and their elite ideas.[31] These habits were impersonal, collective, recurring,

[24] Quentin Skinner, Meaning and Understanding in the History of Ideas, 8 *History and Theory* 3 (1969), p. 4.

[25] See, e.g., Peter Novick, *That Noble Dream: The 'Objectivity Question' and the American Historical Profession (Ideas in Context)* (Cambridge: Cambridge University Press, 1988).

[26] Quentin Skinner, *Visions of Politics* (Cambridge: Cambridge University Press, 2002), p. 1.

[27] Skinner, Meaning and Understanding in the History of Ideas, supra note 24, at 29.

[28] See, e.g., Francois Dosse, *New History in France: The Triumph of the* Annales (Urbana: University of Illinois Press, 1994). See also Jo Guldi and David Armitage, *The History Manifesto* (Cambridge: Cambridge University Press, 2014).

[29] Roger Chartier, "Intellectual History or Sociocultural History?" in *Modern European Intellectual History: Reappraisals and New Perspectives* (Dominick LaCapra and Steven Kaplan, eds.) (London: Cornell University Press, 1982), p. 16. For the Cambridge School's version, see J. G. A. Pocock, Machiavelli, Harrington, and English Political Ideologies in the Eighteenth Century, 22 *William and Mary Quarterly* 549 (1965) ("It should be clear already that I will be dealing with that vexed yet favorite topic of the relation of ideas to social reality, but I shall be doing so in tones of extreme caution.")

[30] Arthur Lovejoy, *The Great Chain of Being: A Study of the History of an Idea* (New York: Harper, 1936).

[31] Chartier, Intellectual History, supra note 29, at 18.

but were not necessarily universal or transcendental. They were social, local, and contingent habits of mind, particular to no great thinker but rather to the very material out of which the thinker produced his great thoughts.

As Roger Chartier put the contrast, "To an intellectual history of unbridled minds and ideas without support structure is opposed a history of collective representation, of intellectual equipment and categories available and shared at a given epoch."[32] And as Lynn Hunt suggested in one of her round-ups of the *Annales* school, "In contrast to these earlier forms of historical analysis, the *Annales* school emphasized serial, functional, and structural approaches to understanding society as a total, inter-related system."[33] Famously, this totalizing approach to the geography and demographics of society was delineated into three layers of time: (1) that of the *longue duree*, a structure of habits immanent in some geographical milieu, (2) a medium, intermediary sensibility, and (3) the most superficial level of the event, associated with individual consciousness. Fernand Braudel's most well-known work focused on the "geo-historical structuralism" of the *longue duree*.[34]

The *Annales* school, along with an influx of Marxist historiography,[35] has been said to have influenced the emergence of an "old" cultural history, a view of the historical method interested in the distinction between discursive and non-discursive practice, with a predilection for the latter.[36] The "new" cultural history, if it still is new here in 2018, was similarly interested in getting away from the desiccated realm of ideas and back to the material, but now toward a linguistic understanding of dedifferentiated cultural hybrids.[37] What's more, the new mode often

[32] Id. at 21.

[33] Lynn Hunt, French History in the Last Twenty Years: The Rise and Fall of the Annales Paradigm, 21 *Journal of Contemporary History* 209, 211 (1986). See also Stuart Clark, *The Annales Historians, in The Return of Grand Theory* (Quentin Skinner, ed.) (Cambridge: Cambridge University Press, 1985).

[34] Hunt, supra note 33, at 211.

[35] See, e.g., EP Thompson, *The Making of the English Working Class* (New York: Vintage, 1966); Perry Anderson, *In the Tracks of Historical Materialism* (Chicago: University of Chicago Press, 1984); Walter Benjamin, *The Arcades Project* (Howard Eiland and Kevin McLaughlin, trans.) (Cambridge, MA: Harvard University Press, 2002). See also G. A. Cohen, *Karl Marx's Theory of History: A Defence* (Princeton, NJ: Princeton University Press, 2001).

[36] Roger Chartier, "The Chimera of the Origin Archaeology of Knowledge, Cultural History, and the French Revolution," in *Foucault and the Writing of History* (Jan Goldstein, ed.) (Oxford: Blackwell, 1994), p. 176; Donald Kelley, The Old Cultural History, 9 *History of the Human Sciences* 101 (1996).

[37] Lynn Hunt, "Introduction," in *The New Cultural History* (Lynn Hunt, ed.) (Berkeley: University of California Press, 1989), p. 1.

defined itself as against the search for long-range structures, such as the geographical milieu over the long haul, or the means of economic production, and instead set its sights on that rich texture of popular culture and its labyrinthine nodes of sexuality, media, identity, and so much else. Sometimes framed as microhistory,[38] this was above all an *embodied* history, finding inspiration in Clifford Geertz's great mantra, "thick description."[39] This shift in emphasis largely took its cue from the sea changes taking place in cultural studies in the 1970s and 1980s, where culture came to be seen as both indispensable and irreducible in historical explication.[40] Attending to "conditions of communication, the terms of representation, the interactions between structures," cultural history sees society as a web of textualities.[41] As Appleby, Hunt, and Jacob put it, "all historians of culture must grapple with how to relate the cultural artifact – text, painting, or steam engine – with the other beliefs, knowledge systems, interests, and structures affecting the human agents who gave rise to it."[42]

Similarly at work in "the linguistic turn" was a set of developments in intellectual history.[43] But whereas cultural historians (and some intellectual historians), understood "discourse" in the light of continental thinking, I want to focus briefly here on intellectual historians generally more influenced by the analytics of Austin and Wittgenstein, and associated

38 See, e.g., Matti Peltonen, Clues, Margins, and Monads: The Micro-Macro Link in Historical Research, 40 *History and Theory* 347 (2001).

39 Clifford Geertz, *The Interpretation of Cultures* (New York: Basic Books, 1979). See also William Sewell, *Logics of History: Social Theory and Social Transformation* (Chicago: University of Chicago Press, 2005), p. 153.

40 Richard Biernacki, "Method and Metaphor after the New Cultural History," in *Beyond the Cultural Turn: New Directions in the Study of Society and Culture* (Victoria Bonnell and Lynn Hunt, eds.) (Berkeley: University of California Press, 1999), p. 65.

41 Miri Rubin, "What Is Cultural History Now?" in *What Is History Now?* (David Cannadine, ed.) (New York: Palgrave, 2002), p. 81. Of course, cultural historians weren't the only ones interested in the idea that societies are textual structures. See, e.g., Dominick La Capra, Rethinking Intellectual History and Reading Texts, 19 *History and Theory* 245 (1980).

42 Joyce Appleby et al., *Telling the Truth about History* (New York: Norton, 1994), p. 225.

43 Dominick LaCapra, *History and Reading: Tocqueville, Foucault, French Studies* (Toronto: University of Toronto Press, 2000); John Toews, Intellectual History after the Linguistic Turn: The Autonomy of Meaning and the Irreducibility of Experience, 92 *American Historical Review* 879 (1987); Ethan Kleinberg, Haunting History: Deconstruction and the Spirit of Revision, 46 *History and Theory* 113 (2007); Judith Surkis, When Was the Linguistic Turn? A Genealogy, 117 *American Historical Review* 700 (2012).

with the Cambridge School.[44] Famously articulated by Quentin Skinner, John Pocock, and John Dunn, Cambridge intellectual history saw the task of the historian as situating "the texts we study within such intellectual contexts as enable us to make sense of what the authors were doing in writing them . . . to see things their way."[45] As Skinner continued, in this Austinian register, "[t]he aim is to see such texts as contributions to particular discourses, and thereby to recognize the ways in which they followed or challenged or subverted the conventional terms of those discourses themselves. More generally, the aim is to return the specific texts we study to the precise cultural contexts in which they were originally formed."[46] The purpose here is to uncover the intentionality of the historical subject, and in order to do this, the historical subject is located in ever-widening fields of intellectual context. "The social context figures as the ultimate framework for helping to decide what conventionally recognizable meanings it might in principle have been possible for someone to have intended to communicate."[47]

To put all of this another way, Cambridge school contextualism sought to reveal the true intentions of the speaker by way of a search for discursive origins, the "proper" context of meaning and intelligibility, or at least, "a promising context with which to begin."[48] This is, after all, the purpose of intellectual history, to tell us what happened, and why.[49] But this search for origins is still "postmodern," if you like; it proceeds with an eye for discontinuity and rupture, and is far more likely to relish the absence of any coherent system or doctrine, such as a unified history of political philosophy. As Pocock suggested in this regard, "any historian who tries to provide himself with a model of political philosophies as the products of historical processes is bound to ask the question whether what he is studying is in fact the record of a continuous activity with a history of its own."[50] Political philosophy, Pocock continued, is "simply too diverse and disorderly – being of the groundstuff of history itself – to have a

44 See, e.g., J. G. A. Pocock, *Political Thought and History: Essays on Theory and Method* (Cambridge: Cambridge University Press, 2009), pp. 76–77; Quentin Skinner, *The Foundations of Modern Political Thought, Vol. Two: The Age of Reformation* (Cambridge: Cambridge University Press, 1978), pp. 127–134. For discussion of the linguistic turn as it manifested in Germany, see Martin Jay, "Should Intellectual History Take a Linguistic Turn? Reflections on the Habermas-Gadamer Debate," in LaCapra and Kaplan, supra note 30.

45 Skinner, Visions, supra note 26, at 3. See also *Meaning and Context* (James Tulley, ed.) (Princeton, NJ: Princeton University Press, 1988).

46 Skinner, Visions, supra note 26, at 125. 47 Id. at 87.

48 Pocock, Political Thought and History, supra note 44, at 88. 49 Id. 50 Id. at 52.

single evolving pattern of history."[51] The historian's task, in this valence, is to ask of those discursive contexts that *led* to classical republican theory from an originary center in Machiavelli's conceptual vocabulary.[52] Or, perhaps, we ask of those contexts that *did not* lead to liberal theory, but were rather themselves a product of Christianity.[53] And so on...

The historical methods of the *Annales* school, the "new" cultural history, and intellectual history, are all suggestive of both what structuralist historiography is and is not. From the *Annales* school there is belief in structure, the totalizing historical unity. From cultural history there is allegiance to Foucault, Derrida, and what we could call a general commitment to poststructuralist historicism: the endless multiplication of context and the hunt for the discursive trace. From intellectual history, at least in its Cambridge school form, there is the emphasis on origins, origins to be found in the discursivity of political, economic, and religious thought.

Structuralist historiography has something in common with the *Annales* historians, to the extent that structuralist historians are also interested in seemingly (but not really) anachronistic "totalities." It has something in common with cultural history's poststructuralist historicism, to the extent that structuralist historians believe that totalities and sweeping swaths of time are a waste of time, and that the historical terrain can never be gobbled up in monumentally coherent narratives. And finally, structuralist historians have something in common with the intellectual historians, to the extent they are after a language of *thought*. But, like poststructuralist genealogy, structuralist history lacks a taste for origins, committed only to the *how* of structural transformation.[54]

[51] Id.

[52] See J. G. A. Pocock, *The Machiavellian Moment: Florentine Political Thought and the Atlantic Republican Tradition* (Princeton, NJ: Princeton University Press, 1975). See also *Machiavelli and Republicanism (Ideas in Context)* (Gisela Bock et al., eds.) (Cambridge: Cambridge University Press, 1990).

[53] This, of course, is a reference to John Dunn's work on John Locke, to which I return in Chapter 6. At once a demolition project out to destroy what in 1968 appeared as the consensus view of a unified totality called "Locke," and an effort to substitute in its stead a more local, particularly *true* context in which to understood what Locke *himself* had meant. The origin of Locke's intentions, the answer to the critical *why* Locke meant what Dunn meant Locke to mean, it turned out, was the broader context of Christianity. See John Dunn, *The Political Thought of John Locke: An Historical Account of the Argument of the 'Two Treatises of Government'* (Cambridge: Cambridge University Press, 1969). See also John Dunn, *Western Political Theory in the Face of the Future* (Cambridge: Cambridge University Press, 1993).

[54] Foucault, Archaeology, supra note 4, at 164.

What of the problem of context? If social, cultural, and intellectual histories all have their favored contexts, in what context does structuralist history operate? The central question is whether, in its pursuit of argumentative practice, structuralist legal history is oblivious to the need for contextualism. If it is, structuralist legal history reflects just the sort of generalizing and totalizing account of legal history that poststructuralist historicism was pitched against.[55] As we saw in Chapter 1 with respect to Trubek's complaints about Kennedy's work on Blackstone, Kennedy's work was flatly anachronistic. If the purpose in exhuming Blackstone was to appropriate past philosophy in the service of a present interest – showing jurists how they argue right now – Kennedy's history so badly failed to take account of historical context, that it could not be, as one commentator has suggested in a different context, "worthy of the name of 'history' of philosophy. What is offered in that name is in fact a species of textual exegesis or critical commentary, with no more connection to history than the fact that the authors are dead."[56] But even if a theorist tries to escape presentism with the excuse of doing nothing more than ahistorical critical commentary, the excuse will not appease for long, since "the reading of philosophy of the past cannot ignore the historical circumstances of their production without risk of serious distortion."[57]

Was the Harvard School's work lacking in proper contextualization, and "dogged by debilitating anachronism and presentism"?[58] As Peter Gordon has recently argued, in order to answer this question we ought to ask, which contexts are necessary for a "history" to be appropriately historicized, and therefore, excused of presentism?[59] My argument is that, despite all appearances, structuralist legal history *is* contextualist historiography. Structuralist legal history is not ahistorical, is actually legal history – just not *intellectual* legal history, not *cultural* legal history, not *social* legal history. What has been misunderstood is that the targeted context is a *legal* context. Now, the misunderstanding is certainly understandable, for at first blush the idea of "putting law in legal context" seems nonsense.

55 See Harry Harootunian, Remembering the Historical Present, 33 *Critical Inquiry* 471, 484 (2007).

56 Sarah Hutton, Intellectual History and the History of Philosophy, 40 *History of European Ideas* 925, 926 (2014).

57 Id.

58 Ian Hunter, The Figure of Man and the Territorialisation of Justice in Enlightenment Natural Law: Pufendorf and Vattel, 23 *Intellectual History Review* 289 (2012).

59 Peter Gordon, "Contextualism and Criticism in the History of Ideas," in *Rethinking Modern European Intellectual History* (Darrin McMahon and Samuel Moyn, eds.) (New York: Oxford University Press, 2014).

So here is what I mean: For the structuralist, the identification of a *legal context* entails the identification of a particular mode of *legal thought*. Legal thought in turn refers to the figures of argumentative practice. To put the point another way, when the structuralist historian constructs a mode of legal thought, she is constructing a legal grammar as well as styles of legal argument, layers in the legal structure that are both something other than the doctrinal rules immanent in legal concepts. The realm of doctrine, of course, is also relevant to legal thought. But rather than focus solely on the content of rules in concepts, the structuralist historian constructs legal thought as a structure encompassing grammar, concept, and style. It is the relation between concept on the one side and grammar and style on the other that fills out the meaning of a *legal context*.

Structuralist Legal History

Let me say that again, but a bit more slowly this time. A familiar move in legal analysis "places" a legal rule in its proper social context. For example, in order to properly understand the life of the law, perhaps we need to see law in its political or economic contexts, as Charles Beard, Willard Hurst, Lawrence Friedman, or Morton Horwitz have suggested.[60] Unless and until we are alive to these social contexts, we only get partial glimpses of what law is really all about. Perhaps in order to understand the American Constitution, we need to place those rules in the context of its drafters' experience.[61] Or perhaps so that we can to come to grips with the contemporary configuration of the administrative state, we need a thick account of the institutional order.[62] Or perhaps legal history as

[60] See, e.g., Charles Beard, *An Economic Interpretation of the Constitution of the United States* (New York: Free Press, 1986); James Willard Hurst, *Law and the Conditions of Freedom in the Nineteenth-Century United States* (Madison: University of Wisconsin Press, 1956); *American Law and the Constitutional Order: Historical Perspectives* (Lawrence Friedman and Harry Scheiber, eds.) (Cambridge, MA: Harvard University Press, 1978); Morton Horwitz, *The Transformation of American Law, 1870–1960: The Crisis of Legal Orthodoxy* (New York: Oxford University Press, 1992).

[61] See, e.g., Mary Bilder, *Madison's Hand: Revising the Constitutional Convention* (Cambridge, MA: Harvard University Press, 2015); Jennifer Nedelsky, *Private Property and the Limits of American Constitutionalism: The Madisonian Framework and Its Legacy* (Chicago: University of Chicago Press, 1990).

[62] Daniel Ernst, *Tocqueville's Nightmare: The Administrative State Emerges in America, 1900–1940* (New York: Oxford University Press, 2014); Brian Balogh, *A Government Out of Sight: The Mystery of National Authority in Nineteenth-Century America* (New York: Cambridge University Press, 2009); William Novak, *The People's Welfare: Law*

the history of ideas.[63] Clearly, there are any number of contexts we could choose from in giving our historical account, and to be sure, many of them are fantastic.

Like these historical works, structuralist histories also place law in context, but contexts that will neither be politico-economic nor cultural, about neither the history of the Constitution nor the "legal process." It will instead be a history that places "doctrine" in the distinctive context of legal thought. For the structuralist, legal thought presents an elaborate and complex context for research and study. It refers to the structure of background practices in the grammar that constitutes a legal language. It refers to the mechanics of legal style – the patterns of argumentative practice jurists manifest in the process of putting legal rules into action, giving the rules momentum, and when done successfully, giving the rules a gloss of necessity. It refers to the lexical terrain of technical knowledge immanent in legal concepts, what we might otherwise call rules or "doctrines." The legal context of legal thought is about all of this: the structure's basic grammar, its argumentative style, and its lexicon. Consequently, while a structuralist history of legal thought *is* about legal concepts (the language's lexicon), a concept's rules are not the end but only the beginning of the story. Rather than focus solely on the content of rules, or on the settled state of those rules as the aim of the pursuit, structuralist legal history uses the legal concept as an open passageway for exploring legal thought. Thus, while the structuralist places doctrine in context, she does not put it in anything that looks like a familiar historical context: political, economic, cultural, etc. She puts doctrine in the historical context of legal thought.

The example developed in this book is that of political economy. A structuralist history of political economy begins with political economy's legal context, and the search for legal context begins with a lexicon, the terrain of legal concepts.[64] Which concepts? In the context of liberal legal

and Regulation in Nineteenth-Century America (Chapel Hill: University of North Carolina Press, 1996).

63 See, e.g., Grant Gilmore, *The Ages of American Law* (New Haven, CT: Yale University Press, 1977); Gregory Alexander, *Commodity & Propriety: Competing Visions of Property in American Legal Thought, 1776–1970* (Chicago: University of Chicago Press, 1997); Rudolph Pertitz, *Competition Policy in America, 1888–1992* (New York: Oxford University Press, 1996); Herbert Hovenkamp, *The Opening of American Law: Neoclassical Legal Thought, 1870–1970* (New York: Oxford University Press, 2015).

64 Reinhart Koselleck's conceptual history is a helpful example of how to think about legal concepts as an open-ended lexicon of technical knowledge. For Koselleck, a concept,

thought, we know to at least consider property and contract as provisional starting points. But these are so-called bodies of law, disciplinary fields in need of demolition.[65] What comes into view is a veritable sea of legal concepts, pieces of technical knowledge strewn about in a litter of rules. Now, it hardly makes sense to assume that every legal field will present its lexicon in the same way, or that all structuralists will similarly compose. But when we come to the lexical sea of "property law," with its concepts of trespass, nuisance, estates, trusts, servitudes, and so on, we meet a list of open-ended choices, and very little in the way of "settled" doctrines. Let us take, very briefly, a lexical view of the concept of the servitude as an example. As the jurist looks for the rules, perhaps he encounters something like the following.[66]

unlike an "idea," is an entity that aspires toward a rich semantic diversity. This suggests that a given word only becomes a concept once "the entirety of meaning and experience within a sociopolitical context within which and for which a word is used can be condensed into one word." Reinhart Koselleck, *Futures Past: On the Semantics of Historical Time* (Cambridge, MA: MIT Press, 1985), p. 121. Immanent in a concept, on this view, are a plurality of pathways – pathways which themselves give the concept its contingent form. Reinhart Koselleck, *The Practice of Conceptual History: Timing History, Spacing Concepts* (Stanford, CA: Stanford University Press, 2002); Reinhart Koselleck, *Critique and Crisis: Enlightenment and the Pathogenesis of Modern Society* (Cambridge, MA: MIT Press, 1998). For discussions of the difference between conceptual history and contextualist history, see Melvin Richter, Conceptual History (Begriffsgeschichte) and Political Theory, 14 *Political Theory* 604, 620–621 (1986); J.G.A. Pocock, "Concepts and Discourses: A Difference in Culture? Comment on a Paper by Melvin Richter," in *The Meaning of Historical Terms and Concepts* (Hartmut Lehman and Melvin Richter, eds.) (Washington, DC: German Historical Institute,1996); Donald Kelley, On The Margins of Begriffsgeschichte, in Lehman and Melvin, supra note 64; Quentin Skinner, Rhetoric and Conceptual Change, 3 *Finnish Yearbook of Political Thought* 60 (1999); Kari Palonen, Rhetorical and Temporal Perspectives on Conceptual Change, 3 *Finnish Yearbook of Political Thought* 41 (1999); *Political Concepts and Time: New Approaches to Conceptual History* (Javier Fernandez Sebastian, ed.) (Santander, Spain: Cantabria University Press, 2011). For general discussion, see John Zammito, Koselleck's Philosophy of Historical Time(s) and the Practice of History', 43 *History & Theory* 126 (2004); Helge Jordheim, Against Periodization: Koselleck's Theory of Multiple Temporalities, 51 *History & Theory* 151 (2012); Elias Jose Palti, From Ideas to Concepts to Metaphors: The German Tradition of Intellectual History and the Complex Fabric of Language, 49 *History & Theory* 194 (2010); Lynn Hunt, *Measuring Time, Making History* (Budapest: Central European University Press, 2008).

65 Foucault, Archaeology, supra note 4, at 117.

66 I have populated this list of rules entirely from law school textbooks and restatements purely in order to keep the provenance of these rules separate from juridical arguments. Of course, this separation is facile, as the rules taken from these sources typically rely on citations to case law. Also, I do not mean to suggest that this list is in any way comprehensive; it is partial and merely illustrative.

Pair 1

(a) *Servitudes represent nonpossessory interests of people in things over which they hold no title.*[67] *The thing that is subject to the servitude is known as the burdened estate.*[68] *The thing that benefits from the servitude is known as the benefited estate.*[69] *An easement is appurtenant when the benefit attaches to another piece of land, regardless of who the owner of that benefited land might be.*[70] *An easement is in gross when the benefit attaches to a particular person.*[71]

vs.

(b) *Whether a servitude is regarded as "nonpossessory" or a "possessory" interest depends on the various incidents of "ownership" ultimately determined by a court in the context of the relevant community policies.*[72] *For example, this issue may be resolved by looking to the extent that the beneficiary of a servitude enjoys the right to exclude third parties from the benefited estate.*[73]

Pair 2

(a) *Servitudes are the creation of private agreements, in contrast with public use restrictions as found in zoning laws.*[74]

vs.

(b) *Servitudes are the creation of public agreements, since the laws of property are enforced by positively enacted legal authorities.*[75]

67 Jesse Dukeminier et al., *Property* (6th ed.) (New York: Aspen, 2006), p. 671; Restatement (Third) of Property (Servitudes) (2000), 1.2 (Comment D).

68 Sheldon Kurtz et al., *Cases and Materials on American Property* (6th ed.) (St. Paul: West, 2012), pp. 613–614.

69 Id.

70 Thomas Merrill and Henry Smith, *Property: Principles and Policies* (2nd ed.) (New York: Foundation Press, 2012), p. 983.

71 Id. at 987.

72 Luther McDougal and Myres McDougal, *Property, Wealth, Land: Allocation, Planning and Development* (2nd ed.) (Indianapolis: Bobbs-Merrill, 1981), pp. 379, 447.

73 Id. at 476–477; Charles Clark, *Real Covenants and other Interests which Run with the Land: Including licenses, easements, profits, equitable restrictions, and rent* (Callaghan, 1947), pp. 2–3; Harry Bigelow, *Cases and Materials on Rights in Land* (St. Paul: West, 1945), pp. 41–42; Restatement, supra note 67, at 1.2 (Comment C).

74 Kurtz, supra note 68, at 607; Restatement, supra note 67, at Introductory Note.

75 McDougal & McDougal, supra note 72, at 417.

> *The source of authority for and the functions of zoning laws and the law of servitudes are indistinguishable once the dogma of the public-private distinction is ignored.*[76]

Pair 3

(a) *Whereas the holder of land in fee simple can use her land for any number of purposes, the holder of a nonpossessory interest is highly constrained.*[77]

vs.

(b) *Beneficiaries of a servitude may enjoy rights of use that were never contemplated when the servitude was originally created and are reasonably necessary for the enjoyment of the servitude.*[78] *Furthermore, the rights of use incident to ownership in fee simple are constrained by a host of legal doctrines, and the content of such rights is unknowable when analyzed independently of a concrete legal controversy.*[79]

Pair 4

(a) *Servitudes are rights and duties that pass automatically to subsequent owners and possessors.*[80]

vs.

(b) *Servitudes never pass automatically to subsequent owners and possessors, since the passage of a servitude always depends on the judicial negotiation of conflicting policy concerns.*[81]

Pair 5

(a) *Easements are affirmative servitudes, meaning that an easement offers its holder a right to use another's land.*[82] *The beneficiary*

[76] Kurtz, supra note 68, at 607.
[77] Dukeminier, supra note 67, at 671; McDougal & McDougal, supra note 72, at 475–476.
[78] Dukeminier, supra note 67, at 724; Restatement 4.8 (Comment d); Restatement, supra note 67, at 4.10.
[79] Joseph Singer et al., *Property Law: Rules Policies and Practices* (6th ed.) (Frederick, MD: Wolters Kluwer, 2014), p. 40; McDougal & McDougal, supra note 72, at 475–476.
[80] Merrill and Smith, supra note, at 983; Dukeminier, supra note 67, at 709.
[81] Singer, supra note, at 513; Clark, supra note 73, at 4–5.
[82] Charles Harr and Lance Liebman, *Property and Law* (Boston: Little, Brown and Company, 1977), p. 706; McDougal & McDougal, supra note 72, at 476.

of an easement can only use the burdened land for its specified purpose.[83] *Additionally, owners of easements may engage in reasonable maintenance and improvements, but are restricted from causing undue burdens on the burdened estate.*[84]

vs.

(b) *The beneficiary of an easement may use the burdened land for purposes other than the originally specified purpose.*[85]

Pair 6

(a) *Owners of the burdened estate must acquire the consent of the easement holder if they wish to change the location of the easement.*[86]

vs.

(b) *Owners of the burdened estate need not acquire the consent of the easement holder if they wish to change the location of the easement.*[87]

Pair 7

(a) *Easements "run with the land." This means that easements pass automatically to subsequent owners and possessors, but an easement is only enforceable if (a) it is written in the original deed, (b) there was notice to the burdened estate holder of the easement, and (c) the grantor of the easement intended the easement.*[88]

vs.

(b) *In order to be enforceable, easements need not be in writing, holders of burdened estates need not have actual notice, and it is unnecessary to find evidence of the grantor's express intent to create an easement. A party can seek legal enforcement of an easement through equitable doctrines of estoppel, prescription, prior use, and necessity.*[89]

[83] Merrill and Smith, supra note 70, at 986.
[84] Singer, supra note 79, at 514.
[85] Restatement, supra note 67, at 4.10.
[86] Dukeminier, supra note 67, at 725.
[87] Restatement, supra note 67, at 4.8(3).
[88] Singer, supra note 79, at 517.
[89] Restatement, supra note 67, at 2.1(2).

Pair 8

(a) *Easements are contracts, having arisen out of a bargaining process between free and equal members of civil society.*[90]

vs.

(b) *Easements are irrevocable conveyances, typically found in deeds and not contracts and are more apiece with the in rem aspects of a property law that is the law of things.*[91]

Pair 9

(a) *Real covenants are negative servitudes, meaning that the owner subject to a covenant is restrained in how he can use his land.*[92] *To be enforceable, real covenants must be in writing and have been intended by the original drafters of the covenant.*[93]

vs.

(b) *Real covenants are enforceable in the absence of express writing, as in the case of estoppel.*[94] *Real covenants are similarly enforceable in the absence of express intent.*[95]

Pair 10

(a) *To be enforceable, real covenants must "touch and concern" the thing that is the object of the covenant.*[96]

vs.

(b) *Real covenants are enforceable even when the thing that is the object of the covenant is unaffected.*[97] *The operative question will focus on the legal relations and interests therein affected by the covenant.*[98]

[90] Merrill and Smith, supra note 70, at 983; Kurtz, supra note 68, at 607.
[91] Merrill Smith, supra note 70, at 986; Kurtz, supra note 68, at 607.
[92] Merrill and Smith, supra note 70, at 1025.
[93] Singer, supra note 79, at 557–559; Merrill and Smith, supra note 70, at 1038.
[94] Singer, supra note 79, at 565.
[95] Id. at 567; Merrill and Smith, supra note 70, at 1038–1039.
[96] Singer, supra note 79, at 557–559; Merrill and Smith, supra note 70, at 1039.
[97] Singer, supra note 79, at 557–559.
[98] Clark, supra note 73, at 97.

Pair 11

(a) *To be enforceable, there must be privity of estate between the covenanting parties, and the benefits and burdens of the covenant must run to the succeeding owners of the burdened and benefited estates.*[99]

vs.

(b) *Real covenants are enforceable despite a lack of privity of estate between the covenanting parties. This is sometimes established through a substitution of "notice" for "privity" and "equitable servitude" for "real covenant."*[100] *It is sometimes established simply by doing away with the privity requirement altogether.*[101]

Pair 12

(a) *Beneficiaries of real covenants may obtain relief against owners of servient estates, either in the form of damages or injunctive remedies, depending on whether the covenant is cast as an equitable servitude.*[102]

vs.

(b) *Beneficiaries of real covenants cannot obtain relief when an official determines the covenant to be unreasonable, unconscionable, or in violation of a statutory prescription.*[103]

For most readers, an encounter with a list like this is a little (or a lot) unpleasant.[104] The experience is one of dissonance. Presented as a series

[99] Singer, supra note 79, at 557–559; Merrill and Smith, supra note 70, at 1039–1040.
[100] Singer, supra note 79, at 557–559; Merrill and Smith, supra note 70, at 1025.
[101] Singer, supra note 79, at 567; Merrill and Smith, supra note 70, at 1040.
[102] Singer, supra note 79, at 564. [103] Restatement, supra note 67, at 3.1, 3.7.
[104] Here was Oliver Wendell Holmes' view of the situation back in 1881, already anticipating the realist interpretation of the bundle of rights: "The language of the law of easements was built up out of similes drawn from persons at a time when the *noxae deditio* was still familiar; and then, as often happens, language reacted upon thought, so that conclusions were drawn as to the rights themselves in terms of which they happened to be expressed. When one estate was said to be enslaved to another, or a right of way was to be a quality or incident of the neighboring piece of land, men's minds were not alert enough to see that these phrases were only so many personifying metaphors, which explained nothing unless the figure of speech was true . . . All that can be said is, that the metaphors and similes employed naturally led to the rule which has prevailed, and that, as this rule was just as good as any other, or at least was unobjectionable, it was drawn from figures of speech without attracting attention, and before anyone had seen

of pairs emphasizing tension without resolution, fragmentation without harmony, there are few markers of majority and minority rules, and little sense of a settled terrain. It looks, above else, like a demand for juridical choice, an open invitation for judicial activism, with little hope for an impersonal rule of law. But maybe not! The sense in which this list appears to the jurist depends on that jurist's training. Many jurists are likely amateurs in the context of building arguments out of the legal concept of the servitude. And if the jurist is an amateur, the legal concept appears as a menu of indeterminate and technical rules. The business of concluding for one rule over another, and fashioning that conclusion in a way that looks legally necessitated, will be challenging. If, on the other hand, the jurist is a master, the lexicon manifests quite differently. Rather than flinch in the bracing dissonance, the experienced jurist will make his moves fluidly, flowing from background practice oh-so-easily into a neutral and natural conclusion. Certain pairs will draw the jurist, others will recede. Certain choices in the pairs will sing out as majority rules, while others will fall away as exceptions. Certain choices emerge as *right* and others *wrong*. And as the master jurist, that jurist trained in the rituals and techniques of legal argument, finds a source of momentum carrying him from the facts, into the technical space of the concept, and out into a conclusion, he practices a certain *style*.[105]

that they were only figures, which proved nothing and justified no conclusion . . . We must take it that easements have become an incident of land by an unconscious and unreasoned assumption that a piece of land can have rights. It need not be said that this is absurd, although the rules of law which are based upon it are not so." Oliver Wendell Holmes, Jr., *The Common Law* (New York: Macmillan, 1968), pp. 297–299.

[105] The history of legal style has something in common with what Hayden White calls the "tropics of discourse," the figures, tropes, and grooves in a language-system's terrain, "linking" *langue* and *parole*. White explained that there were several levels here in the space between *langue* and *parole*, but I want to mention just three. The first and deepest orientation is what White referred to as "tropological." "This ground is that of language itself, which, in areas of study such as history, can be said to operate tropologically in order to prefigure a field of perception in a particular modality of relationships." Hayden White, *Tropics of Discourse: Essays in Cultural Criticism* (Baltimore: Johns Hopkins University Press, 1978), p. 72. White may very well be conflating the tropological ground with Saussure's *langue*, but we will take it as an orientation toward the *langue*, and not as identical with it. White suggested that the tropics of discourse are inhabited by the four master tropes of metaphor, metonymy, synechdoche, and irony. Hayden White, *Metahistory: The Historical Imagination in Nineteenth Century Europe* (Baltimore: Johns Hopkins University Press, 1975), p. xi. These tropes are interpretive strategies, and it is through these strategies that we endow experience with meaning. White, Tropics of Discourse, supra note 105, at 72. The strategy of metaphor, for example, takes our experiences of difference and finds in those differences deeper similarities. Metonymic strategies construct the whole out of the prioritized part, assuming in the

This master jurist is the real target of structuralist legal history.[106] For like Merleau-Ponty's soccer player, this jurist's practice of legal argument comes so naturally that a great deal of the conceptual indeterminacy – the raw fact of ideological choice – very rarely comes into conscious view. It is not that this master jurist is unthinking or on autopilot. It is rather that, in his juridical expertise he has become so utterly familiar with the lexicon that the lexicon draws him in certain directions just as the "lines of force" operating on a soccer field draw the player. For the master jurist, in other words, a substantial amount of the argumentative work is in the background. Only when there is a glitch, a novel legal question requiring unfamiliar answers, does the argument enter a rational foreground, encountering the dissonance of the legal concept.[107]

process the distinction between universal and particular. The strategy of synecdoche, in contrast, relies on the universal/particular distinction but in order to prioritize the totality. As White explains, the important point is that in metaphor, metonymy, and synecdoche alike language provides us with models of the *direction* that thought itself might take in its effort to provide meaning to areas of experience not already regarded as being cognitively secured by either common sense, tradition, or science. Id. at 73. Thus, the first plane of tropological orientation concerns the way in which the historian approaches the *langue* in order to secure meaning. Hayden White, *Figural Realism: Studies in the Mimesis Effect* (Baltimore: Johns Hopkins University Press, 1999), p. 8. This orientation sets the table for the analysis to follow, though it does not strictly determine the subsequent cognitive and rhetorical moves. As for the cognitive move, this involves a pre-figurative choice of the historian about the kind of explanation she will make of the materials. This is a choice about "what a set of historical events will look like *once they have been explained.*" White, Tropics of Discourse, supra note 105, at 63. Beyond what White referred to as this pre-figurative, explanatory orientation lies another plane, moving closer in the direction of *parole* and away from the deep rules of the *langue*: the rhetorical mode. Id. at 66. As opposed to the historian's semi-conscious explanatory orientation, this next phase is about the sort of plot to be used in the explanation. Id. What *form* of narrative is to be deployed? The rhetorical orientation concerns the aesthetic choice to present the materials as a quest, a tragedy, a satire, or some other plot structure.

106 And it is here that the structuralist turns to case law, not for statements of the rule but for examples of argumentative practice. See, e.g., *Neponsit Property Owners Association v. Emigrant Industrial Savings Bank*, 278 N.Y. 248 (1938) (arguing in the modern liberal style); *Eagle Enterprises v. Gross*, 349 N.E. 2d 816 (1976) (arguing in the classic liberal style).

107 What I have been describing so far largely takes place in the foreground; this is a rational working of the technical rules, in which the jurist makes choices in the context of a relatively indeterminate legal concept. But the navigation of the concept also happens at a deeper, preconceptual level, in which the jurist performs a grammar without having any necessarily rational control over the performance. "The mass of coping is an *essential support to the episodes of conceptual focus* in our lives, not just in an infrastructural sense that something has to be carrying our mind around from library to laboratory and back. More fundamentally, the background understanding we need to make the sense

This is the point at which structuralist legal history comes, interrogating the jurist's background practices and asking whether, when, and why these practices recur.[108] If they do, perhaps we have happened upon a legal style, and perhaps in turn we compose a legal grammar that figures in from the background. Structuralist legal history is therefore a composition of the various styles manifested by different jurists at different moments in time. It is not a composition of the rules, situated in some nonlegal context. It is a composition of the rules situated in the legal context of legal thought, or, if you like, the context of what it means to think like a lawyer. As it turns out, over time, these styles change. Structuralist legal history explores the historical structure of these styles, in their basic grammar and lexical comportment, and how they transform in the lexical context of various legal concepts.

Before turning to a discussion of the historical structures of liberal legal thought, explored throughout the remainder of this book, let me summarize where we have been so far:

1. *The Structuralist Activity.* With its roots in the ideas of Merleau-Ponty, Foucault, and Barthes, the structuralist activity begins in a state of apparent contradiction. It suggests an experience with a juridical world of legal material that neither precedes him nor is of his own making, a world that is neither subjectivity nor *the real.* The structuralist activity is an encounter with indeterminacy and a mode of being that composes linguistic unities and totalities in the midst of that encounter. The structuralist sensibility is chiastic, but we can think of chiasmus as a field of opportunity just as easily as a blockade.[109] Hopefully, the structuralist embraces her chiastic compositions in the light of the former.
2. *Jurist and Office.* If the structuralist sensibility is a reflection of the structuralist's own persona as a composer, the composition is a legal language. But which language of legal thought, and where? Here the structuralist turns to the jurist and the office in which the jurist has been trained. The jurist is that legal professional familiar

we do of the pieces of thinking we engage in resides in our ordinary coping." Hubert Dreyfus and Charles Taylor, *Retrieving Realism* (Cambridge, MA: Harvard University Press, 2015), p. 52.

108 I turn to the "why" only in Chapter 9, on the mystifying and legitimating effects of liberal legal thought.

109 Judith Butler, *Senses of the Subject* (New York: Fordham University Press, 2015).

with the practices of legal argument. Office is the site of training and professionalization, the place in which the jurist learns to be a jurist. In this rendering of the structuralist activity, the target is the office of liberal legalism, the place in which liberal legal thought is produced and reproduced. The office of liberal legal thought knows no necessary social or cultural boundaries, and knows no necessary institutional home.

3. *Structure, Concept, and Style.* Once the structuralist turns to the work of the jurist in the language of liberal legal thought, she composes a series of practices. At the most basic level in the structure is the grammar of liberal legal thought. This master grammar constitutes the language system and constrains the choices of the jurist in his decisions about how to fashion an argumentative practice. Separate from the grammar is the lexicon of liberal legal thought. Unlike the closed space of the grammar, the lexicon is relatively open-ended. It is filled with a wide expanse of legal concepts, which are in turn filled out by technical rules. Sometimes "settled," more often these technical doctrines offer the jurist a choice of ideological maneuvers rather than impersonal rules. It is in the idea of style that we answer the question of how a jurist uses the language of liberal legal thought, moving from the background practice of the grammar and through the lexical indeterminacy of legal concepts on the way to a conclusion. A legal style is a recurring pattern of argumentative practice, at once constrained by the unity of the *langue* and at the same time open to the jurist's ideological choice. For amateur jurists, the ideological aspect is highlighted and conceptual analysis is prevalent, given their lack of familiarity with the relevant background practices. This is the jurist in his first couple years at the firm, the new law clerk, and so on. They are less trained in the "skilled coping" necessary for mastery. For master jurists, much of the argument flows out of the background practice, ideology is pushed deep in the blind spots, and conceptual analysis is at a minimum. This is the jurist on the soccer field.
4. *Legal Contexts.* The structures of legal thought composed by the structuralist are neither universal nor timeless.[110] They are

[110] For the suggestion that structures are problematic for this reason, see Sewell, supra note 39, at 125. In contrast, Hayden White explained that in historical practice, "Narrativization produces a meaning... by imposing a discursive form on the events that its own chronicle comprises by means that are poetic in nature... This is what Barthes meant

contingent, historically situated languages of legal argument. However, the structuralist does not rely on conventional contextualism when she crafts this history of legal structures. That is, the structuralist historian leaves for others the business of placing legal rules in political, social, and cultural contexts. These contexts are both important and illuminating, but on their own they miss the value of the legal context, the context of legal thought. The context of legal thought is grammar and style, the layers in the structure from and through which the lexicon is motivated. A history of legal context, as a result, is a history of juridical practice, the structure of and style in which jurists argue for legally-necessitated conclusions, and how one form of practice morphs into another. The history of legal context, as a result, is silent with respect to origins and the causes of change. As Hayden White has said,

> A history is . . . less like a picture intended to resemble the objects of which it speaks or a model . . . than 'a complex linguistic structure specifically built for the purpose of showing a part of the past.' In this view, historical discourse is not to be likened to a picture that permits us to see more clearly an object that would otherwise remain vague and imprecisely apprehended. Nor is it a representation of an explanatory procedure intended to finally provide a definitive answer to the problem of 'what really happened' in some given domain of the past. On the contrary . . . historical discourse is less a matching of an image or a model with some extrinsic reality than a making of a verbal structure, a discursive 'thing' that interferes with our perception of its putative referent even while fixing our attention on and illuminating it.[111]

We now have the elements of a jurisprudence of style, what I take to be the intellectual descendant of the Harvard School's path-breaking adventures in structuralism and phenomenology. It is in the light of these elements that this book's remaining chapters explore the structure and style of liberal legal thought, in its classic, modern, and pragmatic manifestations.

when he said: 'Narrative does not *show*, does not *imitate* . . . [Its] function is not to *represent*, it is to *constitute* a spectacle. Hayden White, *The Content of the Form: Narrative Discourse and Historical Representation* (Baltimore: Johns Hopkins University Press, 1987), pp. 42–43.

111 White, Figural, supra note 105, at 6.

PART II

LIBERAL LEGAL THOUGHT

4

The Classical Style

The discussion of liberal legalism in this and following chapters takes Chapter 1's elaboration of the liberal structure as its point of departure. It is worth a brief restatement of what that structure entailed. First is the idea that liberal legal thought is a distinctive and relatively autonomous semiotic system. At the deepest layers of the *langue* – the system's grammatical horizon – is a relation between two theses, the theses of competition and control. The thesis of free competition holds that society is merely a device enabled by the organic will of equally independent rights-bearing individuals. Founding society on the autonomous, rights-bearing individual is both natural and just. Society, in contrast, is only an artifice. It comes into being as a derivative *good* to the extent that the clash of individual wills yields natural outcomes. There is no a priori definition of the good superseding the right of individual pursuit of self-interest. The second thesis of social control holds that the contest of individual wills does not produce a stable environment. By their nature, individuals pursue their interests to the detriment of themselves and others. Free competition does not naturally yield derivative goods. Free competition naturally yields chaos, and in the end, a society devoid of the competitive impulse initially understood as the good fruit of a competitive individualism. The thesis of social control therefore holds it a necessary correlative of the rights-bearing individual that there exist an authoritative police power. Society is still artificial, individual right is still organic. But in order to realize good competition in society, the thesis of social control demands the subjection of individual rights to the restraints of the state's police power.

A second characteristic concerns the relation between these two theses. Together, the two theses present an antinomy. As discussed in Chapter 1, the thesis of free competition is defined by its belief in a rights-bearing individual always sovereign in the sphere of what counts as just. What is *good* is whatever comes as a result, for definitions of the good life cannot precede individual will. But the thesis of social control rejects the sovereign right of the individual to decide matters of social justice. The freedom to exercise one's rights depend in the last resort on a police power able and willing to limit and destroy those rights. But the thesis of free competition rejects the existence of any power over and above that of the autonomous individual that might define the proper limits of rights. And round and round we go.[1] Like a serpent swallowing its tail, the two theses of competition and control form the syntactical practice of the deep background structure of liberal legal thought.

Third, the hard constraints of the *langue* sit in contrast with the open space of legal concepts. It is here that we most directly experience the language system's relative indeterminacy. Indeed, discretion reigns at the lexical level of the concept and its doctrines. Shall it be *sic utere tuo ut alienum non laedas* or *damnum absque injuria*? Shall we emphasize an abstract and general field of competition, or the rights of property and contract that are its conditions of possibility? The background grammar sets up choices between the forms, and the styles coalesce around particular series of argumentative practices, but the jurist is rarely compelled to conclude one way rather than another. Nevertheless, jurists cannot say anything. As we will see, jurists very rarely leave the grammatical structure or the dominant styles of making the passage from facts and rules to justification to conclusion. It is dangerous to leave these patterns, for the consequence is either a shift into an entirely different legal language, or a shift into nonsense.

Fourth, a third grammatical thesis in liberal legal thought is that of a naturalizing juridical science. The purpose of the third thesis is mediation. It mediates both the sense of conflict between the twin theses of competition and control, and anxiety over the indeterminacy of concepts and doctrines. This third thesis, with its mediating mission, places faith in the jurist to harmonize dissonance through a resolution in an impersonal, scientific consonance. The jurist's role, in other words, involves the

[1] This hamster-wheel effect is demonstrated exceptionally well in Martti Koskenniemi, *From Apology to Utopia: The Structure of International Legal Argument* (Cambridge: Cambridge University Press, 2006), p. 63.

transformation of historical settlements into legal harmonies – harmonies that come to appear as nature's gift to man. The process in which the jurist produces these harmonies, in which he is "driven to having either to unveil or to liquidate"[2] the antinomy, involves a naturalizing distortion, a legal *trompe l'oeil*.[3] In the hands of the master jurist, these distortions rationalize, legitimatize, and universalize, creating as tight a fit as possible between argumentative practice and "natural reality." Alternative ideas about what nature might entail, or what might be possible in the argumentative structure, disappear. The harmonious legal argument reifies the twin theses of liberal legal thought and banishes their dissonance beyond the bounds of the thinkable. The signature melody in this naturalizing practice: "It goes without saying."[4]

Fifth, there is in the structure of liberal legal thought a rhetorical space between the *langue* and the jurist's holding, a space filled out with legal concepts and styles of argumentative practice. It is useful to think about the relation between grammar, concept, and style in terms of background and foreground. The more the jurist is engaged with background practice, the more that the liberal theses have become preconceptual and prereflective. An aspect of what defines legal consciousness in the milieu of liberal legalism is precisely the expert capacity to handle these background constraints with little conceptual difficulty. Think of the orator who has "fallen" into her work, so "in the zone" that there is hardly any awareness on her part of the rational coupling of sentences, much less the deeper space of grammar. It just flows. That said, it is unusual, save perhaps in the cases of the greatest juridical masters, that a jurist experiences the work of legal argument in this way, or at least, all of it in this way all of the time. Sure, there is the typical ease with which the sophisticated jurist enters the field, as legal arguments come ready-to-hand. But often enough, conscious choices unsettle the smooth textures, we face unusual facts, unfamiliar concepts, technical terrain to be mastered, conclusions to be justified. That is, the more unfamiliar the terrain of legal argument, the more foregrounded the work becomes. It is in this way that jurists begin with the "facts," the unworked material to be explained. There is nothing in the facts themselves that can rationally instruct the jurist on what to make of them. The data does not come preloaded with a "figurative

2 Barthes, *Mythologies: The Complete Edition, in a New Translation* (Richard Howard and Annette Lavers, trans.) (New York: Hill and Wang, 2013), pp. 239–240.

3 Id. at 231.

4 Id. at 256. See also Karl Marx and Friedrich Engels, *The German Ideology* (New York: Prometheus Books, 1998).

language" that might assist the jurist in crafting his narrative. This figurative language, absolutely necessary to the making of an argumentative justification, must come from someplace *other* than the facts themselves.

In the legal context of liberal thought, in this chapter and the next I focus on the styles in which jurists experience this gradual shifting from background to foreground. These are the classic and modern styles of liberal legal thought. Rather than introduce them as originating at different points in legal history, I suggest that we see both the classic and modern styles as already constituted by 1870.[5] It is true that as styles of argumentative practice, jurists were not equally disposed between the classic and the modern – a situation something like I will describe as having taken place in the early years of the twenty-first century in the context of the pragmatic style. The classic style may have been more popular in 1870, the modern style might have been more popular in 1950, a retro-classic style might have been more popular once again in 1990.[6] But the question of "popularity," of how many jurists were engaged in one style of legal thought rather than another, is beyond the scope of the structuralist activity. Nevertheless, I want to suggest that, rather than see the modern style as a reaction to the fall of the classic style, we instead see the two styles as rhetorical strategies both already at work in the last decades of the nineteenth century. The classic and modern styles are deeply complementary, the one just as thoroughly committed to the grammatical horizon of the *langue* as the other.

The classic style that serves as the object of the next several pages combines the theses of free competition and social control in such a way that competition has the appearance of priority over control. The thesis of control, in other words, is always at the service of the thesis of competition. A first aspect of the style is a beginning with statements in support of the autonomous, rights-bearing individual, and the goods derived in the contest of will. The thesis of control is affirmed as well, though typically in a position of subordination to the thesis of competition. It is not,

5 My claim is not that liberal legal thought begins after the end of the US Civil War. It is rather that by this time, both the classic and modern styles are already established. For discussion of 1870 as a point of orientation, see Thomas Grey, Langdell's Orthodoxy, 45 *University of Pittsburgh Law Review* 1 (1983); Robert Gordon, "Legal Thought and Legal Practice in the Age of American Enterprise," in *Professions and Professional Ideologies in America, 1730–1940* (Gerald Geison, ed.) (Chapel Hill: University of North Carolina Press, 1983).

6 See, e.g., Justin Desautels-Stein, A Structuralist Approach to the Two State Action Doctrines, 7 *New York University Journal of Law and Liberty* 254 (2013).

however, that the superiority of the thesis of free competition results from the consequences assumed to result; free competition has natural priority over social control. A second aspect in the classic style is a tendency to believe that the theses of competition and control refer to sharply differentiated domains of power. The field of free competition, or what we can also call "the market," is *private*. In the abstract, this is a field in which free and equal rights-bearing individuals clash. The field of social control, on the other hand, is *public*. This is the locus of the state and its police powers, including the power to control market forces. In the classic style, these two fields present themselves in strict separation. This separation suggests a third important element in the classical style: a priority of legal formalism over legal functionalism. I'll say more on both of these below, but for now, what we need to know of formalism in the classic style is its way of making good on the belief in naturalizing juridical science, the belief that the jurist will harmoniously (objectively) resolve liberalism's antinomies in the apolitical work of adjudication. The classic style, for example, crafts a pattern of legal argument about the priority of the thesis of competition over the thesis of control through the elaboration of first principles and the "scientific" application of those principles to the facts at hand. When done well, the elegance of the classic style is such that the jurist produces a legal justification that hardly seems to have had a style at all; it comes off as simply *right*, casting alternatives as the indicia of judicial activism. When done not-so-well, the argumentative practice comes off as more obviously the work of ideology, an ideology of justification.

What follows is an illustrative survey of six jurists deciding six controversies in the general arena of political economy and the market as a legal concept. As will also occur in Chapters 5 and 8, the survey may aggravate. Not only is there a blatant lack of intellectual, social, political, and economic context for these controversies, I don't even include the case names or the names of the judges. I apologize for the irritation, as I understand just as well as the reader the gravitational pull of these extralegal contexts with which we have become so accustomed. What, we want to know, was the influence of the coal industry in Scranton or the steel industry in Pittsburgh? What was *really* going on in Wisconsin with the navigation of the Fox River or in Chicago with its "virtual monopolies"? What of the political battles between Justices Peckham and White? In keeping with the jurisprudential and historiographic claims from Part I, these questions and many more about what was "really going on" are neither asked nor answered. Instead, I offer first a pattern of argumentative practice in the classic liberal style. Second, I locate that style in the *context* of legal thought.

So Says the Jurist

We begin in Pennsylvania. The year is 1886, and our jurist sits on the state's supreme court. The dispute demanding resolution is this.[7] The Pennsylvania Coal Company is the owner of 1600 acres of anthracite coal in close proximity to Mrs. Sanderson's home. Mrs. Sanderson is the owner of an estate near the mouth of the basin of the Lackawanna River, known as Meadow brook. As an owner in fee, the Pennsylvania Coal Company can, in the light of the thesis of free competition, use its property in any way it likes. Here, it means that the Coal Company ought to be legally justified in its desire to dig tunnels for the extraction of coal. But it also means, as Mrs. Sanderson owns her lands in fee as well, that she should be similarly able to build a home, along with a fish and ice pond. The trouble is that in the course of digging its tunnels, the Coal Company has dumped "large volumes" of "corrupted" water into the Meadow brook basin. The harm to the brook is dramatic and complete, to such an extent that it is now "totally unfit for domestic use . . . the fish in the brook have been totally destroyed, the plaintiff's pipes corroded, and [her] entire apparatus for the utilization of the water rendered wholly worthless."[8] Having suffered this total loss in value, Mrs. Sanderson sues the Coal Company for damages.

Our jurist knows he must choose for one or the other, and in all likelihood, he has a sense for how he wants to come out. He needs, at bottom, to *constitute* the field he will soon navigate. Of course, he might be undecided if perhaps this is a novel problem for him or if there is an unfamiliar wrinkle. But more often, the jurist knows what he wants to happen, and the question is about how to make it happen, and how to *justify* it. In getting started, the jurist orients the argument to come with a statement about competition in society. The coal industry in Pennsylvania, he explains, is of tremendous social value.[9] In competition with the industry is the group of riparian owners of which Mrs. Sanderson is a member. It is useful to compare these two groups, since if Mrs. Sanderson's claim bests that of the Coal Company, all riparian owners will enjoy the same. The resolution of this clash will not present, says the jurist, a narrow

[7] *Pennsylvania Coal Co. v. Sanderson*, 113 Pa. 126 (1886).
[8] Id. at 143. [9] Id. at 144.

precedent.[10] Something about the facts suggests a broad, universalizable, question. It is not local and ad hoc. And because the contest between Mrs. Sanderson and the Coal Company turns out to be universal and not local, "the consequences must be that mining cannot be conducted except by the general consent of all parties affected."[11] Notice what our jurist has already accomplished, merely in having oriented the argument by way of these social considerations. The momentum of the argument is no longer at a standstill, caught between competing claims from two equal owners. The momentum is in motion, begging for an explanation of why the more general rights of the Coal Company ought to suffer at the hands of Pennsylvania's Mrs. Sandersons.

With this orientation in place, the jurist makes what we come to see as a characteristically classic move: "It will be observed that the defendants have done nothing to change the character of the water, or to diminish its purity, save what results from the *natural* use and enjoyment of their own property. They have brought nothing onto the land *artificially*."[12] Now, our jurist is not claiming that Mrs. Sanderson has not suffered a harm; the water is filthy and Mrs. Sanderson cannot exercise her right to use her land as she likes. Her use-rights are destroyed. But what is beginning to emerge in the argument is the idea that if the Coal Company was exercising *its* will in such a way that the use was natural, and not artificial, then Mrs. Sanderson will have suffered a harm for which there is no legal remedy. The Coal Company, says the jurist, "had a right to mine the coal. It may be stated, as a general proposition, that every man has the right to natural use and enjoyment of his own property."[13] When an owner, like the Coal Company, exercises these natural rights in a reasonable way, the harms done to others are not legal wrongs, for the harm is *damnum absque injuria*, a harm for which no legal compensation is required.[14] Here we have the lexical statement: "Where the owner of land, without willfulness or negligence, uses his land in the ordinary manner of its use, though mischief should thereby be occasioned to his neighbor, he will not be liable for damages."[15]

On the other hand, if the Coal Company uses artificial means in its efforts to mine the coal, Mrs. Sanderson's claim for damages, and the claims of everyone similarly situated, become legally cognizable. A clash between two actors in the exercise of their natural will, in other words, can be reconciled in the private, prelegal space of free competition. A will that gains superior standing through *artificial* means, in contrast, is bad

[10] Id. at 145. [11] Id. [12] Id. [13] Id. at 146. [14] Id. [15] Id. at 151.

competition, and very likely, a public nuisance.[16] Given that the jurist has already noted the natural way in which polluted water left the tunnels for the brook, and that the Coal Company extracted the coal in a natural manner, Mrs. Sanderson is likely out of luck.[17]

There are, however, two possible counterarguments. First is the question of whether it is appropriate to describe the Coal Company's activities as "natural." In the course of the extraction, the Coal Company installed "powerful engines" in order to pump water up from the tunnels and out toward the brook. As a result, a greater amount of polluted water descended on Mrs. Sanderson's land than would have otherwise taken place, without the use of the engines. The Coal Company concedes as much. Is this a case of bad competition between rights of use, since the Coal Company has clearly introduced "artificial" means in its mining operations? Our jurist responds, "the water cannot be discharged by gravity alone, it must necessarily, as part of the process of mining, be lifted to the surface by artificial means, and thence be discharged through the ordinary natural channels for the drainage of the country."[18] Mining is a natural right, and, says the jurist, "the usual and ordinary way" of mining includes the use of artificial operations. In this way, the use of powerful engines is, *actually*, completely natural. "The water flowed into Meadow brook just as it was found in the mine. Its impurities were from natural, and not from artificial causes."[19]

A second possible problem with justifying the Coal Company's rights as against Mrs. Sanderson is a problem of public welfare. Is it the case that the Coal Company's propulsion of the dirty water into the brook might cause health problems for the community at large, thus constituting a public nuisance? Perhaps, that is, what we have here is something more than a competitive clash between equal rights-holders? Perhaps this is a situation in which the play of competition demands a certain quotient of state control. Not so, says the jurist. For while it is plain that the state does enjoy a police power, the exercise of that power ought to enable and facilitate the industry it was created to defend. In this case, it turns out, it's an easy call. There is a total lack of harm to the general health and well-being of the community, "the community does not complain on any ground."[20] The harm done is, *actually*, a "mere personal inconvenience" that "must yield to the necessities of a great public industry, which although in the hands of a private corporation, subserves a great public interest."[21] Do the mining practices of the Pennsylvania Coal Company

[16] Id. at 149. [17] Id. at 146–147. [18] Id. at 148 [19] Id. at 155. [20] Id. at 149.

present a public nuisance, calling for an exercise of the police power in the name of public health and safety? Quite the contrary! The mining practices of the Coal Company are a service to the community's well-being, not a harm, and the trivial inconveniences done to Mrs. Sanderson are exactly that. What looked at first to be a contradiction in the competing equal rights of neighboring owners turns out to be nothing of the sort. A harmonious consonance unfolds, as we come to understand the natural and indisputable priority of the one claim over the other.

Let us stay in Pennsylvania for a bit longer, but move along to 1904. We are still with the state's supreme court, but now we have a dispute between a Mrs. Sullivan and the Jones & Laughlin Steel Company.[22] The problem is similar to the one resolved so harmoniously back in 1886. On the one side is the Steel Company and its right to blast certain furnaces for the purpose of burning ore in the manufacture of pig iron. The Steel Company recently built some new furnaces with a greater capacity, and as the jurist says, "These furnaces are rebuilt, improved, and enlarged, are constructed in accordance with modern and approved plans, and in their construction are in every respect equipped with modern appliances and improvements, and are equal, in many respects superior, to other furnaces in this locality . . . "[23] They are good, normal furnaces, much like the good and normal pumps that helped destroy Mrs. Sanderson's fish pond. In addition to maintaining the furnaces in the natural and ordinary way, the furnaces were operated "in a careful and skillful manner, and no effort or money was spared to keep them in constant good order and repair."[24] As for the pollution resulting from the burning of the ore, the Steel Company "has been diligent in its efforts to find means, or to adopt appliances or inventions, which will prevent the escape of dust from its furnaces."[25] On the other side is Mrs. Sullivan. Her property is located on a bluff just above the Steel Company's furnaces, and her pear orchard has suffered for it. The trees are destroyed, and "the whole property has been blackened and disfigured."[26] Furthermore, the structure of the home is in jeopardy, as the smoke and dust has corroded the tin and metal work; doors and windows must be kept closed, but even still, a coating of greasy dust is everywhere, on the people, on the food, on the furniture, on the pets.[27]

The jurist begins in what we will begin to recognize as a familiar posture. He may or may not know how he wants to conclude, though we do

[21] Id. [22] *Sullivan v. Jones & Laughlin Steel Co.*, 208 Pa. 540 (1904).
[23] Id. at 543. [24] Id. at 544. [25] Id. [26] Id. [27] Id. at 545–546.

notice a much more substantial amount of text dedicated to Mrs. Sullivan's pear orchard than we were given for Mrs. Sanderson's fish pond. That may end up meaning something, might not. Once again, the jurist orients the argument with a statement that seems to suggest a way of prioritizing the competing claims: the steel industry, like the coal industry, is an "important and lawful business."[28] Mrs. Sullivan is engaged in no industry worth naming. What's worse, Mrs. Sullivan knew she was living in a manufacturing district, and could have only expected to suffer from "the smoke and dust without which the fires of the furnaces and factories could not burn."[29] True, we have in the abstract two equal claims in this competition of uses – manufacture of iron versus maintenance of an orchard – but in practice some equal claims seem greater than others.

Still, something feels off, the melodies are unstable; the jurist seems to be going out of his way to convince us that good Mrs. Sullivan has nothing in common with that whiny Mrs. Sanderson. Mrs. Sullivan, the jurist explains, for years was content with her lot, suffering the expected amount of smoke and dust. But with the *new* furnaces, Mrs. Sullivan has, however humbly, now submitted a request that the Steel Company be enjoined. Taking your lumps is one thing. Having your property totally ruined is another. Mrs. Sanderson's property, of course, was ruined as well, to such an extent that it had to be abandoned.

As we may have been starting to suspect, the jurist's next move stalls the momentum that was just before moving to the advantage of the Steel Company. Every rights-bearing individual, says the jurist now, stands in an initial situation of equality; no individual enjoys an a priori capacity to know better than another what the good life entails.[30] So what to do in a dissonant clash between two equal wills? Having seemed to backtrack now from the industrial disposition that had caused so much trouble for Mrs. Sanderson, the jurist asks of the party with the most *natural* use going. Pear orchards are very natural. Steel manufacturing – also very natural. But what of the new furnaces that are producing so much more smoke than the older ones? Are these furnaces "natural"?[31] "No!" says the jurist.[32]

[28] Id. at 546. [29] Id. [30] Id. at 548. [31] Id. at 549.

[32] In a typical reading we'd now "distinguish" the facts of Mrs. Sullivan's case from the facts in Mrs. Sanderson's case, finding a reasonable explanation for the determination of furnaces as artificial (and therefore bad competition) and the pump engines as natural (and therefore good competition). As I will suggest throughout this and the next chapter, to accept these so-called "distinctions" is to misunderstand the structure in which the

In his examination of the dispute, the jurist tells us that "the furnaces were artificially brought by appellee onto its lands by being built there by it, and the Mesaba ore converted by the furnaces into iron is also artificially brought there by it."[33] Okay, but does this suggest that anytime someone uses their property in a way that incorporates machines, the use is artificial? If so, the jurist seems on the verge of overturning Mrs. Sanderson's case. Not at all, says the jurist. "By this we are not to be understood as saying, or even intimating, that the large furnaces could not be erected and operated, that Mesaba ore cannot be used, or that if, in the operation of the furnaces and the use of this fine ore, the discomfort and annoyance of the appellants had simply been increased in degree, they would be entitled to relief."[34] The use of the furnaces are *potentially* artificial, and not intrinsically so, since the furnaces, like the pump engines, are incidental to a natural use of property. What makes the use of the furnaces artificial in this case, the jurist explains, is that rather than having produced a trivial inconvenience, the smoke and dust have actually destroyed Mrs. Sullivan's property.[35] The jurist explains that once an owner uses his property in such a way, no matter how natural the means might have been at the first, that it destroys the use of another, the first owner's use transitions from natural use to artificial use, from good competition to bad. *Sic utere tuo ut alienum non laedas*.[36]

But now come two possible counterarguments. First, how can the jurist enjoin the Steel Company when an injunction will surely create more harm to the great and public industry to which the Steel Company is dedicated, than to the harm suffered by Mrs. Sullivan? Is not the jurist's role to secure the resolution with the greatest amount of good and the least amount of harm? The jurist's answer is as clear as it is powerful: To weigh and balance the interests between competing claims is not the role of a naturalizing juridical science, "and although it continues to be repeated occasionally, it has no rightful place in the jurisprudence of a free commonwealth, and ought to be relegated to the age in which it was appropriate."[37] The jurist continues,

> [I]t cannot be said that injury would result from an injunction, for no man can complain that he is injured by being prevented from doing to the hurt of another that which he has no right to do. Nor can it make the slightest difference that the

jurist is arguing, as this would suggest a "right" way to decide, as opposed to a structure in which the jurist makes choices.

[33] Id. at 549. [34] Id. at 549–550. [35] Id. at 550. [36] Id. [37] Id. at 554.

> plaintiff's property is of insignificant value to him as compared with the advantages that would accrue to the defendants from its occupation. There can be no balancing of conveniences when such balancing involves preservation of an established right, though possessed by a peasant only to a cottage as his home, and which will be extinguished if relief is not granted against one who would destroy it in artificially using his own land.[38]

For this jurist, it is not the abstract generality of free competition that matters as much as the guarantee of its essential prerequisites. And chief among the prerequisites of free competition is an equality of right.

A second objection: How can our jurist satisfy himself with the finding that Mrs. Sullivan suffered a total deprivation and not a trivial inconvenience? What standard separates the two? The jurist's answer is similar. There is a standard, a fine and bright line to draw between trivial inconvenience and total deprivation. The separation is sharp, at least at first – for a use that results in the former for a neighbor is natural, a use that results in the latter is artificial, and it is naturalizing juridical science that conceives the difference. This is not a balancing act, a gray area deserving a nimble hand. This is black and white, right and wrong, and where Mrs. Sanderson's rights were inconvenienced, Mrs. Sullivan's were destroyed. Did you see what the jurist did there? If you didn't, fear not, for you are not alone. This is *trompe l'oeil* in the classic style.

Next, we find ourselves in Wisconsin in the year 1871, though rather than visit the state's supreme court, we now sit with the Supreme Court of the United States. The dispute is between a Mr. Pumpelly and the Green Bay and Mississippi Canal Company.[39] The Canal Company, in accordance with a Wisconsin Act relating to Mills and Mill-dams, built a dam across the Fox River for hydraulic purposes.[40] The Wisconsin Board of Public Works "adopted" the dam as a part of its "system of improving the navigation of the Fox River," though the dam itself remained the property of the Canal Company.[41] As a result of the dam, Mr. Pumpelly's lands adjacent to the lake to which the river connects were flooded. The waters came "with such a violence," Mr. Pumpelly declared, "as to tear up his trees and grass by the roots, and wash them, with his hay by the tons ... to choke up his drains and fill up his ditches," and to otherwise cause him great injuries.[42] Mr. Pumpelly's damages are not disputed; the question is once again which of these parties has the superior claim: The Canal

[38] Id. at 555. [39] *Pumpelly v. Green Bay & Mississippi Canal Co.*, 80 U.S. 166 (1871).
[40] Id. at 167. [41] Id. at 168. [42] Id. at 167.

Company's right to build its dam as against Mr. Pumpelly's right to farm his land. The added wrinkle here is that, in contrast with Mrs. Sanderson and Mrs. Sullivan's claims, Mr. Pumpelly is competing with an actor with "public" dimensions. Thus, this dispute triggers a "public-private" distinction.

For the jurist, it is the addition of the public element that necessitates something other than the form of argument deployed in the contests with the Coal and Steel companies. For in those disputes the jurist faced a clash of abstractly equal claimants, both acting in the private space of the market. What of a clash between a private actor and the state? After disposing of the Canal Company's first defense – a technical reading of the relevant Act that might have justified the Company's erection of the dam and the resulting flooding – the jurist turned to the business of getting his argument off the ground.

The orienting move here is a beginning with the Wisconsin Constitution.[43] Like the US Constitution, the Wisconsin document reads: "the property of no person shall be taken for public use without just compensation therefor."[44] With the intermingling between the Wisconsin legislature's effort to improve the navigability of the state's waterways and the property rights of the Canal Company in the dam, the jurist senses a need for a shift in legal concepts, from that of "nuisance" to that of "taking," and now the question becomes whether Mr. Pumpelly has suffered a "taking" in violation of the Wisconsin Constitution. Nevertheless, and despite the shifting in lexical terrain, the argumentative structure remains identical to the Pennsylvania disputes we have already witnessed. Now, however, we see the jurist's invocation of a public-private distinction, in which the problem of "nuisance" is gently transformed into the problem of "takings." Mr. Pumpelly is similarly situated with respect to Mrs. Sanderson (suffering a total loss of use, but not ownership) and Mrs. Sullivan (the same). He has suffered "an almost complete destruction of the value of the land," but neither the Canal Company nor the State of Wisconsin has deprived Mr. Pumpelly of ownership. Deprivation of use-rights, yes. Deprivation of title, no. And aren't takings, as opposed to nuisance claims, exactly about situations in which individuals have been deprived of title?

Well, what good are ownership rights if an owner has no rights of use? No good at all, says the jurist. "It would be a very curious and unsatisfactory result . . . [if so long as] the government refrains from the absolute

[43] Id. at 176–177. [44] Id. at 177.

conversion of the real property to the uses of the public it can destroy its value entirely . . . because in the narrowest sense of that word, it is not *taken* for the public use."[45] If we read a taking to be so different from nuisance, the result is backwards. For rather than understand the constitution as a restriction on the state's desires to restrict individual rights, this perverted understanding of a taking amounts to restriction on individual will, making the constitution "an instrument of oppression" rather than a shield for individual rights.[46] Indeed, this does have it backwards. The state's police power ought to enable and facilitate individual will and free competition, not control them.

With that, we can see the outline of the jurist's argumentative form. When a private individual suffers a harm in the nature of a diminution of a use-right, the analysis depends on what side of the public-private distinction we are operating. If it is on the private side, we argue in the conceptual lexicon of nuisance. If it is on the public side, meaning that the state has intervened in a way that the jurist now wishes to foreground, we argue in the conceptual lexicon of takings.[47] In either case, the problem is a contest between two competing interests about what to do with one's property. This competition takes on a particular gloss when, as here, the state is implicated in favor of one of the competitors. The jurist faces a choice: should the harmed individual have to show that they have been deprived of ownership in order to win damages against the state, or can the individual argue as if the state is just another private actor, claiming a diminution of use-rights? The jurist chooses the latter argument. Why? Because in the light of the thesis of free competition, to choose the former would turn the Constitution inside-out, favoring a view of state control as having a value independent of its capacity to facilitate the free competition of individual will.

Before the jurist can conclude, however, a counterargument awaits. As we will encounter more thoroughly after our imminent arrival in Illinois, the Wisconsin legislature enjoys the police power, the power of the state to overcome individual rights when the communal well-being so demands. "Improvements of roads, streets, rivers, and other highways," these improvements properly fall within the scope of the police power.[48]

[45] Id. at 177–178. [46] Id. at 178–179.

[47] When I say that the "jurist chooses to foreground," I do not mean to suggest that this is necessarily a conscious choice. As I discussed in Chapters 2 and 3, the reversion into this style of argument may very well have far more to do with background familiarity and skilled coping than rational decision.

[48] Id. at 180–181.

Indeed, says the jurist, "we do not deny that the principle [of the police power] is a sound one."[49] Then comes a lexical statement: if a jurist decides that the state is *naturally* exercising the police power, and the state has refrained from *actually* confiscating the property, then the individual has suffered a harm for which there is no legal remedy. This is simply the price for living in a civilized society, *damnum absque injuria*. And so, why is Wisconsin barred from using its police power in this instance? Why must it pay Mr. Pumpelly for his damages? Is this not a natural rather than an artificial exercise of the police power?

The jurist's answer is very similar to what we saw in Mrs. Sullivan's case. It cannot be a question of balancing the good served by Wisconsin's waterways program as against the harms done to Mr. Pumpelly. The Rule of Law knows of no such balancing tests that might pay respect to the objectivity required of a naturalizing juridical science. For while there will be cases in which Wisconsin will be in the right, justifying its harm to individuals in the name of the police power, this is simply not one of them. There is a sharp line separating the natural exercise of the police power from the exercise of the takings power, where in the former the state may harm without worry of compensation. But in the latter, if the state wishes to act, it will have to pay for it. That line is like a force of nature, and says the jurist, "beyond this we do not go, and this case calls us to go no further."[50] Mr. Pumpelly wins. Has the jurist actually identified the line beyond which he will not go? It feels like the line must be there. Can you see it?

On to Illinois! We arrive in the year 1876, once again in the care of the US Supreme Court. Here we see a slightly different factual milieu. Rather than a dispute between two private persons, or a between one private person and another acting under the color of state authority (if you will), here the contest is between two private persons – a Mr. Munn and a Mr. Scott – and the state of Illinois.[51] Limiting ourselves to the facts as presented by the jurist, the difficulty for Mr. Munn and Mr. Scott began after the adoption by the Illinois General Assembly of an Act regulating the operation of grain warehouses. Warehouses of a certain size and type, as articulated in the Act, were deemed "public," and as a result, the owners of such warehouses were required to procure a license and bond for their operation.[52] Furthermore, when receiving grain from various locations around the United States for storage, warehouse operators

[49] Id. at 181. [50] Id. [51] *Munn v. People of State of Illinois*, 94 U.S. 113 (1876).
[52] Id. at 116.

were barred from charging rates higher than those already stipulated by the state.[53] Mr. Munn and Mr. Scott were the managers and proprietors of just such a grain warehouse in Chicago. The operations of the warehouse satisfied the criteria for regulation, as spelled out in the Act, but they refused to file for license or bond, and charged rates beyond the prices fixed by the state.[54] The question put before our jurist was what ought to happen in the clash between the individual right of an individual to use his property as he wishes, here in the service of a great and noble commerce, and a state's exercise of its police power in the regulation of those rights. Does the Illinois Act represent a point at which the police power has simply gone too far, crossing the constitutional line "expounded" in the case of Mr. Pumpelly?[55]

The jurist begins with the newly enacted Fourteenth Amendment to the US Constitution, which in relevant part forbids states from depriving persons of life, liberty, or property, without due process of law.[56] We take note of the jurist's choice to begin with this language, though we are unsure as of yet what sort of explanatory story is brewing. Our first clue: the jurist chooses to focus on the word "deprive," and look to history for assistance in figuring out whether our Chicagoans have been deprived of their property in a way that makes sense here in the context of the Fourteenth Amendment. What light is shed in this intellectual history? The jurist explains that the idea of government prohibited from depriving individuals of their rights without due process "is old as a principle of civilized government."[57] Establishing a strong pedigree, the jurist suggests the beginnings of some argumentative momentum – perhaps he is setting up an argument that will look like the one favoring Pumpelly, an argument favoring individual rights as the groundwork for good competition and a good society.

But no, the jurist takes a switchback. While it is fundamentally true that our social system recognized the priority of individual right and the prohibition of wrongful deprivation, the jurist alerts us to a competing aspect of the social system that has an equally powerful pedigree. This is the liberal idea that as persons contract into political society, they are forced to renounce the full panoply of rights they had enjoined in the prepolitical condition.[58] Indeed, the price of civilization is precisely that of having to give up a full freedom of right in exchange for a political power capable of creating order.[59] Thus, the jurist now insists, the basic

[53] Id. at 117. [54] Id. at 118. [55] Id. at 123.
[56] Id. [57] Id. [58] Id. at 124. [59] Id.

recognition of *sic utero tuo* gives rise to the state's police power, the power to deprive persons of the full exercise of their rights.[60] And just as the right of the individual to be protected from wrongful deprivation is old as the hills, so too does the police power originate in "time immemorial."[61] As the jurist says,

> Under these powers the government regulates the conduct of its citizens one towards another, and the manner in which each shall use his own property, when such regulation becomes necessary for the public good. In their exercise it is has been customary in England from time immemorial, and in this country from its first colonization, to regulate ferries, common carriers, hackmen, bakers, millers, wharfingers, innkeepers, &c, and in so doing fix a maximum of charge to be made for services rendered, accommodations furnished, and articles sold.[62]

Strangely, the jurist has now done a good bit of running in place. Rather than having drummed up some good momentum for an explanatory argument, the jurist has done the opposite, placing us face-to-face with the basic antinomy of liberal legalism. "The constitution forbids states from depriving persons of their property without due process." "The police power allows states to deprive persons of their power without due process." All we hear is dissonance. Are we stuck in it? Not to worry, the jurist knows what he's doing, for just as soon as the jurist conjures up the tension, he mediates it as his role demands, opening a pathway that at once seems to recognize the simultaneous truths of these two opposing theses, and reconciles them in such a way that we experience a *right* way to argue forward. Once again, we should recall, this mediation will not take place through weighing and balancing, through judicial discretion. What is essential is that the jurist finds a naturally harmonious way of resolving the dissonance, a proper understanding of the principles upon which the police power rests, "in order that we may determine what is within and what without its operative effect."[63]

That understanding turns on a careful appreciation for the public-private distinction. The jurist sets up the argumentative flow in this way. (1) Yes, the constitution's primal mission is to protect individual rights of property and contract. (2) And yes, the state's police power and the attendant capacity for destroying individual rights originates in time out of mind. (3) The natural space in which the state is meant to exercise this power is "public," while the free space of competition between individual persons is "private." (4) When the exercise of individual right crosses this natural line between private and public, when the use of *private* property

[60] Id. at 125. [61] Id. [62] Id. [63] Id. at 124.

has *public* effects, we enter the proper field of the police power. Voila! Harmony! The jurist explains:

> Property does become clothed with a public interest when used in a manner to make it of public consequence, and affect the community at large. When therefore, one devotes his property to a use in which the public as an interest, he, in effect, grants to the public an interest in that use, and must submit to be controlled by the public for the common good, to the extent of the interest he has thus created.[64]

Now the form of the argument is clear. We just need to know whether Mr. Munn and Mr. Scott, in their operation of the grain warehouse, transformed their private property into a kind of property with public effects (i.e., the sort of property over which the police power is meant to apply).[65] As we have seen jurists already arguing, an acquaintance with industry assists the navigation of this natural divide between public and private. As our jurist explains, Mr. Munn and Mr. Scott sit at the "gateway of commerce,"[66] a nexus of a national network of grain transportation, storing grains coming from the west on their way to the east. Ought this simple fact to carry the warehouse over the line from private to public, the fact that the warehouse is doing a substantial amount of business on a national scale? This is unclear, but what disposes of the question is an added flourish: Mr. Munn and Mr. Scott are not merely participating in the ordinary and natural flow of this commerce; they are *controlling* it through *extraordinary* means. "Thus it is apparent that all the elevating facilities through which these vast productions 'of seven or eight great States of the West' must pass on the way 'to four or five of the States on the seashore' may be a virtual *monopoly*."[67] And if this is the case, that the grain warehouse has become the vehicle for a virtual monopoly over a national stream of commerce, then, says the jurist, we have undeniably made that passage from purely private uses of property to those uses "clothed with a public interest." In making that passage, we find ourselves in the proper field of the police power.

Does this mean, however, that the theme of the police power trumps the theme of constitutional rights? It does not. For what the jurist has done here is only to restate the basic mission of the state: to protect a society in which the free play of free individuals results in free competition. But rather than focus on the frustrated rights of Mr. Munn and Mr. Scott, the jurist focuses on the abstract generality of free competition. For what Mr. Munn and Mr. Scott are doing in Chicago is precisely to frustrate

[64] Id. at 126. [65] Id. at 130. [66] Id. at 132. [67] Id. at 131.

that basic mission, frustrating the field of free competition in the instantiation of a virtual monopoly. This is, at any rate, the jurist's argument: the mediating device of "public interest" naturally and harmoniously resolves the tension between the theses of competition and control, and the operation of that device is both objective and apolitical, just as the thesis of naturalizing juridical science demands.

We arrive in Missouri in the year 1897. Or, at least, it might be Missouri, but it could really be anywhere, as this case presents us with a broader geography.[68] The dispute is between the Trans-Missouri Freight Association, a collection of railroad companies with a headquarters in Kansas City, and the US government. It concerns the Sherman Anti-Trust Act, the federal government's first attempt to statutorily address the problem of "bad competition," and the question of whether the Association has run afoul of the sprit, if not the letter, of the Act. The government claimed that in the effort to "unjustly and oppressively to increase" their rates, prevent any of the Railroads from reducing rates, "thereby exact and procure great sums of money from the people," monopolize "the trade, traffic, and commerce among and between the states, and more generally, "counteract the effect of free competition," close to twenty railroads "did combine, conspire, confederate, and unlawfully agree" to form the Trans-Missouri Freight Association.[69] But what do these allegations amount to? Did the Railroad Companies do anything other than exercise their private rights of property and contract, making themselves more competitive, avoiding the inevitable harms of a "ruinous competition"?[70]

Here we see the jurist confronted with a question lurking in the background of Mr. Munn and Mr. Scott's case: What happens when we press harder on the thesis of free competition? If most competitors are destroyed in the process of competition, is this not a natural outcome, and therefore a good outcome? Or are the emergence of trusts and monopolies perversions of the competitive process? The jurist sees, in the structure of legal argument confronting him, two possible routes of justification. On the one side is an emphasis on the generality of competition as a good in itself, and on the other is competition as something that may or may not be good. Our jurist chooses the first path.

If competition is a "good in itself," that means, says the jurist, that it is not his business to ask or answer the question of whether certain

[68] *U.S. v. Trans-Missouri Freight Assn.*, 166 U.S. 290 (1897).
[69] Id. at 299. [70] Id. at 368–369.

forms of competition are better than others. Thus, when the Sherman Act prohibits agreements in restraint of trade – and there is no denying that the agreement constituting the Freight Association is exactly that – the jurist's role is to assist in the work of identifying those situations in which trade has been restrained; it is not, in contrast, to assist in the very different work of figuring out when certain restraints are good and others bad. Or to put it another way, the agreement constituting the Freight Association is exactly bad competition because it has stifled the competitive process, just as the grain warehouse in Chicago was stifling in a similar way. But might it be the case that "stifling competition," on further review, proves to be a "good thing"? It is not the jurist's role to find out.

Perhaps Mr. Munn and Mr. Scott's "virtual monopoly" was actually a very different thing. For while theirs was a case in which private actors were caught in the sway of Illinois' police power, the case of the Railroads is something else. For one thing, the Railroad companies enjoy a public dimension lacking in the Chicago case, and for another, while there is no disputing the police power of Illinois, of what power does the federal government claim in restricting freedom of contract and property right?

The jurist navigates the first concern through a review of the public-private lexicon. The Railroad company argued that the market treats various industries differently, and that certain forms of competition will be good in one sector and bad in another: "[There are evils arising from unrestricted competition in regard to railroads which do not exist in regard to any other kind of property ... The difference between railroad property on the one hand, and all other kinds of property, on the other, is so plain that entirely different economic results follow from unrestricted competition among railroads from those that obtain in regard to all other kinds of business."[71] Due to the special nature of the Railroads, the Companies claimed, it is a mistake to understand them as governed by the same rules of the private sphere.[72] Not so, says the jurist. There is the state on one side of the divide, and the market on the other.[73] While it is certainly true that the state may bestow special rights and privileges to private actors, such bestowals are incapable of transforming a private phenomenon into a public one, as if it had the power to make the color red into green, by fiat.

Why should not a railroad company be included in general legislation aimed at the prevention of that kind of agreement made in restraint of trade, which may

[71] Id. at 320. [72] Id. at 329–330. [73] Id. at 322–323.

> exist in all companies, *which is substantially of the same nature wherever found, and which tends very much towards the same results* whether put in practice by a trading or manufacturing or railroad company? It is true the results of trusts, or combinations of that nature, may be different in different kinds of corporations, *and yet they all have an essential similarity*, and have been induced by motives of aggrandizement as against the public interest.[74]

So much for the idea that railroads might flee the competitive process by piercing the veil between private and public spheres.[75] What of the second concern, that of whether there is a decent analogy between the state's police power and the federal government's regulatory power under the commerce clause? As we have seen, the police power is both deep and broad in this structure of legal argument, but it is as only as deep and broad as the conception of individual rights that this power is meant to facilitate. The federal power to regulate the competitive process among and between the states is similarly situated: it goes just as far as necessary to facilitate healthy interstate commerce. And here, says the jurist, is the rub: is it within the ambit of that federal power to prohibit *all* agreements in restraint of trade, or only those agreements that restrain trade, *unreasonably*?[76] The Railroad companies argue for this latter construction, that it would be inconceivable to imagine a congressional intention to abrogate such an extensive power over the states. To press such limitations on the federal power both underestimates the nature of that power and overestimates the role of the jurist.

Our background conception here is one in which the free play of individual expressions of will (though the concept of private ownership) generates a field of competition that is *good*. However, when individuals use their property in such a way as to clog the field, as in Mrs. Sullivan's case or the case of Mr. Munn and Mr. Scott, the basic intuition of *sic utere tuo* is undermined. As a consequence, it is the chief duty of the state – and now here, this is the federal state – to stop individuals from clogging the field. This is an imperative to keep competition pure at a level of generality, for we want competition free of perversion, and not merely "reasonable competition." This brings us to the problem in overestimating the capacity of the jurist. For if the question really did come down to those agreements that unreasonably constrain the competitive

74 Id. at 322–323.

75 And when the public nature of railroads is conceded, which it must be, this only suggests even greater reasons to demand competitiveness, not less. Id.

76 Id. at 327.

process, how would one know? It is worth quoting the jurist's worries at length:

> If only that kind of contract which is in unreasonable restraint of trade be within the meaning of the statute, and declared therein to be illegal, it is at once apparent that the subject of what is a reasonable rate is attended with great uncertainty. What is a proper standard by which to judge the fact of reasonable rates? Must the rate be so high as to enable the return for the whole business done to amount to a sum sufficient to afford the shareholder a fair and reasonable profit upon his investment? If so, what is a fair and reasonable profit? That depends sometimes upon the risk incurred, and the rate itself differs in different localities. Which is the one to which reference is to be made as the standard? Or is the reasonableness of the profit to be limited to a fair return upon the capital that would have been sufficient to build and equip the road, if honestly expended? Or is still another standard to be created, and the reasonableness of the charges tried by the cost of the carriage of the article, and a reasonable profit allowed on that? And, in such case, would contribution to a sinking fund to make repairs upon the roadbed and renewal of cars, etc., be assumed as a proper item? or is the reasonableness of the charge to be tested by reference to the charges for the transportation of the same kind of property made by other roads similarly situated? If the latter, a combination among such roads as to rates would, of course, furnish no means of answering the question. It is quite apparent, therefore, that it is exceedingly difficult to formulate even the term of the rule itself which should govern in the matter of determining what would be reasonable rates for transporting: while, even after the standard should be determined, there is such an infinite variety of facts entering into the question of what is a reasonable rate, no matter what standard is adopted, that any individual shipper would in most cases be apt to abandon the effort to show the unreasonable character of a charge, sooner than hazard the great expense in time and money necessary to prove the fact, and at the same time incur the ill will of the road itself in all his future dealings with it. To say, therefore, that the act excludes agreements which are not in unreasonable restraint of trade, and which tend simply to keep up reasonable rates for transportation, is substantially to leave the question of reasonableness to the companies themselves.[77]

To sum up, our jurist deployed a form of argument we have now seen five times. Begin with a background commitment to the inviolability of individual right, and a foregrounded appreciation for the field of competition that results from the free play of these rights. Next, contrast this with a strong commitment to the power of the state to govern the field, and more importantly, provide those grounds that make both the enjoyment of individual right and free competition possible. But a newer twist: even if we accept the essential foundations of property and contract, how do we know when the state's power (either in the guise of the police power or

[77] Id. at 331–332.

the commerce power) is properly facilitating "competition"? The jurist's answer here in the context of the Freight Association is clear: you look to the field of free competition as a generality, in the abstract, and remove those perversions warping the free play. These perversions are most obvious at the level of price-fixing and monopolization. To get deeper into the question of what amounts to a "reasonable" form of competitive restraint is to move the jurist away from realm of naturalizing juridical science and into the ideological and political.

Welcome to Ohio. Or New Jersey. Welcome, in any case. The year is 1911, and we find a dispute between John Rockefeller's Standard Oil Company of Ohio and the United States.[78] The Oil Company was a combination of most of the oil refineries in Cleveland, and with this "complete mastery over the oil industry, controlling 90 percent of the business of producing, shipping, refining, and selling petroleum,"[79] the government claimed, Standard Oil fixed the prices of crude and refined oil, limited its production, controlled its transportation, forced its competitors to either join the Company or go out of business, and thereby restrained and monopolized trade and commerce among the states.[80] For its part, the Oil Company made a basic defense: its actions were merely coincident with its rights of property and freedom of contract, "essentially necessary to the well-being of society" and "protected by the constitutional guarantee of due process of law."[81]

The jurist began in what he called a "jungle"[82] of conflicting pathways. Nothing is familiar here, not the law, not the facts.[83] The jurist looks more analyst than athlete, unclear of the lines of force.[84] Looking for a foothold with which to get some orientation, the jurist explains that while none of the parties agree on what the Sherman Act means, they at least concede that this is the statement of the legislature with which to constitute the field.[85] "We shall therefore . . . make this one point of harmony the initial basis of our examination" in the hope that, once the "true meaning" of the Act's view of competition is uncovered, a "harmonious resonance" will shape everything to come after. It is as if the legal argument is a tremendous quilt, and the family is all twisted up in its kinks and folds. If, says the

78 *Standard Oil Co. of New Jersey v. U.S.*, 221 U.S. 1 (1911).

79 Id. at 33. 80 Id. at 32–33. 81 Id. at 69. 82 Id. at 48. 83 Id. at 47–48.

84 Keep in mind, *saying* that you're confused and out of sorts may very well be more tactical than confessionary.

85 Id. at 48–49.

jurist, he can give it a great and mighty tug, the rest will unfurl naturally, or to switch back the metaphor, the dissonance resolved.

How then, can our jurist find this "true meaning"? One possibility is to look at the political debates over the adoption of the Act and "the economic conditions of the times."[86] But this wouldn't lead us toward a principle with which to properly orient ourselves, and so the jurist evades contemporary debates in favor of "elementary and indisputable conceptions" of what amounts to a "contract in restraint of trade."[87] These elementary and indisputable conceptions are independent of whatever the drafters of the Act may have actually had in mind, and independent of what progressives had thought about it. Rather, these conceptions await the jurist in the objective archives of legal history. Once the jurist looks, with a clear head and clear heart, he finds that while certain past jurists may have viewed *any* restraints on competition as prohibited,[88] a new lexical statement rises to the surface.

Monopolies and contracts *unduly* in restraint of trade have the same unwanted effect of limiting the rights of individuals to alienate their property interests via the freedom of contract. That is, rather than think about the Sherman Act as having the purpose of shielding free competition itself from certain perversions, it is more appropriate to see it as shielding rights of property and contract from unreasonable restraint. "[B]y the common law," says the jurist, "monopolies were unlawful because of their restriction upon individual freedom of contract and their injury to the public."[89] And further, "That to protect the freedom of contract of the individual, not only in his own interest, but principally in the interest of the common weal, a contract of an individual by which he put an unreasonable restraint upon himself as to carrying on his trade or business was void."[90] The effect on competition itself – the "common weal" – is only a happy consequence of the first-order work of facilitating the reasonable exercise of individual freedom. To get this backwards has ridiculous implications, for if we read the prohibition on monopolies and contracts in restraint of trade as having competition as its proper object, we make the mistake of viewing competition as an abstract generality.[91] It is through an

[86] Id. at 50. "That is, the vast accumulation of wealth in the hands of corporations and individuals, the enormous development of corporate organization, the facility for combination which such organizations afforded, the fact that the facility was being used, and that combinations known as trusts were being multiplied, and the widespread impression that their power had been and would be exerted to oppress individuals and injure the public generally."

[87] Id. at 51. [88] Id. at 51–52. [89] Id. at 54. [90] Id. at 54–55. [91] Id. at 58.

essential understanding of individual rights that competition takes flight, not the other way around:

> [The Sherman Act] indicates a consciousness that the freedom of the individual right to contract, *when not unduly or improperly exercised*, was the most efficient means for the prevention of monopoly, since the operation of the centrifugal and centripetal forces resulting from the right to freely contract was the means by which monopoly would be inevitably prevented... In other words, that freedom of contract was the essence of freedom from undue restraint on the right to contract.[92]

The elementary and indisputable view of the Act shows us that the question has always been whether we are dealing with an unreasonable exercise of individual freedom, presumably like what we have already seen from the Steel Company in Pittsburgh (though not like the Coal Company in Scranton). Therefore, the question before the jurist is not whether the field of free competition has been perverted, but whether property has been used in an unnatural/unreasonable way. As the jurist says, "it becomes obvious that the criteria to be resorted to in any given case for the purpose of ascertaining whether violations of the section have been committed is the rule of reason guided by the established law and by the plain duty to ... [serve] the public policy which its restrictions were obviously enacted to subserve."[93]

What then of the concern that jurists have no role to play in the definition of what should count as "reasonable competition"? Alas, says the jurist, the question of "reasonable competition" is not before us. Indeed, such an exploration would very well take a jurist well beyond the proper confines naturalizing juridical science. What the rule of reason is doing here, when understood in its true form, is nothing other than the judicial examination of when and whether an individual's use of his property is reasonable. And what kind of examination is more squarely in the jurist's wheelhouse than *that*?[94] This is no more than the same line-drawing exercise we have seen in the last five disputes. "This is so clear," says the jurist in the ringing tones of a triumphant mythology, "as to require no elaboration."[95]

Finally, we can ask, were the creation of the Standard Oil trusts an undue restraint on trade? Did they pose unreasonable exercises of the rights of property and contract? We are right back to where we in the cases of Mrs. Sullivan and Mrs. Sanderson. Remember that Mrs. Sanderson suffered "a trivial inconvenience" in her contest with the Coal Company,

[92] Id. at 62. [93] Id. at 62. [94] Id. at 69–70. [95] Id. at 70.

and that Mrs. Sullivan's rights were "destroyed" by the Steel Company. Here, says the jurist, the Oil Company has acted unreasonably, exercising its rights in violation of the *sic utere tuo* principle. Unlike the businessman interested in exercising his rights in such a way as not to cause unreasonable harm to his neighbors, like the Coal Company, Mr. Rockefeller has shown an intent to go beyond the "normal methods of industrial development" to achieve greater power than would "otherwise have arisen had normal methods been followed."[96] The reasonable exercise of individual rights is to use them so as to at once find success and still not exclude others from the industry. In Mr. Rockefeller's case, he fell on the wrong side of the rule of reason. Beginning with a "genius for commercial development," he soon succumbed to an irrational desire for a total mastery that would deny others the right to use and sell their own property.[97] This desire, with its attendant practices, says the jurist, "lead the mind up to a conviction of a purpose and intent which we think is so certain as practically to cause the subject not to be within the domain of reasonable contention."[98]

Summing Up the Classic Liberal Style

There is a tendency to see some of these decisions as standing in contradiction. Mrs. Sanderson's case came out one way, Mrs. Sullivan's case came out the other. Mr. Pumpelly's rights against the state were vindicated, while Mr. Munn and Mr. Scott's were not. Competition was the order of the day in the Railroad case, while Competition was little more than an afterthought in the case of Standard Oil. Nevertheless, what I have been trying to emphasize in the argumentative practice of these six jurists is a certain recurring pattern, a certain form of justification that unites what might otherwise be thought of as a collection of irreconcilable opinions about private rights in the marketplace.

All six jurists found themselves working with a structure of legal argument that seemed very much to precede them, a structure having very little to do with "rules" or "legal precedents." The structure of legal argument had its deepest moorings in an idea about the relation between individual rights, competition, and control. Every jurist had this milieu of ideas ready-to-hand. They were not foreign and arcane, technical and obscure; they were background givens. These background givens presented the jurist with certain argumentative pathways, pathways that seemed to

[96] Id. at 75. [97] Id. at 76–77. [98] Id. at 77.

repeat over and again. If we present these pathways in something like a decision tree, we might end up with something like this:

1. If this is a private dispute between equals, do you want to emphasize a general field of free competition or the priority of individual rights?
   (a) If you want to emphasize the general field of free competition, do you want to use an industrial referent to provide argumentative momentum for the benefit of one of the parties?
      (i) If yes, do you want to stall that momentum by labeling industrial means artificial?
      (ii) If no, continue on to 1(b), since your argument entails a belief that competition is merely the product of clashing rights of property and contract.
   (b) If you want to emphasize a tension between equal rights of use, do you want to find that one of the parties has diminished the use-rights of another?
      (i) If yes, you can either use *sic utere tuo* or *damnum absque injuria* and carry the momentum through to a decision.
         (1) If you choose *sic utere tuo*, emphasize that the artificial/unreasonable acts have resulted in a legally cognizable harm (Mrs. Sullivan's case).
         (2) If you choose *damnum absque injuria*, emphasize that the natural/reasonable acts resulted in a harm for which there is no legal remedy (Mrs. Sanderson's case).
      (ii) If no, remember that you are barred from justifying this conclusion through a balancing of the interests of the two parties. If you feel the need to balance the rights against one another, you must either return to 1(a) or 1(b), or shift into the modern style elaborated in the next chapter.
2. If there is public aspect of the dispute, regardless of whether you are dealing with the police power or the commerce power, do you want to emphasize a general field of free competition or the priority of individual rights?
   (a) If you want to emphasize the general field of free competition, has the state confiscated an individual's property?
      (i) If yes, the state may be justified in the confiscation, but it has to pay for it.
      (ii) If no, continue to 2(b).

(b) Has the state crossed the line in its attempt to purify the competitive field of artificial distortions?
  (i) If no, you can choose *damnum absque injuria*, emphasize that the natural/reasonable acts of the state resulted in a harm for which there is no legal remedy (Mr. Munn's case, Trans-Missouri Freight Association's case).
  (ii) If yes, continue on to 2(c).

(c) If you want to emphasize the priority of individual rights, has the individual used his rights in a natural/reasonable way?
  (i) If yes, carry the momentum through to a decision (Mr. Pumpelly's case).
  (ii) If no, carry the momentum through to a decision (Mr. Rockefeller's case).

As this suggests, all six jurists were practicing in the classic style of liberal legal thought. The questions simply turn on which lexical points get picked up and pushed along by the style. Shall we emphasize a society in which industry competes, competes vigorously, and all for the good? This is what the jurist did in Mrs. Sanderson's case, emphasizing the benefits in choosing the Coal Companies of the world over the Mrs. Sandersons, before showing that the Coal Company's particular uses were natural, despite the operation of pump engines. This is what the jurist did as well in Mr. Munn and Mr. Scott's case, emphasizing the importance of a field of free competition over their individual rights of property and contract. And while the jurist might have found the state's intervention too much here, he didn't, claiming that the state's control of virtual monopolies is exactly what the police power is meant to do. The jurist followed the same pattern again in the Railroad case, emphasizing the importance of a purified field of free competition and natural place of the federal government in seeking such an end.

In the other three cases, the jurist uses exactly the same style of argument, but simply emphasizes different points along the way. Mrs. Sullivan trumps the Steel Company because the jurist now emphasizes individual right over the field of competition. Mr. Pumpelly wins against the state of Wisconsin for the same reason. And while Mr. Rockefeller ultimately loses his case, it is not due to the force of a different rule. The jurist in that case, as in the cases of Mrs. Sullivan and Mr. Pumpelly, emphasized the priority of individual rights, but more relevant now, the natural/reasonable use of those rights. And while Mrs. Sullivan and Mr. Pumpelly had been absolutely reasonable in their uses, Mr. Rockefeller had not. But this was an unreasonableness, once again, not focused on "unreasonable competition," but the unreasonableness of the *sic utere tuo* principle.

There is more to the classic style than I have outlined here, principally in the techniques used in the service of naturalizing juridical science: the practice of legal formalism. I come to this aspect of the classic style in Chapter 6. But before formalism, we need a presentation of the modern style, and that is the task of the next chapter.

5

The Modern Style

The modern liberal style is in keeping with the same general outline that began in the last chapter. In that review, I emphasized five aspects of liberal legal thought. First, liberal legalism is a semiotic structure. Second, it is a semiotic structure grammatically generated out of a twin set of theses, those of free competition and social control. Third, the grammar is figured as an antinomy. This antinomy is fixed and governs the argumentative forms in which the whole of the liberal language is spoken. Fourth, the antinomy triggers a third thesis in the liberal grammar, that of a belief in naturalizing juridical science. Fifth, the jurist experiences the structure in terms of foreground and background and, as he moves from the former to the latter, engages a legal style. In the last chapter, I outlined the classic liberal style of argument through a reading of six adjudications of political economy. In what follows I do the same for the modern style. As with classic liberalism, the modern style marshals a style of argumentative practice out of the five aspects I have just mentioned. As we will see, the modern style emphasizes aspects of the structure that were less clearly visible in the classic renditions. The modern style foregrounds the following moves.

First, whereas the classic style combined the theses of competition and control in such a way that free competition always took priority, in the modern style the thesis of social control predominates. It is important to be clear here: the moderns discard neither the idea of individual rights of property and contract, nor the idea of good competition. These are still grammatically immovable – remember, we are still in the language of liberal legalism. Now, however, instead of seeing society as always an artifice, we take the idea of "social interdependence" as an orienting figure. Second, the modern style continues to regard the two fields of competition and control as separate. Rather than view the separation as inviolable, moderns view it as blurry and make a point of having little patience with efforts at pretending to know where the line lies. To be sure, the modern jurist concedes that there is a private core, but on the whole, the public-private distinction is thought to have far less use for them that it did for the classic jurists. Third, the modern style has a different relationship with the thesis of naturalizing juridical science. For whereas the classic style regarded juridical adventures beyond the legal material as running afoul of the jurist's training in the Rule of Law, the modern style regards law's purpose as the satisfaction of social needs. As a result, the jurist must either develop a degree of expertise in the diagnosis of social problems, or defer to those social scientists in government or elsewhere who understand the world in which law is located. As I discuss further in Chapter 6, this is the modern preference for legal functionalism, in contrast with the classic preference for legal formalism. While functionalism and formalism are certainly different, they are nonetheless unified in the service of liberalism's third thesis: adjudication must be objective and apolitical, that is, naturally harmonious. The classic style, as we have seen, crafts a pattern of legal argument about the priority of the thesis of free competition over the thesis of social control through the elaboration of first principles and the "scientific" application of those principles to the facts at hand. The moderns are just as committed to juridical objectivity, but in a different style. Here, the jurist tends to regard the legal material as generally indeterminate. What stands in its place is the determinacy of empirical social science. So while it might be true that jurists in the classic style deluded themselves in an argumentative *trompe l'oeil*, the modern style has faith in the power of social science to identify society's problems and prescribe its solutions. The jurist's task, as a result, lies in bringing those solutions into legal reality. This, as I discuss further in the next chapter, is as much a practice of harmonious illusion as anything developed in the classic arsenal.

In what follows is a reading of six jurists deciding disputes in the modern liberal style of legal argument. These disputes continue the theme developed in the last chapter, that of political economy in the crux of competition and control. After the jurists have finished with their arguments, I offer a summary.

So Says the Jurist

Welcome to the Appalachian mountains, and in particular, to a coal-bearing area stretching through Virginia, West Virginia, Kentucky, and Tennessee.[1] The year is 1933, a bad year for the coal industry.[2] In the midst of what our jurist calls "deplorable" economic conditions, 137 coal companies have joined together to form Appalachian Coals, an exclusive selling agency. The Agency agreed, among other things "to establish standard classifications, to sell all the coal of all its principals at the best prices obtainable and, if all cannot be sold, to apportion order upon a stated basis," and to fix prices at its central office.[3] The United States claimed that this combination into Appalachian Coals violated the Sherman Act through the elimination of competition among the defendant coal companies, as well as through its power to fix the price of coal.[4] The response of the Coal Companies was that the creation of Appalachian Coals was in the service of facilitating competition, and not ending it, for without a unified approach, said the Companies, the industry would soon go belly up.[5]

The jurist faced the now-familiar question of whether the Coal Companies were engaged in good competition, or bad. In the classic style, a jurist would choose between two familiar pathways: begin with a nuisance model of conflicting rights, or begin with the generality of free competition understood to be an aftereffect of those rights. In the modern style, the jurist begins in a different posture. True, the jurist starts with language we may very well have heard in Mr. Rockefeller's case: the purpose of antitrust law is to prevent undue restraints on interstate commerce.[6] However, rather than unpack the idea of undue restraints as a formal analysis of individual rights and the natural trumping of one over the other, the jurist here rejects formal analysis in favor of exactly the kind of juridical behavior that had so frightened the classical jurists. The Sherman Act is a charter for freedom, says the jurist, and as such it is flexible, adaptable, and intended to conform to the needs of society as those needs shift over time. Gone is the paradigm of an abstract mathematics; for what the jurist must do now is look away from a legal dogmatism and turn to the market's *real* math.

In applying this version of the rule of reason – a version quite at odds with that espoused in Mr. Rockefeller's case – the jurist has no use for lines

[1] *Appalachian Coals v. US*, 288 U.S. 344, 357 (1933). [2] Id. at 359. [3] Id. at 358.
[4] Id. at 358–359. [5] Id. at 359. [6] Id.

of black and white, lines beyond which a jurist cannot pass. This rule of reason unfolds in shades of gray. In applying this rule, says the jurist, "a close and objective scrutiny of particular conditions and purposes is necessary in each case. *Realities must dominate the judgment.* The mere fact that the parties to an agreement eliminate competition between themselves is not enough to condemn it."[7] It is no longer acceptable to deduce what counts as a perversion in the competitive process from first principles. Instead, the jurist must "consider the economic conditions peculiar to the coal industry, the practices which have obtained, the nature of defendant's plan of making sales, the reasons which led it its adoption, and the probably consequences of the carrying out of that plan in relation to market prices and other matters affecting the public interest in interstate commerce in bituminous coal."[8] In order to effectively satisfy the goals of antitrust *law*, jurists must first understand *market society*.

This is precisely what the jurist hoped to do. First, what is the reality of the coal industry? Citing a substantial amount of material from the District Court, we can summarize the jurist's discussion of the economic conditions facing the Appalachian coal companies as very bad.[9] "Numerous producing companies have gone into bankruptcy or into the hands of receivers, many mines have been shut down, the number of days of operation per week have been greatly curtailed, wages to labor have been substantially lessened, and the states in which coal producing companies are located have found it increasingly difficult to collect taxes."[10] For their part, the Coal Companies came together in an effort to save themselves, taking advantage of economies of scale, gathering research, and avoiding a host of other inefficiencies, all the while avoiding the need to limit production.[11] Second, what will be the effect of the coal combination on competition in that industry? The jurist, as is typical in the modern style (and in a move reminiscent of the classic tendency to posit the existence of a sharp line but never explain where it really might be), amasses as much data as possible on the social scene, but laments that "it would be impossible to make even a condensed statement of this evidence."[12] But jurists must often do the impossible, and so, says the jurist, this evidence cannot be understood as achieving with a certainty that the combination will prove anticompetitive.[13]

The jurist therefore faces the following: On the one side is the reality of a distressed industry and "the evidence leaves no doubt of the existence

[7] Id. at 360. [8] Id. at 361. [9] Id. at 361–364. [10] Id. at 365.
[11] Id. at 366–367. [12] Id. at 368. [13] Id. at 368.

of the evils at which defendant's plan was addressed ... When industry is grievously hurt, when producing concerns fail, when unemployment mounts and communities dependent upon profitable production are prostrated, the wells of commerce go dry."[14] This is certain. What is uncertain is an understanding of what would *really* be the effects of the coal combination on prices.[15] As a result, and when we take into consideration the social purpose of the Sherman Act, the correct course of action is to follow what the jurist can say with *objectivity* about our *social reality*, and the only thing he feels comfortable in saying is that competition in the coal industry needs help. Is Appalachian Coals the answer? Maybe, maybe not, but the combination cannot be rendered illegal on the basis of an abstraction. Going with what he feels is the scientifically justifiable course of action, the jurist rejects the federal claim of a Sherman Act violation.

Next, we arrive in sunny California. It is ten years later, 1943, and the topic is raisins.[16] Or rather, the California legislature is discussing raisins in the context of its Agricultural Prorate Act. The purpose of the Act in relevant part was to "conserve the agricultural wealth of the state" and "prevent economic waste" by restricting competition among growers and maintaining prices in the distribution from growers to packers.[17] Mr. Brown was both a grower and a packer of California raisins, and his business had fallen under the shadow of the Act. As determined by a program committee established under the Act, all raisins grown in California were first classified in terms of quality. When Mr. Brown was ready with his raisin crop, he was required to attend a receiving station at which his raisins would be sifted for those fit for sale. Twenty percent of his saleable crop would go into a "surplus pool," while 50 percent would go into a "stabilization pool." Mr. Brown received fixed payments for his contributions to the pool, but could sell his remaining 30 percent through ordinary commercial means, allowing his payments for a certificate fee per ton sold.[18] Mr. Brown's complaint is that the Prorate Act violates the Sherman Act, stifling the raisin market through price fixing and reduction of supply.

In the last dispute between the coal companies and the United States, the question was whether the combination manifested in Appalachian Coals was anticompetitive. This question sent the jurist on an

[14] Id. at 372. [15] Id. at 373. [16] *Parker v. Brown*, 317 U.S. 341 (1943).
[17] Id. at 346. [18] Id. at 348.

argumentative journey into "the real world" of the coal industry in order to distinguish, on the basis of the data, the good from the bad. Here, in Mr. Brown's case, the jurist faces an entirely different scenario. The route of argument, however, proves no less modern. The jurist's argument begins with a concession: "We may assume for present purposes that the California prorate program would violate the Sherman Act if it were organized ... [by] private persons, individual or corporate."[19] What's more, says the jurist, we can assume that Congress could invalidate the program through the exercise of its commerce power, if it sought to do so.[20] This is all to say, there is little doubt in the jurist's mind that California's prorate program is harmful to competition. Does Mr. Brown win?

He does not. What makes conduct anticompetitive in the context of private action needn't make conduct anticompetitive in the context of public action. Or to put this another way, consider what is happening here with regard to the public-private distinction as it is rendered in the structure of liberal legal thought. Perhaps this is like the case of the Trans-Missouri Freight Association, where in the classic style the jurist suggested that when the state acts in the market, it is doing exactly that: *acting in the market*. And as a result, said the jurist in that instance, simply having a public quality did not shield the railroads from the demands of free competition. The public-private distinction in that case was sharp, for once a public actor crossed the Rubicon and into the private domain, private rules ruled. Here in Mr. Brown's case, in the modern liberal style something very different is going on. It is not that the public-private distinction has vanished. It's still here, but functioning differently as a result of the jurist's choice to foreground the state's power to control the market. Even though the California program would be patently anticompetitive if it had been the product of private action, and even though the state is clearly participating in the private domain of the market, the jurist's orienting move here is to give deference in the direction of the state. The state *retains* its public capacity, regardless of its deep immersion in the private domain, since the jurist is interested in making the Sherman Act now about something analytically other than the protection of "free competition" or "individual rights of property and contract." It is about the state's power to control the market,[21] as the Sherman Act "gives no hint that it was intended to restrain state action or official action directed by a state."[22] Indeed, says the jurist, "the state in adopting and enforcing the prorate program" acted as "sovereign [and] imposed the

[19] Id. at 350. [20] Id. [21] Id. at 352. [22] Id. at 351.

restraint as an act of government which the Sherman Act did not undertake to prohibit."[23] The state has the right to control the market, precisely because it is a definitively public entity. While this idea was certainly present in the classic style, what has transformed is both the scope and nature of the power of social control.

The jurist faces a second objection. Mr. Brown asks, does not the anti-competitive nature of the California program affect other states as well, thus coming into conflict with the federal commerce power? In a typically modern move, the jurist rejects a "mechanical test" which might sharply delineate the frontiers of interstate commerce.[24] In cases where the federal government has not acted, and a state regulation of local affairs affects interstate commerce, says the jurist, a proper accommodation emerges through an identification of the purposes of the regulation.[25] This focus on purpose, function, and interest takes the jurist away from first principles and toward "a consideration of all the relevant facts and circumstances [bearing on] the safety, health, and well-being of local communities, and which, because of its local character and the practical difficulties involved, may never be adequately dealt with by Congress."[26] As with the Appalachian coal industry, the jurist sees an all-things-considered approach to the reality of social need as the crucible for legal argument.

Looking to the raisin industry in California, the jurist once again finds deplorable conditions. The evidence all suggests the presence of certain "evils attending the production and marketing of raisins," resulting in an unstable industry on the verge of collapse. The raisin industry, like the coal industry, demands an economic response.[27] Of this condition the jurist has no doubt – society's problems are transparent, and California's program is focused on this social need. What's more, the raisin industry is a particularly local issue demanding local solutions, and while the state's program necessarily has spillover effects, the effect of the raisin program on interstate commerce is neither "greater than [nor] substantially different in kind from that contemplated by [similar] stabilization programs authorized by federal statutes."[28] Is this merely a political decision masquerading as impersonal adjudication? So long as the form of legal argument tracks the social problem and merely applies governmental expertise to the resolution of that problem, the argument remains free of ideology and in the service of a naturalizing juridical science. True, the argument is not harmonious in the abstract; but that is no longer the aspiration. The

[23] Id. at 352. [24] Id. at 362. [25] Id. at 362. [26] Id. at 362–363.
[27] Id. at 363. [28] Id. at 368.

argument is harmonious because it finds a perfect consonance between the needs of society and the efforts of the state to meet those needs. Is the consonance real? Are the needs really there, are the efforts really on point? Better not to ask.

From the west coast over to the east, we arrive in Washington, DC, in the year 1954.[29] The dispute is between a Mr. Morris,[30] owner of a department store in Southwest DC, and Congress, acting in its capacity as wielder of the police power in Washington, DC.[31] Mr. Morris questioned the constitutionality of the District of Columbia Redevelopment Act, a congressional effort to rehabilitate DC's substandard housing and blighted areas, "injurious to the public health, safety, morals, and welfare..."[32] The Act was expansive. With little confidence in the market's capacity to effect meaningful change through the force of free competition, Congress doubted progress without a "comprehensive and coordinated planning of the whole territory of the District of Columbia..."[33] This comprehensive planning would be the work of a body of experts in urban planning, the National Capital Planning Commission, which in turn would submit its views to the Columbia Redevelopment Land Agency.[34] Among other things, the Commission could recommend to the Agency that certain real estate be acquired for redevelopment. Under the Act, the Agency should give a preference to private enterprise in executing the development plan.[35] Mr. Morris owned a department store in the midst of the area targeted by the Commission for redevelopment, claimed that his property was in good condition, and that it would be a violation of the Fifth Amendment for the Agency to forcibly confiscate his department store and hand it over to another private actor in order to create a "better balanced, more attractive community."[36]

Our jurist's style is swift and confidant. There is little need here for line-drawing, or the hard work of navigating the relationship between the constitution, the police power, and property rights. Rather, the style manifests in the thesis of social control. What we are dealing with here in DC, says the jurist, is nothing other than the police power. Unlike jurists operating in the classic style, this jurist explains that "an attempt to define its reach or trace its outer limits is fruitless, for each case must

[29] *Berman v. Parker*, 348 U.S. 26 (1954).
[30] *Schneider v. District of Columbia*, 117 F. Supp. 705 (1953).
[31] Berman, supra note 29, at 32. [32] Id. at 28. [33] Id. at 29.
[34] Id. at 29–30. [35] Id. at 30. [36] Id. at 31.

turn on its own facts."[37] While there is surely an outer frontier to the power, says the jurist, we don't know where it is, and nothing about its exercise here are suggestive of it. Indeed, the jurist's role is minor: "the legislature, not the judiciary, is the main guardian of the public needs to be served by social legislation."[38] What's more, says the jurist, the service of social needs such as public safety, public health, morality, peace and quiet, law and order – this is merely the threshold of what the police power entails, not its limit. "Miserable and disreputable housing conditions may do more than spread disease and crime and immorality. They may also suffocate the spirit by reducing the people who live there to the status of cattle . . . The concept of the public welfare is broad and inclusive. The values it represents are spiritual as well as physical, aesthetic as well as monetary."[39]

With so much momentum in place, the jurist has little to do but just let it rush on to a lexical resting point. Is there a problem with not merely restricting Mr. Morris' use of the property, but actually confiscating it as a part of the redevelopment plan? Not at all, says the jurist. The power of eminent domain is merely one of the state's many weapons in the fight against social decay and disorder. Yes, the confiscation must be for a public purpose, but the land will be used with regard to the public needs of the community. We can say this with confidence, since it is the work of scientific expertise: "The experts concluded that if the community were to be healthy, if it were not to revert again to a blighted or slum area, as though possessed of a congenital disease, the area must be planned *as a whole*."[40] Is there a problem with taking Mr. Morris' property and giving it to a private firm for redevelopment? Not at all, says the jurist. "The public end may be as well or better served through an agency of private enterprise than through a department of government . . . We cannot say that public ownership is the sole method for promoting the public purposes of community redevelopment projects."[41]

The jurist concludes, the argument is clear. It is natural that in the exercise of the police power Congress would take the needs of the whole, of society, as its proper point of departure. In assigning the task of redevelopment to a commission of experts, a comprehensive plan came about with a view toward confiscating certain properties in the effort to transform the total area. It matters little whether private or public actors take custody of the confiscated property, so long as the confiscation is in the service of a public purpose. The object of the police power is broad, very

[37] Id. at 32. [38] Id. [39] Id. at 32–33.
[40] Id. at 34. [41] Id. at 33–34.

broad. Mr. Morris cannot object to the taking, assuming of course that he is justly compensated for it. No dissonance here, the jurist assures.

The Big Apple, 1963. We sit with the New York Court of Appeals, looking over a dispute between the Port of New York Authority and the owner of one Courtesy Sandwich Shop, located in lower Manhattan.[42] In some respects the problem was much like that in Mr. Morris' case. On the one side is the interest expressed by the state of New York in establishing "a facility of commerce" that would facilitate "the centralized accommodation of functions, activities and services for or incidental to the transportation of persons, the exchange, buying, selling and transportation of commodities . . . in world trade and commerce."[43] In short, and in accordance with New York statute, the Port Authority wants to make New York City more competitive through the creation of a new economic center, a World Trade Center. In the process, the Port Authority seeks to condemn property in the area, including the Courtesy Sandwich Shop. The question is whether the statute runs afoul of the Constitution in granting the Port Authority the power to condemn private property for an economic purpose, and not a public purpose. As above, the question is not whether the state can do this without paying for it; the question is whether the state can do it at all.

Recall what we have already seen in both the classic and modern styles of legal argument. In the classic style, a jurist sets up a very sharp distinction between a private and a public sphere. In each sphere, certain rules dominate with a kind of mathematical force, and so the line between the two spheres resonates in a natural harmony. In this classic style, the constitutional power of eminent domain is characterized as fairly narrow: private property can only be confiscated when the confiscation is for a public purpose, and, it will be remembered, the public purpose of the constitution is the protection of property and contract. Thus, the range of purposes for which the state can destroy rights of ownership will be limited. One way to think about this, in terms of the relation between the public and private spheres, is that the public sphere is always in a subordinated posture with respect to the natural authority of the private sphere; the public was created to assist the private, not dominate it.

In contrast is the modern style, where our practice in constructing the public sphere figures differently. Now, the public power is "broad and inclusive," capable of retaining its character even in the midst of

[42] *Courtesy Sandwich Shop v. Port of N.Y. Auth.*, 12 N.Y. 2d 379 (1963).
[43] Id. at 387.

decisively private matters. The public purpose to which the power of eminent domain is attached need no longer be restricted to the demands of the private sphere of property and contract. In the context of the Courtesy Sandwich Shop, the jurist faces an exercise of the police power so far beyond what we saw in Washington, DC, that one is forced to wonder whether there is any line at all between the public and private. For what is New York claiming as the "public purpose" justifying its use of eminent domain? The exercise of social control, here in the context of the World Trade Center, is made in the effort to make New York City more economically competitive. We have come some way from public blight.

New York State's pursuit of a more competitive environment is something other than what the jurist allowed in Mr. Rockefeller's case, as well as in the case of Mr. Munn and Mr. Scott. New York is neither prohibiting unreasonable contracts nor cleansing the competitive field of perversions and impurities. Rather, New York is directly intervening in the market, destroying rights of private ownership in order to create new rights for other, private owners. Does this seeming collapse of the public-private distinction, in which the word "public" ceases to have meaning in the context of the "public purpose" requirement, worry the modern jurist? Nope.

> It is the gathering together of all business relating to world trade that is supposed to be the great convenience held out to those who use American ports and which is supposed to attract trade with a resultant stimulus to the economic well-being of the Port of New York. This benefit is not too remote or speculative as to render the means chosen to achieve it *patently unreasonable*; nor is the benefit sought itself an improper concern of government. The history of western civilization demonstrates the cause and effect relationship between a great port and a great city. Fostering harbor facilities has long been recognized by this court as the legitimate concern of government. Even the centralization of inland trade has supported the exercise of the power of eminent domain for the establishment of public markets wherein private merchants plied their trades. *No further demonstration is required* that improvement of the Port of New York by facilitating the flow of commerce and centralizing all activity incident thereto is a public purpose supporting the condemnation of property for any activity functionally related to that purpose.[44]

Our jurist brushes aside the old lines that so worried jurists in the past. The police power not only begins with the kind of social blight and public health addressed in Washington, DC, it continues on to include the concept of "economic well-being." Is it "patently unreasonable" that the

[44] Id. at 388–389 (citations omitted) (italics mine).

police power might extend so far, defining "public purpose" in such a way as to now mean, "any reasonable purpose"? After all, this isn't like the situation in Washington, DC, in which a department store was condemned in the service of public health concerns. Here, one merchant – the Courtesy Sandwich Shop – will be pushed aside (and bought out) in favor of another, more competitive merchant. There is only a problem here, says the jurist, if one holds a slavish attitude toward what ought to count as a "public purpose." And here comes the mantra of the mythical: "No further demonstration is required."[45]

Let's head back down to Washington, DC, and jump ahead to 1968 and the DC Circuit. It has been fourteen years since Mr. Morris lost his department store, but housing conditions in the nation's capital are still pretty bad.[46] The current manifestation of the problem has arisen in the context of a dispute between a landlord, Mr. Habib, and his month-to-month tenant, Mrs. Edwards. Shortly after moving into her apartment, Mrs. Edwards complained to the Department of Licenses and Inspections of sanitary code violations Mr. Habib had failed to correct.[47] After an inspection, the Department found more than forty violations and ordered Mr. Habib to fix them. In response, and rather than repair the dwelling, Mr. Habib obtained a default judgment and evicted Mrs. Edwards in accordance with local regulations.[48] Mrs. Edwards sought to reopen the judgment on the basis that Mr. Habib's eviction was an illegal retaliation for her report of the housing code violations.[49]

The jurist's train of argument is really a tour de force in the modern style, for it highlights at every turn a modern mastery of liberal legal thought. This is, without a doubt, a jurist immersed in a legal flow, grasping the affordances of the ready-to-hand in the legal material. The jurist begins with Mrs. Edwards' constitutional objection to her eviction. Now, in a classic style we could imagine a jurist moving very quickly through the question of constitutional state action: Is the state action requirement satisfied here, such that Mr. Habib is either a state official or acting under the color of state authority? No, he's not; with a clear appreciation for the public-private distinction, a jurist in the classic style could dispose of the claim easily. But here, the jurist spends pages of lengthy discussion on the question.[50] And he does so after saying at the outset that he won't even reach the question of constitutional prohibition.[51] Why dedicate,

[45] Id. at 389. [46] *Edwards v. Habib*, 397 F. 2d 687 (1968).
[47] Id. at 688. [48] Id. at 689. [49] Id. [50] Id. at 129–137. [51] Id. at 129.

then, a lengthy argument to a claim that he will not decide? "Because," says the jurist, "constitutional considerations inform the statutory construction on which our decision rests."[52]

I will not outline the full breadth of this first stage in the argument, but only summarize the basic "consideration" the jurist uses to orient his explanatory argument. The essential problem for Mrs. Edwards in her attempt to bring a free speech claim against Mr. Habib is the state action doctrine. If Mr. Habib is a private actor, and he is, then Mrs. Edwards has no constitutional claim.[53] This is the point at which a classic jurist might choose to end the matter and settle on a lexical statement. This jurist, however, takes the modern view, and airs the question of whether the state action requirement might be satisfied even in the case of a private dispute. Mrs. Edwards' argument is that the state action requirement can be satisfied when a private actor seeks the assistance of the state in effecting their will as against another private actor; critically, the organ providing the "assistance of the state" in this argument is a *court*. Is a court a state actor, a *political* agent? If so, was there not a substantial amount of state action involved when Mr. Habib sought a default judgment in order to prompt the police to send Mrs. Edwards on her way? The jurist has already explained that he will not rely on this argument, not in the context of nailing Mr. Habib for violating Mrs. Edwards' rights of free speech. However, the jurist does say that

> There can be no doubt that the application by the judiciary of the state's common law, even in a lawsuit between private parties, may constitute state action which must conform to the constitutional strictures which constrain the government. This may be so even when where the court is simply enforcing a privately negotiated contract. But the nature and extent of the judicial involvement required to bring into play these constitutional constraints is unclear.[54]

The classic worry, of course, is that if a judge takes this way of thinking very far, "the distinction between private and governmental action will be obliterated,"[55] and judges will be political in the same way as legislators. In modern manner, the jurist suggests that while there is at the end of the day a final distinction between public and private, we need to concede, as the Courtesy Sandwich Shop needed to concede, that the difference is now very, very dull.[56] The important consideration is that, regardless of wherever the final frontier might lie between the spheres of private and state action, a jurist can never avoid the fact that he *is* a state actor, and

[52] Id. [53] Id. at 129–130. [54] Id. at 130. [55] Id. [56] Id. at 132.

that in deciding for one claimant over another in a private dispute, the state coerces one individual at the behest of another.

It is this highly politicized view of the state action doctrine that ferries the jurist on to the next move in the argument. Indeed, the jurist comes in with a full head of steam, the momentum all pushing away from the idea that Mr. Habib had only employed a neutral procedure in obtaining a default judgment. The suggestion rather seems to be that there *are no* neutral procedures. After quoting the relevant sections of the DC Code dealing with default judgments, and what happens after a tenant receives notice of termination, some other jurist might have ended the matter here. There is nothing in the Code that suggests Mr. Habib did anything wrong in terminating Mrs. Edwards' tenancy. Once again, our jurist takes a left turn where we might have otherwise gone right. The Code, says the jurist, nowhere states that a tenant is barred from providing evidence of improper motives as a defense against termination and possessory actions.[57] Of course, this is right; the Code is silent because the received understanding is that a landlord can terminate for *any reason at all*. The jurist makes a move with dramatic implications: landlords may evict for any *legal* reason, not for any reason at all.[58]

Now we can justifiably ask, how did the jurist end up with such a strange reading of the DC Code's eviction procedure? "Any *legal* reason"? It is here that the jurist's argumentative run-up starts to do its work, for when we recall the "constitutional considerations" leading up to this point, the jurist's point does not seem strange at all, but almost natural. Does it make sense for the state to bestow its sovereign powers of coercion upon a private actor, allowing that private actor to wield that power in the marketplace as against another private actor, *when the reasons for doing so undermine the public welfare?*[59] A blurred public-private distinction and a foregrounded view of the court as a state actor, in other words, assist the jurist in now making out what was a perfunctory use of a neutral procedure into something ridiculous. No, says the jurist, Mr. Habib cannot deploy the power of the state against Mrs. Edwards because he wants to punish her for reporting his failure to remedy a dilapidated dwelling.

In the classic style, a jurist might arrive at this last point by way of natural right. The jurist here, however, arrives by way of the modern version of a naturalizing juridical science. First, he notes the social context in which the dispute takes place. "The housing and sanitary codes," says the

[57] Id. at 138. [58] Id. at 139. [59] Id. at 139–141.

jurist, "indicate a strong and pervasive congressional concern to secure for the city's slum dwellers decent, or at least safe and sanitary, places to live."[60] In order to effectuate the will of Congress and realize the purpose of the statutes, tenants must be able to report violations without fear of reprisal. It cannot matter that the statutes do not give individuals standing to bring claims. "The notion that the effectiveness of remedial legislation will be inhibited if those reporting violations of it can be legally intimidated is so fundamental that a presumption against the legality of such intimidation can be inferred as inherent in the legislation even if it is not expressed in the statute itself."[61] In looking to the needs of the community in the "light of the appalling condition and shortage of housing in Washington, the expense of moving, the inequality of bargaining power between tenant and landlord, and the social and economic importance" of making the sanitary and housing codes effective, the jurist utters, Mr. Habib cannot rely on state action in order to realize his interest in punishing Mrs. Edwards. This conclusion necessarily *follows*.

Finally, we head back to the New York Court of Appeals, in 1970. The dispute is between Mr. and Mrs. Boomer (and their neighbors), and the Atlantic Cement Company.[62] As with the case of Mr. Habib and Mrs. Edwards, we find ourselves back in the space of a clash between individual wills. On the one side is the right of the Boomers to the use of their home in peaceable enjoyment. On the other is the right of the Cement Company to make cement. The problem is that in the making of the cement, the Company has discharged substantial amounts of dust, and through its blasting procedures caused excessive vibrations in the Boomers' neighborhood. In this "competition" between owners, the jurist must choose a winner.

As in Mr. Brown's case, where the jurist was excused from deciding whether California's program was anticompetitive (because it clearly was), our jurist needn't decide whether the Boomers have suffered a wrong for which there is a legal remedy. They have. But should they get a payment for damages, thus allowing the Cement Company to continue operations, or ought the jurist to enjoin the Company from further work?[63] The jurist begins in the modern style, orienting the argument in the light of social need. Says the jurist, "The public concern with air pollution arising from many sources in industry and in transportation is currently

[60] Id. at 139. [61] Id. at 140–141.

[62] *Boomer v. Atlantic Cement Co*, 26 N.Y. 2d 219 (1970). [63] Id. at 222.

accorded ever wider recognition accompanied by a general sense of responsibility in State and Federal governments to control it. Cement plants are obvious sources of air pollution in the neighborhoods where they operate."[64] Ought the jurist to resolve the problem through an injunction, stopping the pollution and thereby "seeking promotion of the general public welfare"?[65] The jurist's modern answer: No.

That was the sound of a record screeching, for as you will have noticed, this answer does not seem modern at all. Is not the modern style precisely about seeking the promotion of the general welfare? Is not the approach one of social function, and making sure that law serves social ends? Indeed it is, and on the face of it, our jurist seems to be doing something other than arguing in the modern style. But appearances can be deceiving.

In making out what seems like an effort to stall the momentum generated on behalf of the Boomers, the jurist reclaims the public-private distinction that has been so battered in the cases of Courtesy Sandwich Shop and Mr. Habib. The resolution of private disputes sometimes has public effects, says the jurist. But "it is a rare exercise of judicial power to use a decision in private litigation as a purposeful mechanism to achieve direct public objectives greatly beyond the rights and interests before the court."[66] Now while this claim is certainly dubious – using the judicial power in such a way is in fact a hallmark of the modern style – the jurist then shifts into an explicitly modern mode. Air pollution, says the jurist, is a serious social problem, and indeed the law should cater to a resolution of that problem. But here, and in contrast with our prior disputes, there is a total lack of any relevant exercise of the police power. There are no experts here, no comprehensive plan, no agency, nothing at all in terms of the indicia of the police power at work. While a jurist's role is to adjudicate questions about the exercise of that power, in the dispute here between the Boomers and the Cement Company, the state has been silent.

> A court should not try to do this on its own as a by-product of private litigation and it seems manifest that the judicial establishment is neither equipped in the limited nature of any judgment it can pronounce nor prepared to lay down and implement an effective policy for the elimination of air pollution. This is an area beyond the circumference of one private lawsuit. It is a direct responsibility for government and should not thus be undertaken as an incident to solving a dispute between property owners and a single cement plant – one of many – in the Hudson River valley.[67]

[64] Id. [65] Id. [66] Id. [67] Id. at 223.

What seems to be happening in the jurist's argument, then, is merely an affirmation of the jurist's proper deference to the legislature's expertise in using law to solve social problems. Jurists, given that they are not experts in the social and natural sciences, cannot do this on their own. Thus we can understand what the jurist means when he says that he is barred from adjudicating the dispute in the absence of any relevant expertise.

Nevertheless, the argument is far from finished, and its most modern flourish awaits. In what looks like a turning away from "the general public welfare," which we can now understand as a reference to air pollution, the jurist moves on to decide the question of whether to issue an injunction on the basis of what is best characterized as . . . the general public welfare! No longer functioning as a reference to the environment, "general welfare" now functions as a reference to the market. Back in the classic style the argument might have gone like this: So long as the Cement Company is making its products in a reasonable (natural) way, which it is, and so long as we want to characterize the harm to the Boomers as an inconvenience (*damnum absque injuria*), we should allow the Cement Company to continue production. In this argument, the Boomers likely get nothing at all. In the modern style the jurist proceeds differently. The harm to the Boomers is not *damnum absque injuria*. They have suffered a harm for which they ought to be compensated. But how should the jurist decide whether they should be bought out, or whether the Company should get shut down?

Despite the jurist's insistence that his argument would avoid all reference to the public welfare, this is precisely the consideration that generates his next move. The analysis is decidedly utilitarian, asking of the solution likely to yield the greatest economic benefit. Again, this has nothing to do with natural lines between good competition and bad; this is an economic analysis of utility. "The total damage to plaintiffs' properties is . . . relatively small in comparison with the value of defendant's operation and with the consequences of the injunction which plaintiffs seek."[68] Thus, the reason for avoiding the problem of equal rights of use, which would land us in a classic posture, "is the large disparity in economic consequences of the nuisance and of the injunction."[69] The damages to all the plaintiffs, including the Boomers but not limited to them, is $185,000. The investment in the Cement Company, in contrast, is $45 million. To enjoin the Company, as a consequence, "is a drastic remedy" with no economic sense. The "public interest"[70] clearly lies in keeping the

[68] Id. [69] Id. [70] Id. at 227.

plant open, as the market will suffer, not only with respect to the fortunes of the Cement Company, but also for the 300 employees who would suffer as well.

So what has happened here? Whether the jurist knew it or not, the argument turned a modern bait-and-switch. There are social problems that require legislative solutions, and air pollution is a good example. In the absence of expert help and comprehensive plans, it is beyond the abilities of juridical argument to reach for social remedies in the context of private disputes. Even in the jurist's dramatic treatment of the dispute between Mr. Habib and Mrs. Edwards, there was still in the background a legislative exercise of the police power. Even so, just as the jurist pushes the public welfare away with one hand, he *expertly* brings it back in with the other. For while it might be beyond the jurist's ability to effectively deal with environmental problems, welfare analysis of market conditions in Albany, apparently, is not. A view of social need, and an interest in interpreting the clash of individual will in the light of those social needs, carries the day. The twist is that rather than define social needs in the register of environmental protection, the jurist defines it in the register of the market. There is too much dissonance in the field of climate change. In the market, well, it is here that the jurist finds harmony's law.

Summing Up the Modern Style

As I suggested in Chapter 4, what I have tried to emphasize in these six readings was less a summary of rules than a sense for the argumentative style in which the jurists were working. The modern style, like the classic style, operates in the basic grammar of competition and control. The modern style, like the classic style, suggests certain styles of argument in the light of that grammar. It is, however, suggestive only of style, not of lexical settlement, for the question of how a jurist might come out is never answered by identifying the style in which the argument was made. Does the modern style mandate a preference for the state in disputes with private actors? It does not. As we saw in the case of Appalachian Coals, what was determinate for the jurist was not a preference for state control as much as was an appreciation for market failure. The coal industry was dying, and given these awful conditions, the jurist saw a social need in demand of a proper response. That response, in this case, came from private actors and not the state. As far as the jurist could see, it was these actors in their assessment of the realities of market failure, and not the antitrust enforcers, who best understood the reality of the industry.

To be sure, the modern style entails a heavy privileging of the state's power to control the field of competition. Going further, the modern style even allows for the argument that it is the state that *defines* competition. In the California raisins case, the jurist encountered what would have been easily considered, *by market standards*, state legislation and enforcement with patently anticompetitive effects. The jurist did not care to apply market standards to the state, since it is the political power of control which precedes the private sphere of competition, and not the other way around. Now, this sounds like a principled approach, and at the end of the day, it certainly is. Nevertheless, with respect to the style in which the jurist makes the argument, principles are dispensed with in favor of realities and social functions. The power of political control precedes private competition because political control is morally or scientifically superior; it precedes it, says the modern jurist, because this is the way the world really works. Mechanical, bright-line tests are of no use here. Interests and purpose are the watchwords.

This modern disavowal of bright-line distinctions was especially apparent in the cases of the World Trade Center and DC Housing Code. In the former dispute, the jurist expanded the meaning of "public purpose" into "any reasonable purpose," allowing for the private property of an individual to be taken and sold to another individual when doings so would be more competitive. In the latter dispute, the jurist suggested the virtual impossibility of a purely private dispute, when the dispute involved a court. A court, said the jurist there, is as much a state actor as any other, and in the process of going to court an individual seeks to bring the coercive power of the sovereign to bear against another private actor. The result is something close to losing all sight of the public-private distinction. Once again, these argumentative moves take place in the context of social needs and the state's effort to meet those needs. The jurist must effectuate those needs, objectively and harmoniously, and it is this naturalizing task that orients his immersion in the legal material.

To say once more, however, none of this demands that the jurist conclude in any one direction over another, or favor one kind of rule. Yes, the thesis of social control is favored over the thesis of free competition. Yes, juridical pursuit of the thesis of control projects a trajectory toward the expertise of social science in order to give the modern style its needed "objectivity." But all of this is still deeply indeterminate, as we saw in the Boomers' case. In what seemed like a persistent effort at misdirection, the jurist denied the hallmarks of the modern style on his way toward vindicating the rights of industry as against a group of homeowners. And yet, the jurist's style was distinctly modern. As in every other dispute surveyed here, the jurist once again looked at social needs in order to compel a decision that enjoyed a gloss of objectivity and that met those needs. While the jurist may not have had the necessary expertise to adjudicate the social problem of air pollution, he had enough of it to ensure that the market remained properly competitive. In doing so, however, the jurist employed none of the classic moves, but relied instead on the characteristically modern emphasis on public welfare through an analysis of costs and benefits.

These are the practices of the modern style. It is fluid, energetic, looking for the stuff of legal argument in a constantly changing yet empirically knowable society. It prioritizes the power of the state to address social problems, while backgrounding the sanctity of individual rights of property and contract. It asks of expertise and bureaucratic involvement, and the social purpose to be served in a given legal dispute. It avoids bright-line rules and asks of results. It rejects a classical harmony between juridical science and nature, and worships a modern harmony among social science, social need, and law.

6

Liberal Legalism and the Context of Legal Thought

The last two chapters elaborated the classic and modern styles of liberal legal thought. Moving out from the liberal theses of free competition and social control, we watched as twelve jurists wrestled with a political economy of legal concepts, ranging from nuisance and takings to monopolies, and broader concepts such as competition, the police power, and the market itself. Some readers were likely disappointed, reading it as an inadequate explanation of "what was really going on" in those disputes, falling over 100 years between 1870 and 1970, all over the United States. For some, the failure might have been linked to an insufficient survey of the relevant lexicon: in order to understand what these jurists were *really* saying, we need to contextualize their statements with more statements still.[1] For others, the problem might lie in the insufficient contextualization in a "broader" extralegal context.[2] As I argued in Chapter 3, however, the discussion of these twelve cases is intended to explain neither the full lexicon of "property law" or "antitrust law," nor the intellectual or social contexts in which the decisions were made. The broader context I was offering is the *legal context* of *legal thought*. I shall summarize that legal context below, but first, it is useful to contrast that contextualization with the more typical sorts.

[1] I take this as what Barry Cushman was up to in his own doctrinal contextualization of Duncan Kennedy's *Rise and Fall of Classical Legal Thought*. See Barry Cushman, The Structure of Classical Public Law, 75 *University of Chicago Law Review* 1917 (2008).

[2] See, e.g., David Rabban, *Law's History* (New York: Cambridge University Press, 2013); Robert Steinfeld, *Coercion, Contract, and Free Labor in the Nineteenth Century* (Cambridge: Cambridge University Press, 2001).

General Contexts

There are numerous extralegal contexts to choose from when thinking about our twelve cases, and I certainly cannot cover them all here, even briefly. One way of grouping the choices is to separate very general contexts from those that will be more narrow and particular. General contexts are offered as a way of showing the meaning of the cases, even over a very long stretch of time. For example, one such context could be what is now an old-fashioned intellectual history of "American Thought."[3] For if one of my claims is that these twelve cases demonstrate certain commitments to an autonomous, rights-bearing individual, as well as the view that it is in the clash of these rights-bearing individuals that good competition reveals the good society, does this not amount to the claim that the American legal tradition is itself deeply liberal?[4] Louis Hartz famously argued for a variation of this now unpopular idea, that American thought was thoroughly Lockean.[5] In this and similar views, the United States enjoyed a particularly distinctive political tradition, without analogy to the nations of Europe and their struggles with socialism.[6] As historians like Bernard Bailyn and John Pocock made famous, Hartz' liberal story became increasingly difficult to accept.[7] Instead of a Lockean consciousness, these scholars explained, the United States' had its origins in an entirely different political tradition, that of republicanism.[8] As Frank Michelman representatively argued, "I believe

[3] Morris Cohen, *American Thought: A Critical Sketch* (New York: Free Press,1954).

[4] Contextual histories in this vein might also establish feudalism as a marker for the emergence of liberalism. See, e.g., Daniel Coquillette, *The Anglo-American Legal Heritage* (Durham, NC: Carolina Academic Press, 1999); Walton Hamilton, Property – According to Locke, 41 *Yale Law Journal* 864 (1932); Frank Sharman, An Introduction to the Enclosure Acts, 10 *Journal of Legal History* 45 (1989).

[5] Louis Hartz, *The Liberal Tradition in America: An Interpretation of American Political Thought Since the Revolution* (New York: Harcourt, 1955). For discussion, see James Kloppenberg, *The Virtues of Liberalism* (New York: Oxford University Press, 1988). See also James Kloppenberg, "In Retrospect: Louis Hartz' 'The Liberal Tradition in America,'" 29 *Reviews in American History* 460 (2001).

[6] See, e.g., Richard Hofstadter, *The American Political Tradition and the Men Who Made It* (New York: Vintage, 1973); Daniel Boorstin, *The Genius of American Politics* (Chicago: University of Chicago Press, 1953).

[7] Bernard Bailyn, *The Ideological Origins of the American Revolution* (Cambridge: Harvard University Press, 1967); G. A. Pocock, *The Machiavellian Moment: Florentine Political Thought and the Atlantic Republican Tradition* (Princeton, NJ: Princeton University Press, 1975). See also Staughton Lynd, *Intellectual Origins of American Radicalism* (Cambridge: Cambridge University Press, 2009).

[8] Gordon Wood, *The Creation of the American Republic, 1776–1787* (Chapel Hill: University of North Carolina Press, 1998); Joyce Appleby, *Liberalism and Republicanism.*

that a close consideration of certain implications of historical republican constitutional thought can point us toward an account of the relation between law, politics, and democracy . . . that Americans also will, upon reflection, recognize as truer in other respects to their most basic understandings of what constitutionalism is all about."[9] To place the discussion of the twelve jurists in this intellectual context would therefore prioritize the power of certain ideas, whether "liberal" or "republican," to influence jurists in the making of their decisions, over a span of a hundred years. Very likely a decent attempt at such contextualizing would have to take care in grappling with the differences between 1870 and 1890 and 1930 and 1968 and so on. But the sense of what would happen is clear enough: we would come to understand the meaning of these twelve cases by way of their insertion in the intellectual milieu of republicanism, or liberalism, or perhaps some blending of the two.[10]

Another related and very general context in which we might read our jurists is that of religion.[11] Obviously, a religious context might develop along any number of fronts.[12] Following from the prior point about liberalism and republicanism, one route might be to ask not of some rival to the

in the Historical Imagination (Cambridge, MA: Harvard University Press, 1992); Dorothy Ross, "The Liberal Tradition Revisited and the Republican Tradition Addressed," in *New Directions in American Intellectual History* (John Higham and Paul Conkin, eds.) (Baltimore: Johns Hopkins University Press, 1980); J. G. A. Pocock, *The Ancient Constitution and the Feudal Law: A Study of English Historical Thought in the Seventeenth Century* (Cambridge: Cambridge University Press, 1957); Quentin Skinner, "The Republican Ideal of Political Liberty," in *Machiavelli and Republicanism* (Gisela Bock et al., eds.) (Cambridge: Cambridge University Press, 1990).

9 Frank Michelman, Law's Republic, 97 *Yale Law Journal* 1493, 1499 (1988). See also William Novak, *The People's Welfare* (Chapel Hill: University of North Carolina Press, 1996); Gregory Alexander, *Commodity & Propriety* (Chicago: University of Chicago Press, 1997).

10 See generally, Rudolph Peritz, *Competition Policy in America, 1888–1992: History, Rhetoric, Law* (New York: Oxford University Press, 1996); Stanley Katz, Republicanism and the Law of Inheritance in the American Revolutionary Era, 76 *Michigan Law Review* 1 (1977); Isaac Kramnick, The 'Great National Discussion': The Discourse of Politics in 1787, 45 *William & Mary Quarterly* 3 (1988); Elizabeth Mensch, The Colonial Origins of Liberal Property Rights, 31 *Buffalo Law Review* 635 (1982); Robert Steinfeld, Property and Suffrage in the Early American Republic, 41 *Stanford Law Review* 335 (1989).

11 William Fisher III, Ideology, Religion, and the Constitutional Protection of Private Property: 1760–1860, 39 *Emory Law Journal* 65 (1990).

12 See, e.g., Max Weber, *The Protestant Ethic and the 'Spirit' of Capitalism and other Writings* (Peter Baehr and Gordon Wells, trans.) (New York: Penguin, 2002); Harold Berman, *Law and Revolution II: The Impact of the Protestant Reformations on the Western Legal Tradition* (Cambridge, MA: Harvard University Press, 2003).

liberal tradition, but of liberalism's true identity.[13] Here, to take the example of John Dunn, what we find when we look closely at the protagonist-in-chief, John Locke, is a deeply theological thinker.[14] As Dunn explained, Locke's argument in *The Second Treatise* was incomprehensible in the absence of certain assumptions about God's role in the creation of the universe and of man. Just to take a few snippets, what of Locke's view of individual rights? "All rights except those of God himself are circumscribed by the fact that they are exercised by one part of the created order over another part. All of them must serve... God's purpose in the creation of that order."[15] What of Locke's view of ownership? "[I]f God had created all of it for some good purpose, clearly none of it should be destroyed without good purpose. Hence that other axiom of Lockean politics, the duty to maximize preservation and its curious consequence, the iniquity of waste. Everything which cannot be used must be preserved and no being may make use by right of another being of his own species."[16] Locke's view of the state of nature? "In itself it is simply an axiom of theology. It sets human beings in the teleology of divine purposes. The story of how ineptly men have carried these out is the classic Christian story." With views like Dunn's in mind, liberalism, at least if we focus on Locke as a central representative, turns out to be as theistic as the arguments of Thomas Aquinas.[17] And Saint Thomas is a good representative of the "medieval Aristotle," a signification which in many circles liberalism is meant to reject.[18] Arguably, all of this might be a meaningful context for a "proper" understanding of the twelve jurists.

13 See, e.g., Quentin Skinner, *The Foundations of Modern Political Thought* (Volume Two: The Age of Reformation) (Cambridge: Cambridge University Press, 1978).

14 John Dunn, *The Political Thought of John Locke* (Cambridge: Cambridge University Press, 1969). See also John Locke, *Vindications of the Reasonableness of Christianity* (Oxford: Oxford University Press, 2012).

15 Dunn, Locke, supra note 14, at 94. 16 Id. at 95.

17 For a debate along these lines, see Timothy Stanton, Authority and Freedom in the Interpretation of Locke's Political Theory, 39 *Political Theory* 6 (2011); John William Tate, Locke, God, and Civil Society: Response to Stanton, 40 *Political Theory* 222 (2012); Timothy Stanton, On (Mis)Interpreting Locke: A Reply to Tate, 40 *Political Theory* 229 (2012).

18 See, e.g., Roberto Unger, *Knowledge and Politics* (New York: Free Press, 1975), p. 5; Ian Shapiro, *The Evolution of Rights in Liberal Theory* (Cambridge: Cambridge University Press, 1986); Harold Laski, *The Rise of European Liberalism: An Essay in Interpretation* (New Brunswick: Transaction Publishers, 1997); Arthur Monahan, *The Circle of Rights Expands: Modern Political Thought After the Reformation, 1521 (Luther) to 1762 (Rousseau)* (Montreal: McGill-Queens University Press, 2007); J. W. Burrow, *Whigs and Liberals: Continuity and Change in English Political Thought* (Oxford: Oxford University Press, 1988); Alan Ryan, *The Making of Modern Liberalism* (Princeton, NJ: Princeton University Press, 2012).

A third candidate in the search for meaning is that of the rise of the social sciences and the expertise they would come to produce.[19] This kind of discussion could cut in a number of directions as well.[20] Given the persistent theme of competition in the arguments of the twelve jurists, one direction might head toward the sociology of Herbert Spencer and Social Darwinism.[21] Perhaps the whole idea of a clash of will and good progress, as the twelve jurists argued, is most explicable in the light of a natural process of social elimination and vindication.[22] As Kunal Parker has suggested, "If one is to make sense of the late-nineteenth century debate between laissez-faire and social democracy, we must turn to Spencer's thought."[23] Spencer's shadow, Parker argues, hovered over not only those jurists arguing from the thesis of competition, but just as much as over those arguing from the thesis of control.[24] Or, moving in the direction of the economic study of society, perhaps a second and better route here would be to place our jurists in the context of what was happening in the late nineteenth-century transition from political economy to "economics."[25] In this transition was the revolutionary rise of the marginalists, who believed that in certain cases the involuntary transfer of wealth from some individuals to others could be in the interest of social welfare.[26] Through new mathematical understandings of concepts

[19] Dorothy Ross, *The Origins of American Social Science* (Cambridge: Cambridge University Press, 1991).

[20] Not only might we follow the social sciences in their disciplinary trajectories, asking of what political science or anthropology might say about our twelve jurists. But we could follow the rise of social theory as well, putting the cases in the context of some thinker, say a Karl Marx, Emile Durkheim, or Pierre Bourdieu. For a well-known example, see Bruno Latour, *The Making of Law: An Ethnography of the Conseil d'Etat* (Cambridge: Polity Press, 2010).

[21] See, e.g., Richard Hofstadter, *Social Darwinism in American Thought* (New York: G. Braziller, 1959); Mike Hawkins, *Social Darwinism in European and American Thought, 1860–1945: Nature as Model and Nature as Threat* (Cambridge: Cambridge University Press, 1997).

[22] Herbert Hovenkamp, *The Opening of American Law* (New York: Oxford University Press, 2015).

[23] Kunal Parker, *Common Law, History, and Democracy in America, 1790–1900* (New York: Cambridge University Press, 2011), p. 220.

[24] Id. at 230.

[25] Herbert Hovenkamp, *Enterprise and American Law, 1836–1937: Neoclassical Legal Thought, 1870-1970* (Cambridge, MA: Harvard University Press, 1991). For an interesting discussion of the emergence of law and economics in this context, see Edmund W. Kitch, The Fire of Truth: A Remembrance of Law and Economics at Chicago, 1932–1970, 26 *Journal of Law and Economics* 163, 181 (1983).

[26] See, e.g., Alfred Marshall and Mary Paley Marshall, *The Economics of Industry* (London: Macmillan, 1884); Peter Groenewegen, "English Marginalism: Jevons, Marshall, and

like marginal utility, diminishing returns, and supply and demand,[27] the marginalists argued for what was a major element in the modern liberal style: an entrenched suspicion that markets were not self-regulating after all, and that when "left alone," they failed.[28] In the midst of the marginalists were the rebel economists – institutional economists like Henry Carter Adams or Thorstein Veblen – who argued that *society* was the key concept, the concept around which the idea of free competition could usefully be deployed.[29] In espousing this new notion of the social, Adams, for example, argued for a new orientation toward the state.[30] Adams explained how the key elements in a properly competitive marketplace demanded a great deal of state intervention, and in some cases, state ownership.[31]

Economic thought between 1870 and 1970 is surely an edifying context in which to place our twelve jurists. Why stop there? Shifting only slightly into a related fourth context, still in the category of the very

Pigou," in *A Companion to the History of Economic Thought* (Warren Samuels et al., eds.) (Malden, UK: Blackwell, 2003).

[27] See, e.g., W. W. Rostow, *Theorists of Economic Growth from David Hume to the Present: With a Perspective on the Next Century* (New York: Oxford University Press, 1990), pp. 153–160.

[28] See, e.g., John Maynard Keynes, *The End of Laissez-Faire* (London: Hogarth Press, 1926), pp. 49–59. Proposals for more muscular state action were pushed far more aggressively, however, in the work of institutional economists like Thorstein Veblen, Richard Ely, and John Commons. See Joseph Dorfman, "The Background of Institutional Economics," in *Institutional Economics: Veblen, Commons, and Mitchell Reconsidered* (Berkeley: University of California Press, 1963), p. 30; Herbert Hovenkamp, Coase, Institutionalism, and the Origins of Law and Economics, 86 *Indiana Law Journal* 499, 521–529 (2011). The idea that the promotion of individual self-interest could guarantee social well-being certainly did fall out of favor by the middle of the twentieth century. However, my point is that in the modern style the thesis of free competition never really goes out of favor as a central organizing principle for society. Modern liberals did not believe, as was put forward from some on the left, that the very concept of free competition itself was fundamentally problematic – that the basic background rules themselves were somehow complicit in the problem of social inequality. In the context of economic thought, we could say that the perspective of economists like Harrod, Domar, or Keynes never did away with the basic assumptions of the neoclassical marginalists. It was rather that the marginalists failed to see how conditions of uncertainty and equilibria might prove much more socially problematic than had been otherwise assumed.

[29] Henry Carter Adams, Relation of the State to Industrial Action, 1 *Publications of the American Economic Association* 7, 34 (1887). See also Felix Cohen, Dialogue on Private Property, 9 *Rutgers Law Review* 357 (1954).

[30] Adams, supra note 29, at 65–66.

[31] Later examinations of ownership rights from a similarly left-oriented law and economics include Duncan Kennedy and Frank Michelman, Are Property and Contract Efficient? 8 *Hofstra Law Review* 711 (1980); Pierre Schlag, Coase Minus the Coase Theorem? Some Problems with Chicago Transaction Cost Analysis, 99 *Iowa Law Review* 175 (2013).

general, is that of the Gilded Age, progressivism, and the political transformation of capitalism.[32] There is obviously a lot to say here, but only in the briefest terms, this general context is also a postbellum story in which laissez-faire emerges,[33] followed by massive transformations in social consciousness,[34] which gave rise to a steady consensus about the widening gap between the rich and poor,[35] between management and

[32] A very eclectic list: Ernest Mandel, *Late Capitalism* (London: Humanities Press, 1975); Joseph Schumpeter, *Capitalism, Socialism, and Democracy* (New York: Harper, 1962); Giovanni Arrighi, *The Long Twentieth Century: Money, Power, and the Origin of Our Times* (London: Verso, 2010); Joyce Appleby, *The Relentless Revolution: A History of Capitalism* (New York: Newton, 2010); Joseph Singer, *No Freedom without Regulation: The Hidden Lesson of the Subprime Crisis* (New Haven, CT: Yale University Press, 2015); Richard Hofstadter, *The Age of Reform* (New York: Vintage, 1960); Eric Hobsbawm, *The Age of Empire: 1875–1914* (New York: Vintage, 1989); Eric Hobsbawm, *The Age of Extremes: A History of the World, 1914–1991* (New York: Vintage, 1996); Richard Hofstadter, "What Happened to the Antitrust Movement," in *The Paranoid Style in American Politics: -And Other Essays* (New York: Vintage, 1967); David Abraham, Liberty Without Equality: The Property Rights Connection in a 'Negative Citizenship' Regime, 21 *Law & Social Inquiry* 1 (1996).

[33] See, e.g., Jacob Viner, *Essays on the Intellectual History of Economics* (Douglass A. Irvin, ed.) (Princeton, NJ: Princeton University Press, 2014); Michael Les Benedict, Laissez-Faire and Liberty: A Re-Evaluation of the Meaning and Origins of Laissez-Faire Constitutionalism, 3 *Law & History Review* 293, 293–331 (1985); Stephen A. Siegel, Lochner Era Jurisprudence and the American Constitutional Tradition, 70 *North Carolina Law Review* 1 (1991); Stephen A. Siegel, Understanding the Lochner Era: Lessons from the Controversy over Railroad and Utility Rate Regulation, 70 *Virginia Law Review* 187 (1984); Cass R. Sunstein, Lochner's Legacy, 87 *Columbia Law Review* 873 (1987); Harry Scheiber, Regulation, Property Rights, and Definition of the "Market": Law and the American Economy, 41 *Journal of Economic History* 103 (1981); Harry Scheiber, Property Law, Expropriation, and Resource Allocation by Government, 33 *Journal of Economic History* 232 (1973).

[34] See, e.g., H. Stuart Hughes, *Consciousness and Society* (New Brunswick: Transaction Publishers, 2008); Christopher Lasch, *The New Radicalism in America 1889–1963: The Intellectual as a Social Type* (New York: Newton, 1997); Christopher Lasch, *The True and Only Heaven: Progress and Its Critics* (New York: Newton, 1991); Perry Anderson, *The Origins of Postmodernity* (London: Verso, 1998); Perry Anderson, *A Zone of Engagement* (London: Verso, 1992); Edmund Wilson, *Axel's Castle: A Study of the Imaginative Literature of 1870–1930* (New York: Farrar, Straus, and Giroux, 2004). Morton White, *Social Thought in America: The Revolt Against Formalism* (Boston: Beacon, 1969); James Kloppenberg, *Uncertain Victory: Social Democracy and Progressivism in European and American Thought, 1870–1920* (New York: Oxford University Press, 1988).

[35] See, e.g., Charles Beard, *An Economic Interpretation of the Constitution of the United States* (New York: Macmillan, 1913); Richard Ely, *Property and Contract in their Relations to the Distribution of Wealth* (New York: Macmillan, 1914); L. T. Hobhouse: *Liberalism and Other Writings* (James Meadowcroft, ed.) (Cambridge: Cambridge University Press, 1994); *The Cry for Justice: An Anthology of the Literature of Social Protest* (Upton Sinclair, ed.) (New York: L. Stuart, 1963).

labor,[36] and the need for an enlarged political apparatus to manage the "captains of industry" and plan the economy.[37]

On this last point, and in this age of the great Robber Baron, many became increasingly anxious about the "curse of bigness."[38] It is in the 1870s that historians have noticed the development of these trends, much having to do on the one hand with the substantial depression of trade in the period from the 1870s to the 1890s, and on the other the effects of the infrastructure put in place by the revolution in communication and transportation technologies.[39] The advent of the combined corporate enterprise, which evolved into that legal device called a trust, had several implications for the traditional image of the market pattern: combinations or trusts would advance at the expense of an abstract idea of perfect competition, big business mergers would advance at the expense of small business owners,[40] and the business entity would gain rights of a measure comparable to that of the private individual.[41] Further, as Alfred Chandler has explained, it is here that we see market actors willing to forego Adam Smith's picture of the invisible hand and its allocation of resources in favor of the "visible hand" in the new science of business management.[42]

36 See, e.g., William Forbath, *Law and the Shaping of the American Labor Movement* (Cambridge: Harvard University Press, 1991); Daniel Ernst, *Lawyers Against Labor: From Individual Rights to Corporate Liberalism* (Urbana: University of Illinois Press, 1995); Ahmed White, *The Last Great Strike: Little Steel, the CIO, and the Struggle for Labor Rights in New Deal America* (Oakland: University of California Press, 2016).

37 See, e.g., Karl Polanyi, *The Great Transformation: The Political and Economic Origins of Our Time* (Boston: Beacon Press, 2001); Daniel Yergin and Joseph Stanislaw, *The Commanding Heights: The Battle for the World Economy* (New York: Free Press, 2008); Sidney Fine, *Laissez-Faire and the General Welfare State: A Study of Conflict in American Thought, 1865–1901* (Ann Arbor: University of Michigan Press, 1964); Arthur Schlesinger, Jr., *The Crisis of the Old Order: 1913–1933, The Age of Roosevelt* (New York: Mariner, 2002); Daniel Ernst, *Tocqueville's Nightmare: The Administrative State Emerges in America, 1900-1940* (New York: Oxford University Press, 2014).

38 Louis D. Brandeis, *The Curse of Bigness: The Miscellaneous Papers of Louis D. Brandeis* (Osmond K. Frankel, ed.) (Port Washington, NY: Kennikat Press, 1935).

39 Herbert Hovenkamp, The First Great Law & Economics Movement, 42 *Stanford Law Review* 997 (1990).

40 Hobsbawm, Age of Empire, supra note 32, at 44.

41 Morton Horwitz, *The Transformation of American Law, 1870–1960* (New York: Oxford University Press, 1992), pp. 74–76. On the history of trusts, see Gregory Alexander, The Dead Hand and the Law of Trusts in the Nineteenth Century, 37 *Stanford Law Review* 1189 (1985); Gregory Alexander, The Transformation of Trusts as a Legal Category, 1800–1914, 5 *Law & History Review* 303 (1987); Herbert Hovenkamp, Antitrust Policy, Federalism, and the Theory of the Firm: An Historical Perspective, 59 *Antitrust Law Journal* 75 (1990), pp. 79–87.

42 Alfred Chandler, Jr., *The Visible Hand: The Managerial Revolution in American Business* (Cambridge, MA: Harvard University Press, 1977). See also David Harvey, *The*

Although the "market remained the generator of demand for goods and services ... modern business enterprise took over the functions of coordinating flows of goods through existing processes of production and distribution, and of allocating funds and personnel for future production and distribution."[43] These changes, along with the tendency toward the new form of trusts and syndicates popping up in the United States and Germany, led Chandler to conclude that the new economic man, in his acquisition of certain fundamental responsibilities previously allotted to the natural market, had simultaneously acquired vast amounts of power.[44] Concerns about economic concentration accelerated in the 1880s and 1890s as the public became more aware and more skeptical of big trusts like Standard Oil, American Cotton Oil, National Linseed Oil, National Lead, and the Whiskey and Sugar trusts.[45] The issue bubbling to the surface was what sort of public policy would make the best response. All of this and more might offer helpful explanations for why our jurists argued as they did.

Particular Contexts

We now have on the table a number of compelling choices about how to contextualize our twelve jurists. There is the debate between liberalism and republicanism, the debate over liberalism's theological commitments, the question of Social Darwinism and the transition from Political Economy to Economics, and the transformation of capitalism and the rise of the welfare state. As I have said, these are general contexts, and they often provide great explanatory power. These general contexts, however, do not exhaust the menu of choices, for even at this level of generality the proliferation of contexts could surely continue. That being said, the proliferation that ensues at this general level is nothing compared with what we see in the shift toward more particular contexts into which we might place the twelve cases.[46] For the sake of argument, let us now deny that

Condition of Postmodernity: An Enquiry into the Origins of Cultural Change (Oxford: Blackwell, 1991).

43 Chandler, supra note 42, at 1.   44 Id. at 323–332.

45 Horwitz, supra note 41, at 80–81.

46 This list of potential contexts could obviously just go on and on. But here's a brief sampling, limited by way of legal sub-field: On law and economics, Harold Demsetz, Toward a Theory of Property Rights, 57 *American Economic Review* 347 (1967); Robert Ellickson, Property in Land, 102 *Yale Law Journal* 1315 (1993); Richard Posner, *Antitrust Law: An Economic Perspective* (Chicago: University of Chicago Press, 1978). On law and gender, Reva Siegel, Home as Work: The First Woman's Rights Claims Concerning Wives'

any context of a general sort can meaningfully explain a dozen decisions stretching over 100 years and 2,800 miles. Instead, we need much smaller groupings, if not contexts that proceed case by case.

Unlike in the general contexts of economic thought or the stages of capitalism, here the proper context would be, say, the coal, steel, or railroad industry of a particular time and place.[47] We would want to know of the influence that industry exerted on the jurists or legislatures, or of the socio-economic demands on particular regions or towns.[48] Or, perhaps, we need even more particular contextualizations, such as the biographical context of the jurist. Where did he come from, what was his race, his sex, his politics, what did he want? Doesn't it matter if our jurist is a William Douglas or Skelly Wright, a Rufus Peckham or Edward White?[49]

All of these particularized contexts, like the general ones already discussed, take us "away" from the text of the twelve decisions and into some

Household Labor, 1850–1880, 103 *Yale Law Journal* 1073 (1994); Reva Siegel, The Modernization of Marital Status Law: Adjudicating Wives' Rights to Earnings, 1860–1930, 82 *Georgetown Law Journal* 2127 (1994). On law and race, Ian Haney Lopez, *White by Law: The Legal Construction of Race* (New York: New York University Press, 2006); David Roediger, *The Wages of Whiteness: Race and the Making of the American Working Class* (London: Verso, 2007). On law and politics, Arthur Schlesinger, Jr., *The Cycles of American History* (New York: Mariner, 1999). On law and international relations, Andrew Fitzmaurice, *Sovereignty, Property, and Empire, 1500–2000* (Cambridge: Cambridge University Press, 2014). On law and philosophy, Ronald Dworkin, *Law's Empire* (Cambridge, MA: Harvard University Press, 1986); R. H. Helmholz, *Natural Law in Court: A History of Legal Theory in Practice* (Cambridge, MA: Harvard University Press, 2015); Peter Stein, *Legal Evolution: The Story of an Idea* (Cambridge: Cambridge University Press, 1980).

47 See, e.g., James Willard Hurst, *Law and Economic Growth: The Legal History of the Lumber Industry in Wisconsin, 1836–1915* (Cambridge, MA: Harvard University Press, 1964); Barbara Young Welke, *Recasting American Liberty: Gender, Race, Law, and the Railroad Revolution, 1865–1920* (Cambridge: Cambridge University Press, 2001); Robert Nelson, *The Making of Federal Coal Policy* (Durham, NC: Duke University Press, 2012).

48 See, e.g., Andrew Wender Cohen, *The Racketeer's Progress: Chicago and the Struggle for the Modern American Economy, 1900–1940* (Cambridge: Cambridge University Press, 2004); Howard Gillete, Jr., *Between Justice and Beauty: Race, Planning, and the Failure of Urban Policy in Washington, D.C.* (Philadelphia: University of Pennsylvania Press, 2006).

49 See, e.g., Barry Cushman, The Secret Lives of the Four Horsemen, 83 *Virginia Law Review* 559 (1997); Richard Fallon, Greatness in a Lower Federal Court Judge: The Case of J. Skelly Wright, 61 *Loyola Law Review* 29 (2015); Morton Horwitz, The Warren Court: Rediscovering the Link Between Law and Culture, 55 *University of Chicago Law Review* 4450 (1988); Melvin Urofsky, Conflict Among the Brethren: Felix Frankfurter, William O. Douglas and the Clash of Personalities and Philosophies on the United States Supreme Court, 1988 *Duke Law Journal* 71 (1988).

context ostensibly "outside" of law and beyond it. Before turning to the legal context with which I'm concerned, I want to distinguish a related and much more familiar kind of particularizing context. This move away from the case and toward a particular context is what I want to call the move toward the "Body of Law." Here we would expect an effort to pull out those cases that "belong" to certain Bodies, such as Property Law,[50] Constitutional Law,[51] or Antitrust Law.[52] Thus the nuisance cases would get contextualized by positioning them along with other nuisance cases, as well as with "related" doctrines such as trespass or servitudes. The takings cases might go in either the Property Law body or the Constitutional Law body or both, and would need contextualization by citing other decisions related to eminent domain and the police power, implementing these rules in both similar and differing factual disputes. Or, in addition to contextualizing the takings cases with more takings cases, we might contextualize them with more constitutional decisions dealing with other amendments, such as the Fourteenth. The Sherman Act cases go in the body of Antitrust Law, with similar contextual demands. The assumption underlying each of these groupings into discrete Bodies of Law is this: We understand the meaning of a rule by contrasting it with other fact patterns in which that rule has been articulated, as well as with other rules that are different in an important way but similar enough that we would still claim them in the same Body. All of this goes to what we can call the "doctrinal context" for a given decision, which is basically the association of rules with other rules, concepts with other concepts, all in the service of fleshing out the lexicon.

A second and related context is what is often called the "policy" context. Here, we stick within the confines of the Body of Law, but instead of seeking meaning through a slideshow of various fact patterns in which the rule is implemented (this is basically the norm in the law school classroom), we look for law's meaning in its normative implications (this happens in the classroom as well, but it is a marginal activity compared with the search for doctrinal or lexical context). What is the policy favored by the rule, who wins, who loses, what might happen if the rule is tweaked this way or that? What is the most reasonable way in which the rule can

[50] See, e.g., Joseph Singer et al., *Property Law* (6th ed.) (Frederick, MD: Wolters Kluwer, 2014).

[51] See, e.g., Lawrence Tribe, *American Constitutional Law, Issue 1* (New York: Foundation Press, 1978).

[52] See, e.g., Einer Elhague and Damien Geradin, *Global Antitrust Law and Economics* (New York: Foundation Press, 2011).

be elaborated? Again, the context here is still lexical, in the sense that the scene of meaning is restricted to those rules thought to constitute the body. The context shifts a bit, though, as we emphasize the policy consequence in choosing one lexical statement over another.[53]

The Context of Legal Thought

What all of this goes to show is a widespread expectation that a decent analysis of the twelve jurists must involve at least one of the three

53 A great deal of legal scholarship is of this kind. Helpful examples, often blending nonlegal contexts with normative analysis, include the following. On nuisance, see e.g., John McLaren, Nuisance Law and the Industrial Revolution – Some Lessons from Social History, 3 *Oxford Journal of Legal Studies* 155 (1983); Joel Brenner, Nuisance Law and the Industrial Revolution, 3 *Journal of Legal Studies* 403 (1974); John Edward Cribbet, Concepts in Transition: The Search for a New Definition of Property, *University of Illinois Law Review* 1 (1986); Robert Bone, Normative Theory and Legal Doctrine in American Nuisance Law: 1850–1920, 59 *Southern California Law Review* 1101 (1986); Henry Smith, Exclusion and Property Rules in the Law of Nuisance, 90 *Virginia Law Review* 965 (2004); Gregory Alexander, The Social-Obligation Norm in American Property Law, 94 *Cornell Law Rev* 745 (2009). On takings, see, e.g., Frank Michelman, Possession versus Distribution in the Constitutional Idea of Property, 72 *Iowa Law Rev* 1319 (1987); Frank Michelman, Property, Utility, and Fairness: Comments on the Ethical Foundations of "Just Compensation" Law, 80 *Harvard Law Review* 1165 (1967); Harry Scheiber, *The Road to Munn: Eminent Domain and the Concept of Public Purpose in the State Courts, in Perspectives of American History* (Donald Fleming and Bernard Bailyn, eds.) (Cambridge, MA: Harvard University Press, 1970); Joseph Sax, Takings, Private Property, and Public Rights, 81 *Yale Law Journal* 149 (1971). On housing, see, e.g., Edward Rabin, The Revolution in Landlord-Tenant Law: Causes and Consequences, 69 *Cornell Law Rev* 517 (1984); Lawrence Friedman, Comments on Edward H. Rabin, The Revolution in Residential Landlord-Tenant Law: Causes and Consequences, 69 *Cornell Law Rev* 585 (1984); Bruce Ackerman, Regulating Slum Housing Markets on Behalf of the Poor: Of Housing Codes, Housing Subsidies and Income Redistribution Policy, 80 *Yale Law Journal* 1093 (1971); Samuel Abbot, Housing Policy, Housing Codes, and Tenant Remedies: An Integration, 56 *Boston University Law Review* 1 (1976). On the Sherman Act, see, e.g., Robert H. Bork, *The Antitrust Paradox: A Policy at War with Itself* (New York: Free Press, 1978); Tony Freyer, *Antitrust and Global Capitalism, 1930–2004* (Cambridge: Cambridge University Press, 2006); Peritz, supra note 10; Eleanor M. Fox, The Sherman Antitrust Act and the World – Let Freedom Ring, 59 *Antitrust Law Journal* 109 (1990). On constitutional intersections with antitrust issues, see, e.g., Herbert Hovenkamp, Regulatory Conflict in the Gilded Age: Federalism and the Railroad Problem, 97 *Yale Law Journal* 1017 (1988); Herbert Hovenkamp, The Antitrust Movement and the Rise of Industrial Organization, 68 *Texas Law Review* 105 (1989); James May, Antitrust in the Formative Era: Political and Economic Theory in Constitutional and Antitrust Analysis, 1880–1918, 50 *Ohio State Law Journal* 257 (1989); Alan Meese, Liberty and Antitrust in the Formative Era, 79 *Boston University Law Review* 1 (1999); William H. Page, Legal Realism and the Shaping of Modern Antitrust, 44 *Emory Law Journal* 1 (1995).

contextualizations I have just outlined: (1) general contexts, such as shifts in the history of capitalism or social theory, (2) particular nonlegal contexts, such as industrial influence, region, or biography, and (3) the doctrinal context, conventionally understood as collections of legal concepts and rules. Why violate these expectations? Continuing from the discussion in Chapter 3, I want to suggest a fourth contextualization for our twelve jurists, that of the *legal context*. The legal context, in its way, combines aspects of the prior three. It is structural and therefore a kind of general context. It is also generated out of close attention to a jurist's practice of legal argument, and as it is so thoroughly about practice, it is a context that is also "concrete." The legal context is also concerned with the lexical terrain of doctrine, though rather than seeing legal concepts as the settled outcome, the view of legal context understands doctrine as an open-ended passageway inviting a style of practice. Nevertheless, despite these connections between the historical context of legal thought and the three contexts I have surveyed over the last few pages, this fourth contextualization – the context of legal thought – remains distinct. It will be useful to review the elements of the historical context of legal thought before highlighting the legal context in which I have placed the twelve jurists.

At a preconceptual level of legal thought is a jurist's *legal grammar*. In the language system of liberal legalism, this grammar is constituted by an antinomy and a mediation. The antinomy emerges out of the contest between the twin theses of free competition and social control. In the valence of ongoing work in political economy, we saw these theses swirling in and around the last two chapters. The mediation of the antinomy is offered by way of a third thesis, that of a naturalizing juridical science. I will come back to this mediating work momentarily. In contrast with the legal grammar is the plane of *legal concepts*. Legal concepts are clusters of rules, fragments of technical knowledge. We expect legal concepts to be "settled," or, at least, we expect the work of adjudication to be focused on their settlement. Once a jurist knows the rules of the concept, according to this belief, he just needs to apply them in the context of particular facts. However, in the jurisprudence of style we expect legal concepts to have a pervasive indeterminacy. Knowing the technical space of the rules is necessary for the jurist to do his work, but it is hardly sufficient in the effort to know the full legal context. For example, knowing the rules of nuisance or eminent domain or the police power or the commerce clause or monopolization is important, but this knowledge only presents a threshold for the jurist's work to begin, not its end. The end of the work is the *legal decision*, that juridical choice to offer a lexical statement as the end of the line.

There are now three points in the history of this legal context: the three theses in the constitutive grammar of liberal legal thought, legal concepts (such as nuisance, etc.), and the jurist's ultimate resolution of the dispute, the decision. If we remove the grammar from the equation, we get what above I was calling "doctrinal contextualization." Legal concepts, in this familiar view, are filled out through a review of cases that appear relevant to a particular "Body of Law," where rules gain meaning on the one hand through application in certain factual scenarios and on the other hand through their association with other rules. In contrast, what I emphasized in the discussion of the twelve jurists in Chapters 4 and 5 was both the background grammar and the *style* of argumentative practice. A jurist's style of argumentative practice therefore represents a fourth point in the elaboration of legal context, and yet another point missed in the three traditional forms of historical contextualization. As I have suggested, a style of argumentative practice is the way in which jurists, operating from certain grammatical presumptions (i.e., the three theses), gain intellectual momentum as they move from the grammar through the open terrain of the lexicon and out toward a legal decision. That is, given the absence of any neutral or necessary way in which to choose among the available rule-applications in a given legal concept, jurists resort to recurring argumentative pathways in their operation of the lexicon.

All together now, placing the twelve jurists in the context of legal thought requires an identification of (1) the background grammar, (2) the relevant lexicon, (3) the decision, and (4) the style in which the jurist fashions an argumentative practice in the passage from the grammar to the decision. In my discussion of the twelve jurists, I attempted to do exactly that. If I had been developing a doctrinal context, the discussion would have looked much more like that of a hornbook. If I had been developing the cases in a more general context, it might have looked more like Rudolph Peritz' *Competition Policy in America* or Gregory Alexander's *Commodity and Propriety*. Instead, the discussion focused on their legal context, the flow of argumentative practice in which jurists moved from grammar through concepts to decision.

That flow – the legal context – was this. The founding elements of civil society are rights-bearing individuals. These rights-bearing individuals are natural owners, since they come into the world possessing natural ownership over their bodies. As they own their bodies, they also own the labor their bodies produce. All individuals are equal in this respect, since no person comes into the world with natural superiority over another. In this equality of ownership, all rights-bearing individuals have an equal right to express their will through the use of their labor, and the things they acquire with that labor. However, while there is a founding premise of equality of use, it needn't follow that all uses are equal. In fact, some uses are naturally beneficial, others are not. Or, if you like, some uses are reasonable, while others are not. In either case, civil society is bettered through the proliferation of good uses, and harmed in the spread of the bad. The proliferation of good uses, in labor and things, makes for good social progress through the vehicle of competition.

The equal right of the individual in the exercise of his will is the spark in the engine of good competition, the engine driving civil society forward. But there are problems here that necessitate the intervention of the state. First, a political society must form in order to protect the equal rights of individuals. Crime, tort, and war are constant threats to freedom. A constitution comes into being in response, and the chief aim of the supreme public law is the protection of individual rights as against the state itself. The constitutional power to regulate interstate commerce is of a piece with this central mandate. Further, private laws are required to protect individuals as against one another. Second, political society must decide important questions about how the engine of social progress really works. When does the exercise of individualism go wrong, failing to spark the competitive engine? What if the sparks are firing, but firing so hard the engine runs too hot? These questions unpack in two different ways, though these ways end up being very largely the same thing.

On the one side, political society assigns the task of distinguishing the good from the bad to the legislature. Through its police power, the state decides when certain uses of property are unnatural, unreasonable, or otherwise harmful to society. In the exercise of this power, the state prohibits certain uses while allowing the individual to retain ownership. However, the state may also confiscate the property entirely if the confiscation is in the service of the social good, and the state has paid the owner for his loss. Similarly, the federal commerce power aims at the maintenance of good uses as against the bad. In the exercise of the police power, the power of eminent domain, or the commerce power, state action is decidedly *political*. The exercise is taken, by definition, because it is thought to make society *better*. On the other side, political society assigns the task of distinguishing good from bad uses to the jurist. This determination might be dressed as a competition between purely individual wills. If so, the jurist can answer by navigating the rules of a legal concept, such as private nuisance or monopoly. Or the determination might be dressed as a competition between an individual will and the will of the state. If so, the jurist can answer by navigating the rules of concepts such as public nuisance or eminent domain or "competition" itself. Of course, the jurist's work concerns the political economy of free competition in every case, just as it concerns the operation of social control. In certain contexts the jurist foregrounds "competition" as a legal concept, but in others leaves it as a background premise.

Now what should begin to come into view is the mediating project of naturalizing juridical science, the third grammatical thesis in liberal legal thought. This mediating project offers jurists two historical styles – the classic and the modern – and each of the two styles offer two distinctive forms of practice. In the classic style, at the peak of its power in the late nineteenth century and the early decades of the twentieth, jurists practice either of these two forms of naturalizing juridical science:

1. A jurist begins with the premise of equal rights of ownership and use, and then chooses to emphasize particular industries as midwives for the kind of good society competition breeds. In this way, the jurist backgrounds *equal rights* of use through the foregrounding of *free competition.*

or

2. A jurist begins with the premise of equal rights of ownership and use, and then highlights a perversion in a competitive field that is otherwise sound. In this way, the jurist backgrounds the value of *free competition* in and of itself and foregrounds the importance of *equal rights* of use as the basis for free competition.

In *Sanderson*, *Munn*, and *Trans-Missouri Freight Association*, jurists practiced the first form. In each case, the jurist acknowledged the priority of individual ownership and equal rights of use. This acknowledgment was quickly backgrounded, however, as the jurist shifted toward the field of competition itself, and the way in which competition is fueled by good industrial production. Of course, the seam in the argument is what counts as "good" production. For while the coal company in *Sanderson* was on the right side of reason, the grain elevator operators and the freight association in *Munn* and *Trans-Missouri*, respectively, were in the wrong. In *Sullivan*, *Pumpelly*, and *Standard Oil*, jurists practiced the classic style in its second form. In each case, the jurist acknowledged the priority of individual ownership and equal rights of use. However, and unlike in the prior three cases, here the jurists gave the priority of individual rights momentum by pointing to a defect in the competitive field. In *Sullivan*, that defect arose in the steel company's use of artificial means, whereas in *Standard Oil* it arose in the oil company's unreasonable abuses of competitor's rights of use, which all amounts to the same thing. In *Pumpelly*, the defect arose in the state's interference in the market's prerequisite, namely, individual rights.

How does the classic style morph into the modern style? Again, jurists practice two forms:

1. A jurist begins with the premise of *social control* and an assumption about the prevalence of market failure, and while noting the relevance of equal rights of use, emphasizes the importance of *regulating competition* for the greater scheme of the social good.

or

2. A jurist begins with the premise of *social control* and an assumption about the prevalence of market failure, and while noting the relevance of the competitive impulse in individual will, emphasizes the importance of *equal rights* of use.

In *Parker, Berman*, and *Courtesy Sandwich*, jurists practiced the first form. These argumentative practices dutifully nod in the direction of the thesis of free competition, but are soaked in the thesis of social control. Markets fail persistently, and as a result, they are managed aggressively. Typically, it is the state that does the managing, as was the case in each of these three disputes, in California, Washington, DC, and New York. Interestingly, however, the jurist in *Appalachian Coals* suggested that, if need be, private actors might also do well at the managing. The coal market was failing, and so it required significant intervention. The state wasn't doing it, but it needed getting done. That said, *Appalachian Coals*, along with *Edwards* and *Boomer*, reflect the second form in the modern style. Here, social control over failing markets is acknowledged, but the momentum turns toward the protection of individual rights as a fundamental prerequisite of social well-being.

Chapters 4 and 5 suggested how the classic and modern styles flow from a preconceptual grammatical plane through the indeterminate space of legal concepts on the way to legal decisions. The classic style foregrounds the thesis of free competition over the thesis of social control, but jurists still have discretion to choose at various hinge points, hence the break into two forms. Similarly, in the modern style jurists foreground the thesis of social control over free competition, but once again, there is a hinge point when it comes to whether the social good is best served in deferring to the larger social field or in the more particular space of individual rights. What still needs answering is the question of why these jurists never balked at what seemed an outright contradiction between the two theses and the unmasking of impersonal adjudication as ideological maneuver. The answer here involves another aspect of the classic and modern styles, and this is the way that they each in their different ways achieve the effect of legal necessity, offering the audience harmony's law. These styles of legal argument are "scientific" in character. In the classic style, natural science is taken as the preferred analogue, whereas in the modern style, it is the expertise of the social sciences. In both cases, a naturalizing juridical science ostensibly brings a settling and stabilizing consonance to what is always only an *appearance* of dissonance in the legal conflict.

In the classic style, the name for naturalizing juridical science is *formalism*. Formalism, in other words, is the classic manifestation of the third thesis in liberal legal thought, the thesis demanding resolution of the antinomies wrought in the contest between the first two theses. The function of formalism is therefore to justify the practice of legal argument as something other than politics or morality. Its commitment is to uncover the inherent *legal* content of society's economic, political, and social organization, and to expound the system as a structure of concepts and rules. By uncovering this legal immanence in society, the jurist is doing what jurists do – *finding* the law, never creating it. To accuse formalism of ideology or political influence is akin to accusing mathematics of ideology in its disclosure of the golden mean. What makes formalism *formalism* is its decisive failure to actually achieve anything like this kind of certainty. The formalist production of harmony is always an illusion.

With the six jurists discussed in Chapter 4, formalism was the style of argumentative practice. In *Sanderson*, the jurist claimed that the coal company's use of an engine was not artificial and therefore a reasonable use, while the jurist in *Sullivan* claimed the use of an engine as artificial and therefore an unreasonable use. There was a natural line between reasonable use and unreasonable use, and while the line was not crossed in the first case, it was crossed in the second. We can call the style in which the jurist distinguished the arguments formalistic because of the presence of two blended elements: (1) the promise of a mathematical precision (2) that never delivers. This is the essence of formalistic justification – the classic manifestation of the third liberal thesis – the combination of a claim for the identification of some sharp line and a practice that is always ambiguous about where that line might be.

In *Sanderson* and *Sullivan*, how did our jurists know of the line, or the process in which the line could be "crossed"? The idea is that once you begin with a first principle, such as *sic utere tuo* or *damnum absque injuria*, the jurist can calculate an answer, as if it were a math problem, or find a proper consonance, as if it were a problem of counterpoint. Harmony, in any case, is forthcoming. There is no room for balancing or calculations of utility in this formalistic practice, as this would concede too much power to the jurist's own discretion. In a formalistic practice, the jurist enjoys as much dominion over the immanent world of legal principles as does the mathematician over the immanent world of numbers. These worlds preexist the juridical scientist, and his task lies only in the correct application. The task of the jurist is therefore to decide disputes about these lines with apolitical justifications, without regard to social consequences but rather with an eye toward proper renderings of the principles themselves. Where is the line between an appropriate exercise of the police power and that of eminent domain? Or the line between a perversion of the competitive impulse and good industrial innovation? The line is that drawn by nature itself, in the language of the first thesis of competition. But in the formalistic practice as we have seen it, the jurist never follows through. All we get is the illusion of closure, the illusion of a harmonious result. We are never told precisely where the lines are drawn, or how we could even know of the line's existence in the first place. Thus, for every hinge in the argument, formalism requires the jurist to mask over the presence of the hinge through *trompe l'oeil*, references to nature's most "reasonable" dictates. We know we are in the presence of formalism when a jurist articulates a principle, states that a party is either safely within or uncomfortably without the confines of that principle, and punctuates the argument with the ideologically prominent flourish of "No further demonstration required." Why is no further demonstration required, we might ask? Because there is only the illusion of demonstration, nothing more. Need the jurist be aware of the illusion himself? Not at all. Remember, this is about depicting the elements of a style of practice, not a juridical psychology.

The modern style has its own form of naturalizing juridical science, and it is called *functionalism*. Just like formalism in the classic style, functionalism is a modern liberal thesis for bringing harmony to the dissonance between the theses of free competition and social control. Indeed, functionalism and formalism have the same function, to justify the practice of legal argument as something other than politics or morality. And like formalism, functionalism has a particular form. Functionalism sees law with purposive eyes, constituting it as a perfectible approximation to a prescriptive plan of social life. However, and unlike formalism, while functionalism makes a point of not fetishizing its form, it fetishizes all the same in its teleological commitments.

With the six jurists discussed in Chapter 5, the style of argumentative practice was functionalist. In every case the jurist oriented his path by the lights of the thesis of social control. Competition, still understood as a social good, was no longer only about the clash of individual wills. Good competition was rather a function of state planning, measurable by the social welfare. How can a jurist know when state planning has gone too far, vanquishing the individual rights the jurist was tasked with protecting? When is the state properly exercising the police power? Formalist practice answered these questions by way of an analogy to the natural sciences, through resort to "natural" (reasonable) lines drawn in the universe of legal materials. In functionalist practice, the jurist avoids line-drawing exercises whenever possible, and instead seeks to answer these questions through resort to law's purpose and society's needs. The analogy is no longer to the natural science, but to the scientific expertise of its social sibling.

Did it matter in *Berman* that a private owner's property was taken and conveyed to other private owners? Or did it matter in *Courtesy Sandwich* that a private owner's property was taken for a classically *private* purpose, that of promoting economic development? Or did it matter in *Parker* that a public actor was engaged in blatantly anticompetitive behavior? Sure, it mattered. But the better questions for a functionalist style of practice are these: What have the experts identified as the relevant social problem? What social purpose is served in the legal remedy? Designations like "public" and "private" have little meaning here.

Now, it might be objected that while formalism is understandable as a juridical science because of its fidelity to an impersonal rule of law, it is more difficult to see how functionalism meets the needs of this third legal thesis. For is not the jurist's resort to social needs and consequences undeniably *political*? Does not the modern style collapse the distinction between legislation and adjudication, thereby undermining the capacity for juridical science to bring a natural harmony to the antinomy of free competition and social control? No, says the modern jurist. This is still a juridical science, but the classic jurist's reliance on form and principle is exchanged for a reliance on function and purpose, *understood in the clear light of empirical social science*. Because of the availability of social science, experts are able to understand society's needs objectively. So long as sociologists, economists, political scientists, urban planners, and all the rest can do *their* jobs, jurists can maintain faith in the thesis of naturalizing juridical science because legal rules can be tailed objectively in the meeting of the experts' prescriptions. To be sure, argumentative practices may no longer be natural in the sense that the golden mean is natural. But how much more *natural* can it be to use law as the servant of society, configuring law's purpose as the satisfaction of social need? Indeed, harmony is still very much the aim. Rather than seeking to harmonize the theses of competition and control through the disclosure of a natural legal immanence, the theses now harmonize by bringing law and society into consonance. All that has changed in the transformation from the classic to the modern style is first a switch in emphasis from the thesis of free competition to the thesis of social control, and second, a switch away from an analogue in the natural sciences and toward an analogue in the social.

Furthermore, functionalism similarly resembles formalism in its blend of precision and ambiguity, its *trompe l'oeil*. As I mentioned above, we know a formalistic practice when the jurist says that he will justify a choice for a lexical statement through a precise, line-drawing exercise. This use is reasonable, that use is not. This exercise of the police power goes too far, that exercise does not, etc. These limits are not drawn from contingent situations, but from the natural fabric of our institutions. Then, in the act of justifying this line, the jurist consistently fails to explain why the line was here and not there, or how or where this natural fabric was conceived. The jurist offers precision in puffs of smoke. A very similar effect is at work in the functionalist practice of argument. The jurist will justify a choice for some lexical statement through a precise connection between that rule's purpose and a social problem. In order to keep the impersonal and apolitical tenor of the work in sight, the jurist keeps this connection tight: it is very clear what the rule's purpose is, there is no controversy about how that purpose might realize itself in its social application; it is very clear what the social problem is, and there is no controversy about how to fix it. Nevertheless, in its effort to meet the demands of naturalizing juridical science, the functionalist style suffers just as the formalist style suffered. Functionalist justifications rely on the disclosure of right answers about the various purposes of a legal concept, the various problems in society, the right kinds of social expert to invite for support, and the rightness of social expertise in any given field. And while functionalist practice promises that the DC housing plan or California's regulation of the raisin industry or New York's interest in promoting economic development is fortified in social expertise and will meet social needs, it is always only a promise. Once again, the jurist turns out an illusion of harmony and balance, an illusion that the legal choice of one lexical statement over another is impersonal rather than ideological. It is still an illusion, all the same.

To round out this discussion of the legal context in which I situated our twelve jurists, let me remind the reader of how this contextualization was atypical as legal historiography. What *is* typical is to place a legal decision in a general historical context, or a more particular context, or to read a case for its "rule" and then place that rule in the doctrinal context of some "Body of Law." A fourth historical context, and the one that I am highlighting here, is the legal context of liberal legal thought. Legal thought is the name for the entirety of a language system's structure and style. The *legal structure* includes legal grammar and the lexicon of legal concepts. The manner in which a jurist moves from grammar through concept and toward decision is *legal style*. A basic feature of a legal style is its capacity to track the demands of the thesis of juridical science. A successful legal style therefore generates a harmonious gloss of necessity. In the classic liberal style, the way of achieving this sense of legal necessity is *formalism*, whereas in the modern liberal style that way is called *functionalism*. Both forms of practice combine aspirations toward scientific justifiability with sleight-of-hand. Once again, I must emphasize that it is not at all necessary for the jurist to have intentionally engaged in a deception. It is simply an aspect of the style.

Unavoidably, the structure of legal thought and its styles of argumentative practice are historical. Time is real, and these structures exist in a past that from moment to moment take part in a never-ending process of recession and becoming. The structures are not eternal, or at least if they are, we have no way of knowing as much. In any case, we can see them change, in time and space. We have met jurists arguing all over the United States, in California, Illinois, Wisconsin, New York, Washington, DC, and Pennsylvania. In the classic style, these jurists argued in 1871, 1876, 1886, 1897, 1904, and 1911. In the modern style, they argued in 1933, 1943, 1954, 1963, 1968, and 1970. The classic style, as a result of my sample, tends to look more popular in those years after the Civil War and before World War II, while the modern style dominates between World War II and the Vietnam War. Is this right? Is this what was really happening? If so, *why*? These are excellent questions for intellectual, social, and cultural historians, but the task of the structuralist historian is to answer a different set: What does it mean to think like a lawyer in the language of liberal legal thought? What does this entail? Are there patterns of argument, and if so, what are they, and what accounts for their recurrence? Do these styles persist over time? Do they change, and if so, how?

In the next several chapters I continue to explore these questions, but now in the shift from the classic and modern styles of legal argument to a *contemporary* one. My presumption is that, between 1870 and 1970, the classic and modern styles of liberal legal thought reigned. Between 1970 and the present, in contrast, liberal legal thought transformed once more. It is to the story of this transformation that I now turn.

PART III

PRAGMATIC LIBERALISM

7

American Pragmatism

In Part I of this book I introduced the structuralist jurisprudence of style, and applied it to a history of liberal legal thought in Part II. In the book's third and final part, I turn to the contemporary structure of liberal legal thought, what I call pragmatic liberalism. In my approach to this contemporary structure, I go beyond the legal terrain of liberalism and introduce a cultural sensibility called American Pragmatism. As I explain, it is in the late twentieth-century encounter between American Pragmatism and liberal legal thought that pragmatic liberalism comes about. After acquainting ourselves with the cultural sensibility of American Pragmatism here in Chapter 7, Chapter 8 explores the legal style of pragmatic liberalism. Chapter 9 offers a structuralist critique.

My route toward American Pragmatism begins where the last chapter left off, in the legal context of naturalizing juridical science. That discussion examined the historical practices of the classic and modern liberal styles, and how the one morphed into the other. What I avoided, however, was the explicit rivalry between these two styles. True, I noted the antinomy that exists at the level of the basic grammar, and the conflict between the twin theses of competition and control. But by "rivalry" I mean the existence, over the span of 100 years, of an intellectual debate between jurists over the right way of doing naturalizing juridical science.[1] The first wave of criticism began in the late nineteenth century. With the classic style in the public eye and the modern as the marginal upstart, jurists initially focused their critical energies on the more popular target.

[1] See, e.g., David Kennedy and William W. Fisher III, *The Canon of American Legal Thought* (Princeton, NJ: Princeton University Press, 2006).

To be sure, juridical criticism took a number of forms, and certainly, it was not all trained on the classic liberal jurists.[2] Still, an important task of what we commonly understand today as late nineteenth- and early twentieth-century legal critique (what we now often call "legal realism") was the demolition of the classic style.[3]

It is too much to sketch the intellectual history of legal realism and the left-economics that came into its own in this period of American history.[4] It is nevertheless important to say, however briefly, how this thread of critique was something other than modern liberalism.[5] Now, I do not mean to suggest that the weakening of the classic style or the arrival of legal realism caused the modern style. It is clear that the modern style was already in use, prior to the writings of many "realist" writers.[6] But what is certain is the ballooning popularity of the critical trend, spreading throughout legal academia and the courts. Of course, it may be true that in certain quarters legal realism acted as a kind of catalyst for the modern style.[7] It is still useful to distinguish the realist critique from the

[2] Famous targets included Christopher Columbus Langdell and Joseph Beale. See, e.g., Christopher Columbus Langdell, *A Selection of Cases on the Law of Contracts with References and Citations* (Boston: Little, Brown, 1871); Joseph Beale, *A Treatise on the Conflict of Laws, or Private International Law* (New York: Baker, Voorhis & Co., 1935).

[3] There are fewer areas in American jurisprudence more riddled with confusion and contrast than the question of what legal realism was "really" all about. I will not attempt to solve any of these problems here. As I suggest, I do believe that it is productive to separate out a "critical realism," which I associate with the antinomian sensibility, from a reconstructive legal realism that may or may not – it just depends on who you've designated as a realist – lead to modern liberalism. It is tempting to provide a massive list of works on legal realism, but instead I will simply offer what is possibly the most famous citation, and one of the most disputed: Karl Llewellyn, Some Realism about Realism – Responding to Dean Pound, 44 *Harvard Law Review* 1222 (1931).

[4] See, e.g., John Henry Schlegel, *American Legal Realism and Social Science* (Chapel Hill: University of North Carolina Press, 1995); G. Edward White, From Sociological Jurisprudence to Realism: Jurisprudence and Social Change in Early Twentieth Century America, 58 *Virginia Law Review* 999 (1972).

[5] Duncan Kennedy, *Three Globalizations of Legal Thought: 1850–2000* (Princeton, NJ: Princeton University Press, 2010), p. 40. Kennedy distinguishes between the antiformalist realists on the one side and "the social people," often captured in the label of "legal process," on the other. I call the "social people" modern liberals.

[6] Id. at 37–40. See also Roscoe Pound's discussion of the influence of Rudolph von Jhering in The Scope and Development of Sociological Jurisprudence, 25 *Harvard Law Review* 140 (1911).

[7] This is something like Leiter's argument with respect to the idea, for example, that the contemporary manifestation of legal realism was law and economics, rather than critical legal studies. Brian Leiter, *Naturalizing Jurisprudence: Essays on American Legal Realism and Naturalism in Legal Philosophy* (New York: Oxford University Press, 2007), p. 96. On a recent criticism of the misunderstanding of legal realism in critical legal studies,

modern practice of legal argument, and the central way in which I want to emphasize that distinction is by way of the realist critique of juridical science.

This strand of critical legal realism attacked the third thesis in the liberal legal grammar. As we have seen, classical formalism offered the jurist a route for harmonizing the antinomy between the theses of competition and control, giving the legal language both stability and a necessarily apolitical consonance.[8] The realist critique illuminated the illusory character of formalist practice, or what I have been calling the classic style of *trompe l'oeil*. When, for example, a jurist encounters a decision between a use of property that is either inappropriate because it harms others in their equal rights of use, or appropriate because it is natural and therefore conducive to good competition, we come face to face with, says the critical realist, a political choice. There is simply no way to avoid this political reality, since the so-called natural condition giving the jurist his orders is a figment of his imagination. The choice between *sic utere tuo* and *damnum absque injuria* is always about choosing winners and losers, and in the effort to dress the decision up in the language of juridical science, says the critical realist, all he does is hide that choice.

The same applies at every other hinge in classic liberal practice. Where is the line between an appropriate exercise of the police power and that of eminent domain? Where is the line between eminent domain and unconstitutional confiscation? Where is the line between a use of property that makes for good competition, and one that makes for the bad? These are the questions asked and "answered" with "mathematical precision" in the classic liberal style, since the lines are "real." Not so, says the critical realist. There are no lines, and there are no meaningful *legal* conceptions of right and wrong that preexist the jurist. The answers never exist *out there*, awaiting juridical revelation. Law only comes into being, a real law with real consequences anyway, at the moment a judge decides a dispute.[9] The stuff of decision concerns political questions of distribution, wins and losses.[10] A realist law confronts these realities.

see Brian Leiter, Legal Realism and Legal Doctrine, 163 *University of Pennsylvania Law review* 1975 (2015).

[8] Walter Wheeler Cook's trashing of Joseph Beale is a fine example. See The Logical and Legal Bases of the Conflict of Laws, 33 *Yale Law Journal* 457(1924), p. 470.

[9] Oliver Wendell Holmes, Jr., The Path of the Law, 10 *Harvard Law Review* 457 (1897).

[10] This focus on distribution is what opens the door to the modern liberal style. For discussion in the context of the legal process school, see Charles Barzun, The Forgotten Foundations of Hart and Sacks, 99 *Virginia Law Review* 1 (2013).

As I have said, this attack on juridical science is consistent with what I am calling *critical* realism.[11] "Legal realism," as a larger and largely contested movement of various personalities, was something more. For many of the realists, versions of the critique just rehearsed *called for* a particular solution, a solution sometimes framed in the modern style that soon come to dominate juridical practice. In one sense it easy to see why: the attack on liberal legalism's third thesis might have been fatal to the system. Without its mediating influence, the antinomy of liberal legalism could have caught fire, exposing the work of jurists as the activist work of often-unelected politicians. To be sure, many were keen on destroying the classic liberal style. But the destruction of the entire edifice of liberal legalism was a different and more frightening prospect. What would come in its place? In any case, what may have happened is that, in so thoroughly undermining the classic liberal manifestation of the third thesis, in its place came a new modern manifestation of that thesis. As we have already seen, indeed the modern liberal style has its own understanding of juridical science, paying partial respect to the realist critique.

I say "partial" for the following reason, a reason that would emerge in the 1970s, a full generation after the modern style entered its maturity. The modern liberal style made it unfashionable to believe in the classic juridical science of legal formalism. In this sense, modern liberals followed critical realism in rejecting the classic liberal understanding of the third thesis. Modern liberalism, however, was still *liberal*. It was at bottom a rescue operation, and so the modern liberal style retained the third thesis, but transformed it. As we have already seen, it was transformed in the light of functionalism, the modern operationalization of juridical science. Thus, modern liberalism was only partially in line with critical realism, given its refurbished faith in the third thesis. Critical realism, taken to a logical conclusion, would have been just as hostile to functionalism as it ever was to formalism.

It is this "logical" conclusion that brings us to the 1970s, the point at which my survey of the twelve jurists came to an end. I chose to end it there because, at around this time, a new wave of criticism had crashed once again on the shores of liberal legal thought. This time, however, the critique was doubled. On the one side was the second coming of a kind of retro-classical liberalism. Sometimes dubbed "neoliberalism," this was

[11] In this sense, I am basically talking of a leftist realist analysis. A wonderful contemporary example is Duncan Kennedy, The Role of Law in Economic Thought: Essays on the Fetishism of Commodities, 34 *American University Law Review* 939 (1985).

not merely a reincarnation of the classic style.[12] Rather, the emphasis of the critique drummed up the spirit of the classic style, but filtered that spirit through new economic understandings of the relation between competition and control.[13] Thus, it became a commonplace to concede the existence of market failures, a basic presumption of the modern style. However, rather than attribute that failure to the operation of individual rights in a competitive marketplace, the "new" liberals argued that the failures were actually due to state intervention.[14] And while these critics would similarly concede the unavailability of "natural law" as a means for deciding line-drawing exercises, they often replaced "nature" with "reasonableness," typically coming to the same effect.[15] Finally, the new retro-classical critics argued that functionalism was simply a form of politics, and that in having indulged this subservient view of the jurist, the Rule of Law had been denigrated, and the third thesis destroyed. It was up to the new liberals to restore the system.[16] Again, it is beyond the scope of this book to answer the question of just how prevalent neoliberalism came to be as a distinctive argumentative practice. My sense, and it will have to remain only a sense, is that it was very prevalent.

The other form of critique applied to the moderns here in the 1970s, though really coming into its own in the 1980s, was the critical realist assault on functionalism. As I have already suggested, a version of this critique was available as early as the first assault on classical formalism.[17] For while the modern style recoiled at much of the classic liberal posture, it went on to motivate the thesis of juridical science all the same. Critical realism, in its militant stance against reification, might as well have been

[12] Henry Smith's work is a good example of the effort to reinvent the classic style without falling prey to some of its classic failings. See, e.g., Henry Smith, Property as the Law of Things, 125 *Harvard Law Review* 1691 (2012).

[13] A popular example of the debate is expressed in an exchange between Ronald Dworkin and Richard Posner. See Richard Posner, The Ethical and Political Bases of the Efficiency Norm in Common Law Adjudication, 8 *Hofstra Law Review* 487 (1980); Ronald Dworkin, Why Efficiency? A Response to Professors Calabresi and Posner, 8 *Hofstra Law Review* 563 (1980).

[14] See, e.g., Friedrich Hayek, *The Constitution of Liberty* (Chicago: University of Chicago Press, 1978).

[15] For contemporary examples, see Lief Carter and Thomas Burke, *Reason in Law* (Chicago: Chicago University Press, 2016); Martin Shapiro and Alec Stone Sweet, *On Law, Politics, and Judicialization* (New York: Oxford University Press, 2002).

[16] See, e.g., Richard Epstein, *The Classic Liberal Constitution* (Cambridge, MA: Harvard University Press, 2014).

[17] Indeed, it is apparent how Felix Cohen's assault on classic legal thought was just as apt with regard to his own functionalist reconstruction. Felix Cohen, Transcendental Nonsense and the Functional Approach, 35 *Columbia Law Review* 809 (1935).

directed against the moderns. (Though, again, there seemed to be little taste for the alternatives.) According to the new critics, the modern search for objectivism through appeals to the social sciences revealed nothing but the perspective an expert adopts when doing the work experts do.[18] Just as the classic style was undermined in its failure to find objectivity in the immanent universe of legal material, so too did the modern style fail to find objectivity in the social world. Questions accumulate, unanswered: Why the needs of society over the needs of the subordinated? Why the needs of society over the needs of the elite? Who are the subordinated, anyway, and why? What is society, anyway, and where? What counts as a need, and not an interest? Who decides? Social scientists? Why, and which ones? In this version of the critique, realism was deployed now in the 1970s and 1980s against the moderns in symmetry with the critique raised against the classicists at the turn of the twentieth century: law is politics, through and through.[19]

In the last third of the twentieth century, jurists working in the language of liberal legal thought increasingly found themselves painted into a corner. The game was up, and liberal legalism was in retreat. What to do? Keep on practicing as a modern liberal, but now in bad faith? Start practicing as a retro-classical liberal, also in bad faith?[20] Neither option made much sense, and with the basic styles of liberal legalism undermined, one might have expected a reasonable outcome for the practicing jurist: the final eclipse of liberal legal thought and the emergence of some other dominant language system in the world of law.[21] However reasonable this might have been, liberal legal thought did not die. Curiously, after its encounter with what were surely fatal critiques, the two legal styles of liberal legal thought simply . . . *continued on*. Sometimes oblivious of one another, sometimes at work in a single argumentative pattern, the two

[18] In the register of Science and Technology Studies, see, e.g., *States of Knowledge: The Co-Production of Science and the Social Order* (Sheila Jasanoff, ed.) (New York: Routledge, 2004). In law, see, e.g., Annelise Riles, *Collateral Knowledge: Legal Reasoning in the Global Financial Markets* (Chicago: University of Chicago Press, 2011).

[19] For this critique in the register of critical legal studies, see Gary Peller, The Metaphysics of American Law, 73 *California Law Review* 1151 (1985).

[20] For a recent treatment, see Duncan Kennedy, "A Social Psychological Interpretation of the Hermeneutic of Suspicion in Contemporary American Legal Thought," in *Searching for Contemporary Legal Thought* (Justin Desautels-Stein and Christopher Tomlins, eds.) (New York: Cambridge University Press, 2017).

[21] This is what Unger had in mind: Roberto Unger, *Democracy Realized: The Progressive Alternative* (London: Verso, 2000).

enemy styles marched ever forward, zombie-like, defeated and buried on the field of battle, but unwilling to remain in their graves.

In the rest of what follows, I tell the story of how this situation became possible. The quick answer is this. In the 1970s and 1980s, liberal legalism was in crisis. With its third thesis in jeopardy, the grammar of liberal legalism was teetering toward a collapse into nonsense. With nothing left to mediate the conflict between the theses of competition and control, and now with all of the affirmative evidence available for undermining its coherence, the language of liberal legal thought might have disintegrated. This is the point at which the cultural sensibility of American Pragmatism resurrects the slaughtered remains of liberal legalism and, breathing an unearthly life into what was a dying language, brings that language back from the dead.

The most well-known form of American Pragmatism, at least in the academic world, is surely the one traced to the writings of William James, John Dewey, and Richard Rorty, among others. I will call this form "philosophical pragmatism."[22] However, the form of American Pragmatism responsible for transforming the liberal legalism of the twentieth century into the "pragmatic liberalism" of the twenty-first is something very different, in some important ways at odds with the ideas of the philosophical pragmatists. In the discussion that follows here, I will simply call it American Pragmatism, with the understanding that I do not mean to refer to its philosophical sibling, but rather its status as a cultural sensibility in the United States.

Who is this new cultural character, "American Pragmatism"?[23] I approach it from the vantage of the arts, and in particular, music and painting. My intention is not, however, either to give an explanation of

[22] There is of course far too much to put in a single footnote, so here's just a sample of three. My apologies to Charles Sanders Peirce and Hilary Putnam, among many others. See, e.g., William James, *Pragmatism (A New Name for Some Old Ways of Thinking)* (New York: Longmans, Green, and Co., 1946); William James, *Essays on Faith and Morals* (Longmans, Green, and Co., 1947); John Dewey, *The Quest for Certainty: A Study of the Relation of Knowledge and Action* (New York: Putnam, 1960); John Dewey, *Experience and Nature* (La Salle, IL: Open Court, 1958); John Dewey, *Reconstruction in Philosophy* (Boston: Beacon Press, 1957); Richard Rorty, *Philosophy and the Mirror of Nature* (Princeton, NJ: Princeton University Press, 1979); Richard Rorty, *Philosophy and Social Hope* (London: Penguin Books, 1999); *The Philosophy of Richard Rorty* (Randalle Auxier and Lewis Edwin Hahn, eds.) (Chicago: Open Court, 2010).

[23] I want to remind the reader that in this chapter's discussion of American Pragmatism I do not attempt a structuralist history. When I turn to pragmatic *liberalism* in the next chapter, I resume the structuralist history of liberal legal thought begun in Chapter 4.

classical art and the rise of modernism, or to situate music and painting in those traditions. My point is rather to use music and painting, as they lived mostly in Europe and mostly between the days of the early Renaissance and World War II, to evoke two broad sensibilities. It is the relation with these two sensibilities that colors my depiction of American Pragmatism. The first is a "naturalizing sensibility." We will know it is near when some medium conjures up a mimetic effect, a work intended to disclose natural reality through its representational technology.[24] I hope that this sounds familiar. The naturalizing juridical science of liberal legal thought is a direct descendant of this naturalizing sensibility. The second is what I call an "antinomian sensibility." I might very well have called it any number of things, but "antinomian" captures a mood in which the author is working to undermine the very idea of nature's rules, invested in giving the lie to mimesis and the naturalizing sensibility.[25] Just as critical realism offered the jurist an anti-necessitarian posture, so too did the antinomian sensibility lack a program that might move artists "forward."[26] (I also like this label because it is suggests a kind of welcome for antinomies and

[24] For discussion, see *Erich Auerbach, Mimesis* (Willard Trask, trans.) (Garden City, NJ: Doubleday, 1957); *Refiguring Mimesis: The Representation of Reality in Western Literature* (Jonathan Holmes and Adrian Streete, eds.) (Hatfield, UK: University of Hertfordshire Press, 2005); Fredric Jameson, *The Antinomies of Realism* (London: Verso, 2015); Frank Ankersmit, Why Realism? Auerbach on the Representation of Reality, 20 *Poetics Today* 53 (1999); Hayden White, *Figural Realism: Studies in the Mimesis Effect* (Baltimore: Johns Hopkins University Press, 1999); Michel Foucault, *The Order of Things: An Archaeology of Human Sciences* (New York: Vintage Books, 1994).

[25] See, e.g., Barthes' discussion of the semiotic attack on the mythological transition from *antiphysis* to *physis*. The antinomian sensibility, as I hear it, reflects a mood in which the performer (be it musician, painter, philosopher, or jurist) experiences a naturalizing transition from *antiphysis* to *nomos* and, for some reason troubled by that experience, seeks to destabilize or destroy that turning of historical artifact into natural rule by exposing the ideological name that has been lost in the passage from history to nature. Roland Barthes, *Mythologies: The Complete Edition, in a New Translation* (Richard Howard and Annette Lavers, trans.) (New York: Hill and Wang, 2013), pp. 254–255. For a distinct but spiritually similar source, I think, see Walter Benjamin, *The Arcades Project*, (Howard Eiland and Kevin McLaughlin, trans.) (Cambridge, MA: Harvard University Press, 2002); Beatrice Hanssen, "Benjamin or Heidegger: Aesthetics and Politics in an Age of Technology," in *Walter Benjamin and Art* (Andrew Benjamin, ed.) (London: Continuum, 2005).

[26] This split between critique and reconstruction is some ways reflects the split between leftism and modernism that emerged in the early decades of the twentieth century. Or, to put this another way, while many modernists defined themselves in taking an antinomian stance, only a selection believed that Marxism or any other particular raft of political views followed from that stance. For discussion, see Martin Jay, *The Dialectical Imagination: A History of the Frankfurt School and the Institute of Social Research, 1923–1950* (Berkeley: University of California Press, 1973); *Aesthetics and Politics* (Fredric

chiasma, a welcome I further elaborate at the book's end.) What I will suggest later, moving to the context of the arts in the United States, is that between World War II and the 1970s, there arrived a particular way of dealing with the collision between the naturalizing and antinomian sensibilities. In a nutshell, and as I describe further below, the idea was to give the antinomian sensibility full reign at the level of the *personal*, and banish it entirely at the level of the *political*. That "way of dealing" via a powerful public-private distinction is the very stuff of American Pragmatism, the cultural sensibility that will later join the grammar of liberal legal thought, yielding a third moment in the liberal life span: from classic to modern to contemporary legal pragmatism.

A Naturalizing Sensibility

There is in the history of the arts the presence of a *naturalizing* sensibility.[27] At a very general level, it is a mood or disposition in which the artist's art intends to rope in, reflect, represent, or reveal a natural reality.[28] The aspiration of the art, in one way or another, is to explain the world to us, for the art sees what we cannot. This mood is therefore motivated: it seeks to *naturalize* experience by way of an effort to match the medium with the real by a presentation of the real through the medium.[29] As Philippe Descola has suggested, by the early seventeenth century the business of revealing Nature's true character was booming: "Now the construction of Nature had really begun! It was, to be sure, a social and ideological construction, but it was also a practical one thanks to the expertise of clockmakers, glass producers, and lens grinders and of all the craftsmen who made laboratory experimentation possible."[30]

Jameson, ed.) (London: Verso, 2007); Fredric Jameson, *The Modernist Papers* (London: Verso, 2007).

[27] Quine's view and the naturalistic "turn" in philosophy represents a narrower case of the broader naturalizing sensibility that I am after. W. V. Quine, *Ontological Relativity and Other Essays* (New York: Columbia University Press, 1969). For discussion, see, e.g., John Ryder, "Reconciling Pragmatism and Naturalism," in *Pragmatic Naturalism* (John Shook, ed.) (New York: Prometheus, 2003); Roger Gibson, Jr., Quine on Naturalism and Epistemology, 27 *Erkenntnis* 57 (1987).

[28] See, e.g., Georg Lukács, *Realism in Our Time: Literature and the Class Struggle* (John and Necke Mander, trans.) (New York: Harper & Row, 1971); Nelson Goodman, *Languages of Art* (Indianapolis: Hacket, 1976); Rorty, Mirror, supra note 22.

[29] For an overview, see Nick Zangwill, "Aesthetic Realism I," in *The Oxford Handbook of Aesthetics* (Jerrold Levinson, ed.) (Oxford: Oxford University Press, 2003).

[30] Philippe Descola, *Beyond Nature and Culture* (Chicago: University of Chicago Press, 2013), p. 62.

At the philosophical center of this emerging paradigm was its "founding father," as Martin Jay has called Rene Descartes.[31] As Jay pointed out: "Descartes was still enough of an ontological realist with a strong correspondence theory of truth to believe that the mind's natural geometry – its intellectual sign-system, if you will – was congruent with that in the natural world. Like the Albertian perspectivalists he so resembled, he had no qualms about naturalizing a particular visual practice and lifting it outside history."[32]

This Renaissance construction of the naturalizing sensibility might have been ubiquitous, but I will focus on two of its early sites in the arts: music and painting. As we traditionally encounter it today in a place like the United States, the naturalizing sensibility pivots around an idea that has made passing mention over the last three chapters: *harmony*. On this view, natural reality is itself harmonious. It is the vagrancy of human experience that is not. The end of art is to *prove* to the audience that harmony belies nature, if only we could see and hear.[33] Art's task is to demonstrate this harmony through representation of the real, and not through mere analogy.[34] Well before Descartes' "natural geometry of the mind" made it on the scene, somewhere around the time of Charlemagne medieval monks discovered the beginnings of a "natural" harmony of sound.[35] They found that if you plucked a string of a certain length, and then plucked it a second time, but after the string had been cut exactly in half, you would hear the same note, only plucked at a different pitch. The monks called the latter pitch an "octave" higher than the former. Later on, it was found that if you divided the octave into twelve notes, there would be ten notes to choose from in the space between the two notes you had already plucked.[36] Hence the series of twelve in the octave, referred to as

[31] Martin Jay, *Downcast Eyes: The Denigration of Vision in Twentieth-Century French Thought* (Berkeley: University of California Press, 1994), at 70.

[32] Id. at 80.

[33] For a discussion on the early Greek development of harmony, see J. Peter Burkholder et al., *A History of Western Music* (New York: W.W. Norton & Company, 2014), pp. 11–18.

[34] Foucault, Order of Things, supra note 23, at 17.

[35] Burkholder, History, supra note 33, at 29.

[36] Originally the Church called this an octave because in banning the use of certain pitches for being too "seductive," the "natural" number of pitches came to eight, hence the label "octave." Later on, as the church's hold relaxed and the outlawed pitches were allowed use, we ended up with twelve pitches. But the old label "octave" was retained anyway. See Howard Goodall, *The Story of Music: From Babylon to the Beatles: How Music Has Shaped Civilization* (New York: Pegasus Books, 2013), p. 20.

the chromatic scale.[37] This series of twelve, already on its way toward naturalizing our sense of sound, is "chromatic" because the series exhausts the palette of colors from which the artist may choose. The idea of harmony comes into play once we start to think about how to arrange the colors, or tones, or laws, whatever you like, by plucking various notes, and then clusters of notes called chords, simultaneously. The essence of harmony is reconciliation. It is the reconciliation of disagreement; perhaps a disagreement between dissonant sounds, dissonant colors, dissonant figures, and so on. In music, harmony comes about either vertically, in the context of a harmonious chord of pitches, or horizontally, in the contrapuntal sequence of consonance *resolving* dissonance. The rub, of course, inheres in the ability to pronounce first on when there is dissonance, and second, when the dissonance resolves in harmonious consonance. Who decides?[38]

Indeed, if we imagine our monks examining their stretched-out strings, one might wonder how one could ever know which notes (those twelve points in a given octave) might harmoniously "unite," and which would not. The question was conventionally answered in the register of mathematics. If you pluck a string and, let's say, we hear an A, and at the same time pluck that string five steps up from A, giving us an E, the A and the E together formed a perfect mathematical ratio, a harmonic consonance.[39] These ratios in the harmonic series comprised the circle of fifths, the entire point of which was to give musicians a skeleton key for decoding the natural harmony of sound.[40] Armed with devices like the circle of fifths,

[37] Interestingly, given the present interest in showing the presence of a naturalizing sensibility across disciplines, it is worth reminding the reader that the scale that uses all of the twelve pitches, each separated by the smallest intervals in the system (semitones), is called the *chromatic* scale. The more common *diatonic* scales include only two semitones and five whole tones. For further discussions of harmony, see Heinrich Schenker, *Harmony* (Elizabeth Mann Borgese, trans.) (Chicago: University of Chicago Press, 1954).

[38] For a well-known discussion of interpretation in music, see Theodor Adorno, *Essays on Music* (Berkeley: University of California Press 2002), pp. 115–120. See also Peter Kivy, *Introduction to a Philosophy of Music* (Oxford: Oxford University Press, 2002); Peter Kivy, *Music, Language, and Cognition* (Oxford: Oxford University Press, 2007); Jerrold Levinson, *Musical Concerns* (Oxford: Oxford University Press, 2015); Jerrold Levinson, *Music, Art, and Metaphysics* (Ithaca, NY: Cornell University Press, 1991).

[39] For discussion, see Kenneth Levy, Is Tonality a Natural Law? 132 *Proceedings of the American Philosophical Society* 299 (1988). See also *The New Harvard Dictionary of Music* (Don Randel, ed.) (Cambridge, MA: Harvard University Press: 1986), pp. 197–199.

[40] See, e.g., Theodor Adorno, *Philosophy of New Music* (Robert Hullot-Kentor, trans.) (Minneapolis: University of Minnesota Press, 2006), p. 53.

natural harmonies were created by playing notes and chords destined for one another, and by avoiding those that did not.[41]

The production of naturalizing harmonies represented a major development in the work of composers, as they increasingly used mathematical ratios (whether consciously or not) to "reveal" a natural order of sound, an order that existed independently of the artist. And yet, for all of the power disclosed in the discoveries of the harmonic series, it was not until the seventeenth century that music began, in the eyes of its authors, to really track the real. In the work of Arcangelo Corelli, for instance, a new tactic joined the naturalizing effort.[42] For Corelli, the music of the time failed to transition well between loud and soft. Usually the instruments were such that the composer had to choose one or the other – loud or soft – without being able to switch easily between the two. In working out the notion of dynamics, Corelli found a more "realistic" sound that at times might break off disjointedly in the handing of a loud voice over to a soft and back again. Or, in the effort to punctuate the music with smooth and undulating waves, softening the rough edges between loud and soft, instruments could gradually shift between borders rather than violently changing planes.[43] As Howard Goodall has written, "What composers could impose instead of incremental change were more abrupt contrasts of loud and soft, like the juxtaposition of light and shade, chiaroscuro, in painting."[44] This tactic, so familiar to us today, became identified with the new term *concerto*.[45]

In the early eighteenth century, Johann Bach Sebastian pushed the revelation of the natural order of harmonic progression to new heights.[46] This natural order was, for Bach, above all else a set of musical laws.[47] Like Corelli's reliance on clocklike rhythmic patterns, Bach understood the point of music as that of laying down the law, the law of what came

41 On the "diabolical" combinations of tones, see Goodall, The Story of Music, supra note 36, at 35.

42 Burkholder, History, supra note33, at 387. See also Hans Joachim Marx, Some Corelli Attributions Assessed, 56 *The Musical Quarterly* 88 (1970).

43 Notice here the typical use in discussions of music in which the sound is analogized to figures in nature, like waves, clouds, breeze, and the like. For general discussion, see Suzanne Langer, *Philosophy in a New Key* (Cambridge, MA: Harvard University Press, 1942); Jennifer Robinson, The Expression and Arousal of Emotion in Music, 52 *Journal of Aesthetics and Art Criticism* 13 (1994).

44 Goodall, The Story of Music, supra note 36, at 84.

45 Randel, The New Harvard Dictionary of Music, supra note 39, at 186–187.

46 See generally, Malcolm Boyd, *Bach* (Oxford: Oxford University Press, 2000).

47 See, e.g., Wylie Sypher, *Four Stages of Renaissance Style: Transformations in Art and Literature 1400–1700* (New York: Doubleday, 1955).

to be known as counterpoint.[48] Revealing a lattice-like world of musical order, Bach's use of counterpoint in the vehicle of the fugue established some melody for a given organ, then repeated by another, and another still, repeated at various tempos and pitches. This layering of voices over and behind and in front and all over one another fashioned webs of mesmerizing complexity. Importantly for the naturalizing sensibility of which I take Bach as a formidable representative, the creation of these musical patterns of sequences and cadences was *not* the creation of music for music's sake. Bach's point was to use music in order to reveal the natural beauty of God's plan for humankind. In creating his music, Bach hoped to open a portal through which humans could better understand the harmonious world in which they lived but failed to understand. That portal, it had turned out, was built from the physics of sound.[49]

In painting, as with so many media, a similar mood had been at work.[50] Just as sound was subject to harmonious resolution, so too was color:

> Color is light, that is, it is the visible spectrum of electromagnetic waves; it therefore has to do with physics. Color is substance, that is, the material with which we can represent it; it therefore has to do with chemistry. Color is perception, that is, the process taking place in our eyes; it therefore has to do with physiology . . . Color also involves another science, mathematics, which deals with color as a structural problem. It orders the multiplicity of colors according to objective parameters, and devises models in which each individual hue has its place. Efforts to systematize color go back to antiquity, but they never grew beyond rudimentary metaphysical speculations. It was only with the advent of the exact sciences in the seventeenth century that more sophisticated models appeared.[51]

The naturalizing sensibility is sometimes rooted in the work of the fourteenth century Florentine Giotto di Bondone, a so-called father of Western pictorial art.[52] For Giotto, the purpose of the painted image was, once again, to reveal the natural world, a world that had for far too long gone

[48] For an eighteenth-century distillation of the "fundamental rules" of counterpoint, as bestowed by an "Almighty God," see Joseph Fux, *Gradus ad Parnassum* (Alfred Mann, trans.) (New York: W.W. Norton & Company, 1971), pp. 22–23.

[49] See, e.g., Peter Kivy, *Sound and Semblance: Reflections on Musical Representation* (Princeton, NJ: Princeton University Press, 1984), pp. 152–155.

[50] For a discussion of representation in painting and music and how the modes differ, see, e.g., Roger Scruton, *The Aesthetics of Music* (Oxford: Oxford University Press, 1997); Roger Scruton, *Understanding Music: Philosophy and Interpretation* (London: Bloomsbury, 2016).

[51] Karl Gerstner, *The Forms of Color: The Interaction of Visual Elements* (Cambridge, MA: MIT Press, 1990), p. 13.

[52] *Gardener's Art Through the Ages*, Vol. II (Richard Tansey and Fred Kleiner, eds.) (10th ed.) (Orlando, FL: Harcourt Brace, 1996), p. 634. See also Giorgio Vasari, *Lives of the*

obscured. Painting needed to be more "realistic," and in order to make it so the composition of the image needed to represent the coherence of a harmonious world, rationally and mathematically precise. Deploying "scientific" techniques that would "revolutionize" the trajectory of visual art, Giotto's images could reveal the secrets of the real, the secrets of nature.[53] The trick, and trick it was, involved *trompe l'oeil*, giving an illusory depth to what was the indisputably flat surface of the canvas.[54] Giotto's new art would give his painted images the dimensionality of sculptural form through the use of highlighted foreground and shadowy background, and reconceived ideas about perspective. As with Corelli's dynamics, now aided by the development of chiaroscuro and foreground/background spatiality, Giotto's figures looked "realer" than anything seen since the time of the Greeks.

The effort to make paintings look ever more real, once again meaning a harmonious agreement between human artifact and natural reality, accelerated throughout the Renaissance.[55] In an "early" phase, painters like Masaccio pushed Giotto's naturalizing art a step ahead, further developing the link between painting and more exact, mathematical observations. In particular, Masaccio relied on a novel use of aerial perspective from which the viewer of the painting experienced a diminution of light and precision as the image receded in the distance.[56] At the center of the painting, the place where the lines of perspective converge, Masaccio realized the fulcrum of illusion: a vanishing point drawing the eye into the depths of infinity, giving the two-dimensional canvas the "lifelike" appearance of three dimensions.[57]

Most Eminent Painters, Sculptors, and Architects (London: Macmillan, 1912); Heinrich Wölfflin, *Classic Art: An Introduction to the Italian Renaissance* (London: Phaidon, 1953).

[53] Ernst Gombrich, *The Story of Art* (London: Phaidon, 1951), pp. 144–147.

[54] See, e.g., Ernst Gombrich, *Art and Illusion: A Study in the Psychology of Pictorial Representation* (Princeton, NJ: Princeton University Press, 1956); Fred Leeman, *Hidden Images* (New York: HN Abrams, 1976).

[55] A selection of well-known works include Samuel Edgerton, Jr, *The Renaissance Rediscovery of Linear Perspective* (New York: Basic Books, 1975); Erwin Panofsky, *Perspective as Symbolic Form* (Christopher Wood, trans.) (New York: Zone Books, 1991); E.J. Dijksterhuis, *The Mechanization of the World Picture* (Oxford: Clarendon Press, 1961); Kartsen Harries, Descartes, Perspective, and the Angelic Eye, 49 *Yale French Studies* 28 (1973); Norman Bryson, *Word and Image: French Painting of the Ancien Régime* (Cambridge: Cambridge University Press, 1981); William Ivins, *On the Rationalization of Sight* (New York: Da Capo Press, 1973).

[56] Tansey and Kleiner, Gardener's, supra note 52, at 694–698.

[57] For discussion, see Charles Bouleau, *The Painter's Secret Geometry: A Study of Composition in Art* (New York: Harcourt Brace, 2014); William Ivins, *Art and Geometry: A Study in Space Intuitions* (Cambridge, MA: Harvard University Press, 1946).

These techniques reached something of a climax in the "high" phase of the Renaissance, most famously in the works of Raphael and Leonardo.[58] With respect to the naturalizing sensibility, what unites these and others of the time is a culminating commitment to the combination of mathematics and *trompe l'oeil*.[59] It is here in the promise of mathematical disambiguation and deliverance of the abstruse that, as Ernst Gombrich suggested, "harmony [was] attained."[60] In Raphael's *Philosophy*, Plato and Aristotle are at the center of a vast hall filled with the great thinkers of the ages. With its various groupings flanking the two central philosophers, and hemmed in by Apollo on the one side and Athena on the other, Raphael's painting is a mathematical marvel, creating a symmetry of forms receding toward infinity at a central vanishing point just between the heads of Plato and Aristotle. As one commentator explained, "That this stagelike space is projected on a two-dimensional surface is the consequence of the union of mathematics with pictorial science, here mastered completely."[61]

Likely the most famous of all Renaissance painters was Leonardo, an artist perhaps without rival in the use of painting to produce the experience of a naturalized artifact. The key, as we have already seen, was the pairing of an expert deployment of measured, pictorial space with a technique aimed at *confusing* the precision of that geometrical space.[62] Of a piece with the use of aerial perspective and the vanishing point to produce an illusion of depth, Leonardo's famous practice of making the math breathe, so to speak, was *sfumato*.[63] The union of these two apparently contradictory themes – spatial precision and expert ambiguity – came together in many of Leonardo's works, including his *Mona Lisa* of 1502. Leonardo's genius was to create a portrait in which the geometric precision of perspective, elevated to a masterly degree, was intentionally made ambiguous through the blurring of the sharp boundary lines demanded by the contours of Lisa's true face. That is, while Lisa, *in fact*, possessed human eyes and a human mouth and so on, with all of their "actual" features, Leonardo found that to represent those features in the most "realistic" way was to make the boundaries marking the eyes

[58] See, e.g., Gombrich, The Story of Art, supra note 53, at 218–219; Dan Pedoe, *Geometry and the Visual Arts* (New York: Dover, 2011).

[59] Jay discusses this same combination in Downcast Eyes, supra note 31, at 76.

[60] Gombrich, The Story of Art, supra note 53, at 209.

[61] Tansey and Kleiner, Gardener's, supra note 52, at 742.

[62] See, e.g., Jonathan Crary, *Modernizing Vision, in Vision and Visuality* (Hal Foster, ed.) (Seattle: Bay Press, 1988).

[63] Gombrich, The Story of Art, supra note 53, at 219.

and the corners of the mouth ambiguous, smudged, drifting in shadow. This was *sfumato*, the purpose of which was to create a mellowing in the viewer's perception, a sensation of soft confusion about what Lisa was looking at, whether she was smiling, etc.[64] Leonardo, in this high Renaissance moment, performed the naturalizing sensibility to a T. By relying at once on the promise of mathematical precision and the deliverance of smoky, smeared boundaries, Leonardo naturalized the *real* human image. It is easy enough to see how Bach's mesmerizing fugues were descendants, at once a mathematical marvel and yet entirely elusive in immanent experience.

The naturalizing sensibility, as it emerged in the fourteenth century and crystallized in the sixteenth, would proceed in various veneers.[65] By the end of the nineteenth century, that veneer was increasingly Impressionist.[66] While it might be argued that the Impressionists broke with the naturalizing sensibility, rejecting the impulse to create an image that mirrored reality, consider the converse. As Arthur Danto suggested, Impressionism was "concerned with the conquest of visual appearances, with natural differences between light and shade."[67] A reason for thinking that the effort to reveal nature in art collapsed by the time of, say, Manet's *Luncheon on the Grass*, is the notable shift away from *trompe l'oeil* and Euclidean geometry and toward a more "raw" presentation of nature's facts, of physical reality.[68] But what Manet and his followers were after was still natural reality, the way it *really* looks.[69] This meant getting away from the highly contrived effects of the vanishing point and shading that trick the mind into seeing depth where there is only surface. Rather, in turning toward a new and more "realistic" form of painting, the Impressionists sought "sincerely" to report the facts of the world, with

64 Id. 65 Typical examples include David, Poussin, Courbet, Turner, and Delacroix.

66 Classical music is sometimes said to have itself entered an impressionist phase. See, e.g., Therese Dolan, *Manet, Wagner, and Musical Culture of Their Time* (Burlington, VT: Ashgate, 2013). On the beginnings of impressionism in painting, see Sam Hunter and John Jacobus, *Modern Art: Painting, Sculpture, Architecture, Photography* (New York: Vendome Press, 1992), pp. 9–22.

67 Arthur Danto, *After the End of Art: Contemporary Art and the Pale of History* (Princeton, NJ: Princeton University Press, 1997), p. 55.

68 Clement Greenberg, "Modernist Painting," in *Aesthetics* (David Goldblatt and Lee Brown, eds.) (Upper Saddle River, NJ: Pearson, 2005), p. 28.

69 For discussion, see, e.g., Jonathan Crary, *Suspensions of Perception: Attention, Spectacle, and Modern Culture* (Cambridge, MA: MIT Press, 2001); Michael Fried, *Manet's Modernism or, The Face of Painting in the 1860s* (Chicago: University of Chicago Press, 1996).

disinterest and objectivity.[70] Striving toward beauty at reality's expense – this had been the classical tradition. As Clement Greenberg put it, "Realistic, illusionist art had dissembled the medium, using art to conceal art. Modernism used art to call attention to art."[71] Similarly, Gombrich explained, "If we trust our eyes, and not our preconceived ideas of what nature *ought to look like* according to academic rules, we shall make the most exciting discoveries."[72]

The Impressionists discovered that if we look at nature in the open, we do not see individual objects each with its own color but rather a blending of a *bright medley of tones*. (Recall the introduction of the *chromatic scale* in music, the entanglement of color and sound.) By the time Monet, Renoir, and Degas pushed Impressionism into high gear, the smooth blends of chiaroscuro and geometric perspective were eliminated in favor of quick, staccato movements of the brush, bright colors, thick crusts of paint, and an allowance for the free play of "natural" light. Why dispense with the techniques that had revealed nature so wonderfully over the past several hundred years? For the Impressionists, the real world simply did not look so neat and manicured. Natural reality was much messier, demanding a more complex rendering of the artist. In the end, Impressionism was certainly committed to the naturalizing sensibility; it was only that these artists now found a more "realistic" way of capturing the real.

Nevertheless, Impressionism does mark an important moment in the development of the naturalizing sensibility. As Renoir said toward the close of the century, "A short break came in my work about 1883. I had wrung Impressionism dry and I finally came to the conclusion that I knew neither how to paint nor to draw. In a word, Impressionism was a blind alley."[73] If the natural world was more complex in its appearance than the traditionalists had understood, and if Impressionism began the project of complicating the image in order to make it more "real," where could all of this lead? For artists that would get gobbled up under the label "Post-Impressionism,"[74] the route toward the revelation of the real truly was

[70] Manet's explanation from an 1862 catalogue is quoted in Hunter and Jacobus, Modern Art, supra note 66, at 18.

[71] Greenberg, Modernist Painting, supra note 68, at 28.

[72] Gombrich, The Story of Art, supra note 53, at 385.

[73] Hunter and Jacobus, Modern Art, supra note 66, at 20.

[74] For discussion, see Roger Fry, *Cézanne: A Study of His Development* (London: Hogarth Press, 1952); *Art Made Modern: Roger Fry's Vision of Art* (Christopher Green, ed.) (London: Merrell Holberton, 1999); Caroline Elam, *Roger Fry's Journey: From*

becoming something of a dead end. Terry Eagleton sums up the critical stance of the antinomian that was increasingly gaining traction:

> Works of realism know the truth, but pretend in a crafty act of prestidigitation that they do not: the work must first of all abstract the essence of the real, then conceal this essence by recreating it in all its supposed immediacy. The realist artefact is therefore a kind of tromp l'oeil, a surface which is also a depth, a regulative law everywhere absolute yet nowhere visible. The richly specified elements of the text are at once equivalent to and less than the totality which constitutes them; and the price which these elements pay for their privileged mediation through the whole is the loss of any real power to react critically upon it.[75]

The way forward, as we are about to see, was a turn *away* from something called natural reality. Where could that turn lead?

An Antinomian Sensibility

In many accounts, it leads to "modernism."[76] As Post-Impressionism flowered in the paintings of the Fauvists, Cubists, Surrealists, Constructivists, Dadaists, and Abstract Expressionists, the "modern" was spreading through Paris, eventually conquering New York and beyond.[77] However, rather than abide by the terms of that larger totality – modernism – I want to follow the lead of the antinomian sensibility. I use the term antinomian here to express a disposition toward insurrection, a rejection of the belief in the possibility of achieving harmonious consonance from some neutral standpoint. Its essence lies in a willing confrontation with, rather than an evasion of, a situation of antinomy. In music and painting, this antinomian sensibility involved a loss of faith in a law of harmonics in sound and color. Now the vital domain of personal experience would serve as the engine of artistic production, where one might make art *for*

the Primitives to the Post-Impressionists (Edinburgh: National Galleries of Scotland, 2006).

75 Terry Eagleton, *Ideology of the Aesthetic* (Oxford: Blackwell, 1990), pp. 324–325.

76 For discussion, see *Modernism and Modernity: The Vancouver Conference Papers* (Benjamin H. D. Buchloch et al., eds.) (Halifax: The Press of the Nova Scotia College of Art and Design, 1983); Hal Foster, *The Return of the Real* (Cambridge, MA: MIT Press, 1996); Yve-Alain Bois, *Painting as Model* (Cambridge, MA: MIT Press, 1990); Rosalind Krauss, *The Originality of the Avant-Garde and Other Modernist Myths* (Cambridge, MA: MIT Press, 1985); *Peter Burger, Theory of the Avant-Garde* (Michael Shaw, trans.) (Minneapolis: University of Minnesota Press, 1984).

77 See, e.g., Serge Guilbaut, *How New York Stole the Idea of Modern Art* (Chicago: University of Chicago Press, 1985).

art's sake. In the effort to capture natural reality, even in its Impressionist mode, art had little meaning beyond its representational aspirations, which, to be sure, were immense. But now, in the wake of the antinomian sensibility and its rejection of the representational ideal, art might fill itself with meanings the naturalizing sensibility had worked so hard to empty out.

It is worth emphasizing that nothing follows logically from having adopted this antinomian stance. There is, in other words, no one way in which this sensibility manifests a series of sounds or images. There were, and are, many. What unites them is a belief in the autonomy of the image, its necessary existence as something set off and apart from a natural motif. If we continue with painting, we find one manifestation of the antinomian sensibility in Cubism.[78] If a viewer places Leonardo's *Mona Lisa* next to Manet's *Luncheon on the Grass*, and then brings in Pablo Picasso's *Les Demoiselles d'Avignon*, perhaps we can see how that progression morphs in the acid of the antinomian sensibility.[79] Picasso's depiction of five women in their contrasting poses with their increasingly unhuman faces begs the question of whether these are "truly" women at all. Move on to Marcel Duchamp's *Nude Descending a Staircase*[80] or Georges Braque's *The Portuguese*,[81] a super pile-on in which the viewer encounters what might seem a flattened conjuring of conflicting perspectives, and one finds in Cubism an explicit rejection of the naturalizing vocation, any singular vision of the real. As the diversity of perspectives suggests, there *is no* singular vision of the real, but rather a plurality. While Cubism certainly comes back to geometry as a painter's tool, it is a science no longer pressed in the service of naturalizing anything other than the idea that nature has exploded.[82]

A second direction in which the antinomian sensibility might lead was found by abstract expressionists working in Germany, like Wassily

[78] See, e.g., Henry Kahnweiler, *The Rise of Cubism* (Henry Aronson, trans.) (New York: Wittenborn, 1949); Patricia Dee Leighten, *Re-ordering the Universe: Picasso and Anarchism, 1897–1914* (Princeton, NJ: Princeton University Press, 1989); Robert Rosenblum, *Cubism and Twentieth Century Art* (New York: Abrams, 1960).

[79] For discussion of *Les Demoiselles d'Avignon*, see Leo Steinberg, The Philosophical Brothel, 44 *October* 7 (1988).

[80] See, e.g., Thierry de Duve, *Pictorial Nominalism on Marcel Duchamp's Passage from Painting to the Readymade* (Minneapolis: University of Minnesota Press, 1991); Dada Symposium, 105 *October* (2003).

[81] See, e.g., *Picasso and Braque, a Symposium* (Lynn Zelevansky, ed.) (New York: Museum of Modern Art, 1992).

[82] See, e.g., Greenberg, Modernist Painting, supra note 68, at 29–30.

Kandinsky and Paul Klee.[83] Kandinsky's *Black Lines* from 1913, for example, inaugurated a mode of painting in which color had been "emancipated" from nature's representations, dispensing with the apparent need to match art and object. Unlike Leonardo's attempt to breathe life into his geometry, or Manet's effort to make art more real by eliminating geometry and illusion, or even in Picasso's non-Euclidean geometrical shattering of the object, here in Kandinsky the image isn't intended to describe anything natural at all.[84] Or, at any rate, nothing natural existing in the physical world. Kandinsky's exploding color formations, zigzags, and crosshatch scratches – these forms and more were, for Kandinsky, indicative of something very real, indeed, an independent *spiritual* reality.[85] Similarly, Klee understood abstract expression as a mystical enterprise, aiming at the realization of universals, sometimes in the register of an autonomous series of signs. Klee's *Around a Fish* from 1927 is indicative, with a fish immersed in a sea of unrecognizable figures. His earlier *Once Emerged from the Gray of Night* strikes a similarly nonsensical tone, albeit aiming "toward the wisdom of the stars."[86] The aspiration toward natural harmony, Klee suggested, belonged to the past.[87] Now, in contrast, "Art des not render the visible; rather it makes visible."[88]

A third but by no means final direction is Surrealism.[89] One branch of the surrealist movement was known for its attachment to automatism. In this explicitly psychoanalytic approach, the artist disengages consciousness to the extent she can, and "allows" without reason a parade of unconscious impulses, a psychic automatism to lead the way.[90] Andre Masson's *Battle of Fishes* of 1927 exemplifies this so-called automatic writing, with its writhing squiggles, birdlike creatures, and mountain peaks. Images like these sat somewhere between that of the German expressionists and what

[83] Starr Figura, *German Expressionism: The Graphic Impulse* (New York: Museum of Modern Art, 2011).

[84] Of course, abstraction can cut in many ways. It may be liberated from the object, or perhaps the image gives us the purest form in which the object is rendered. In this latter vein, we're veering back toward a naturalizing sensibility. See *Art Since 1900: 1900 to 1945, Vol. I* (Hal Foster et al., eds.) (London: Thames and Hudson, 2011), pp. 120–124.

[85] Wassily Kandinsky, *Concerning the Spiritual in Art* (M. T. H Sadler, trans.) (New York: Dover, 1977).

[86] These are the last words inscribed by Klee on the painting.

[87] See, e.g., Klee's *Ancient Harmony* from 1925.

[88] Klee, quoted in Hunter and Jacobus, Modern Art, supra note 66, at 123.

[89] William Rubin, *Dada and Surrealist Art* (New York: Abrams, 1985); Sidra Stitch, *Anxious Visions* (New York: Abbeville Press, 1990).

[90] André Breton and Philippe Soupault, *The Magnetic Fields* (London: Atlas Press, 1985).

was soon to come, most notably in the work of Salvador Dali. In this second branch of Surrealism, the abstractions of automatism were discarded in favor of a theme held dear by the naturalists: realism through illusion. In his explorations of what he called a paranoiac and delusional program aimed at the "discrediting of the world of reality,"[91] Dali produced hyper-realized images of scenes that could only exist in dreams and nightmares. As a result, *trompe l'oeil* was not put to use in the naturalization of a harmonious world, but rather in making the world more dreamlike, decidedly *unnatural*. Dali's famous painting from 1936, *Soft Construction with Boiled Beans: Premonition of Civil War*, speaks for itself.[92]

Again, similar developments in the antinomian mood were at work in the world of sound.[93] For much of its existence, musical compositions leaned on the physicality of dance or the revelation of God's image in the search for structure. Music, after all, does not have a "canvas" in the same way that painters, say, have a canvas. Once these "natural" platforms became less popular, the need for an internal architecture nevertheless continued, a need soon satisfied in the development of the sonata form. The sonata form provided composers with a readymade map for building their compositions, compositions increasingly seen as ends in and of themselves. Already in 1854, Eduard Hanslick was arguing against music's essence as the invisible fabric of a natural plan. For Hanslick, the "essence of music is sound and motion," nothing more. The nature of music "is specifically musical. By this we mean that the beautiful is not contingent upon nor in need of any subject from without."[94]

By the end of the nineteenth century, the antinomian mood was cresting. Building off of the increasing use of dissonance in the works of Franz Liszt, Gustav Mahler, and Richard Strauss, gaining momentum through Claude Debussy, and climaxing in the radical compositions of Igor Stravinsky, Arnold Schoenberg, Alban Berg, and Anton Webern, the idea that music was fundamentally in thrall to a law of harmonic

91 Dali, quoted in Hunter and Jacobus, Modern Art, supra note 66, at 183.

92 Or, to hear him speak for it, see Salvador Dali, *The Secret Life of Salvador Dali* (New York: Dover, 1993).

93 Painters and musicians and other artists often found themselves in one another's company; Schoenberg and Kandinsky were friends, for example.

94 Eduard Hanslick, *The Beautiful in Music: A Contribution to the Revisal of Musical Aesthetics* (Gustav Cohen, trans.) (Indianapolis: The Library of Liberal Arts, 1957), pp. 47–48.

progressions blew apart.[95] Everything was up for grabs. The regularity of rhythm was abandoned in Stravinsky's well-known *Rite of Spring*, trading in Corelli's clocks for the very irregular percussive blasts of nature's time. The hierarchy of harmonic combinations, as represented in the circle of fifths and families of keys, was melted down in Schoenberg's pursuit of an egalitarian atonality. Whereas in the past composers had obeyed the "laws" of perfect ratios – the octave, the fifth, the fourth – the idea was to now give the twelve tones free play without reliance on orienting roots and families.[96] The tones became orphans, happily ripping traditional expectations of the harmonious image to shreds, relying on the coming of new and unfamiliar harmonies.[97] The result was a liberating ice bath of dissonance,[98] and as Alex Ross has suggested, it was here in works like Webern's 1909 *Six Pieces* that "the age of noise" began.[99]

Obviously, there is more, much more, to be said about music and painting in the twentieth century. Thankfully, my task has been narrow. In this brief survey of painting and music I have described two sensibilities, the one exemplified in the posture of Bach, Leonardo, and Manet, the other in Schoenberg, Picasso, and Kandinsky. The purpose in outlining these naturalizing and antinomian sensibilities, as I have already said, is to provide a context for the emergence of American Pragmatism. As I will suggest, the distinctive character of American Pragmatism lies in its straggling of the two sensibilities, unwilling to either reject or accept either in their totality. But before listing the features of American Pragmatism, I want first to introduce a third layer (in addition to the first two of music and painting): that of philosophy. Once again, however, my intention is not to

95 Bryan Sims provides a helpful overview of the avant-garde as it developed in Germany and France in Bryan Sims, *Music of the Twentieth Century: Style and Structure* (New York: Schirmer Books, 1996), pp. 123–202.

96 Arnold Schoenberg, *Theory of Harmony* (Roy Carter, trans.) (Berkeley: University of California Press, 1983), pp. 238–267.

97 Or, in other words, the very idea of harmony must be expanded to include any simultaneous cluster of pitches. As Alban Berg put it, "Generally speaking, to understand this [new] language in its entirety and details means recognizing the entrance, duration, and end of all melodies, hearing the simultaneous sounding (*Zusammenklang*) of the voices not as random occurrences, but as harmonies, and experiencing the small and large concatenations and contrasts as such." Alban Berg, "Why Is Schoenberg's Music So Hard to Understand?" in *Contemporary Composers on Contemporary Music* (Elliott Schwartz and Barney Childs, eds.) (New York: Holt, Rinehart and Winston, 1967), p. 60.

98 Igor Stravinsky, *Poetics of Music in the Form of Six Lessons* (Arthur Knodel and Ingolf Dahl, trans.) (Cambridge, MA: Harvard University Press, 1942); Sims, Music of the Twentieth Century, supra note 95, at 22.

99 Alex Ross, *The Rest Is Noise: Listening to the Twentieth Century* (New York: Picador, 2007), p. 68.

explain or describe everything that was happening in philosophy at the turn of the twentieth century. Rather, my focus is only on philosophical pragmatism.[100] The reason for this is that in the work of pragmatists like William James and John Dewey, we can see, as we can also see in the works of Stravinsky and Duchamp and others, an attempt to make art *after* the antinomian encounter. To put this point another way, James and Dewey wanted to develop a philosophical sensibility that somehow continued the naturalizing theme right *through* the antinomian. This attempt was not successful, at least not in capturing the hearts and minds of the generations that followed. It is this failure that will mark the moment at which American Pragmatism took flight.

Is Philosophical Pragmatism an Antinomian Naturalism?

Delivered within a few years of the arrival of Picasso's *Demoiselles* and Stravinsky's *Rite*, over on the other side of the pond William James was inaugurating a new philosophical mood.[101] In a set of lectures delivered in Cambridge, Massachusetts (1906–1907), James spoke of a "new dawn"[102] for philosophy, in something like the way the Reformation had reworked the Christian tradition. This was the time to cast off the naturalizing sensibility, cast off philosophy as much as the arts.[103] James explained,

> When the first mathematical, logical, and natural uniformities, the first *laws*, were discovered, men were so carried away by the clearness, beauty, and simplification that resulted, that they believed themselves to have deciphered authentically the eternal thoughts of the Almighty. His mind also thundered and reverberated in syllogisms. He also thought in conic sections, squares and roots and ratios, and

[100] For historical accounts, see, e.g., Cheryl Misak, *The American Pragmatists* (Oxford: Oxford University Press, 2013); James Kloppenberg, *Uncertain Victory: Social Democracy and Progressivism in European and American Thought, 1870–1920* (Oxford: Oxford University Press, 1988); John Diggins, *The Promise of Pragmatism: Modernism and the Crisis of Knowledge and Authority* (Chicago: University of Chicago Press, 1994); David Hollinger, The Problem of Pragmatism in American History, 67 *Journal of American History* 88 (1980).

[101] It was new*ish* anyway, at least in the United States. For similar interventions abroad, see, e.g., Henri Bergson, *Key Writings* (John Mullarkey and Keith Ansell Pearson, eds.) (London: Bloomsbury, 2014); Mark Okrent, *Heidegger's Pragmatism: Understanding, Being, and the Critique of Metaphysics* (Ithaca, NY: Cornell University Press, 1988).

[102] James, Pragmatism, supra note 22, at 6.

[103] Id. at 30; John Dewey, *The Quest for Certainty* (New York: Minton, Balch and Co., 1929). For a summary of Peirce's critique of Descartes, see Richard Bernstein, *The Pragmatic Turn* (Cambridge: Polity Press, 2010), pp. 32–52.

geometrized like Euclid. He made Kepler's laws for the planets to follow; he made velocity increase proportionally to the time in falling bodies; he made the law of the sines for light to obey when refracted; he established the classes, order, families, and genera of plants and animals, and fixed the distances between them. He thought the archetypes of all things, and devised their variations; and when we rediscover any of these wondrous institutions, we seize his mind in its very literal intention. But as the sciences have developed farther, the notion has gained ground that most, perhaps all of our laws are only approximations. The laws themselves, moreover, have grown so numerous that there is no counting them; and so many rival formulations are proposed in all the branches of science that investigators have become accustomed to the notion that no theory is absolutely a transcript of reality.[104]

Here was the falling of the naturalizing sensibility on the swords of the antinomians.[105] The desire to articulate a world in conformity with the natural order of a preexisting and true reality, James explained, was and has always been a terribly infectious mystification. Nevertheless, the naturalizing sensibility can never fulfill its promise of revealing the real, precisely because it inappropriately substitutes an ideal vision of reality for the "dirt and sweat," the hard and unavoidably material and endlessly multiple facts of our actual worlds. This mystification was due in part to what James derided as rationalism, intellectualism, or spiritualism, the belief in truths that exist eternally, independently of human experience. The fault, however, was not rationalism's alone. The mystifying effects of the naturalizing sensibility were just as much the result of empirical science, exchanging a crass idealism for an equally crass materialism.[106] To be sure, empiricism, like pragmatism, is premised on experience and verification, and to a certain extent, these are sibling sensibilities.[107] And to be sure, James spoke of the need for a *radical* empiricism.[108] But the

[104] James, Pragmatism, supra note 22, at 56–57.

[105] Later, a sword of a similar sort belonged to Ludwig Wittgenstein. For discussion, see Cheryl Misak, *Cambridge Pragmatism: From Peirce and James to Ramsey and Wittgenstein* (Oxford: Oxford University Press, 2016), pp. 117–128.

[106] James, Pragmatism, supra note 22, at 72. See also Bernstein, The Pragmatic Turn, supra note 103, at 56–60; Marianne Janack, *What We Mean by Experience* (Stanford, CA: Stanford University Press, 2012), pp. 7–11.

[107] For the view that pragmatist philosophy is best read as a kind of "scientific realism," see John Shook, *Dewey's Empirical Theory of Knowledge and Reality* (Nashville: Vanderbilt University Press, 2000); John Shook, A Pragmatically Realistic Philosophy of Science, in Shook, Pragmatic Naturalism, supra note 27; Leiter, Naturalizing Jurisprudence, supra note 7, at 46–52. See also Susan Haack, *Evidence and Inquiry: A Pragmatist Reconstruction of Epistemology* (New York: Prometheus, 2009).

[108] William James, *Essays in Radical Empiricism* (Longmans, Green, and Co., 1938).

empiricist's restricted preference for sense-driven experience is not what interests the pragmatist; the pragmatist denies the subject-object relation at the heart of the empirical paradigm, denies the view that the natural sciences have a monopoly of knowledge, and seeks out instead a broader, holistic, interactive world of being.[109] As John Dewey explained a decade later, "The fact that a strictly empirical philosophy was taken by so many critics to imply an *a priori* dogma about the kind of consequences capable of existence is evidence, I think, of the inability of many philosophers to think in *concretely* empirical terms. Since the critics were themselves accustomed to get results by manipulating the concepts of consequences and practice, they assumed that even a would-be empiricist must be doing the same sort of thing."[110] Speaking further to the different views of experience sought out by the pragmatists, Dewey wrote:

> if modern tendencies are justified in putting art and creation first, then the implications of this position should be avowed and carried through. It would then be seen that science is an art, that art is practice, and that the only distinction worth drawing is not between practice and theory, but between those modes of practice that are not intelligent, not inherently and immediately enjoyable, and those which are full of enjoyed meanings. When this perception dawns, it will be a commonplace that art – the mode of activity that is charged with meanings capable of immediately enjoyed possession – is the complete culmination of nature, and that "science" is properly a handmaiden that conducts natural events to this happy issue. Thus would disappear the separations that trouble present thinking: division of everything into nature *and* experience, of experience into practice *and* theory, art *and* science, of art into useful *and* fine, menial *and* free.[111]

Rather than continue the project of mystifying concepts, in either the empiricist or rationalist versions of the naturalizing sensibility, James and Dewey both argued for the necessity of embracing a practical definition of reality and truth, where the question was never about the existence of an object, but rather the effects our conception of an object

[109] As John Ryder succinctly put it, "In a nutshell, for pragmatism experiences subsume nature, and for naturalism nature subsumes experience." Ryder, Reconciling Pragmatism and Naturalism, in Shook, Pragmatic Naturalism, supra note 27, at 62.

[110] John Dewey, The Need for a Recovery in Philosophy, in *The Pragmatism Reader* (Robert Talisse and Scott Aiken, eds.) (Princeton, NJ: Princeton University Press, 2011), p. 136. See also John Dewey, *The Development of American Pragmatism: Twentieth Century Philosophy Living School of Thought* (Literary Licensing, 2011).

[111] John Dewey, *Experience and Nature* (London: George Allen, 1929), p. 358. For further discussion of James and Dewey on this point, see Martin Jay, *Songs of Experience: Modern American and European Variations on a Universal Theme* (Berkeley: University of California Press, 2005), pp. 262–280.

are likely to have on personal experience.[112] Here we can see the pragmatic transition from the antinomian back to naturalism, a shift from the critique of nature to its embrace. For James and Dewey, as (say) for Klee, reality and truth are constantly mutating, changing, up for grabs, all too many truths and realities, only and ever to be understood in precise context.[113]

As for how we can measure the value of a given practice in personal terms, this new pragmatism offered an alternative both to the Cartesian effort to constitute truth through a matching or agreement between the artifact and a natural reality, and the neoclassical effort to gauge marginal utility. Instead, a practice was true if a practice was useful, if it *paid* us with results, and the practice was useful only and always to the extent that it could be verified and validated through actual and concrete experience.[114] The problems, as James explained, were the laborious and sometimes overwhelming demands of this holistic view of verification. It is human nature, James suggested, that we take on faith what we have never *actually* verified as having proved its usefulness; the process of verification, in other words, is all too often incomplete or not even begun, replaced with mental shortcuts, *beliefs* in the shortcut.[115] But this natural inclination to take the usefulness of concepts on faith was itself useful. As James explained, "For one truth-process completed [i.e. verified through concrete experience] there are a million in our lives that function in this state

[112] Of the many objectors to this conception, see, e.g., Bertrand Russell, *History of Western Philosophy and Its Connection with Political and Social Circumstances from the Earliest Times to the Present Day* (New York: Touchstone, 1972), p. 818. I have intentionally left Peirce out. For Peirce's articulation, see Charles Sanders Peirce, "How to Make Our Ideas Clear," in Talisse and Aiken, The Pragmatism Reader, supra note 110.

[113] James, Pragmatism, supra note 22, at 212–213. See also Alan Malachowski, James' Holism: The Human Continuum, in *The Cambridge Companion to Pragmatism* (Alan Malachowski, ed.) (New York: Cambridge University Press, 2013); Larry Hickman, *Pragmatism and Post-Postmodernism: Lessons from John Dewey* (New York: Fordham University Press, 2007), pp. 131–139. Hilary Putnam is well known for arguing that James was actually offering a view of philosophical realism. For an overview, see Hilary Putnam, *Pragmatism* (Oxford: Blackwell, 1995). For discussion, see David Hildebrand, *Beyond Realism and Antirealism: John Dewey and the Neopragmatists* (Nashville: Vanderbilt University Press, 2003); Joseph Margolis, *Pragmatism without Foundations* (Oxford: Basil Blackwell, 1986).

[114] James, Pragmatism, supra note 22, at 222. Again, the temptation to equate the pragmatic maxim with empiricism is strong. For an attempt to tease out the differences in detail, see Cheryl Misak, *Verificationism: Its History and Prospects* (New York: Routledge, 2005).

[115] For one way of making good on this presumption, see Herbert Simon, Rational Choice and the Structure of the Environment, 63 *Psychological Review* 129 (1956).

of nascency. They turn us *towards* direct verification; lead us into the *surroundings* of the objects they envisage; and then, *if everything runs on harmoniously*, we are so sure that verification is possible that we omit it, and are usually justified by all that happens. Truth lives, in fact, for the most part on a credit system."[116]

Nevertheless, James argued that as with any system of credit, we must pay up when the bill comes due. At some point, we must ask ourselves and ask each other, *is it* running harmoniously? *Are we really sure about our background practices?* That is, while it is all well and good for us to take on faith that our practices are useful – meaning that they are supported by ethical investigations of the structure of experience – and that the practice pays off, these shortcuts are not self-generating. At some point, we must take the hard look. James continued, "this all points to direct face-to-face verifications somewhere, without which the fabric of truth collapses like a financial system with no cash-basis whatever . . . But beliefs verified concretely by *somebody* are the posts of the whole superstructure."[117] If the rock-bottom necessity of facing off against common sense is lost, if the debt accumulates forever, we lose track of pragmatism's first higher-order proposal about the world: the naturalizing sensibility à la Descartes is a mystification, and nature is a space in which nothing is necessary or neutral.[118] The antinomian view of nature discloses a natural indeterminacy, but a natural indeterminacy with an "open air and possibility" where "every sort of permutation and combination is possible."[119]

James, Dewey, and others developed a powerful philosophy, homegrown in the United States, with its focus on these themes of pure experience, truth and nature, experimentalism and democracy, and more.[120] As has often been recounted, however, pragmatist philosophy in the

[116] James, Pragmatism, supra note 22, at 208. [117] Id.

[118] An influential example of this idea, but in the context of law, is John Dewey, Logical Method and Law, 10 *Cornell Law Quarterly* 17 (1924).

[119] James, Pragmatism, supra note 22, at 10. This openness has long been viewed as deeply problematic. See, e.g., Randolph Bourne, Twilight of Idols, 2 *The Seven Arts* 688 (1917). What's more, many scholars don't even see this as the critical lesson at all. See, e.g., Susan Haack, *Defending Science – within Reason: Between Scientism and Cynicism* (New York: Prometheus, 2003); Susan Haack, "Not Cynicism, but Synechism: Lessons from Classical Pragmatism," in *A Companion to Pragmatism* (John Shook and Joseph Margolis, eds.) (Malden, UK: Blackwell, 2006). For more like-minded readings, see Roberto Unger, *The Self Awakened: Pragmatism Unbound* (Cambridge, MA: Harvard University Press, 2007); Colin Koopan, *Pragmatism as Transition: Historicity and Hope in James, Dewey, and Rorty* (New York: Columbia University Press, 2009).

[120] A fun intellectual history is Louis Menand, *The Metaphysical Club: A Story of Ideas in America* (New York: Farrar, Straus and Giroux, 2001).

United States went out of fashion by the middle decades of the twentieth century.[121] Various explanations abound for this downward trend: the rise of logical empiricism, the rise of existentialism and critical theory, the fall of the economy, World War II.[122] And although any of these contexts are likely important and valuable, the one I want to emphasize now is the story of music, painting, and the naturalizing sensibility I've already been telling. That is, one way to think about the eclipse of James and Dewey after the middle decades of the twentieth century is in the register of the naturalizing and antinomian sensibilities, and the curious way in which pragmatist philosophy attempted to arrange a relation between the two. It was an arrangement, or at least, the suggestion of an arrangement, that did not catch on.[123]

I want to suggest that we can see James and Dewey as trying to have it both ways. Imagine for a moment that we land J. S. Bach or Leonardo da Vinci at James' Harvard lectures on the collapse of the naturalizing sensibility. And imagine – and it may take some Herculean leaps to imagine it – that Bach and Leonardo are at once young and impressionable but also retain something essential about their distinctive spirits. Perhaps, like James, they devise a plan for sound and color in the orienting mood of the antinomian. The antinomian sensibility is their starting point, their north star. And yet, somehow, they pursue the naturalizing impulse *anyway*. What could that mean? It would not mean that Bach, in this fictive moment, will see his fugues as revealing nature's immanent order. He no longer believes in it. And Leonardo's *Mona Lisa*, painted now in 1910, still blends *tromp l'oeil* and geometry, but perhaps, like Dali, Leonardo no longer believes that these tactics are the key for representing reality. Maybe, we could say that James, Dewey, and our imagined versions of Bach and Leonardo want to experiment with nature after having already absorbed the terrors of the antinomian. An idea of harmony's law would somehow persist in the very midst of an anti-naturalizing mood.

As this Kierkegaardian image certainly suggests, the philosophical pragmatists were asking a lot. They wanted to orient a new philosophical mood in opposition with the naturalizing sensibility while at the same

121 Morris Dickstein, "Introduction: Pragmatism Then and Now," in *The Revival of Pragmatism* (Morris Dickstein, ed.) (Durham, NH: Duke University Press, 1998), p. 9.

122 See, e.g., Bernstein, The Pragmatic Turn, supra note 103, at 11–13.

123 When philosophers speak today of pragmatism's "miraculous" resurgence, this is not the arrangement they usually have in mind. See, e.g., Joseph Margolis, *Pragmatism Ascendant: A Yard of Narrative, a Touch of Prophecy* (Stanford, CA: Stanford University Press, 2012), p. 111.

time offer a program for moving forward, beyond the antinomian stalemate. This notion of a beyond, in which philosophy would nurture a vision of an experimentalist nature, is what distinguishes philosophical pragmatism from the pragmatism that became a cultural dominant in the last third of the twentieth century: American Pragmatism. The central practice, slowly emerging after World War II, coming into its own by the 1970s, and then sliding into hegemony by the first decades of the twenty-first century, was a way of interfacing with a world in which it simply didn't matter anymore if the modes of the naturalizing sensibility continued to dominate art, music, or philosophy, or anything else for that matter, *so long as the sensibility was working*. Of course, this crass instrumentalism, divorced on the one side from a theory of the good (thus distinguishing itself from a more sophisticated form of consequentialism), and divorced on the other from a theory of an experimental nature (thus distinguishing itself from philosophical pragmatism), was something very much like the thing James and Dewey had worried about.[124] If we simply take truth to be the compliment for whatever happens to be working, and forever distance ourselves from the need to ask the hard questions about what it means for a system to be working at all, we end up worshipping the fetishes that are our shortcuts.

When philosophical pragmatism made its "neopragmatist revival" in the last third of the twentieth century, these glimpses of an "antinomian naturalism" were lost.[125] For thinkers like Richard Rorty and Stanley Fish, the antinomian sensibility was in full effect. The lessons of James and Dewey with respect to the failures of rationalism and empiricism were absorbed, soaked in the antinomian acid bath. But a striking change had taken place. James and Dewey, perhaps, were interested in pursuing antinomianism right through a naturalizing sensibility, marshaling the antinomies forward, experimentally. But for Rorty and Fish, what may have been true of the antinomian acid in the context of philosophical questions

[124] James, Pragmatism, supra note 22, at 212–218.

[125] On "neopragmatism" in the work of Rorty and Fish, see Richard Rorty, *Consequences of Pragmatism: Essays, 1972–1980* (Minneapolis: University of Minnesota Press, 1982); Richard Rorty, *Contingency, Irony, and Solidarity* (Cambridge: Cambridge University Press, 1989); Stanley Fish, *Is There a Text in This Class?: The Authority of Interpretive Communities* (Cambridge, MA: Harvard University Press, 1982); Stanley Fish, *Doing What Comes Naturally: Change, Rhetoric, and the Practice of Theory in Literary and Legal Studies* (Durham, NC: Duke University Press, 1990). See also *Deconstruction and Pragmatism* (Chantal Mouffe, ed.) (London: Routledge, 1996); *Against Theory: Literary Studies and the New Pragmatism* (W. J. T. Mitchell, ed.) (Chicago: University of Chicago Press, 1982).

about truth and knowledge was simply not true at all in the context of political and legal questions about the arrangement of our social institutions. What was hot and loud at the level of a personal metaphysics was soft and quiet, reserved and status-quo, at the level of political economy. Why? Why raise a wall between the practices of the philosopher and the practices of the jurist?

One reason for doing so concerns the worry that pragmatists will make the mistake of "marshaling the antinomies," believing that one or another political position *follows* from the antinomian sensibility. As Fish has argued, "If I am a pragmatist and hold that beliefs are internal to practices and cannot be justified by independent and general criteria, *this* belief will not lead me to lose confidence in my other beliefs or inhabit them more loosely than would be the case if I had another account of them... If you know that someone has a pragmatist account of belief, you know nothing about what he or she will do in a moment of crisis or decision."[126] Like Fish, Rorty's forays in jurisprudence similarly led him to the conclusion that the application of philosophical pragmatism to legal thought could only have banal results. Aligning himself with Richard Posner, Rorty agreed that philosophical pragmatism might be a little handy at clearing out a jurisprudential underbrush, but was useless when it came to planting the forest.[127] As Fish put it more directly, "in the wake of formalism's failure, *everything remains as it was*."[128] At bottom, the idea is that since jurists actually need to make decisions – that this is their central task – and that since philosophical pragmatism cannot help a jurist make decisions, pragmatism in law is necessarily banal.[129] Fiery at the heart, cold to the touch: there's the neopragmatist maxim for a politics of law.

I will return to this issue in Chapters 8 and 9, as I think Rorty and Fish make a serious mistake in misunderstanding all that has changed in the twentieth-century history of American legal thought. For nothing could be more misleading than the suggestion that, after the fall of formalistic practice, everything remained as it had been. Because it didn't. The

[126] Stanley Fish, "Truth and Toilets: Pragmatism and the Practices of Life," in Dickstein, The Revival of Pragmatism, supra note 121, at 420.

[127] Richard Rorty, The Banality of Pragmatism and the Poetry of Justice, 63 *Southern California Law Review* 1811 (1990), p. 1815.

[128] Dickstein, The Revival of Pragmatism, supra note 121, at 419.

[129] See also Thomas Grey, Hear the Other Side: Wallace Stevens and Pragmatist Legal Theory, 63 *Southern California Law Review* 1569 (1990); Thomas Grey, Freestanding Legal Pragmatism, 18 *Cardozo Law Review* 21 (1996).

practices of legal argument transformed after the critique of the classic liberal style, and yet again after the assault on legal functionalism. Nevertheless, it is precisely this walled-off view of pragmatism and the squandered possibility of an antinomian naturalism that sets the table for the cultural ascent of American Pragmatism.

Doing What Works: The Cultural Sensibility of American Pragmatism

Looking back from 1984, Fredric Jameson already saw the unfolding of this process all across American culture. His name for it, which I take as emblematic for the sensibility of cultural pragmatism, was pastiche.[130] For Jameson, the culture of pastiche climaxed in the United States of the 1970s.[131] Similarly, Roberto Unger has also identified this time with the beginnings of a new cultural mood, one he associates with the kind of "shrunken pragmatism" I just described.[132] Each of these ideas reflects a very particular orientation toward the naturalizing and antinomian sensibilities, and taken together, they provide the basis for the cultural sensibility of today's American Pragmatism. I define this cultural sensibility in five characteristic features. These include a priority of (1) surface over depth, or *parole* over *langue*, (2) eclectic problem solving over higher-order proposals for structural transformation, or practice over theory, (3) the present over the contemporary, (4) populism over elitism, and (5) the total commodification of nature. In each of these features there is a palpable trace of the antinomian; but unlike in the examples from music, painting, and philosophy I sketched above, there is here a general sense that the naturalizing sensibility is problematic, but a confidence in being able to just make it work anyway. American pragmatism, at bottom, is a play of denials. I sketch each of these features in turn.[133]

[130] Fredric Jameson, *Postmodernism, or, The Cultural Logic of Late Capitalism* (Durham, NC: Duke University Press, 1997), p. 9. Perry Anderson has written that in literature, "perhaps more than any other art, the most insistent motif of the new was a – playful or portentous – parasitism of the old. In Jameson's texts, the name of this device is pastiche. The source of this usage lay in Adorno's critique of what he took to be the aggressive eclecticism of Stravinsky in the Philosophy of Modern Music; but Jameson gave it a more pointed definition. Pastiche was a 'blank parody', without satiric impulse, of the styles of the past . . . it had become the most standardized signature of the postmodern." Perry Anderson, *The Origins of Postmodernity* (London: Verso, 1998), at 61.

[131] Jameson, Postmodernism, supra note 130, at 47; Anderson, The Origins of Postmodernity, supra note 130, at 84–85.

[132] Unger, The Self Awakened, supra note 119, at 44–46.

[133] I hope to soon turn in a subsequent work to a more fleshed-out discussion of what is here really a bare-bones treatment.

For Jameson, the paintings of Andy Warhol presented an early and powerful manifestation of the emerging preference for surface and anxiety about depth. Looking to Warhol's *Diamond Dust Shoes*, Jameson saw "a random collection of dead objects hanging together on the canvas like so many turnips, as shorn of their earlier life world as the pile of shoes left over from Auschwitz."[134] Unlike van Gogh's *A Pair of Boots*, visceral in its colorful depth, a conjuring of a true human experience – that of the peasant worker – Jameson suggests *Diamond Dust Shoes* as a supremely surface indication, a colorless, bloodless technology.[135] There is no human experience, no lived-in context with which to understand Warhol's depiction; it presents a "new kind of flatness or depthlessness, a new kind of superficiality in the most literal sense."[136] In what we might term an indication of passage from modern art into the *contemporary*, we can see this flat and essentially nominalist kind of practice as a consequence of the antinomian devastation of the naturalizing impulse. Rather than bear witness to a Picasso or Kandinsky's strong encounter with antinomian uncertainty, however, Warhol is instead awash in the aftermath. Knowing that "depth" no longer makes sense (since the whole terrain of post-Impressionism has apparently run its course), or at any rate, knowing that deep structures are going out of fashion fast, Warhol gave us the shoes of an anti–van Gogh: free-floating signifiers, uprooted forever from deeper conceptual context.[137]

The flatness of pragmatist pastiche is associated with a thoroughgoing eclecticism. While authors working in the antinomian mood may very well have mimicked the works of authors from the past, the mimicry was essentially historical in its effort to argue against the older use, or if not to argue against it exactly, reinvent it in the course of a campaign of change.[138] Compare, for example, Stravinsky or Bartok's adoption of vernacular musical genres in the context of their experiments with rhythm and harmony, with the eclecticism of John Adams in his current symphonies.[139] Stravinsky's music had a historical opposition in mind, a deliberate attempt to fuse scattered fragments that had not been historically understood as natural.[140] Adams' eclecticism is of an entirely

[134] Jameson, Postmodernism, supra note 130, at 8. [135] Id. at 185, 250.
[136] Id. at 9. [137] Id. at 26.
[138] Id. at 17 ("Pastiche is, like parody, the imitation of a peculiar or unique, idiosyncratic style, the wearing of a linguistic mask, speech in a dead language").
[139] Or, back in paint, we could point to Julian Schnabel or Robert Rauschenberg.
[140] Stravinsky wrote, "Of course, we seemed, Eliot and myself, to have exploited an apparent discontinuity, to have made art out of the *disjecta membra*, the quotations from other

different sort – nature needn't be killed off or reoriented in order to build it as a retrofitted point of attack. For a composer like Adams, it is already dead. Here is Alex Ross's description of a supremely eclectic Adams symphony: "It is a cut-up paradise, a stream of familiar sounds arranged in unfamiliar ways. A glitzy Hollywood fanfare gives way to a trance-like sequence of shifting beats; billowing clouds of Wagnerian harmony are dispersed by a quartet of saxophones. It is present-tense American romanticism, honoring the ghosts of Mahler and Sibelius, plugging in to minimalist processes, swiping sounds from jazz and rock, browsing the files of postwar innovation . . . winding its way through a fragmentary culture."[141] Or, in a different register consider Steve Reich's *Come Out* from 1964, among the first tape pieces in which a recording of a young African-American, Daniel Hamm, describing a beating he took in a Harlem police station, is cut up and played over and over again. The line is "I had to, like, open the bruise up and let some of the bruise blood come out to show them." Reich takes this passage, demolishes it, and then recomposes it at various speeds. Nature is rebuilt in a jarring articulation of domination and bloodshed. But now compare Reich's reaching into history and parading the past in the effort to denaturalize racial hatred with the use of the *Come Out* sample in a remix of Tortoise's *Djed*. Like Jameson's interrogation of Warhol's footwear, we can ask of John McIntyre's band, what is Hamm's voice doing there? Why? The historical relation, the deeper context, has been wiped clean. What we are seeing, or hearing if you like, is a blank and blind "imitation of dead styles, speech through all the masks and voices stored up in the imaginary museum of a now global culture."[142] It is a practice "which randomly and without principle but with gusto cannibalizes . . . styles of the past and combines them in overstimulating ensembles."[143]

Whether in the context of painting or music or philosophy or politics or cooking or parenting, etc., flat eclecticism translates the pragmatic maxim into a vernacular mantra. That maxim, as we have seen, instructs us to deal with our problems at the ground level, practically, in context, preferring solutions that *pay* over solutions enslaved to a higher-order intellectualism. Here, in the context of its vernacular manifestation, the maxim is divested of everything that made philosophical pragmatism both

poets and composers . . . the detritus that betokened a wreck. *But we used it, and anything that came to hand, to rebuild.*" Schwartz and Childs, Contemporary Composers, supra note 97, at 54.

[141] Ross, supra note 99, at 559. [142] Jameson, supra note 130, at 18. [143] Id. at 19.

uncomfortable and exciting. "Focus on problems," we are told, "not on grand theories. In solving that problem, do whatever works for you, and in the business of doing it, use whatever resources are ready at hand.[144] Avoid both the depth of structural explanation and the heights of higher-order discourse. These positions are nothing but illusion. All you can do, and all you have ever done, is just get along, doing what works, with whatever works. Stay flat, stay eclectic, and you'll find yourself happily adrift in the New Normal."[145] What is lost is James' warning: this procedure only goes so far, and as a credit system, it will crash if we never dig the depths of structural experience. The response of cultural pragmatism: "Whatever. Don't worry about it, we'll take our problems one problem at a time." Unger's riposte: "Our problem-solving conjectures, on the scale in which thought is able to accompany action, have only the pragmatic residue of the blind man's rod: we judge them by their use in enabling us to walk ahead without being knocked down."[146]

As I have already intimated, the pastiche of this "flat eclecticism" has a particular relation with history. "History," says the cultural pragmatist, "will no longer be understood as a chronology of totalizing grand narratives.[147] There is in history power and play and that's it."[148] If this is right, can we even speak intelligibly of a "modern" or a "contemporary" music, art, pragmatism, or law?[149] The pragmatist counsel to follow is that you should not, and instead tend to local contexts. As Darrin McMahon and Sam Moyn write in their introduction to *Rethinking Modern European Intellectual History*, "Everyone cultivates his or her own private garden as if writing history were a largely personal task."[150] And what of the possibility that this very approach to a flat and eclectic historiography is itself a grand narrative? "For the time being, intellectual historians seem reluctant to fight about these matters. This may represent

144 See, e.g., William Simon, Solving Problems v. Claiming Rights: The Pragmatist Challenge to Legal Liberalism, 46 *William and Mary Law Review* 127 (2004).

145 This, at any rate, is the gist of Unger's critique. Unger, The Self Awakened, supra note 119, at 45.

146 Id. at 70–71.

147 Jameson, Postmodernism, supra note 130, at 400.

148 Foucault is often tagged as the poster boy for this view of history. As I suggested in Chapters 2 and 3, I think this view is mistaken.

149 See, e.g., Kathleen Davis, *Periodization and Sovereignty: How Ideas of Feudalism and Secularization Govern the Politics of Time* (Philadelphia: University of Pennsylvania Press, 2008).

150 *Rethinking Modern European Intellectual History* (Darrin McMahon and Samuel Moyn, eds.) (New York: Oxford University Press, 2014), p. 4.

a belief that eclecticism is a good in its own right, and that intellectual history is an *inherently* eclectic field."[151]

Inherent, indeed. A few years ago the editors of the art journal *October* sent out a questionnaire to about seventy art historians, critics, and curators, asking a question about the relation between the *present* and the *contemporary*. Are these the same thing?[152] The editors asked, is Contemporary art "real or imagined? A merely local perception? A simple effect of the end of grand narratives?"[153] The responses display a certain and inevitable degree of randomness, but also a palpable idea about the current art world – the idea that art in the current conjuncture is intensely multiple, geographically dispersed, historically uncontained and unrecognizable, a time and space in which "self-legitimizing micro-perspectives have replaced grand narratives,"[154] something ultimately like a scene from *The Blob*,[155] "a Babel of unconverging artistic conversations."[156] As for those interested in defending a totality called "Contemporary Art," they face the unenviable task of forcing a world in which totalizing narratives had been displaced into the totalizing narrative of "Contemporary Art," "a paradigm of no paradigm."[157] That's enough to make your head spin. For others the effort to carve out something called "Contemporary" was pointless: either just stupid, or, more generously, "presentist and amnesiac."[158] The "Contemporary," after all, demands a totality against which it might be defined, and the historiography of pastiche simply does not have a taste for that. What is does like, what it seeks, is "a soft consensus on the immanence of the present, the empiricism of the *now*, of

[151] Id. at 11 (italics mine).

[152] Jean-Luc Nancy titled a lecture "Art Today" precisely in order to get past what he took the "contemporary's" problematic relation with the present. "So we understand that art is always contemporary because it always belongs to certain forms in the space of the contemporary, in the space of an actuality." Jean-Luc Nancy, Art Today, 9 *Journal of Visual Culture* 91 (2010), p. 92.

[153] Hal Foster et al., Questionnaire on the Contemporary, 130 *October* 3 (2009), p. 3.

[154] Though, as Jaleh Mansoor also notes, "Part of the effervescent multiplicity of the putative present, and the confusion it generates, is an 'optical allusion' brought to bear by the seeming coherence of the past." Jaleh Mansoor, 130 *October* 105 (2009).

[155] Christopher Heuer et al., 130 *October* 84 (2009).

[156] Danto, After the End of Art, supra note 67, at 148. To be clear, this quote comes from Danto's *After the End of Art*, and not from the *October Questionnaire*, but it expresses the same point.

[157] Suzanne Hudson, 130 *October* 118 (2009).

[158] Miwon Kwon, 130 *October* 13 (2009). I don't read Kwon to think of Contemporary art history this way, but rather she's describing the views of other, less friendly critics.

what we have directly in front of us, and what they have in front of them over there."[159] James Elkins, for example, defined the inquiry into Contemporary art as an inquiry into the "problems of writing *in the current mode*," though he also worried about anyone's right to speak on that current moment's behalf.[160] Still, *contemporary* collapses into the *present*, as it must. As Pamela Lee put it in her response, in the art historian's pursuit of Contemporary art "somehow we have made keeping pace with *the art of today*... a quasi-science, an intellectual cottage industry, as if we desired to enshrine the nervousness about the present moment in a permanent holding pattern."[161] In this view, a view I attribute to the cultural sensibility of American Pragmatism, a contemporary *anything* always discloses a presence everlasting, mindful of nothing but its dogmatic rejection of historical structure.

From another direction, and the direction that I am favoring here, comes the view of historians like Terry Smith and Richard Meyer (and Jameson and Unger).[162] Both concede the etymological connection between the present and the con-tempo (with time), but they reject the cultural pragmatist view that contemporary art is inevitably that art made in "the current moment." As Smith argued, "To me... this attitude [of treating Contemporary art to mean 'the art of today'] amounts to a pluralist happy mix that seeks to pull a bland idiot mask over the most irreducible fact" about Contemporary art.[163] What is that irreducible fact? Smith works through several, but the one I want to highlight here is the connection between the emergence of Contemporary art and the decline of the modern: "In the visual arts, the big story, now so blindingly obvious, is the shift – nascent during the 1950s, emergent in the 1960s, contested during the 1970s, but unmistakable since the 1980s – from modern to contemporary."[164] As for what that shift entails, Smith suggested that whereas the moderns had violently defined themselves in terms of a past overcome, or at least in the process of overcoming, the "'contemporary' comes, on this reading, to mean not 'to be with time' but '*to be out of time*,' to be suspended in a state after or beyond history, a

[159] Julieta Aranda et al., What Is Contemporary Art? Issue Two, 12 *E-Flux Journal* 1 (2010).

[160] James Elkins, 130 *October* 10 (2009).

[161] Pamela Lee, 130 *October* 25 (2009).

[162] Jameson and Unger both argue for the necessity of a totalizing historiography. Jameson, Postmodernism, supra note 130, at 400; Unger, The Self Awakened, supra note 119, at 78.

[163] Terry Smith, *What Is Contemporary Art?* (Chicago: University of Chicago Press, 2009), p. 1.

[164] Id. at 5.

condition of being always and only in a present that is without either past or future."[165] Rising above the flatness of the pragmatist pastiche, and "looking carefully, and listening for the sound behind the bluster, [we] discern a deeper set of currents, unmistakably *historical* ones."[166] In this "structural" view, the contemporary breaks with the present, becoming a proxy for something else, a form of practice immanent in but obscured by the "bland idiot masks" of the present.

Meyer takes a similar tack. "Why are you studying art history," he asked in his *October* response, "if what you really want is to write about *the current moment*?"[167] And woe to you if you do, for the "current moment," Meyer implies, is a total train wreck. For if Contemporary art does indeed possess an inalienable Presence, we will nevertheless never be able to get out of the way of Tom McDonough's question: "contemporary with *what*?"[168] That is, rather than assume that the contemporary is simply code for "our" present routines, Meyer suggests we "look beyond the individual artist or masterwork to a broader field of artistic and cultural production."[169] But unlike Smith, Meyer traces the broader fields of contemporary art history beyond the 1970s and 1980s, and back into the early twentieth-century wheelhouse of the moderns themselves.[170] Sounding a similar theme, as McDonough writes in the concluding sentence of the *October* collection, "The contemporary is not simply a temporal category whose floating free may be remedied by rejoining it to the longer continuum of the history of art; it is, more importantly, *an urgent charge to think in terms of those transversal linkages between aesthetic practice and the contested terrain of social relations*, and to ask where we stand in regard to them."[171] Ultimately, historians on this side of the contemporary/present debate suggest that if we want to know something of "the history of the new," it is this deeper structure of experience and practice that holds the key. "The current moment," "the immediate past," and "the art of today" – these are just red herrings.[172]

If American Pragmatism is a flat eclecticism of the present, it is also a flat eclecticism that eschews theory and elitism in favor of populism and the everyman.[173] This a sensibility catered for the "people," the *real*

[165] Id. at 245. [166] Id. at 246.

[167] Richard Meyer, 130 *October* 18 (2009).

[168] Richard Meyer, *What Was Contemporary Art?* (Cambridge, MA: MIT Press, 2013), p. 16; Tom McDonough, 130 *October* 123 (2009).

[169] Meyer, What was Contemporary Art, supra note 168, at 16. [170] Id. at 37.

[171] McDonough, supra note 168, at 124. [172] Id. at 280.

[173] Jameson, Postmodernism, supra note 130, at 64.

people, not the missionaries with their manifestoes.[174] Again, while a certain populism is identifiable in contemporary music and painting, it is by no means stranded there. Take our President Trump as an example. Desperately hoping to be known as a "pragmatist" and horrified by the idea that he might be labeled a member of the "elite," Trump regularly accused Hilary Clinton of falling on the wrong side of the divide.[175] Sure, *she* was an elite of the worst sort. But Trump? Billionaire, television celebrity, Wharton graduate, white-male-misogynist? Yes. An elite? Never. As Beverly Gage has suggested in a treatment of Trump and this "nastiest" of epithets, ours is a cultural sensibility in which intellectuals, elites, and fanatics get loaded on one side of the cultural fence, while pragmatists, populists, and real people solve real problems on the other.[176] Elites are dangerously out of touch, "a destructive, condescending collective, plotting against the beleaguered masses outside their ranks."[177]

If these are the elites, who exactly are the problem solvers? Once again, the cultural sensibility of American Pragmatism turns the residue of the antinomian into a cloying perfume. The pragmatic problem solver, eclectic and forward-moving, gets the job done so long as he stays true to himself, he keeps it real. But what does that mean? A couple years ago, Colson Whitehead helpfully sussed out what seems to be the pragmatist's answer.[178] "Don't overthink it! You do you, and all will be well, for it is what it is." Denying the (dying) instinct to "think" about who or what we are, or "think" about what ought to be done, Whitehead suggested that a parade of tautophrases have captured our culture of stagnant narcissism.

[174] A classic discussion is Richard Hofstadter, *Anti-Intellectualism in American Life* (New York: Vintage, 1966). See also Christopher Lasch, *The New Radicalism in America 1889–1963: The Intellectual as a Social Type* (New York: Newton, 1997); Christopher Lasch, *The True and Only Heaven: Progress and Its Critics* (New York: Newton, 1991).

[175] See, e.g., Niraj Chokshi, "Trump Accuses Clinton of Guiding Global Elite Against U.S. Working Class," *New York Times*, October 13, 2016 (available at http://www.nytimes.com/2016/10/14/us/politics/trump-comments-linked-to-antisemitism.html). For more on Trump, see, e.g., John Judis, *The Populist Explosion: How the Great Recession Transformed American and European Politics* (New York: Columbia Global Reports, 2016), pp. 63–88.

[176] Beverly Gage, "How 'Elites' Became One of the Nastiest Epithets in American Politics," *The New York Times Magazine*, January 3, 2017 (available at http://www.nytimes.com/2017/01/03/magazine/how-elites-became-one-of-the-nastiest-epithets-in-american-politics.html).

[177] Id.

[178] Colson Whitehead, "How 'You Do You' Perfectly Captures Our Narcissistic Culture," *New York Times Magazine*, March 31, 2015 (available at http://www.nytimes.com/2015/04/05/magazine/how-you-do-you-perfectly-captures-our-narcissistic-culture.html).

Once we encounter directives like "just do it," "get the job done," "it is what it is," "what will be will be," "boys will be boys," "haters gonna hate," or "it's just locker-room talk," we confront the dumb silence of our flat eclecticism. There is literally nothing else to say. As Whitehead writes, "Like black holes, [these phrases] are inviolable. All criticism is destroyed when it hits the horizon of their circular logic, and not even light can escape their immense gravity . . . 'It is what it is' effectively ends the discussion so that we can stop, nod in solemn agreement and move on."[179] These are the call signs of the problem solver, sophisticated enough to understand that in the New Normal it is simply a waste of time to stop and ask whether this is the right problem, if that is the right solution, or if problem solving is itself the problem. It is what it is, now let's get on with it. Coming back to President Trump, Whitehead's critique seems especially relevant. When Trump explained that his sexual transgressions were instances of "locker-room talk," or just a piece of "boys being boys," these tautophrases banish the ideology of sexism from the conversation. Trump's use of this populist anxiety about thinking too hard, as Whitehead suggests, makes Trump look a lot like Popeye: "Popeye's 'I yam what I yam . . . ' remains what it has always been – the pathetic ravings of a man who claims superstrength, when it is obvious to everyone else in the room that spinach merely ameliorates the symptoms of an undiagnosed vitamin deficiency."[180] Sadly, and unlike in Popeye's case, the pragmatic sublimation of the antinomian evidenced in phrases like "it is what it is" isn't obvious at all. In fact, it is the very genius of American Pragmatism that in its very phrasing, the depths of structural experience are kept out of sight, out of mind.[181]

Finally, the cultural sensibility of American Pragmatism boasts a particular consumerism. James and Dewey were naturalists, in the sense that they believed a theory of nature to be critical to the pragmatist program. As James said of pragmatist practice, "Her manners are as various and flexible, her resources as rich and endless, and her conclusions as friendly as those of mother nature."[182] But theirs was a kind of antinomian naturalism, for as I suggested, James and Dewey seemed to suggest the possibility of practicing a naturalizing sensibility right in the throes of the antinomian. As we have seen, cultural pragmatism is something

179 Id. 180 Id.

181 There is no space for the argument here, but it seems obvious how the development of social media is a powerful accomplice in this venture. See generally, Franklin Foer, *World Without Mind: The Existential Threat of Big Tech* (New York: Penguin, 2017).

182 Jameson, Postmodernism, supra note 130, at 81.

else. The pastiche of American Pragmatism, as Jameson explained, "is what you have when the modernization process is complete and nature is gone for good."[183] This is what happens when absolutely everything has been commodified, the market devouring nature whole. It is a situation in which, borrowing from the language of Guy Debord and Perry Anderson, every pore of the culture has been saturated "in the serum of capital."[184]

This "derealization of the whole surrounding world of everyday reality," Jameson argued, is best rendered as a story about capital, a story that moves from a first stage of market capitalism into a monopoly stage, and finally toward a fully capitalized society in which the remnants of a feudal order have been finally expunged. Or, in other words, what defines the contemporary is indeed a historical relation to the moderns; for whereas the power of modernism was found in its cathartic bouts with an early capitalist or pre-capitalist past, the *contemporary* sensibility of American Pragmatism has no cathartic outlet, no historical relation with a past of any kind.[185] For whereas the modern was defined by the process of capital consuming society, the contemporary is defined as the termination of that process, where society is now totally consumed.[186]

> For the moment, we conclude that the keen sense of the New in the modern period was only possible because of the mixed, uneven, transitional nature of that period, in which the old coexisted with what was then coming into being... One way of telling the story of the transition from the modern to the postmodern lies then in showing how at length modernization triumphs and wipes the old completely out: nature is abolished along with the traditional countryside and traditional agriculture; even the surviving historical monuments, now all cleaned up, become glittering simulacra of the past, and not its survival. Now everything is new; but by the same token, the very category of the new then loses its meaning and becomes itself something of a modernist survival.[187]

To summarize this little sketch, we can capture American Pragmatism as a cultural sensibility in the following way. It emerges in the middle decades of the twentieth century in a situation of increasing disorientation. Slowly, the stabilizing effects of the modern negotiation of the antinomian sensibility are wearing off. By the 1970s, those effects are

[183] Id. at ix. I should remind the reader that Jameson was talking about postmodernism, not what I'm calling American Pragmatism.

[184] Anderson, The Origins of Postmodernity, supra note 130, at 55. See also Guy Debord, *The Society of the Spectacle* (London: Black and Red, 2000).

[185] Jameson, Postmodernism, supra note 130, at 309. [186] Id. at 332.

[187] Id. at 311.

nearly gone and the antinomian sensibility is ready to run riot. Disgraced and discounted, the naturalizing sensibility has nowhere to turn save the strongholds of mathematics and the hard sciences. Everywhere else, it is debased. And yet, in its debasement the naturalizing sensibility refuses to die, eventually finding a new home in the cultural sensibility of American Pragmatism. Chastened, the naturalizing sensibility would never again be what it once was, not in music, painting, or philosophy – or, at any rate, it wouldn't be what it once was, any time soon. It would transform itself into a shortcut naturalism, taken on credit for as long as American Pragmatism kept its faith. It became a cultural sensibility enamored with the dogma of a flat and depthless eclecticism stretching out in the mirage of a mesmerizing present; a present in which practical problem solvers fight the good fight against the elites and intellectuals; an imaginary global museum of "bland idiot masks" for sale in an entirely commodified nature. If we don't like our pragmatic problem solving, there's little reason to worry. It is what it is, what will be will be, and haters gonna hate. In the meantime, just be yourself. You do you, you snazzy problem solver.

This chapter began with the situation of liberal legalism in the United States, somewhere in the 1970s. As I suggested, the situation was bleak. Both the classic and modern styles had been brutally undressed. The question in legal thought might have been, whither liberalism? Was it over? Or, in an alternate arrangement, what might liberalism now become? The answer that I will defend in the following chapter concerns the emergence of a third style of liberal legal thought, practiced alongside of and sometimes in the place of the classic and modern styles. That third style was pragmatic liberalism, a practice of legal argument born in the encounter between American Pragmatism and liberal legal thought. The fit, as I have tried to make plain in this chapter, was tailor-made. As I mentioned at the outset, it is no accident that this chapter's discussion of the naturalizing and antinomian sensibilities in music, painting, and philosophy mirrors the presence of naturalism and antinomy in liberal legal thought. The naturalizing sensibility, in its rationalist form, is something of a very close cousin with legal formalism. Right down to the obsession with harmony, mathematical technique, and *trompe l'oeil*, legal formalism is an argumentative practice that resonates in the practices of Bach and Leonardo. On the other hand, Manet, Monet, Mahler, and Strauss, and what James and Dewey criticized as the materialism of empiricism, all manifest a brand of the naturalizing sensibility with which the modern style of legal functionalism has much in common. Similarly, the tradition of critical realism speaks to liberal legalism in very much the same way that the antinomian sensibility spoke to composers, painters, and philosophers, depriving the author of the techniques needed to reveal a naturally harmonious order.

All of which leads us to ask, when American Pragmatism swept in, breathing new life into an old language of law, what did that look like? How did it work? Answering this question is the task of Chapter 8. Answering the question of how legal structuralism helps us think about American Pragmatism, liberal legal thought, and most pointedly, their offspring in the pragmatic style of liberal legal argument, is the task of Chapter 9.

8

Liberal Legalism Is Dead; Long Live Liberal Legalism

The last chapter examined, in the limited contexts of music, painting, and philosophy, American Pragmatism in its relation to the naturalizing and antinomian sensibilities. This chapter moves on to the interface between American Pragmatism and liberal legal thought: pragmatic liberalism. After the classic and modern styles, pragmatic liberalism presents us with a third subsystem or style in the structure of liberal legal thought. I will explore its work at two familiar levels. First, pragmatic liberalism is oriented out of an alteration of the *langue*, the structure's deep grammar. In the classic and modern styles, you will recall, there are three grammatical theses: the first is the promotion of free competition, the second is the necessity of social control, and the third is faith in a naturalizing juridical science. As I discussed in Chapters 4, 5, and 6, the classic and modern styles rely on the same grammatical presumptions, but have different styles for coping and dealing with those presumptions. The grammar of pragmatic liberalism, in contrast, has morphed. Whereas the first two theses are relatively unchanged, American Pragmatism's effect on the third thesis is dramatic. No longer faithful to a juridical science that might naturally harmonize the antinomies of liberal legal thought, the dialect of pragmatic liberalism introduces a new faith, a faith in the debris of liberal legal thought, and doing with that debris whatever *works*. This shift in faith represents the first level of transformation in the changeover from the classic and the modern to the pragmatic.

The second level of change occurs at the level of style and argumentative practice. This practice, like the practice of the classic and modern jurists, is not uniform. Sometimes, a pragmatic jurist deploys an argumentative practice that is highly self-conscious and overtly synthetic. When jurists argue in this style, explicitly favoring something called "the pragmatic" over the functionalist and the formalist, we see pragmatic liberalism's most obvious manifestations, but also its most uncommon. Charles Sabel and William Simon's "experimentalism" and Richard Posner's eclectic pragmatism are well-known examples.[1]

Much more often, however, a jurist practices in such a way that we can see the transformed elements of the modern and classic styles rattling around, banging against one another in the course of the argument, without any explicit reference to "pragmatism" at all. In another world, all this banging and rattling might cause concern or present opportunities for transformation; after all, an encounter between the classic and modern styles, in the abstract, is powerfully dissonant. They devastate each other. And yet, in the practice of the pragmatic jurist, the dissonance is silenced, the antinomies somehow reconciled. Why? How? The pragmatic jurist is not bothered by the antinomies because it *works* to continue treating the antinomies *as if* they were harmonious. It is what it is, and we just need to get on with the work, and so on. As Unger has suggested, the pragmatic jurist has more to lose and less to gain in renouncing his faith:

> What united them, however, was stronger and deeper than what divided them: a passive attitude to the arrangements and assumptions of the established regime; a conviction that these assumptions and arrangements reflected something profound and respectable about the existing order . . . ; the rightwing Hegelian impulse; and a trust in the cadre of experts – jurists and policy specialists – who would improve the institutional design in the light of the rational architecture under the distant watch of an inhibited democracy, impressed by their credentials.[2]

In the pages that follow, I sketch the structure and style of pragmatic liberalism in these terms. First, I begin by summarizing two "theories" of legal pragmatism, popularized by Sabel, Simon, and Posner. Second, I distinguish these theories from what I take to be the pervasive argumentative

[1] Other examples of work on legal pragmatism include Jules Coleman, *The Practice of Principle: In Defense of a Pragmatist Approach to Legal Theory* (Oxford: Oxford University Press, 2001); Benjamin Zipursky, "Legal Pragmatism and Legal Pragmaticism," in *Pragmatism, Law, and Language* (Graham Hubbs and Douglas Lind, eds.) (New York: Routledge, 2014); Benjamin Zipursky, Pragmatic Conceptualism, 6 *Legal Theory* 457 (2000); David Luban, What's Pragmatic about Legal Pragmatism? 18 *Cardozo Law Review* 43 (1996); Steven Smith, The Pursuit of Pragmatism, 100 *Yale Law Journal* 409 (1990); Daniel Farber, Reinventing Brandeis: Legal Pragmatism for the Twenty First Century, 1995 *University of Illinois Law Review* 163 (1995); John Goldberg, Introduction: Pragmatism and Private Law, 125 *Harvard Law Review* 1640 (2012).

[2] Roberto M. Unger, *The Critical Legal Studies Movement: Another Time, A Greater Task* (London: Verso, 2015), p. 42.

practices of pragmatic liberalism. As I developed the classic and modern styles above by way of the jurist's practice, here too I do the same for pragmatic liberalism. Third, I turn to the structure of pragmatic liberalism and explore the naturalizing effects of the grammar's third thesis on legal conflicts.

Theorizing Pragmatism and Law

For many legal scholars interested in pragmatism, the question turns on how or whether "legal pragmatism" ought to be understood in the light of philosophical pragmatism.[3] Two of the more relatively popular models include experimentalism and eclecticism.[4] The first seeks its intellectual home in the work of philosophical pragmatism, while the second grounds itself in the cultural sensibility of American Pragmatism. The experimental theory of legal pragmatism has been most conspicuously developed by Chuck Sabel and Bill Simon.[5] In their hands, experimental pragmatism is a thoroughly Deweyan approach.[6] As Sabel and Simon explain, "Experimentalism takes its name from John Dewey's political philosophy, which aims to precisely accommodate the continuous change and variation that we see as the most pervasive challenge of current public problems. Policies should be 'experimental in the sense that they will be entertained subject to constant and well-equipped observation of the consequences they entail when acted upon, and subject to ready and flexible revision in the light of observed consequences.'"[7] Sabel and Simon understand this prime directive as an effort first to undermine the idea that regulation works best through the articulation of clear goals and the aggressive implementation of those goals. Experimental pragmatists have little interest in the delicate elaboration of a priori goals because goals only come

3 This is one of the crucial lines of difference between scholars like Posner and Rorty on the one side and Sabel and Simon on the other. For discussion, see, e.g., Brian Butler, Law as a Democratic Means: The Pragmatic Jurisprudence of Democratic Experimentalism, 9 *Contemporary Pragmatism* 241 (2012); Brian Butler, Dews, Dworks, and Poses Decide Lochner, 7 *Contemporary Pragmatism* 15 (2010).

4 Justin Desautels-Stein, Experimental Pragmatism in the Third Globalization, 9 *Contemporary Pragmatism* 181 (2012).

5. A helpful overview is Charles Sabel and William Simon, "Democratic Experimentalism," in *Searching for Contemporary Legal Thought* (Justin Desautels-Stein and Christopher Tomlins, eds.) (New York: Cambridge University Press, 2017).

6 See, e.g., William Simon, The Institutional Configuration of Deweyan Democracy, 9 *Contemporary Pragmatism* 5 (2012); Charles Sabel, Dewey, Democracy, and Democratic Experimentalism, 9 *Contemporary Pragmatism* 35 (2012).

7 Charles Sabel and William Simon, Minimalism and Experimentalism in the Administrative State, 100 *Georgetown Law Journal* 53, 78 (2011).

into focus in the actual process of doing, and not before the doing has been done. Sabel and Simon write: "In the realm of uncertainty, policy aims cannot be extensively defined in advance of implementation; they have to be discovered in the course of problem-solving."[8]

For the experimental pragmatist following Dewey, first on the to-do list is finding a very broad framework goal, a provisional sort of goal that you'll press into a constant tinkering and revising. That is, the goal should change at the margins once we see it present itself in the march of the routine. Next, policymakers devolve as much discretion as possible to local actors, since it is in the local that routines are experienced and understood. Local actors produce, record, compile, and report results as regularly as possible back to the center, and together the local actors and the administrators at the center coordinate and evaluate. Framework goals are regularly evaluated in light of the process, helping dissolve the distinction between the initial "value" and the "facts" to which the value is ostensibly applied.

At first blush, one might expect Richard Rorty to have favored the experimental approach, drawing as it does on Dewey, one of Rorty's "most important philosophers of the Twentieth Century."[9] As we have seen in the last chapter, Rorty's walled-off pragmatism was rather more inclined to see law through the cultural lens of American Pragmatism, rather than through Dewey's philosophy. What was good for a personal metaphysics had no place in the public world of law.[10] With an assist from Tom Grey, Rorty offered the curious suggestion that a properly pragmatist approach to legal problems is an approach entirely divorced from the philosophy of pragmatism. A pragmatist judge needn't have knowledge of Dewey or experimentalism or anything so theoretically inclined, Rorty counseled. All he needs to do, as Richard Posner does, is "keep America intact by keeping our political responses to surprising developments in harmony with our moral intuitions and our national traditions."[11] Pragmatist judges, at bottom, "sit down around tables, argue things out, and arrive at reasonable conclusions."[12] If this is what legal pragmatism means, then a "freestanding" legal pragmatism is toothless.[13]

[8] Id. at 56.

[9] Richard Rorty, *Philosophy and the Mirror of Nature* (Princeton, NJ: Princeton University Press, 1979), p. 5.

[10] Richard Rorty, Pragmatism and Law: A Response to David Luban, 18 *Cardozo Law Review* 75 (1996), p. 75.

[11] Id. at 83. [12] Id.

[13] Thomas Grey, Freestanding Legal Pragmatism, 18 *Cardozo Law Review* 21 (1996).

Richard Posner, the expositor of a second and eclectic theory of legal pragmatism, agreed. Posner's fullest explanation of the theory of "pragmatic adjudication" is in his book *Law, Pragmatism, and Democracy*, in which he describes it is as a "disposition to ground policy judgments in facts and consequences,"[14] consequences that are not ad-hoc but understood in light of their systemic implications for the legal system. Posner cautions against treating this focus on systemic consequences as a meta-rule, as this could turn legal pragmatism into a kind of formalism. The solution is to approach formalism as you might approach poison: chew on it from time to time in order to build up a tolerance. Never taking legal formalism as a point of departure (as this would present too large and dangerous a dose), Posner suggested that judges use formalist reasoning as a tool, but never rely on it as a faith. Pragmatic adjudication will, as result, have "formalist pockets"[15] that stand for the values in stability and predictability served by only slowly adjusting the status quo and the expectations that underlie it. Furthermore, since judges cannot be expected to always take an "all-things-considered" account in the decision making, they will sometimes have to be more formalist than they might otherwise like. Why? Because pragmatism counsels above else an emphasis on *reasonableness in context*. Reasonableness might therefore demand formalist reasoning in certain contexts, for example in the form of judicial limits or boundaries. These limits might include those rare times when appellate-level disputes have such clear answers that a decision going the other way would have untoward effects on the legal system, or in those cases where the separation of powers doctrine forbids judges from deciding questions in ways that exceed their jurisdiction.[16] Even if the best consequences demand a decision that would override, say, the political question doctrine, or blatantly flout precedent, the *reasonable* judge will be bound to refrain from making what appears to be the *best* decision.[17]

Posner recognized that this view of eclectic pragmatism might be taken as more a theory of legal consequentialism than legal pragmatism, and he attempted to separate the two with reference to his emphasis on the ultimate criterion of reason. Posner explained, "[i]f a consequentialist is someone who believes than an act, such as a judicial decision, should be judged by whether it produces the best overall consequences, pragmatic adjudication is not consequentialist, at least not consistently so.

[14] Richard Posner, *Law, Pragmatism, and Democracy* (Cambridge, MA: Harvard University Press, 2005), p. 59.

[15] Id. at 59–60. [16] Id. at 64–71. [17] Id. at 66.

That is why I prefer 'reasonableness' to 'best consequences' as the standard for evaluating decisions pragmatically."[18] Nevertheless, it's unclear if this really helps. Posner's eclectic pragmatism sounds like a decision-making process whereby the best judicial act is the one with the most reasonable consequences. Consequentialists, in contrast, replace "reasonable" with "best." But in order to know what "best" means, consequentialists require a theory of the good, a normative ethics.[19] When Posner distanced legal pragmatism from consequentialism by substituting what appeared to be the less foundational and more anti-formalist standard of "reasonable" for "best," he tried to make good on the pragmatist disdain for "theories of the good" and all the rest. Eclectic pragmatism does not have such a theory of the good, according to this view, and is constrained only by those norms a reasonable perspective on the legal order will understandably entail. Therefore, it cannot be lumped in with other foundational moral systems.

It is beyond the scope of this simple introduction to treat this is claim in any more detail, but I will leave it with the following point. Posner's pragmatic view of reasonableness does not stop at "decision-making process whereby the best judicial act will be the one with the most reasonable consequences." If it did, we might wonder about how the judge enacts "reasonableness" at any particular point in time, but we could still recognize it as a move in the vernacular sensibility of cultural pragmatism. But Posner didn't leave it there. Posner explained that "pragmatic reasoning is empiricist, and so theories that seek to guide empirical inquiry are welcomed in pragmatic adjudication."[20] The approach to legal problems that best gives content to reasonable decision making guided by empirical inquiry, in Posner's view, was law and economics. Now, law and economics and legal pragmatism may end up coming to the same thing.[21] Posner's pragmatism, like American Pragmatism more generally, seems little more than a Trojan horse.

Pragmatic Liberalism as a Style of Argumentative Practice

Much more often, jurists are not self-conscious about the use of pragmatism in the course of composing a legal argument. Consider Barack

[18] Id. at 65. [19] Id. at 49. [20] Id. at 77.

[21] For discussion, see, e.g., Thomas Cotter, Legal Pragmatism and the Law and Economics Movement, 84 *Georgetown Law Journal* 2071 (1996).

Obama, for example, a jurist often described as a pragmatist,[22] though not usually associated with Posner, Sabel, or Simon. In the days following the passing of Antonin Scalia, Obama explained his approach to appointing Scalia's successor on the US Supreme Court.[23] Obama's approach is a concise illustration of the "banging around" I discussed earlier, the manner in which a jurist can serve up an eclectic hodgepodge of classic and modern moves.

Obama explained that a Supreme Court justice ought to be a juridical master, and that legal mastery was a function of two dominant juridical qualities. First, a master is a jurist who "understands that a judge's job is to interpret the law, not make the law."[24] The master jurist knows the difference between the pursuit of an intellectual agenda – this is judicial activism – and the pursuit of impartial justice, and always prefers the latter. In this first quality, Obama gestured in the direction of the classic liberal style and the formalist belief in the jurist's capacity to render objective judgments through an apolitical form of scientific reasoning. The master jurist is not, will never be, *political*. But Obama explained that while this formalistic appreciation for the juridical persona is necessary to mastery, it is not sufficient. There is a second quality to legal mastery, namely, "a keen understanding that justice is not about legal theory, nor some footnote in a dusty casebook. It's a kind of life experience ... that suggests he or she views the law not only as an intellectual exercise, but also grasps the way it affects the daily reality of people's lives in a big, complicated democracy, and in rapidly changing times."[25] In this second quality, predictably, Obama gestures toward the modern liberal style and the functionalist belief in tasking jurists with harmonizing laws in the books with the laws in action. Law's purpose is to serve social needs, and this is a very messy business. Society is big and complicated, and the jurist's work needs to be just as big and complicated in its effort to match the daily reality of people's lives.

Of course, the operations of the classic and modern style are hardly new. We have seen them at length, dating back into the last decades of the nineteenth century. But what Obama so deftly conjures, in a statement only a few paragraphs long, is the sense not only that a jurist *can* be

[22] See, e.g., F. Thomas Burke, *What Pragmatism Was* (Indianapolis: Indiana University Press, 2013).

[23] Barack Obama, A Responsibility I Take Seriously, February 26, 2016 (available at http://www.scotusblog.com/2016/02/a-responsibility-i-take-seriously/)

[24] Id. [25] Id.

both a formalist and a functionalist, but that rising to the level of mastery necessitates the practice of both *at the same time*. Indeed, Obama seems to hear a harmony in their tones, whereas for a century jurists have thought of them as the very definition of dissonance. What has changed is the juridical experience of harmony. No longer is it necessary to place faith in either the classic or the modern styles of practice. It is only necessary to place faith in an idea that a hinging of the two styles at the hip will *get the job done* in a way that neither could ever accomplish alone.

Obama was writing in 2016 at a point in time where pragmatic liberalism was already sliding into the background as a hegemonic practice. Back in the 1970s, a generation earlier, it was still getting its bearings as jurists were coming to grips with the potential of a resurrected liberal legalism. To get a sense for this earlier moment, I turn to those juridical masters working in the Garden State circa 1975, masters in the mold Obama may very well have had in mind. We arrive in the township of Mount Laurel, New Jersey.[26] The problem before the New Jersey Supreme Court was Mount Laurel's zoning ordinance, which in the words of the jurist made it "physically and economically impossible to provide low and moderate income housing in the municipality for the various categories of persons who need and want it and thereby, as Mount Laurel has, exclude such people from living within its confines because of the limited extent of their income and resources."[27]

The jurist's argument began with the familiar colors of the modern style. Over several pages of discussion over the nuts and bolts of the land use ordinance, as well as its history and application beyond the narrow confines of Mount Laurel, the jurist hammered themes of social interdependence and social squalor. "There is not the slightest doubt," says the jurist, "that New Jersey has been, and continues to be, faced with a desperate need for housing, especially for decent living accommodations economically suitable for low and moderate income families."[28] Rather than focus on the rights of individuals to use their property in the most natural or reasonable way, the jurist set up the argument in terms of selfish behavior and the tendency to disregard the larger whole. Speaking to the tendency for local governments to present themselves as market actors and little else, the jurist explained, "Almost every [municipality] acts solely in its own selfish and parochial interest and in effect builds a

[26] *Southern Burlington County NAACP v. Township of Mount Laurel*, 336 A.2d 713 (1975).

[27] Id. at 724. [28] Id. at 716.

wall around itself to keep out those people or entities not adding favorably to the tax base, despite the location of the municipality or the demand for various kinds of housing."[29] All in all, the jurist intoned as the argument's momentum got going, the ordinance favored property's economic potential over the "non-fiscal considerations" relevant to, as Obama might have said, the daily reality of people's lives.[30]

In the modern style, as we have seen, the jurist might take this argumentative progression toward a harmonic resolution in the location of social expertise. Once we know the social science on low-income housing, we can then know the proper course for state planning. It will be recalled that in the modern style, the jurist typically defers to the legislature and the comprehensive plan for dealing with social woe. Here, however, the jurist shifts in a way that sounds oddly unmusical in the modern style. The jurist moves to the common law of New Jersey, and now like a classic jurist, introduces a section of the opinion titled "The Legal Issue" with a formalist overture: "We begin with some fundamental principles as applied to the scene before us."[31] With this turn to "fundamental principles," the argument takes on a herky-jerky feel that continues through to the end, shifting back and forth between the themes of social interdependence and function on the one hand and formal rights and justice on the other.

After having slowed the argument's functionalist momentum with this formal flourish, the jurist turned to the twin principles governing the rest of the composition. On the one side is the police power, the power from which Mount Laurel's zoning ordinance necessarily flows.[32] This is the state's power to regulate the market in the service of the general welfare. The jurist immediately qualified that power, pointing to a "classic" line beyond which the police power could not go.[33] But then again, in more of a modern turn, the jurist explained how hard it was to know where the line might hold.[34] Nevertheless, this jurist is unafraid of line-drawing, and in a classical turn offered a second principle for doing so: the "basic state constitutional requirements of substantive due process and equal protection of the laws."[35] What, the jurist asks, ought to happen when a local government's exercise of the police power goes awry of the principle of equal protection? And perhaps more tellingly, how can a jurist know when this has happened? One way to think about it is to ask, when the local municipality zones for the welfare of the people, *which people,*

[29] Id. at 723. [30] Id. at 723. [31] Id. at 725. [32] Id. [33] Id.
[34] Id. at 725–726. [35] Id. at 725.

whose welfare, ought to matter?[36] Or to rephrase as a lexical statement, when a jurist seeks the line beyond which a municipality may not go in its exercise of the police power, recourse ought to be made to the principle of equality.

It is true, says the jurist, that the "people" of concern in such matters are generally the people belonging to that municipality. After all, the charge of a local government is naturally the care of the people under its authority, and not of those living elsewhere. The jurist's claim, however, is that this way of thinking fails to capture the "fundamental" and "essential" point, the social aspect of the welfare power delegated to various municipalities within a given state.[37] As a result, when local zoning ordinances "have a substantial external impact, the welfare of the state's citizens beyond the borders of the particular municipality cannot be disregarded and must be recognized as served."[38] Municipalities cannot, in other words, disregard the effects of their choices on the welfare of those peoples residing within the state but beyond the purview of the ordinance. But what sort of effects will be relevant, and which ones not? Here, the jurist turns not to nature but to society, and society's "most basic human needs."[39] "It is plain beyond dispute that proper provision for adequate housing of all categories of people is certainly an absolute essential in promotion of the general welfare required in all local land use regulation."[40] This is so essential, says the jurist, that a local municipality is barred from pursuing a parochial focus on one population at the expense of another, when the issue of housing is impacted.

In which direction do these principles run? They run in favor of the plaintiffs and against the municipality, to be sure. But the way in which they are running is novel. It is neither in the style of a principled search for natural harmony, nor in that of a purposive search for social needs. Or rather, it is a style deploying elements of both, arguing at once for a quasi-formalist line beyond which the police power must not be exercised, and a quasi-functionalist understanding of how that line ought to be conceived. It is quasi-formalist, or neo-formalist, because the jurist argues for fundamental principles and sharp lines, but for principles and lines rooted in neither nature nor reason. Similarly, it is quasi-functionalist, or neo-functionalist, because the jurist looks to social needs, but rather than defer to the legislative authority for a determination of those needs, he finds within the office of the jurist itself all the resources he'll need to understand how to meet those needs.

[36] Id. at 726. [37] Id. [38] Id. [39] Id. at 727. [40] Id.

Next, the jurist applied these principles to the particulars of Mount Laurel's zoning plan. That plan intentionally prohibited multifamily and low-income housing and allowed only for single-family detached dwellings, often out of financial reach for poorer families.[41] The purpose for zoning in this way might very well have been racially motivated, and indeed, it was the NAACP that brought the claim. But the focus for the jurist here is on economics, not race, as the town's express explanation for excluding low-income residents was market-based. The idea, put simply, was that Mount Laurel sought out good tax "ratables," industrial zones with little need for state services, and sought to exclude bad ratables, areas with lots of school-age children and education costs. According to Mount Laurel, and ostensibly conceded by the jurist, the zoning plan made plenty of economic sense. Is the economic sense of the plan, the fact that Mount Laurel was pursuing what was most economically profitable given the state's tax structure, enough to convince our jurist? The jurist answers with a classic-modern, one-two punch: "Such restrictions are so clearly contrary to the general welfare *as not to require further discussion*."[42] And again: "We have no hesitancy in now saying, and do so emphatically, that considering the basic importance of the opportunity for appropriate housing for all classes of our citizenry, no municipality may exclude or limit categories of housing for [reasons of economic profitability]."[43]

This argumentative finale is surely classical in its tone. Indeed, one of the hallmark flourishes of the classic liberal style was precisely the idea that a line had been crossed, or not crossed, and that the fact of the matter was so obvious that no further discussion was required. But this is legal *trompe l'oeil*; of course further discussion was required! And this was true in 1890 just as much as 1975. Why was the strength of the argument for economic efficiency insufficient in the face of the argument for affordable housing? Apparently, because the social needs for affordable housing were more powerful than the needs for establishing good tax ratables. How did the jurist know this? No further discussion was required.

I want to suggest that we see the jurist's argumentative practice as an innovative performance in the pragmatist style, for there is in the decision a fascinating transposition of the older practices. Consider the classic style as it was rendered in Chapter 4. In the so-called nuisance cases, the jurist resolved a dispute between two parties, where one of the parties engaged in an economically productive activity that nevertheless

[41] Id. at 728–729. [42] Id. at 729. [43] Id. at 731.

destroyed the possibility of use for the other party. Sometimes, the jurist argued in the register of *sic utere tuo*, at others in the register of *damnum absque injuria*. Either way, the basic posture in each of the cases was an argument intended to harmoniously resolve the question of when one actor can behave in a way that harms a neighbor.

The jurist here in Mount Laurel approaches the question of exclusionary zoning in a strikingly similar way, but now with a heavily modern overlay. Looking at the municipality of Mount Laurel, the jurist asks of the harmful effects of its decision to use property in a particular way – here in a way that was concededly the most economically productive way of "using" that property. Despite this zoning plan's economic benefits, the jurist says that equality is a trumping principle, and so long as every municipality behaves like a Mount Laurel, society will suffer. The jurist's argument now starts to look much like in the case of Mrs. Sullivan and her dispute with the steel company, and less like the dispute between Mrs. Sanderson and the coal company. Mount Laurel, like the steel company, is using its property in such a way as to violate – let's just go ahead and say it – the *natural* rights of New Jersey's citizens to decent shelter. The dramatic shift between Sanderson and Mount Laurel, of course, is that substitution of a state legislature for an individual citizen. We have both formalism and functionalism here in the jurist's argument, but neither are what they once were. Hence the tendency to call these the neo-formalist and neo-functionalist features of the pragmatist style.

We can see a different example of a similar sort of transformation if we jump ahead to the year 2004 and the US Supreme Court. The background of the dispute involved a claim, brought by private parties and government agencies against a number of major vitamin manufacturers, of price fixing, market allocation, and the monitored compliance by those companies of the sales volumes of the vitamins, vitamins premixes, and vitamin bulk products in the global market.[44] The major defendants (F. Hoffman LaRoche (Switzerland), Lonza (Switzerland), BASF (Germany), Eisai (Japan), E. Takeda Chemical Industries (Japan), Daiichi Pharmaceuticals (Japan)) had already been nailed for anticompetitive behavior in the vitamins market, were heavily fined under the Sherman Act, and faced criminal charges.[45] Like the California raisins case discussed in

[44] *F. Hoffman-La Roche Ltd v. Empagran S.A.*, 542 U.S. 155 (2004).

[45] The defendants in *Empagran* were corporations all domiciled in foreign countries (Ecuador, Panama, Australia, Ukraine) who had purchased vitamins from foreign defendants for delivery outside the United States. *Empagran, S.A. v. F. Hoffman LaRoche, Ltd.*, 315 F.3d 338 (D.C. Cir. 2003), p. 342.

Chapter 5, the question now before the Supreme Court was *not* whether the vitamin companies had violated the rules of market competition. They had, without question. The question now was what ought to happen if the anticompetitive behavior, still of massive proportion, failed to include any American plaintiffs or defendants, or claims that the market distortions could be felt on US soil.[46] As a result, the question for the jurist had something of the flavor of the question about Mount Laurel: in a market (or community) in which parties are necessarily connected, of what legal concern are the needs of our neighbors?

The statutory scheme confronting the jurist went beyond the Sherman Act and to the Foreign Trade Antitrust Improvement Act ("FTAIA"). The FTAIA, at first blush, seemed to dispose of the problem, for its "basic" rule is that the Sherman Act does not apply to "conduct involving trade or commerce . . . with foreign nations."[47] There are exceptions, however, including the proviso that the Sherman Act *will* apply when "such conduct has a direct, substantial, and reasonably foreseeable effect," and such effect gives rise to a Sherman Act claim.[48] The plaintiffs argued that under the FTAIA it was unnecessary for the anticompetitive effects of an antitrust violation to give rise to the plaintiff's actual claim. Rather, those effects need to have given rise to any claim, and to that extent, prior adjudications of the vitamins case had made clear that such anticompetitive effects had been substantially felt within the United States. The Court of Appeals for the District of Columbia had accepted the plaintiff's reading of the FTAIA, finding the language of the FTAIA too ambiguous to determine whether the statutorily required anticompetitive effects should give rise to any claim on US soil, or only to the plaintiff's own claim. As a result, the Court held that the "harmful effect on United States commerce must give rise to 'a claim' by someone, even if not the foreign plaintiff who is before the court. Although the language of § 6a(2) does not plainly resolve this case, we believe that our holding regarding the jurisdictional reach of FTAIA is faithful to the language of the statute. We reach this conclusion not only by virtue of our literal reading of the statute, but also in light of the statute's legislative history and underlying policies of deterrence."[49]

This was the scene. The stakes seemed high. On the one side was a striking question of political economy: in an increasingly interconnected global market, in what way ought the United States consider the effects of its rules on its neighbors? On the other side, the market was failing,

[46] Empagran, supra note 44, at 159. [47] Id. [48] Id.

[49] *Empagran, S.A. v. F. Hoffman LaRoche, Ltd.*, 315 F.3d 338 (D.C. Cir. 2003), p. 341.

suffering under the weight of what some considered the greatest worldwide price-fixing conspiracy ever. In the middle of it is the Janus-faced FTAIA. The jurist began by orienting the problem as one of neighboring actors in a global marketplace. If we have foreign plaintiffs suing foreign plaintiffs for foreign harms, was it appropriate for these plaintiffs to use US antitrust law in their efforts to correct the market?[50]

The FTAIA suggested, said the jurist, that Congress meant to signal to American business that the Sherman Act prevented them from distorting American markets. However, it was not clear that the FTAIA was meant to stop US actors from acting willy-nilly in foreign markets. These laws regulate our own market structure, but beyond our borders the Sherman Act has no say. Still, said the jurist, Congress did undermine this interpretation by creating an exception for activities taking place abroad that have reasonably foreseeable effects on American interests.[51] Faced now with determining whether the instant controversy might affect US commerce, thus getting the claim within the FTAIA's exception, our jurist made the pragmatic move: "The price-fixing conduct significantly and adversely affects both customers outside the United States and customers within the United States, *but the adverse foreign effect is independent of any adverse domestic effect*."[52] This is, in effect, a shortcut around the question of whether US markets are actually affected. For it might have very well been the case that the effects were not independent at all.

This shortcut, and the apparent dismissal of our global connectivity, was in its way a repudiation of the neighborly approach of the Mount Laurel jurist. Or was it? Finding the harms to be entirely independent of US interests, the jurist asked, why would it be "reasonable" to now assert American antitrust law over parties and conduct with no connection to the United States?[53] Why should American law supplant "Canada's or Great Britain's or Japan's own determination about how to protect Canadian or British or Japanese customers from anticompetitive conduct engaged in significant part by Canadian or British or Japanese or other foreign companies?"[54] Is it reasonable for the United States to push its neighbors out of the way, forcing its own views of property and competition in the place of their own? Impressed with the idea that each and every sovereign actor ought to compete freely in the global marketplace, the jurist could "find no good answer to this question."[55] By allowing each actor its equal say in the global marketplace, and by refusing to impose a

[50] Empagran, supra note 44, at 160–161. [51] Id. at 162. [52] Id. at 164.
[53] Id. at 165. [54] Id. [55] Id. at 166.

chauvinistic regionalism or globalism on our neighbors,[56] we find a pathway toward "harmony – a harmony particularly needed in today's highly interdependent commercial world."[57]

In the modern style, the jurist would pursue harmony through a searching investigation of the social issues at stake, most likely by way of deference to expert studies, thereby harmonizing law with society's needs. In the classic style, the jurist pursues harmony through an identification of law's natural principles and the resolution of competing claims by way of contrapuntal necessity. Here in the pragmatist style, the jurist's pursuit of the harmonious follows neither of these familiar patterns. Should the jurist seek out an empirical basis, either for the claim that the instant harms are somehow "independent" of the harms experienced in the United States, or for the claim that the imposition of the Sherman Act in this case would cause more dissonance than consonance in the world market? Absolutely not. Wary of both the managerial project of comprehensive planning as well as the project of formal justice, the jurist takes the shortcut that gets the job done.

> In our view, however, *this approach is too complex to prove workable.* The Sherman Act covers many different kinds of anticompetitive agreements. Courts would have to examine how foreign law, compared with American law, treats not only price fixing but also, say, information-sharing agreements, patent-licensing price conditions, territorial product resale limitations, and various forms of joint venture, in respect to both primary conduct and remedy. The legally and economically technical nature of that enterprise means lengthier proceedings, appeals, and more proceedings – to the point where procedural costs and delays could themselves threaten interference with a foreign nation's ability to maintain the integrity of its own antitrust enforcement system. Even in this relatively simple price-fixing case, for example, competing briefs tell us (1) that potential treble-damages liability would help enforce widespread anti-price-fixing norms (through added deterrence) and (2) the opposite, namely, that such liability would hinder antitrust enforcement (by reducing incentives to enter amnesty programs). *How could a court seriously interested in resolving so empirical a matter – a matter potentially related to impact on foreign interests – do so simply and expeditiously*?[58]

What is harmony for the jurist here is not quite what it was for the jurist in Mount Laurel. But in both cases, we witness a practice that constitutes an image of the harmonious market, but without regard either to a natural order or to a faith in social science.

We arrive at a final example of the pragmatist style in 2010, once again with the US Supreme Court. The rule at issue is the first amendment to

[56] Id. at 169. [57] Id. at 165–166. [58] Id. at 168–169.

the US Constitution, and the question concerns its scope. In 2008, a non-profit corporation called Citizens United released a ninety-minute film titled *Hillary: The Movie*.[59] The purpose of the film was to persuade the public that Hillary Clinton was an extraordinarily poor choice for filling the office of President of the United States.[60] Under the campaign finance rules of the time barring certain corporate-funded independent expenditures expressly advocating for or against political candidates, Citizens United would very likely have been barred from sharing its property with the public within thirty days of the upcoming primaries. The question for the jurist was whether this restriction on Citizens United's use of its property was an unconstitutional violation of individual rights.[61] One point to notice at the outset is how the orientation toward individual rights has now shifted from its economic orientation in the classic style to a contemporary emphasis on civil liberties. As we will see, the formalist style is still very much in play here, but once again, it is transformed.

The jurist's argument orbits around a familiar idea: equality of participation in the market. It is from this principle of equal participation that the force of competition is forged, yielding the good society. As a result, says the jurist in classic tones, we cannot be too careful when we use state power to control an "uninhibited marketplace of ideas."[62] As it stands, the Federal Election Commission operates in a bewildering labyrinth of state controls: "Campaign finance regulations now impose unique and complex rules on 71 distinct entities. These entities are subject to separate rules for 33 different types of political speech. The FEC has adopted 568 pages of regulations, 1,278 pages of explanations and justifications for those regulations, and 1,771 advisory opinions since 1975, [culminating in] a two-part, 11 factor balancing test."[63] All of this bureaucratic red tape, says the jurist, may not in and of itself operate as a total restriction on an individual's right of participation in the marketplace, but it sure comes close:

> the FEC has created a regime that allows it to select what political speech is safe for public consumption by applying ambiguous tests. If parties want to avoid litigation and the possibility of civil and criminal penalties, they must either refrain from speaking or ask the FEC to issue an advisory opinion approving of the political speech in question. Government officials pore over each word of a text to see if, in their judgment it accords with the 11-factor test they have promulgated. This is an unprecedented governmental intervention.[64]

[59] *Citizens United v. FEC*, 558 U.S. 310 (2010), pp. 319–320. [60] Id. at 325.
[61] Id. at 337. [62] Id. at 335. [63] Id. at 334–335. [64] Id. at 336.

This might all be bad enough; but the FEC rule with which Citizens United is faced – this is "an outright ban, backed by criminal sanctions," a classic example of censorship.[65]

Pushing even harder now against the thesis of social control, the jurist argues how the marketplace of ideas cannot function so long as the state is in the business of silencing certain individuals. "Premised on mistrust of government," constitutional freedoms are there precisely to ensure that the state will not prefer the rights of some individuals to compete at the expense of others.[66] Ought we care who these participants are, discriminating between them, allowing some more competitive space than others? If we choose to do so, we risk violating the basic theme of equal participation in the market. "By taking the right to speak from some and giving it to others," says the jurist, "the Government deprives the disadvantaged person or class the right to use speech to establish worth, standing, and respect for the speaker's voice. The Government may not by these means deprive the public of the right and privilege to determine for itself what speakers and speech are worthy of consideration."[67] To put it more plainly, it ought not to be the job of the state to control the marketplace of ideas; *the market must speak for itself*.[68]

Now, all of this might be plain enough if Citizens United was not Citizens United at all, but rather some wealthy *elite*.[69] Neither the FEC nor prior Court decisions had suggested that wealthy individuals ought to have fewer rights of participation than poorer people. But the issue here is that Citizens United is not an individual, rights-bearing citizen of the United States. It is a corporation. Should that matter?

In his answer the jurist masterfully slides from the classic posture and into a modern form of argumentative practice. Once again, it is a modern practice transformed. The more conventional modern style of argument was floated and rejected, which was this: it is both appropriate and desirable for the state to control the competition of a corporation in the "marketplace of ideas" because it is the government's duty to elevate the competitive opportunities of traditionally subordinated groups. Individuals with more financial resources will be more competitive, and the raw fact of having more resources is inappropriate as a reason for allowing certain players to dominate others. This is the modern thesis of control. In the case of Citizens United, however, the jurist is unpersuaded by such

[65] Id. at 337. [66] Id. at 340. [67] Id. at 340–341.
[68] Id. at 354. [69] Id. at 350–351.

an "aberration."[70] Equal rights of competition are more attractive than a competitive sphere under control.

It is here that the jurist makes its own modern move: The distinction between "natural person" and "artificial person" makes little difference when we direct our attention to the law's purpose and function in serving social needs. And what society needs, says the jurist, is more competition, and not less. In today's world, in which the landscape is so dominated by the corporate form, it simply makes no sense to hold on to such archaic and formalistic distinctions. "The Framers may not have anticipated modern business and media corporations. Yet television networks and major newspapers owned by media corporations have become the most important means of mass communication in modern times."[71] Similarly, "rapid changes in technology . . . counsel against upholding a law that restricts political speech in certain media or by certain speakers."[72] As social media takes us into a brave new world of competitive speech, "categorical distinctions" are simply out of fashion.[73]

It is worth noting that this decision was not favored by then-President Obama. All the same, with its blending of the classic and modern styles of argumentative practice, it is a decision we would expect from Obama's account of the master jurist.

Pragmatic Liberalism as a Grammar of Conflict

Thus far I have described pragmatic liberalism at the site of argumentative practice. At this level of practice, or style, the effects of American Pragmatism on the language of liberal legal thought are obvious. They are obvious at this point, I hope, because I have already spent so much time elaborating the groundstuff of the pragmatic style: the practices of classic and modern liberalism. What changed in the shift from the older styles to the newer was the "harmless" combination of what in the past would have sounded "diabolical." The pragmatist isn't queasy, and grabs from the past with relish. What's more, the pragmatist needn't merely shift between the old formalisms and functionalisms, though they remain available as tactics. In the pragmatist style, the jurist also deploys neo-formalist and neo-functionalist lines of reasoning. Neo-formalist practice entails the deduction of individual rights from somewhere other than society's natural fabric. Neo-functionalist practice entails the identification of social needs and social solutions in the absence of expertise. These practices may

[70] Id. at 349–355. [71] Id. at 353. [72] Id. at 364. [73] Id.

not sound persuasive, but so long as they work, says the pragmatist, who cares?

As we move deeper into the structure of pragmatic liberalism, the effects of the shift from the classic and modern styles and to the pragmatist are subtler. What is going on in the background practices of pragmatic liberalism? As I mentioned at the outset, the constitutive role of the twin theses of competition and control has not changed. Indeed, the very genius of pragmatic liberalism is the disguised maintenance of that basic antinomy. The grammatical transformation takes place instead at the site of the third thesis in liberal legal thought. The third thesis is an argument for faith in harmony, a naturalizing juridical science. The reason for the existence of the third thesis is anxiety. It is an anxiety produced in the close encounters between human experience and liberal legalism's basic antinomy, for we worry about the sudden collapse of such a fragile system. We have no way of making good on the liberal promise of distinguishing law from a concrete politics on the one side, or from a lofty morality on the other. The third thesis stabilizes that promise, and eases that anxiety, assuring us that a belief in juridical science is necessary and natural.

This belief, as we have seen in Chapters 4 and 5, historically comes in two flavors. On the one side is the formalistic belief in law's autonomy and harmony with nature. On the other side is the functionalist belief in law's harmony with society. In either the classic or the modern styles, law can be and ought to be objective, utterly separate from the subjective caprice of politics. As I have recounted, however, the belief in juridical science, in either the classic or the modern styles, became increasingly difficult to sustain in the face of critique. It was a critique that was coming from everywhere, left, right, and center. (And what's more, it was a critique happening well beyond law, as we saw in Chapter 7.) In an alternate universe, liberal legalism might very well have collapsed, yielding the floor to some other, perhaps yet-to-be-known language of legal thought. Or in the guise of an antinomian naturalism, jurists might have transformed liberal legal thought from the inside out. In our world, however, American Pragmatism transformed liberal legal thought, resuscitating or resurrecting, depending on your point of view, a liberal legalism that was at death's door.

The grammatical transformation worked out in the union of American Pragmatism and liberal legal thought takes place at the site of this third thesis. As we might expect, that thesis transforms in the following way. If the formulation of the thesis was originally something like, "The antinomies of the first two theses are resolved, not by some synthesis but through a belief in the availability of a juridical science that may prove an objective harmony between them," in the system of pragmatic liberalism the third thesis becomes, "Neither the antinomies between the first two theses, nor the incoherence of each thesis in its independence, will disrupt the continued use of this system so long as the jurist practices a sustained oscillation between transformed elements of the classic and modern styles, and believes that this use *works*."

What has happened here is a substantial substitution of terms. In the formulation of the third thesis dominating liberal legalism between 1870 and 1970, the antinomy of the twin theses of competition and control never really threatened to break out, since jurists believed so ardently in the objective capacity of law to ensure natural harmony between the spheres. In the formulation that begins to dominate after 1970, the belief in a harmony-producing juridical science is discarded in favor of a belief that has the same function: shielding the jurist from a direct confrontation with antinomy by leading him forever toward the next problem to be solved, the "practical" question of what needs to get done, shortcuts wherever available, the assurance that the system is just fine, so long as what we're doing works. This is American Pragmatism in the language of liberal legal thought.

The grammatical transformation in the pragmatic style has another effect, more systemic than what I was just describing at the level of argumentative practice. These effects are much harder to see in the structure of the language, but their impact is dramatic. It is common to find legal arguments from recent years that look as if they were simply ripped right out of 1870 or 1950, as the jurist performs a tune taken from the classic or modern styles. Often, this isn't really the case, as the style has morphed, at least at the margins. Regardless, there is a sense that our bodies of law are riven, cut down the middle by ideological disagreement in the classic and modern registers. It is tempting to take some large slate of cases from property, constitutional law, or antitrust in order to demonstrate the deeply conflicted situation (not to mention any number of other "bodies of law"). In decision after decision, one finds a jurist here in a neo-formalist posture, and then in the next related decision, a jurist arguing from a neo-functionalist position. Sometimes, you even find decisions that are just straight-up functionalist, still entirely faithful to the "law as the social servant" motif. And while both property and constitutional law are shot through with formalistic reasoning, more often than not "nature" has been traded out for the more reasonable-sounding idea of reasonableness.

What is interesting, however, is not the fact that jurists lack consensus, as perhaps they might have in 1870 or 1950, about whether formalism or functionalism struck the right chord. What is interesting, I think, is how persuasive you find the following: "It is entirely natural that jurists, just like anyone else, will disagree about the best ways to argue, the best ways to conclude, and the best ideals of juridical practice. There is no one right way to think like a lawyer or argue like a lawyer, and all that matters is that the jurist works hard, doing the best she can with the resources at hand." It has not always been that these sentences would have struck the ear so melodiously, resonating as *right on*. For many jurists working in the history of liberal legal thought, there *was* a right way to think like a lawyer. To concede that today in 2018, *it is entirely natural* to believe in a splintered, fragmented, multiple terrain of argumentative practice, is in itself significant evidence of the prevalence of a pragmatist grammar. For it is that grammar, and in particular the transformation of the third thesis, that promotes the view that it is *natural* that the *naturalizing sensibility* collapsed, and that we have nothing to fear from that collapse so long as we act *as if* the collapse never really happened. Pragmatic liberalism *naturalizes* the sense that a body of law *ought* to be riven, that it would be hard to imagine the situation any other way, and that while the dissonant clash of styles is certainly unpleasant, at least, we know, it works. Just look around. It's working, isn't it?[74]

This kind of "enlightened false consciousness"[75] has been a constant in Duncan Kennedy's work over the last couple decades. Most recently, Kennedy has described the scenario by way of the following example.[76] Imagine an associate at a law firm given a routine assignment from a partner, in which the associate needs to research the best argument in favor of a client. At the end of the allotted time for the work, the associate is unable to personally establish a moment of legal necessity: the *aha!* moment in which they say with confidence, *this is the legally necessitated conclusion*. But time has run out, the associate has yet to produce an answer, the

[74] These lines were written on November 11, 2016, days after the U.S. presidential election. More than any time in recent memory, quite a number of people seem less persuaded that "it" is "working," whatever that means.

[75] The phrase belongs to Peter Sloterdijk, *Critique of Cynical Reason* (Minneapolis: University of Minnesota Press, 1988), pp. 5–6.

[76] Duncan Kennedy, "A Social Psychological Interpretation of the Hermeneutic of Suspicion in Contemporary American Legal Thought," in *Searching for Contemporary Legal Thought* (Justin Desautels-Stein and Christopher Tomlins, eds.) (New York: Cambridge University Press, 2017).

partner needs an answer, and so the associate steadily convinces himself that one of the possible routes is the really the necessary route. Which route will that be? It is here that the ideological transforms, literally right before your eyes, into the necessary. Or consider another familiar example, where an assignment leaves open the question of whether to devote a lot of resources or a little to countering a legal rule of first impression. The question of how much to expend in the work is often a measure of time and will – or, to put it differently, the question of how we approach a legal question has much to do with our choice of work path. And the choice of work path is hardly neutral. Nevertheless, in the day-to-day explanations to partners and clients, our justifications for how we conducted the research will surely be dressed as entirely neutral.

In each of these everyday examples from law firm life (which could easily be replicated elsewhere), the amateur jurist confronts an openness in the terrain of legal concepts, and yet, *somehow*, presents his argument at the end of the day as if that terrain were closed. Borrowing from Paul Ricoeur's well-known work, Kennedy describes this paradoxical mindset as a dialectic between a hermeneutic of suspicion and a hermeneutic of restoration. The hermeneutic of suspicion functions for the pragmatic jurist as that critical awareness of the ever-present possibility of ideological influence in legal argument. The hermeneutic of suspicion is what fosters the sharp critical powers of the pragmatic jurist, and what keeps him from getting into the "flow" of the language's background practices. But the aspect of pragmatic liberalism that keeps the jurist from turning the hermeneutic of suspicion upon himself, and that is ultimately seeking to get the jurist "thinking like a lawyer," is a different hermeneutic altogether, the hermeneutic of restoration. While the hermeneutic of suspicion is always on the hunt for inappropriate ideological influence in the work of colleagues and opponents, the hermeneutic of restoration "is a disposition, like the disposition of its twin to doubt and unmask, a tendency, in this case to search for and find values immanent in the body of legal materials, *to believe in those values*, and to deploy the techniques of legal argument to develop and apply them to shape the legal order through time."[77] There is therefore a tension in pragmatic liberalism, where its "suspicious" side incessantly suggests "breakdowns" in both the structure and style of legal argument, and the "restorative" side incessantly suggests harmonies and the prospects of legal necessity.

77 Id. at 366.

Kennedy suggests that this dialectic sustains itself, denying the ideological aspect of legal work in the very midst of ideology-critique, as projective identification.[78] This is a mechanism whereby an individual projects an inner conflict onto others, and in the process of condemnation, the accuser absolves oneself of the conflict. As Kennedy writes, "The actor denies something in himself, something that is bad or conflict-inducing, relocates it in another, and then vigorously condemns it. Condemnation of the other is a diverted form of self-condemnation."[79] As I have suggested, in the context of pragmatic liberalism jurists are more critically self-aware than at any point in American legal history. It has become a typical feature of "thinking like a lawyer" to know the fault lines in formalist and functionalist styles of practice. With this awareness, the experience of legal necessity (and an attendant faithlessness in legal coherence) becomes increasingly expensive. We want coherence, and in order to get it, legal consciousness limits the solvent of critique to others, and resurrects the possibility of legal necessity for the self through the process of projective identification. It is important to emphasize, however, that this is not merely a case of easy self-deception. As Kennedy writes, "ontological instability is denied: in the actor's case felt necessity is real necessity, and in the other's case, claimed necessity is mere error."[80] It is not the jurist's faith in coherence fighting for supremacy; it is rather the jurist's ineradicable sense of self-doubt endlessly projected elsewhere. And in the process of the projection, the coherence of the legal medium is restored, even if it is only an illusory coherence.

Kennedy "social-psychological" explanation might be a sound one, but I leave for elsewhere the study of its empirical validity. My immediate interest lies instead in the possibility that the hermeneutic of suspicion facilitates a game of hide-and-seek, a game in which the pragmatist style systematically obscures what it means to think like a lawyer. The next chapter illuminates both the game and the stakes.

[78] Id. [79] Id. at 368. [80] Id. at 379.

9

Trompe l'Oeil Liberalism

In its diagnosis of a contemporary structure of liberal legal thought, this Part suggested a commingling between American Pragmatism and liberal legalism. By the 1970s, the language of liberal legal thought had darkened. The victories of modern liberalism had passed, and its enemies were everywhere. Functionalism was a hoax, pretending at a kind of legitimation properly uncovered as a series of trace effects, slippages, and dangerous supplements. Or instead, functionalism was criticized less as a hoax and more for its vulgar displays of judicial activism. Viewed from a certain angle, the moderns were doomed. Their language was dying. As we have seen, however, the end was not yet at hand. A rescue operation unfolded unlike anything ever seen in the history of liberal legalism. Without a grand interlocutor, without a John Locke or John Stuart Mill, a Francois Geny or Oliver Wendell Holmes, a Friedrich Hayek or John Rawls, something was seeping in, all over. And this something was American Pragmatism. It was as if out for a stroll among the ruins, hands in pockets, whistling carefree, head in the clouds, Pragmatism happened upon Liberalism, bent and broken, crumpled in the leaves. Eyebrows arched, Pragmatism bent low. She slipped a firm hand beneath Liberalism's limp head. Her lips to Liberalism's ear, Pragmatism whispered,

> Yes, yes, I know. It hurts. Of course it does. You are bleeding, everywhere it seems. But you should know, this is what you get, you asked for this. You knew better than any. You couldn't stop with your risks, could you? You always wanted, so *desperately*, to be natural, to be true, to be true to yourself and to the rest of us. You were born a jealous spirit, jealous of what you weren't, and now you look to die of it. Yes, yes, shhh. I know. You couldn't help yourself, you shouldn't naturalize, I know, shush now, it's bad, very bad, I know. The naturalizing sensibility

confuses us, *distorts* our relations with each other and within ourselves. It *intoxicates* us when we need sobriety, yes, yes, of course, it *limits* our imagination at those moments we need it most. Dreadful. But listen to me, now, listen closely. You want to live, yes? You, you jurists especially, can you hear me in there? Don't throw away your liberalism, it's too good, too old. Keep on with your work. Get up! Are you the Western Tradition or not? What's that you say? You can no longer hear the harmonies? Don't cry now, this is no time for tears. Be strong. Listen to me. Get up, get up and continue on, and *I* will take the blame. That's right! Blame me, I don't mind. I want it! We will continue this work together, and we both know – of course, of course, no doubt, to be sure – your jealousies, your lust for harmony's law – well, this cannot go on. It cannot go on it has, at any rate. But *I* won't tell anyone, and you shouldn't either. So long as what we do *works* (and it is working, just look around you!), why live in fear? We should not! That's right! Now you see! With me at your side, dear jurist, you simply pick and choose, borrowing from the old liberal ways as you like. It's all yours, all of it! Just enjoy yourself, and I shall carry the burden, I shall carry the burden of harmony's law. If you believe in me, give *me* your faith (and turn away from that *Nature's* charms), I will make you both blind and deaf to the antinomian art. You will be safe. And you will be content. And you will live forever.

I don't think it really happened this way. But, if we get the gist, jurists did accept this invitation. In this alliance there crystallized a contemporary style in the history of liberal legal thought, a style I have been calling pragmatic liberalism. As I discussed in Chapter 8, the arrival of American Pragmatism wrought several changes, at the levels of both grammatical structure and the style of argumentative practice. We saw how at the level of the structural *langue*, a new third thesis replaced the old, wherein a past faith in the jurist's naturalizing power was substituted for a faith in Pragmatism itself. We also saw how at the level of style, jurists took to two modes of argumentative practice. First was the practice of oscillation, shifting back and forth between neo-formalist and neo-functionalist techniques, all in the effort to justify a single judgment. Second was a practice of oscillation at the level of the "legal body," wherein a body of law is riven by contrasting usages and yet somehow sustained by a belief in the natural condition of argumentative strife; "it is what it is," etc.

I now turn to the illusions of liberal legal thought. Throughout this book I have discussed tactical deployments of *trompe l'oeil* reasoning in the contexts of legal formalism and legal functionalism. I now wish to look more broadly, and if pragmatic liberalism is indeed playing a masterful game of hide-and-seek, ask if structuralism can be of any help in seeking out the hidden. Before proceeding, however, a caveat. What of the old complaint that structural analysis and critical theory are incompatible? Is it not true that structuralist commitments deprive the structuralist of any point from which he can raise a justifiable critique?[1] In *A Critique of Adjudication*, Duncan Kennedy developed what he called "pink theory," an effort to join (but not synthesize) the two elements of what have been his basic program for the whole of his academic career: leftism and structuralism (or m/pm, in his words). In that book's last chapter in particular, Kennedy followed the tensions between the two elements, and the basic inability of the structuralist strand to "support" the leftist strand. Even worse, in its more aggressive postmodernity the poststructuralist strand devours the left. Nevertheless, Kennedy had little difficulty in blending the structuralist element with his leftist commitments. Need these normative commitments *follow* from the structuralist platform, or seek from that platform "justifiable support"? No, and what's more, they can't. But this is only a problem for those who believe that their normative commitments must enjoy a kind of logical necessity. Roberto Unger, on the other hand, is a different story but with a similar ending. From his first publication of *Knowledge and Politics* and to his recent re-release of *The Critical Legal Studies Movement*, Unger has always claimed that critique is senseless when it has no connection with a leftist program for reconstruction. The basis for his claim is this: if you are going to wage a critique, you need to have an understanding of structure, and if you are to understand a structure, then you have to know the structure in time, and to know the structure in time is to know what it has been and what it might become. The critique of structure, in a word, is to know the structure's alternative futures. If you do not know its alternative futures, you do not know the structure, and if you do not know the structure, your critique is partial. Nevertheless, the question returns: how can we justify a choice of one alternative future over another? Unger and Kennedy together reject the act of justification as necessarily neutral or natural. It is a choice, a political and existential decision, never anything more or less than the following of the promptings of what we believe to be our better selves.

Furthermore, if we regard the critique of adjudication as revealing only a linguistic difference between adjudication and legislation, and if we accept the tremendous impact of law on society (if not law's constitution of society), then it is a mistake to assume that the study of adjudication, and in particular the jurist's unstated background practices, will have only the most minimal of social consequences.[2] As Unger sees it,

[1] See, e.g., David Kennedy, Critical Theory, Structuralism, and Contemporary Legal Scholarship, 21 *New England Law Review* 209 (1985).

[2] Duncan Kennedy, *A Critique of Adjudication* (Cambridge, MA: Harvard University Press, 1999), p. 265.

law is the very structure of society – the basic arrangements and assumptions of the social order – in the "universal history of legal thought."[3] On this view, without developing "a view of structure and structural change," plans for social change will forever remain the dreams of a people merely singing in their chains.[4] Legal structuralism is already, by definition, a social theory. What this further suggests here, in the context of those who criticize the study of legal thought as too theoretical and insufficiently practical, is an outdated commitment of that critic to the distinction between thought and practice. Legal thought *is* practice. There is no other way to understand legal thought, from this perspective, but as a practice of legal argument. There is just no thing as a structure of legal thought somehow cut off from "reality." They are the same thing. When Unger talks of the higher vocation of legal thought, he repeatedly refers to thought *as* practice. When Kennedy talks of the phenomenology of legal structuralism, the point of doing so is not to pair a subject with an object. It is the reverse. The phenomenology of structuralism – the understanding of how the language is experienced by the jurist – collapses thought as practice.

In the pages that follow, I use the structuralist history developed throughout this book to illuminate three illusions generated in the alliance between American Pragmatism and liberal legal thought. These are the structural illusion of eclectic problem solving, the conceptual illusion of settled law, and the historical illusion of the now. In each critique I point to the production of harmony's law, a *trompe l'oeil* whereby mystification begets legitimation begets stagnation, what Unger calls the "dictatorship of no alternatives."

The Illusion of Eclectic Problem Solving

Liberal legalism is a dissonant language. At its most fundamental levels, liberal legalism harbors deep antinomies and discordant themes. The antinomy that has garnered the most attention here has been that between the first two theses, those of free competition and social control. This set of ideas is historically associated with a system called capitalism, and a family of related criticisms. Most visibly, the assault on capitalism has taken aim at its distributive effects. This is the province of traditional leftist critical theory: the task of demonstrating how capitalist ideas perennially favor and systematically entrench certain dominant actors at the expense

[3] Roberto Unger, *The Critical Legal Studies Movement: Another Time, A Greater Task* (London: Verso, 2015), p. 62.

[4] Id.

of subordinated groups. This is largely a materialist exercise, inquiring into the conditions and circumstances of daily life. This exercise, at least as I see it, is indispensable, never more so than today.[5]

In the structuralist approach, however, there is a different consideration of the relation between domination and subordination. What it reveals are the argumentative practices by which the twin theses of liberal legalism continuously generate and regenerate themselves, and the language system that they together engender, as a language of depoliticized speech. Ideological struggle continuously develops into a depoliticized mantra of the Rule of Law. A constantly renewing iterative process of depoliticization begins with mystification. The basic source of mystification in liberal legal thought is its third thesis. It is here that liberal legal thought professes faith in the jurist to harmonize a discretionary and preferential judgment with the impersonal demands of some external reality. This liberal mystification is a relative of the naturalizing sensibility in the arts and humanities. In those contexts, the naturalizing sensibility guides the artist in the composition of a painting or piece of music with the aim of constituting a reality the artwork merely *represents*. In these examples, jurists and artists are magicians, using the tricks of their trade to transform what we know the object to be – an inescapably political artifact – into what we want the object to be – an object of transcendence.

Liberal legal thought hosts three linguistic modes of mystification. The first two are propagated in the fashion of the third thesis as it is spoken in the classic and the modern styles of argument. Both are a function of faith in naturalizing juridical science, a faith lost in the third mode of the pragmatic style. In the first mode, as we saw in Chapter 4, the jurist wants his arguments to look as "real" as possible, and in this style, looking "real" means matching the legal argument with the natural demands of politics, economics, and society. How can the jurist achieve a realistic composition? The most obvious analogy here is Leonardo da Vinci's *sfumato*, that technique by which an image becomes "real" through the combination of mathematical precision and intentional obfuscation. This, as will be recalled, is the blending of linear perspective with the blurring of boundaries, the smudging of those critical spaces in which the eyes and

[5] For general overviews, see David Hoy and Thomas McCarthy, *Critical Theory* (Cambridge: Blackwell, 1994); David Harvey, *The Conditions of Postmodernity: An Enquiry into the Origins of Cultural Change* (Cambridge: Blackwell, 1991); Martin Jay, *Marxism and Totality: The Adventures of a Concept from Lukács to Habermas* (Berkeley: University of California Press, 1986); Fredric Jameson, *Marxism and Form: Twentieth-Century Dialectical Theories of Literature* (Princeton, NJ: Princeton University Press, 1974).

mouth signal their affect. Now, did the classic jurist intentionally imitate Leonardo in crafting legal arguments that might mystify their ideological aspects? I would be shocked as well as pleased to learn that that might have been the case. But it is not remotely necessary. What we are after here is the jurist's background practice, a practice that may hardly be conscious, especially in the case of the juridical master.

As for how the combination of *sfumato* and linear perspective find an analogy in the formalist manifestation of the third thesis in the classic style, the form of legal mystification works like this (again, as we saw back in Chapter 4). Say we have a dispute between two owners, both of whom enjoy an equal right of use. One owner, however, uses their estate in such a way that it deprives the other owner in some basic use-right. What to do? Will this be a case of free competition or social control? In the classic style, the jurist approaches the composition of argument as Leonardo or Bach approached the canvas or harpsichord. The jurist wants the argument to track a natural reality as closely as possible. He will invoke the adjudicative process as a science, governed like all sciences by certain incontrovertible laws. Mathematics is the ur-science, emulated in hopes of achieving something like its natural precision here in the world of human affairs. As a result, the jurist constitutes the field by positing the relevance of certain principles. As in math, however, these principles go only so far, and the chief work of the jurist is in knowing the line beyond which a principle – such as social control – cannot go. The jurist has no trouble telling the audience that a line exists, and that the line's boundary is black and bold. What the jurist very rarely does, and certainly does not do when he's really "in the flow," is actually point to a clear boundary in fact. The *trompe l'oeil* is at its most effective when the jurist uses the prospect of bright lines as an argumentative hinge, but leaves the lines blurred and smudged to such a degree that we actually have no idea about the location of the line between free competition and social control. And that's the genius: we are mystified, believing in the existence of the bright line precisely because the jurist keeps us from seeing it. This is the *Mona Lisa*'s smile, in argumentative form.

In the second mode, as we saw in Chapter 5, the jurist is equally interested in painting the argumentative composition as "realistically" as possible. The mystifying project of the third thesis is still in full effect: the jurist remains the magician, tasked with the transformation of personal preference into impersonal rule. This transformation requires a matching, once again, between juridical composition and reality. In the modern liberal style, however, reality has changed. Having lost faith in the formalism of the classic jurists, the modern jurists adopts a new faith in a new juridical science. There is no natural design for politics, economics, and society that the jurist might uncover in the work of juridical argument. What there is, however, is social science: the capacity to master the social world by way of replicating the mastery of the natural sciences in their view of the physical world. It is by way of faith in social science's mimicry of the natural sciences that the jurist engages in the necessary mystification required by the third thesis. With social science as its proxy for mathematical certainty, the modern jurist gets to work, harmonizing the theses of free competition and social control, harmonizing laws in the books with the law in action, harmonizing the law in action with the needs of society.

This is the advent of legal functionalism, the *trompe l'oeil* technique by which the modern liberal jurist resolves gaps and conflicts by identifying the social purpose of a given legal rule, and then deferring to the available expertise capable of pointing to the objectively correct social solution. While it may seem as if the jurist's modern functionalism fails to transform personal preference into impersonal rule (isn't the jurist simply performing like any politician?), it is the jurist as vehicle of social science expertise that inoculates the legal argument from political contamination. This, at any rate, is the mystifying maneuver. Because there is a single social purpose relevant for the constitution of the field, because there is a single forum of expertise available for addressing that single purpose, and because these experts are fortified by a singularly correct view of the social process, the functionalist technique is every bit as "scientific" and "realistic" as the formalism it is meant to have surpassed. In fact, it is far more realistic, given the obviously ideological character of the classic style.

What became increasingly clear by the final third of the twentieth century, however, was a symmetry between the classic and modern views of juridical science. Just as the classic jurist spoke of black-letter lines while perpetually leaving everything in shades of gray, so too did the modern jurist speak of a law-and-society paradigm that left unsaid everything that needed articulation: Which purpose is the *right* purpose? Which experts are the *right* experts? Which solutions are *really* the most effective? Leaving these questions at the margins, modern liberal jurists mystified the audience by articulating a jurisprudence faithful to an unproblematic view of statistics, sociology, economics, and political science.

In each of these two modes, mystification functions by conjuring the illusion of impersonal rule out of the stuff of personal preference. Ideology is masked in the Rule of Law, because the Rule of Law is science while ideology is politics. The Rule of Law is depoliticized, in each of these two liberal styles, through a faith in the transformative capacity of the jurist. Now, however, a turn to the third liberal mode, the pragmatic style. As I explained in Chapter 8, the third thesis undergoes a transformation in morphing from the modern to the pragmatic. What had once been a thesis demanding faith in the naturalizing power of juridical science shifts into a thesis demanding faith in American Pragmatism. The mystifying effect of this transition, as I will now suggest, is amazingly pragmatic.

When in the 1970s the antinomian sensibility finally caught up with modern liberalism, the third thesis of juridical science was compromised. In an alternate universe, liberal legalism might have experimented with an argumentative practice that proceeded in the absence of the mystifying third thesis altogether. Instead, and in reverse, liberal legal thought amped up its mystifying armaments. In the argumentative practices of the classic and modern styles, the entire structure depends on and is constituted by the mystifying work of the naturalizing sensibility. Undermine that work, and one would guess, a rippling could ensue throughout the entirety of the language. The joining of American Pragmatism with Liberal Legalism, however, inoculates the system from worries about the naturalizing sensibility. Here's why.

The pragmatic response to the antinomian sensibility was exactly that: *pragmatic*. Faced with an existential threat, pragmatic liberalism shifted away from modern liberalism and asked instead for a juridical faith in the pragmatic sensibility itself. This shift suggested that, so long as a flat eclecticism continues to guarantee a familiar consumerism and minimalist constitutionalism, so long as "law" keeps "working," then there is nothing to fear in abandoning the classic and modern faiths in harmony's law. But it is with this promise of abandonment that the pragmatic style operationalizes its own, extremely powerful process of mystification. The naturalizing sensibility, apparently undermined in its encounter with the antinomian, and seemingly abandoned, returns in pragmatist form.

What is that form, pragmatic liberalism's vision for harmony's law? American Pragmatism, as I discussed in Chapter 7, is a sensibility with five features: it is flat, eclectic, presentist, populist, and consumerist. I focus here on the first of these two features. Flatness, or depthlessness, refers to the pragmatic preference for surface over structure, for grassroots over the ivory tower, for the grounded over the meta. Higher-order proposals for "grand theory" are wastes of time, much less preferred over and against first-order proposals for experiential learning and concrete change. The only higher-order proposal that makes sense is the pragmatist one itself: that all other higher-order proposals are either useless or ideologically compromised. The pragmatist ideal, in contrast, is both useful and ideology-free. If this all goes to the flatness of American Pragmatism, its eclecticism points to the appropriate inventory with which to make these first-order proposals for experiential learning and concrete change. This is the inventory – surprise! – of the classic and modern styles of liberal legal thought. In the twenty-first century, that inventory includes both the naturalizing techniques of formalism and functionalism, as well as their pragmatist progeny we witnessed in Chapter 8: neo-formalism and neo-functionalism. The pragmatic jurist can pick and choose as he pleases. Compose an argument in the classic style or the modern, and if too concerned about the onset of ideology-critique (in which his depoliticized speech is outed as ideology), turn to a channel-switching neo-formalist argument for social control, or a neo-functionalist balancing proposal in the midst of social-science agnosticism. With this eclectic spirit, it is no longer necessary to have faith in either the classic or modern styles of juridical science – in fact, it's downright unfashionable. So long as you have faith in the pragmatic back-and-forth between these discredited techniques, the language will continuously refresh and regenerate itself.

What the proponents of this flat eclecticism either intentionally elide or do not happen to realize is that they are in the business of naturalizing liberal legal thought, of establishing a harmony's law for pragmatists. And business is booming. The reason is that while the work of liberal legalism used to come at some cost – the cost of professing faith in some form of juridical science – working in the office of liberal legalism is now easier than ever. The risks have been swallowed up, marginalized to some other elsewhere (think of the Pragmatist seducer from above), for it no longer matters if liberalism is "really" an ideological apparatus. We've already been there, already done that, undergone the trials of the antinomian and come out happily on the other side. But that's the thing: pragmatic liberalism *hasn't* undergone the trials of the antinomian. It is a poser, a dilettante, a trumped-up language of shortcuts, a mere pastiche. And through its pastiche, pragmatic liberalism naturalizes itself all the more elegantly: the situation of flat eclecticism, in which we take the world as forever fragmented, contingent, existing only and ever at the ground, at the level of the concrete – this is the world we take as natural precisely because we know *this is just the way the world is*. What an effect this is; through its grassroots dismissal of the useless dialectic between the naturalizing and the antinomian, pragmatic liberalism paints a world in which the way everything *is* happens to be the way it *must* be. But this naturalization of the pragmatist sensibility does not take place by matching legal thought with an immanent legal design, and it doesn't take place through a matching between legal thought and the demands of social science expertise. The naturalization is more intense. Through its rejection of the totality, of the metaphysical, of history, of structure, of *naming*, pragmatism hides liberalism's ideological formations far more effectively than the classic and modern styles. For at least in those structures of thought, faith in naturalizing legal science was explicit. The naturalizing move of pragmatic liberalism is more subtle: it has erased its name, proselytizing an unnamed faith for a so-called faithless jurist.

In his famous study of myth, Roland Barthes explained that the exnomination of belief – the resistance of a belief to being named – is itself a deep indication of ideological naturalization. Diagnosing the mythology of the bourgeoisie, Barthes pointed to the various registers in which that set of beliefs operates. At the economic level, there is little in the way of denial; the economic system of the bourgeoisie was *capitalism*, plain and simple. At the political level, things get murkier. There has never been a "Bourgeois Party," so named. At the level of ideology, Barthes suggested, bourgeois beliefs disappear completely. "The bourgeoisie has obliterated its name . . . it makes its status undergo a real exnominating operation: the bourgeoisie is defined as the social class which does not want to be named."[6] Ideological success, said Barthes, becomes knowable by way of a "locus of an unceasing hemorrhage: meaning flows out of [the bourgeois] until [its] very name becomes unnecessary."[7] This bleeding of the concept out and into every crevice of the culture signals a naturalization of the concept that becomes hegemonic. As Barthes continues,

> In a bourgeois culture, there is neither proletarian culture nor proletarian morality, there is no proletarian art; ideologically, all that is not bourgeois is obliged to borrow from the bourgeoisie. Bourgeois ideology can therefore spread over everything and in doing so lose its name without risk: no one here will throw this name of *bourgeois* back at it. It can without resistance subsume bourgeois theater, art, and humanity under their eternal analogues; in a word, it can exnominate itself without restraint when there is only one single human nature left: the defection from the name *bourgeois* is here complete.[8]

If we make the easy transition from bourgeois to pragmatist, it becomes apparent how well Barthes' analysis applies. American Pragmatism, after all, is defined in part by its hostility for names. Not only is there disdain

[6] Roland Barthes, *Mythologies: The Complete Edition, in a New Translation* (Richard Howard and Annette Lavers, trans.) (New York: Hill and Wang, 2013), p. 250.
[7] Id. [8] Id. at 251.

for systemic totality or historical periods; American Pragmatism counsels wariness at the personal level: "Be forever suspicious of those who seek to label you! You do you!" This hostility, like so much of the pragmatist sensibility, begins with a good idea: History is necessarily local and contingent and fragmentary, structures and personalities will always change. But American Pragmatism makes a fetish of this starting point, claiming the illusory character of all names, *except its own*. And it is through this exception, the decisive and definitive unwillingness to allow itself a name that the mystifying ideology of American Pragmatism gains so much of its power. The pragmatist sensibility becomes, *tout court*, "just the way it is."

Thus far, I have been discussing a phase of *mystification* in the life of American Pragmatism and in its union with liberal legal thought. This phase of mystification depoliticizes the third thesis in liberal legal thought, losing faith in naturalizing juridical science only to replace it with faith in a naturalizing pragmatism. After the mystification of ideology, pragmatic liberalism enters a second phase of *legitimation*. Whereas mystification here involves a hiding of ideology through a series of argumentative techniques, legitimation involves the different work of consolidating the ideology as not only a natural feature of social life (the way it is), but a legitimate feature of social life (the way it ought to be). If ideology successfully sheds its name in the way the snake sheds its skin, legitimation follows a similar route.

> And just as bourgeois ideology is defined by the abandonment of the name *bourgeois*, so myth is constituted by the loss of the historical quality of things: in it, things lose the memory that they once were made. The world enters languages as a dialectical relation between activities, between human actions; *it comes out of myth as a harmonious display of essences*. A conjuring trick has taken place; it has turned reality inside out, it has emptied it of history and has filled it with nature, it has removed from things their human meaning so as to make them signify a human insignificance.[9]

Once again, at least for Barthes, legitimacy unfolds as harmony. And, once again, pragmatic liberalism *seems* anything but harmonious. From the insider's look at the jurist's argumentative practice, to the fractured "body of law," to its glaring reflection in political life, pragmatic liberalism may be many things, but "harmonious" doesn't look to be among them. In one sense, this must be right. In none of these settings is the jurist, the field of law, or the political culture "harmonized" in the sense that they

[9] Id. at 255.

might have aspired to be in the modern and classic styles. After all, in classic liberalism the jurist's task was an explicit project of finding a natural harmony in the seemingly dissonant pitches of personal preference and impersonal rule. Similarly, the modern jurist's work was all about finding harmony in the apparent dissonance between law and society. For the pragmatic jurist, in contrast, the aesthetic is entirely contemporary; it is the montage, the assemblage, the sampled cut-up, the mix. If there is a legitimation effect in the structure of pragmatic liberalism, harmony hardly seems the mantra.

Nevertheless, consider three counterarguments in the case for seeing pragmatic liberalism as a mythical "harmonious display of essences." First, remember that from within the storehouse of American Pragmatism there is considerable room for reinventing old and discredited styles of legal thought. A recent illustration is a symposium published in the Harvard Law Review on "The New Private Law." In the introductory article, John Goldberg's *Pragmatism and Private Law* begins just as a pragmatist would hope, with a rejection of those "concepts, categories, or methods that claim for themselves a certain kind of essential validity or primacy."[10] And yet, in Goldberg's survey of what he calls "inclusive pragmatism," "private law" emerges as something that certainly *sounds* like a family of concepts and categories that are essentially valid and primal. Goldberg explained that inclusive pragmatism suggests the following: (1) Be wary of conceptualism.[11] Good pragmatist practice distrusts the reification of ideas. And yet... concepts are far more settled and practically directed than we have often thought. Of course, some legal concepts may be "irredeemably confused or unnecessary."[12] And the search for clarity and settled rules won't ultimately eliminate local disagreements about application. But the point is to find the sense *in* our legal concepts, because this is a "necessary and fruitful aspect of legal reasoning."[13] (2) "The world is complicated."[14] Good pragmatist practice distrusts the reduction of complex legal phenomena to a handful of ideas and principles.[15] And yet... while the concepts and categories of private law are certainly complicated, there is nevertheless a general *coherence*, immanent in their very architecture.[16] (3) Theory's for the birds.[17] Good pragmatist practice distrusts legal theories that float free from the real world of law, that want

[10] John Goldberg, Introduction: Pragmatism and Private Law, 125 *Harvard Law Review* 1640 (2012), p. 1650.
[11] Id. at 1652. [12] Id. [13] Id. [14] Id. at 1653. [15] Id.
[16] Id. at 1655. [17] Id. at 1656.

to fly high rather than keep their feet on the ground. And yet ... what we need are, well, *theories of law* that "explicate the ways in which doctrine structures legal analysis."[18] All in all, Goldberg serves up a pragmatist account of a harmonious (new) private law: a private law wary of conceptualism but faithful to concepts that "make sense;" that is enamored with complexity but faithful to private law's internal coherence; that disdains higher order proposals for law but is faithful to a master directive equipped for explicating the way in which legal analysis flows out of doctrine. Not a poor showing of a "harmonious display of essences"!

Second, consider the pragmatic assessment of the law curriculum as a whole. As I have already suggested, there is no shortage of claims about the apparent problems at work within a given field of law. Throughout the fields of property law, constitutional law, antitrust law, and many, many more, it is conventional practice to identify gaps, contradictions, and paths for reform. But at what we might call the disciplinary level, a level that unites the many bodies of law through professional identification more than anything else, it is much less conventional to encounter suggestions for systematic or disciplinary transformation. Ought, perhaps, Contract and Tort be conflated into a single subject, Contorts?[19] Maybe create amalgamations from the detritus of Constitutional Law, Administrative Law, and Leg-Reg? Or create entirely alien bodies of law? On the whole, my guess is that many would respond in the language of pragmatic liberalism:

> Sure, there are problems at every level of Law, in its doctrines, in its theories, in its institutions and processes. There is ample evidence, everywhere. But our job is to make Law as good as it can be, with an eye simultaneously directed at law's life in society, the "law in action," and another eye directed at law's justice, its mission to serve the interests of individual right. At a level of generality, the system that we have, warts and all, is as good a system as humanity has ever known. We want to change it, fix it and make it ever better and better – there is no perfect stopping point – but when it comes to our disciplinary understanding of Law in its totality, if we can even understand it at such a level, we have to concede that there are no realistic alternatives. For if we even glance at the historical menu of systematic alternatives, it becomes indisputable that our basic legal structure is the only real choice. At the end of the day, *this goes without saying*.

A rephrase might suggest, when we take care to listen to the various bodies of law, not in their own keys but in the harmonies they create when we experience them altogether, it is the most harmonious orchestration

[18] Id. at 1655.
[19] Grant Gilmore, *The Death of Contract* (Columbus: Ohio State University Press, 1995).

humanity has yet conceived. It isn't perfect, but it is as at least as perfect as we have ever known.

Third, consider the pragmatic assessment of the relation between the legal discipline, the market, and our democratic institutions. By and large, pragmatism counsels a similar approach as to that of the legal discipline in particular. Of course, most recent polls suggest a majority of Americans desiring "change." Barack Obama was the candidate of change, and so too was Donald Trump. But for supporters of Obama and Trump, what sort of change is hoped for? Presumably, very different sorts. After all, how different are these two presidents? No doubt, there are those who will suggest that there is in fact very little difference at all. But my claim here is another one: while Obama supporters and Trump supporters likely favor different policies tracking a familiar partisan divide, is it wise to assume that *any* of these people want to change our social institutions in a dramatic way? How many might want to do away with received understandings of constitutional rights, a competitive marketplace, a one-person, one-vote electoral system, or a representative mechanism of governance? Sure, we want change, but where? Once again, these institutions, despite their difficulties – of which no one is ignorant – are ultimately legitimate because these are the institutions history has delivered in its convergence in the present moment. Because there are no realistic alternatives, the social institutions we have are, by definition, ultimately legitimate. Here, a third time, is the pragmatist's call for harmony.

In this situation of mystification and legitimation, the prospect of change comes in two varieties. The first variety is a mild reformism, the kind displayed in the concluding sections of most law review articles. Because this mild reformism is constantly suggesting the prospect of change but never changes anything at the structural level, we can call this the reformist deceit. The second variety involves large-scale change on the level of systemic substitution. Here, rather than tinker around with shifts at the level of *parole*, as the reformist variety tends to do, the idea is that real change requires the displacement of an entire system – something like "capitalism" – with another system – something like "socialism." This systemic deceit suffers in two ways. First, it suffers from mistakenly seeing a "system" as a naturalized social totality, of the pre-structuralist sort. Second, it suffers from mistakenly presuming that the only real possibilities for meaningful change take place at this level of systemic substitution. American Pragmatism provides the reformist deceit with an everlasting warrant, and rejects the systemic deceit as unrealistic, i.e., unnatural. Once again, the pragmatist move begins with a good idea. Systemic transformations are not meaningful because structures never come ready-made like huge blocks of ice. They are, at least in the context of liberal legal thought, layers upon layers, riddled with technical choices. The pragmatist sensibility is dimly aware of the deceit of systemic transformation, but its suspicion is of another kind than what I just described. For the pragmatist, systemic transformation is doubtful because it depends on crisis, a malfunction of deep and terrifying proportions. Possibly with a sense for this dynamic in mind, Trump engaged in a presidential campaign of terror for this very reason: the threat of ruin opens the mind to opportunities previously believed beyond the pale.

If we want to bypass the dogma of these twin deceits, we must break their hold. To do that, we must first loosen the grip of flat eclecticism. We cannot dispel its surface illusions if we do not understand its depth. Cleverly, pragmatic liberalism tells us that there are no depths, no structures, not anymore. But as I have tried to suggest, this is itself a naturalizing move, turning the arguments of American Pragmatism into a collection of things that just are, a *fait accompli*. The pragmatist obsession with first-order proposals for problem solving, and total disdain for structural proposals, is a key aspect of the process. In its denial of everything related to deeper discourse, American Pragmatism deprives itself of what it needs in order to make sense of its first-order problem solving. In other words, a failure to understand the unavoidable dependence of first-order problem solving on deeper levels of discourse does not make those deeper levels go away. All such avoidance does is leave the problem-solving program in the grip of the *langue*, of the deeper structure by which its forms are constrained. The avoidance does even more, for not only does it present the dominance of deeper structure as "surface eclecticism," it guarantees that our prospects of change remain imprisoned in the reformist and systemic deceits. In the first deceit, nothing happens. In the second, nothing could ever happen in the absence of crisis.

Structuralism suggests a third possibility for change beyond the reformist and systemic varieties, what we can call structural transformation. Before saying more, however, beyond these surface illusions that is another illusion to unmask. Thus far, the discussion has focused on the illusions wrought at the level of structure in the language of pragmatic liberalism. By way of its flat eclecticism and emphasis on first-order proposals of problem solving, pragmatic liberalism mystifies and legitimates a stagnant status quo of broken-down arguments in the discredited inventory of liberal legal thought. Next, I turn from the level of the structural *langue* to the level of style, that of argumentative practice. Here, the hope for harmony is resounding, blotting out other, more dissonant understandings of the relation between rule and argument. The result of the harmony effect is a situation in which the entire terrain of style is made invisible, and all there is, and all there should be, is the settled body of law. This is the illusion obscuring the path of structural transformation, what I call the illusion of settled law.

The Illusion of Settled Law

In liberal legal thought there is a conventional view of the relation between legislation and adjudication. Legislation, in this view, is a frozen still in a series of political battles. Through a momentary compromise in the natural world of interest-group pluralism, a statutory scheme is never anything other than a temporary truce. Nevertheless, the political character of the statute recedes as we shift into adjudication. As we have seen, adjudication in liberal legal thought aspires for more than a temporary political freeze; it aspires to the impersonal interpretation and application of both statute and common law. In this view, the role of the jurist is to properly identify the facts, the rules of a legal concept, and the application of rule to fact. The rules internal to a legal concept ought to be "settled." This means that legal concepts should be predictable, coherent, and justifiable in their stable relations. If the concept's rules are unsettled, the jurist ought to settle them. In contrast with the settled terrain of the legal concept is the terrain of legal reasoning, which is ad hoc, unpredictable, and indeterminate. The reasoning that takes place from case to case may be more or less complicated, but as a possible entryway for ideology and personal policy preference, reasoning should always be limited by the apolitical force of settled rules.

The image of fact, rule, and ad hoc reasoning is different in the jurisprudence of style. In this view – the view propounded throughout this book – the liberal legal image gets turned inside out. Whereas in the language of liberal legalism the jurist aims for settled and apolitical *legal concepts*, and regards the level of *reasoning* or *justification* as open and ideological, the jurisprudence of style suggests another orientation. The level of the legal concept is revealed as a typically indeterminate and often contradictory space of technical knowledge, requiring juridical *choice*, and the level of justification is revealed as a recurring pattern of argumentative practice. This orientation, as a result, *flips* the liberal image. Rather than marking the rules as the settled and central area of juridical work, and marking patterns of justification as the marginal work of something called "legal theory," it is the structure of argumentative practice that becomes largely settled and certainly central, and the domain of the legal concept that becomes a site of technical and indeterminate knowledge, riddled with ideological choice. What's more, rather than see the activity as a logical sequence moving from justification to settled rule, from the perspective of legal style the activity goes in reverse. The jurist constitutes the field by way of choosing a legal concept, and then in the encounter with the technical disarray and contradictions therein, falls into a constraining pattern of legal argument as a means of justifying his conclusion. This is the structure I developed in Chapters 1, 2, and 3, have tried to illustrate in Chapters 4, 5, 6, and 8.

If it is the patterns of argument that enjoy a particular structure and it is the legal concepts that are open and discretionary, why does the office of liberal legal thought teach it backwards? What is responsible for the persistence of this illusion of settled law? What empowers the marginalization of style in liberal legal thought? As will be recalled, the style of the jurist at work in the office of liberal legalism develops by way of a background-foreground distinction. Deep in the jurist's background practice are those argumentative moves taken largely for granted; in the language of liberal legalism, these relate most fundamentally to the three theses. It is not necessary for the jurist to be consciously aware of them, for like the rules of English grammar, they function at their best when they are invisible in the flow of speech. Of course, while liberal legalism is forever busy with the work of naturalizing these background practices, as I discussed in the previous section, they are anything but natural. In any case, the liberal jurist operates from this basic posture, arguing under the influence of the liberal *langue*. Take care to note, however, that this is not and has not been a claim about an inescapable and universal mental structure. As I discussed in Chapter 2, the point is phenomenological. In the work of a juridical master, there are prefigured preunderstandings always already at work. The jurist enters the world of legal argument already familiarized with an entire set of ways for constituting and negotiating that world. (I don't even mean here to refer to those practices underlying the jurist's work of legal argument, from status identity to a preference for Lexis over Westlaw to the know-how of persuading clerks and colleagues to everything else; I am only dealing with the background practices relevant to the discrete activity of liberal legal thought.) These ways involve, at a prefigured level, the use of equipment for the operationalizing of the three theses of liberal legalism.

For the amateur jurist, however, the process in which the internalization of the liberal grammar takes place has matured only a little. Like the student of a foreign language still grappling with an alien grammar, the background practices of liberal legal thought are not yet backgrounded at all – they are entirely conscious and still vulnerable to overt criticism. Indeed, in many US law schools, this is exactly what takes place as master jurists slowly go about the process of training the amateurs in coming to absorb and then embody the background practice: what will come to be known as "thinking like a lawyer." Once an amateur makes the passage into expertise and mastery, thinking like a lawyer turns out to involve no thinking at all, for *thinking* is what jurists do (in this particular sense) only when something has gone wrong. When a jurist transitions from an amateur who has yet to feel familiar in the world of legal thought and is constantly struggling to rationalize and universalize the legal material, to a master whose arguments *flow*, are in the zone, in the pocket, on a roll, and so on, the composition of legal arguments is much less like the work of law school memo-writing and far more like the composition of paintings or musical pieces when the artist has "fallen" into her work. Falling here means precisely losing oneself in the medium – the distinction between mind and object fades.

What I have so far been describing is the level of background practice in the work of the jurist. It is a level that, by and large, goes completely unnoticed. In contrast with these background practices – the familiarity the jurist experiences in her embodied know-how of the world of legal thought – is the level of the foreground. It is to this broad and amorphous space of the legal structure – the foreground – that I applied the term "legal style." But it would be a mistake to see background as a level of "prefigured preunderstandings" and foreground as a level of rational analysis. I think that the borderland is much more slippery than that. The way to think about it, as I see it, is that we find the jurist more and more in the foreground the more and more she experiences difficulties in her composition of the argument. If the jurist is immediately confronted with gaps and contradictions, vying policies and principles, and if the jurist doesn't find herself soon *getting into a groove*, the style of argument is going to look all the more "constructed," more ideological, less justified, and overall, a less satisfying piece of legal work. Something has gone wrong here – we can't find the smooth and the familiar. We may end up having to balance our way out, knowing that this will, in the end, only be a cover that covers nothing of consequence.

To borrow an analogy of a different sort for the moment, consider a hallway in your home that you travel many times a day. For some reason, in making your way from one end to the other, there are two doorways that always need opening. As you approach them, it never crosses your mind that you'll need to make sure that you are on your feet when you pass through and not lying on your side, or that you should walk through the large open part and not the small open part between the hinge and the wall. Or, that you will need to figure out those pesky "doorknobs." In fact, as you travel from one end to the other, you understand all of these things without the slightest rational analysis. The knowledge is embodied. But now you come to a doorway in the hall and the knob won't turn. At first, this glitch may spark very little "thought," especially if the knob is prone to sticking. But after your typical efforts, the knob still won't turn, the door still won't open, and here you are, in your absolutely familiar hallway handling your absolutely familiar equipment, but your know-how has now run out. The switch from background into foreground has taken place, and the problem is becoming increasingly foregrounded as the doorknob continues in its errancy. Perhaps you give up and turn around, or perhaps you put your foot right through the door, teaching it who's boss. In any case, the background practice that was only moments before so deeply embodied has given way to a rational examination of some frustrating difficulty.

If we come back now to legal thought in the hands of a master, the grammar of liberal legalism functions as the jurist's background practice. These are the moves of expertise, moves requiring very little if any reflection. These are the moves of the normal human being strolling down the hallway, the baseball player scooping up the grounder and firing to first, the sculptor's acceptance of the clay's invitation to mold in this direction rather than that, the orator's "unconscious" shift in rhetorical strategy. The jurist's foreground practice, in contrast, involves the rational negotiation of problems that look complex or recalcitrant. From the perspective of the amateur jurist, the whole business looks like foreground practice. From the perspective of the master, forays in the foreground are the indicia of failure or novelty.

I have been referring to background and foreground as abstractions: the background involves a familiar know-how when arguing from liberalism's three theses; the foreground indicates a breakdown in that familiar know-how. But what of these distinctions in the more specific contexts of the three structures outlined throughout this book? As we move away from the "master grammar" and into the subsystems, background practices shift as well.

In the classic style, the first thesis of free competition expands to incorporate most of the background. That is, the master jurist in the classic liberal style understands the natural and necessary features of society as inscribed in the immanent fabric of law, and that fabric is first and foremost wound up in the thesis of free competition. The second thesis of social control is pushed out of the background and into the foreground. It only becomes necessary to invoke the natural right of the state to regulate free competition when something has gone wrong; it is an exceptional case, and we only end up arguing for social control in cases of defect. Background practices are, consequently, arguments supporting the natural rights of individuals to compete in an artificial society. Foreground practices are those arguments in favor of regulation and government planning. The *style* in which background and foreground relate to one another has everything to do with the third thesis of naturalizing juridical science, and in the classic style we have already had many opportunities to see that this is the style of legal formalism. The "grooves," "zones," "pockets," and what-have-you of formalism shape the argumentative pathways leading from the background practice into the foreground and out into the surface layer of judgment. When the classic liberal style is at its best, all of this is invisible: all we see is a set of facts, a settled law, and a judgment that was necessitated by the application of that settled law to fact. It is like being swept up in one of Bach's fugues, with little ability to sense the intricate structure underneath.

When the classic style morphs into the modern, shifts abound. The first thesis of free competition remains in the background. It is a mistake to think that it travels entirely into the contingent space of the foreground. Modern liberals are as committed to individual rights as the classic liberals ever were, but they also see much more of a role for social control. The argument for regulation, consequently, achieves a more natural bearing, locked in a harmonious balance with the thesis of free competition. In fact, it is this belief in equipoise that best signifies the background practice of the modern style: it is a given that these two theses, seemingly at odds with one another, can be reconciled on an equal footing. The work of the jurist lies in the working out of these details. When the argument is flowing, the modern variant of the third thesis is firing on all cylinders: through a functionalist style, the harmonious convergence of the twin theses is realized through the identification of symmetrical harmony, that between law and society. So long as the purpose of a statute or doctrine can be determined, and that purpose lines up with social science expertise, the dissonance of legal conflicts will be resolved in the consonance of law's serving social ends. But this is still different than in the classic style, because for the modern jurist the line between background and foreground is admittedly problematic. The modern jurist aspires for settled law, and seeks necessitated legal conclusions. But the modern jurist has already encountered the ideological critique of the classical jurist, and understands that the objectivity of her functionalist style ultimately depends on the work of other human beings. Functionalism is therefore already more visibly foregrounded (and therefore compromised) than formalism ever was. With its conventional bleeding into the ideological foreground, legal functionalism demands more from the jurist in terms of rational justification, ever concerned about the criticism that functionalism is result-oriented, activist, and an assault on the Rule of Law. Proponents of the modern style denied these charges, over and over again.

Of course, as we have already seen, by the 1970s there were ever fewer jurists ready to buy the modernist denial. Rather than marshal the rejection of denial in favor of a face-to-face negotiation with the unsettled terrain of legal practice, pragmatic liberalism ends up just reinforcing the need for law's harmony, and repeating the expectation for settled law. Why? If the whole liberal project of naturalizing legal science has failed, why keep on with the illusion of settled law? As I argued above, structural illusions are less likely to involve this issue of denial in the same way. At that deeper level, processes of mystification and legitimation inoculate the jurist, saving her from having to regularly confront the conflicts in her argumentative practice. The antinomies at the level of the *langue* are already hidden in the work of the third thesis. Here at the level of style, however, at the level of the legal concept, the gap between the sort of consonant law we desire and the sort of dissonance we experience in the course of legal argument is more difficult to avoid.

Fortunately for the pragmatist, clever avoidance is a hallmark of pragmatic liberalism. Rather than see legal concepts as open sites of technical knowledge inviting creative deployment, pragmatic liberalism ends up fortifying the older view of the legal concept as, or at least aspiring to be, a settled body of rules. Rather than see legal arguments as abiding by recurring patterns and formal styles, pragmatic liberalism forces a vision of "legal reasoning" that is by turns a matter of higher-order meta-theory, or random and ad hoc instances of policy preference. In each case, pragmatic liberalism obscures an understanding of liberal legal thought illuminated in the jurisprudence of style. As this discussion of the style of argumentative practice in liberal legal thought has been intended to reiterate, the pragmatic presentation of argumentative practice is backwards.

Pragmatic liberalism insists on this conceptual illusion (the illusion of settled law), this backwards understanding of settled concepts and indeterminate modes of reasoning, because it is safe to do so. If we accept the view of the jurisprudence of style and think of concepts as open sites of technical knowledge and ideological battle, and modes of reasoning as styles constrained by deep background practices, the entire edifice of liberal legal thought looks ready to collapse. In their introduction to a spate of property cases thought particularly muddled, consider these scholars in an effort to ease the anxiety of first-year law students:

> [Learning the law of servitudes] is a little like diving into a swamp at night, swimming and floundering in terror, and emerging quite fortuitously on some unknown shore in the morning. When it is all over you're sorry that it happened, you don't understand anything you saw but you know that you didn't like it, and you are extremely grateful that you blundered out.[20]

The reason it is a commonplace to analogize learning a messy legal concept with drowning in the dark is that it really does seem like drowning in the dark. If our legal concepts are not predictable and consonant, adjudication becomes unaccountable lawmaking, law dissolves into political dissonance, and the game's done.

Thankfully, we needn't be taken in by the illusion of settled rules. The open and indeterminate space of the legal concept is, to be sure, a space in which ideology runs riot. Recall my list of twelve pairs of servitudes rules from back in Chapter 3. Surely it is something like the fearsome character of that list that triggers nightmares of swamps and floundering and the rest. Servitudes may turn out to be an extreme case of technical indeterminacy, but I doubt it. I suspect that many (though certainly not all) legal concepts manifest similar states of technical indeterminacy and ideological discretion. The illusion of settled rules suggests that if this is so, we need to get to work, reconciling, resolving, harmonizing, settling. But if we learn to sidestep this illusion, if we learn that legal concepts are sites of technical knowledge demanding decision, and that there are backgrounded practices of legal argument in which those rules and decisions

[20] Sheldon Kurtz et al., *Cases and Materials on American Property* (6th ed.) (St. Paul: West, 2012), p. 608.

are ferried along, perhaps we can make good on the structuralist claim that pragmatic liberalism makes us see backwards.

For if it *is* backwards, let us flip it and see what comes. What if we took conceptual indeterminacy as an invitation for creative engineering, or what Unger calls "experimentalism," rather than as rampant activism and a threat to the Rule of Law? What if it turned out that, rather than seek out a tepid reformism (the reformist deceit) or a substitution of entire systems (the systemic deceit), jurists embraced the contradictions immanent in the legal concept and used them as a lever for piecemeal transformation? Would this amount to judicial activism? I really don't think so, for what I am suggesting as a route for structural transformation is merely the illumination of the jurist's own background practices, practices that pragmatic liberalism works so hard to keep in shadow. If jurists reframed the foreground as less about breakdown and amateurism and more about creative empowerment, this would not turn them into activists. It would rather introduce them to what Unger calls the "higher vocations" of the jurist: celebrating the contradictions of the structure and lurching out new directions, using the hidden corridors of liberal legal thought to generate styles of practice we have yet to discover. The source material for structural transformation, in other words, is the antinomy – that dissonance which jurists have been for 150 years working so hard to resolve.

Even if this is right, how, as Unger has recently asked, "can we achieve structural insight without succumbing to structural dogma?"[21] Unger writes, "Part of the answer lies in the development of institutions and practices that possess, in superior measure, the attribute of corrigibility, allowing us experimentally to discover the path as we advance . . . As law and legal thought deal with structure in the details, they offer a preferred place in which to look for the equipment that the execution of this task requires."[22] And again:

> We cannot [achieve our structuralist ambitions] . . . by taking refuge in the illusion of neutrality, the pretense of the existence of regimes that fail to tilt the scales among competing visions of the good and opposing conceptions of humanity. We can do so only by creating arrangements that to the greatest degree allow themselves to be corrected in the light of experience. As we revise our institutions and practices for the sake our recognized interests and professed ideals, we change our understanding of those ideals and interests. Our reward for this effort is the enhancement of our ability to engage a particular social world without surrendering to it and to trade institutional habits for untried opportunities of cooperation.

[21] Unger, The Critical Legal Studies Movement, supra note 3, at 68. [22] Id. at 23.

No entrenched regime of social division and hierarchy can survive such a strengthening of our powers of initiative.[23]

Indeed, the jurisprudence of style refuses "refuge in the illusion of neutrality," in the illusions of pragmatism. It is a jurisprudence practiced in the spirit of the antinomian sensibility.

The Illusion of the Now

So far, I have discussed two broad forms of depoliticization, cases where pragmatic liberalism systematically hides its ideology in an illusion of harmony. The illusion of eclectic problem solving concerns the failure of jurists to meaningfully engage the mystifying process in which American Pragmatism naturalizes itself in the grammar of liberal legal thought. The illusion of settled law concerns the failure of jurists to confront legal style and the relation between background and foreground. Whereas the first illusion consistently hides the grammar of liberal legal thought, the second illusion distorts the relation between legal concepts and our practices of legal argument. Finally, I want to rehearse the historical illusion propagated in the language of pragmatic liberalism. Whereas the first and second illusions take their momentum from the flat eclecticism of American Pragmatism, it is that sensibility's notion of "the present" that triggers the illusion of the Now.

As I discussed in Chapter 7, in the debate among art historians about what do with the "contemporary," about whether it marks off some deeper and as-of-yet unnamed structure of practice, or whether it is superfluous, I take it to be a common presumption to prefer the latter position. Be that as it may, it is the effort to release the contemporary from the grip of "the Now" that I will press further. I think Arthur Danto's work on contemporary art is helpful in doing so. Danto reminded his audience of the obvious: the terms "modern" and "contemporary" work simultaneously in double registers. On the one hand, modern means "recent," and contemporary means something like being in tandem with time. This is a temporal register, and we casually use both modern and contemporary in this temporal sense. On the other hand, Danto wrote, "just as modern is not simply a temporal concept, meaning, say, 'most recent,' neither is 'contemporary' merely a temporal term, meaning whatever is taking place at the present moment."[24] Danto's "on the other hand" is therefore a

[23] Id. at 68.

[24] Arthur Danto, *After the End of Art: Contemporary Art and the Pale of History* (Princeton, NJ: Princeton University Press, 1997), p. 9.

second register of use, denoting a style, or "deep structure."[25] The modern, that is, suggests a family of forms that will, at some point in the future, no longer be "very recent" at all. What then, of a *contemporary* style? It is this break between the modern and the contemporary that brings us to Danto's infamous thesis: art had ended. Although, of course, that is not really what his thesis suggested.[26] Rather it was that while art continued, and would always continue, after the collapse of modernism the *history* of art had ended.

Danto believed that by the 1960s and 1970s a modern style of thinking had disappeared. This had been a modern style of thinking about both the nature of art, and how that nature contrasted with the art of its traditional antagonists. By the time Andy Warhol set up his pile of store-bought Brillo Boxes in 1964, the story of modern art was finished. Works like Warhol's lacked all the convictions of modern art, "had no brief against the art of the past, no sense that the past is something from which liberation must be won, no sense even that it is at all different as art from modern art generally."[27] Danto continued, "The narrative structures of traditional representational art, and then of modernist art, have eroded in at least the sense that they have no longer an active role to play in the production of contemporary art."[28] Indeed, it is precisely the decoupling from historical narrative that, for Danto, defines the end of art history.

We can now see that, for Danto, the end of art means the end of western historical narratives of art. Again, not the end of art of the Now, which ostensibly includes all art being made everywhere, "of what we have directly in front of us, and what they have in front of them over there." What ended was a discernible structure of modern practice, but, said Danto, it ended in such a way that the art world took no notice. It was this surreptitious conclusion that did so much to conflate contemporaneity with the pragmatic sense of the Now: "It is a characteristic of contemporaneity – but not of modernity – that it should have begun insidiously, without slogan or logo, without anyone being greatly aware that it had happened."[29] Make no mistake, the arrival of *postmodernism* was loud. But I take Danto's point to be that in contrast with the way in which the moderns waged a historical battle, Warhol's art signaled the end

[25] Id. at 147.

[26] For discussion, see the symposium Danto and His Critics: Art History, Historiography and After the End of Art, 37 *History & Theory* (1998).

[27] Id. at 5. [28] Id. at 48. [29] Id. at 5.

of the fight and a situation in which no one anymore even knew who the protagonists might have been.[30] It was now fireworks rather than artillery shells, explosions for excess, not enemies.

And so, what came "after" the end of art? A very *particular* phenomenon: "artists, liberated from the burden of history, were free to make art in whatever way they wished, for any purposes they wished, or for no purposes at all," the very vacancy of the contemporary style coming into focus. The mark of contemporaneity was a broad relation to art in which faith in the singularity of artistic practice – what Danto called the Age of Manifestos – had been replaced by faith in the wonder and usefulness of the many, the plural, the eclectic, "a style of using styles,"[31] with no style to call its own. "It is no longer something available to us as something we can live. Or, in a way, we can live it only in the mode of pastiche and pretense, and that is not really living it since no one lives it with us."[32] As Andy Warhol said, "How can you say any style is better than another? You ought to be able to be an abstract expressionist next week, or a Pop artist, or a realist, without feeling you have given up something."[33] The contemporary, in Danto's understanding, was a dialectical response to the end of the moderns and the formation of a "post-historical" art world.[34] It meant to do work in such a way that the art bore the mark of art's historical conclusion, to do art after the history of art had ended. To make art in the present, by contrast, well, that didn't mean – it couldn't *mean* – anything at all.

In the effort to further tease out the pragmatist production of the "Now" as we make the transition to the history of legal thought, I want to offer a metaphor. Imagine a park ranger, also a naturalist, hiking with her son in the Rocky Mountains, who has come upon a very large, very colorful snakeskin, lying across the trail. The child sees it, and after a bit of noisy surprise, asks his mother for an assessment. She suggests that it was the skin of a rattlesnake, very recently shed by the color of it, and that in all likelihood the snake's home is nearby. The ranger mother scampers off hunting the real thing, while the child stands alone. The child is dazzled with what until moments before *was* the snake – well, not *really* the snake, but an essential part of it, but now nothing more than a kind of strange copy, a frozen image in time. The mother, meanwhile, is looking for the real thing. She is, after all, a *naturalist*.

[30] Id. at 48. [31] Id. at 9–10. [32] Id. at 202.
[33] Id. at 37. [34] Id. at 47.

The punchline, prematurely: the *contemporary* structure is the snakeskin, the pragmatic *Now* is the snake.[35] Bear with me. We have two versions of the snake, one in the Now but actually absent in the sense that neither the ranger nor the child have any idea of its whereabouts. But even in its absence, we know, or at least think we know, that the rattler is alive somewhere very close, and beneath its current skin – its *real* skin – flow the utterly complex processes of life. The life of the real snake, like present time, is a life that is already slipping away, already gone, beneath the cracks. And it is this quasi-chimerical beauty the naturalist hunts, in vain, taking no notice of the skins left behind. The other version of the snake is from the past, a very recent past but a past all the same. The child has the *material* in his hands, right now in the current moment. But this material isn't the *real*, we all know it, this isn't real art, real law, the real snake. The mother suddenly calls out, "There it went, I caught only a glimpse!" The child looks up and listens. He thinks, "But, I can see the snake just fine. I have it in my hands! Look at its colors . . . "

Maybe the mother with her scientific expertise isn't crazy for chasing a rattlesnake, but is the child crazy for confusing the skin for the creature? Had the child made the same claim for the skin just, let's say, one week earlier, we would have seen a live rattlesnake in his trembling hands. A week hence, that very same skin that had, in the current moment, enclosed the muscled totality of the snake's being, encloses nothing. If the child is crazy, I wonder if it is the tiny germ of the kind of crazy untimeliness described by Friedrich Nietzsche, who found his meditations temporally out of whack with *his* present.[36] Or if the child's sense represents a small glimmer of Giorgio Agamben's "Contemporary," a person at once *out* of time in the experience of *his* time.[37] Perhaps with the innocent child, and not with the expert mother, Nietzsche and Agamben might look to a live snake's skin, *precisely as dead skin*, even while bearing witness to skin in its attached, living form. Consider Agamben's suggestion that "Contemporariness is . . . that relationship with time that adheres to it through a disjunction and an anachronism. *Those who coincide too well with the epoch, those who are perfectly tied to it in every respect, are not contemporaries, precisely because they do not manage to see it*; they are not able

[35] I encourage the reader to dwell on the metaphor's many flaws. I only ask that you take it for what it is: a trope.

[36] Friedrich Nietzsche, *Untimely Meditations* (Daniel Breazeale, ed.) (Reginald John Hollingdale, trans.) (Cambridge: Cambridge University Press, 1997).

[37] Giorgio Agamben, *What Is an Apparatus?: And Other Essays* (Stanford, CA: Stanford University Press, 2009), p. 41.

to firmly hold their gaze on it."[38] Those who coincide too well with the epoch – the naturalist hunting the snake – are blinded to the contemporary because their gaze is not on the contemporary but on the Now. As Agamben continues, it is the bright lights of the present that obscure the opacity of contemporaneity, which is at once a "special darkness" inseparable from those present lights.[39] The contemporary, like the snakeskin, is always only a proxy for a deeper set of forms yet to be named, forms obscured by the glare of the Now, the spectacle of the snake itself, everywhere and still nowhere. The *contemporary*, in turn, is similarly a proxy, a shell, a skin-not-yet-shed, a skin-not-yet-dead.

It is here that I want to leave the metaphor behind, or at least change it, for it strikes me that while it makes good sense to see the contemporary as a placeholder for some other thing, a *thing* out of sight for those perfectly tied to their time, we must now say what happens in the transition from the contemporary placeholder to the thing as-yet-unnamed. So, for instance, Danto failed to name the thing for which his post-historical contemporary was only a proxy. We know very well that what he saw was the world of contemporary art, that he saw the skin shedding even as it was still attached to the snake. But what was it – just refuse, just the end of art as he knew it?

There is a similar trajectory at work in Duncan Kennedy's depiction of Contemporary Legal Thought.[40] After his well-known diagnostics of "classical legal thought" and "social legal thought," Kennedy saw the emergence of Contemporary Legal Thought in the same milieu as Danto saw contemporary art, a structure of legal argument coming into dominance in the late 1960s and 1970s. And just as Danto described this as a time in which art had ended, so too did Kennedy suggest that the structures of American Legal Thought had come to an end. Like Danto's vision of a coherent modern practice of art ranging between 1880 and the 1960s, Kennedy described a coherent practice of legal argument covering that same slate of years. To be sure, neither modernism as Danto saw it, nor legal thought as Kennedy saw it, was even remotely uniform. But what was gone by the 1960s, according to both, "was a large integrating concept" parallel to what had gone before.[41] Instead, the deep structure of what Danto and Kennedy both called the contemporary could be

[38] Id. [39] Id. at 45

[40] Kennedy, A Critique of Adjudication, supra note2, at 346–348.

[41] Duncan Kennedy, "Three Globalizations of Law and Legal Thought," in *The New Law and Development: A Critical Appraisal* (David Trubek and Alvaro Santos, eds.) (Cambridge: Cambridge University Press, 2006), p. 63.

understood "as the unsynthesized coexistence of transformed elements" borrowed from earlier, vanquished times.[42] Unlike prior structures of Legal Thought, Kennedy saw Contemporary Legal Thought as an open-ended language, sourced in the scattered debris left over from the demolished remains of the Moderns. Contemporary Legal Thought for Kennedy, like contemporary art for Danto, marks the end of Legal Thought. It is a time of ruin and rule by the dead. At the same time, Kennedy did not think that Legal Thought had stopped in the 1960s. Indeed, a great deal of Kennedy's work over the past few decades has been precisely directed at an understanding of the argumentative practices of jurists living in his generation, his current moment, what came *after* the end of Legal Thought. Nevertheless, Contemporary Legal Thought, like Contemporary Art, has remained a marker, a placeholder, a proxy, awaiting a time in which we can see in that special darkness the skin falling from the snake. Contemporary Legal Thought awaits its name.

As this book nears its end, I hope that it comes as no surprise that my name for a *contemporary* history of legal thought is pragmatic liberalism. As I have suggested, the history of liberal legal thought in the United States is, in the structuralist view, a triptych. We have three images, three constellations, three styles of argumentative practice. The classic and the modern styles have operated throughout the period with which we have been concerned: 1870 to the contemporary. But the relative "strengths" of those styles have been variable. Between 1870 and World War II, the classic style may have witnessed something of a downward trend, only to revive for a season in the 1980s and 1990s. The modern style was in effect between 1870 and World War II, but where the classic style was waning, the moderns were waxing. By the 1980s and 1990s, the modern style was something out of fashion. The "contemporary," a structure of thought ranging from the 1970s and onward, has been regularly identified as a time of decline. What I have tried to suggest, however, is that, despite the pragmatist effort to disguise itself in an everlasting presence, all surface and eclecticism and problem-solving, and no depth or master narrative or totality, it is possible to name it. In naming it as such, do we offer an account of what is *really going on*? Of course not. It is an account of a *contemporary* structure of legal thought, no more, no less.

Pragmatic liberalism's ability to disguise itself as the "Now" is a function of, once again, a good idea gone bad. Pragmatic liberalism flirts – but

[42] Id.

only flirts – with the idea that time is for real. That is, it flirts with a view of historical contingency and contextual necessity. It flirts with an understanding of history as always subject to change, that our current conditions are neither natural nor necessary, that our institutions might have been otherwise. But in a typical move, pragmatic liberalism gestures toward this view of time, but fails to take it seriously.[43] If it consummated the idea that time was for real, pragmatic liberalism would recognize itself for what it is: dogma and ideology masquerading as cool sophistication. It would be forced to give up its commitments to a surface eclecticism, *outside of time*, and plead agnosticism on the question of whether the reality of time allows for, perhaps even *demands*, structures of practice. It could see, perhaps, in that sea of legal concepts and rules a scattering of points as the stars dot the sky. And it could, perhaps, see in that smattering an intelligibility: not the intelligibility of conceptual sense and complex coherence, but the intelligibility that belongs to constellations. Constellations, of course, are human compositions, efforts to "comb the rubble for affinities amid the debris, affinities that accumulate into a montage, an illustration, a narrative, a structure in which the ruins of Law's bodies once more gain effect."[44] Constellations may not be naturally harmonious. But they have their uses.

[43] Roberto Unger and Lee Smolin's notion of temporal naturalism is relevant here. As they suggest, "We would like to have a naturalism that does not reduce human experience and aspirations to illusions . . . The root of the crisis in naturalism is its being wedded to the picture of the universe as a machine. This in turn is a consequence of the idea that nature is governed by laws which are timeless, immutable, and mathematical. The path out of the crisis is to embrace a new form of naturalism based on the reality of time." Roberto Unger and Lee Smolin, *The Singular Universe and the Reality of Time: A Proposal in Natural Philosophy* (Cambridge: Cambridge University Press, 2015), p. 357.

[44] Justin Desautels-Stein and Christopher Tomlins, "Afterword," in *Searching for Contemporary Legal Thought* (Justin Desautels-Stein and Christopher Tomlins, eds.) (New York: Cambridge University Press, 2017), p. 545.

Coda

In 1843 Soren Kierkegaard published *Fear and Trembling*. In this work Kierkegaard, writing under the name Johannes de silentio, articulated a series of stages in the human effort to find faith in God. In the midst of these stages there is a terror, a terrible expense for believing in the universal. All too often, Kierkegaard suggested, human beings claim the mantle of faith without realizing these true costs. In his exploration of this distinction between the shallow and bourgeois Churchgoer buying faith on the cheap, and the *truly* faithful, Kierkegaard famously revisited the Biblical story of Abraham and Isaac.[1] As we know, the Hebrew God tests Abraham's faith by commanding the sacrifice of his son Isaac, thus prompting a moral dilemma: Abraham must either reject the universal dictate of the divine, or disobey the ethical prohibition on murder. In either case, the suspension of either imperative is undesirable, a fact lost on most church gatherings in which, as Kierkegaard laments, sermons regularly praise Abraham's willingness to follow God's will. For Kierkegaard, however, this casual willingness to praise and emulate Abraham's faith comes much too fast – the bourgeois believer "does not want to work and yet wants to understand the story."[2] In the "easy" and

[1] For discussion of this much discussed work, see, e.g., Donald Green, "Developing Fear and Trembling," in *The Cambridge Companion to Kierkegaard* (Alastair Hannay and Gordon Marino, eds.) (Cambridge: Cambridge University Press, 1998); David Lappano, *Soren Kierkegaard's Theology of Encounter: An Edifying and Polemical Life* (Oxford: Oxford University Press, 2017); Kevin Hoffman, Facing Threats to Earthly Fidelity: A Reading of Kierkegaard's Fear and Trembling, 34 *Journal of Religious Ethics* 439 (2006).

[2] Soren Kierkegaard, *Fear and Trembling* (Cambridge: Cambridge University Press, 2006), p. 63.

"bourgeois"[3] version of the moral, Abraham gave up what was most precious for the sake of God, and in this sacrificial attitude, ends up rewarded with the life of his son. But this isn't what the story is about, Kierkegaard explains. What is missed entirely is the brutal *cost* of faith, a cost that is both essential and terrible, but for Kierkegaard, worth it all the same.

At this point there emerges a relation between two of Kierkegaard's figures. On the one side is Kierkegaard's target, the bourgeois believer, the churchgoer who enjoys the world and all its pleasures while professing faith in a transcendent and universal God. And yet, this is a "surface" belief because it is a superficial faith. It never pushes into the depths of faith's fundamental source, its essential irrationality. The surface believer understands his faith as entirely natural, simple, all too human, for he feels God's love and revels in it. There *is no* terrible cost, only the doing of what humans are made to do: take pleasure in a world that was made for them. In contrast with this surface believer, Kierkegaard describes a character he calls the Knight of Faith. The Knight of Faith is a curious being. When we see him strolling down the street, eating at the tavern, cavorting with friends and neighbors, one would never know he was anything other than the typical bourgeois believer. He seems entirely at home in the world. But there is nothing normal about the Knight of Faith; he is a Madman.

To understand this madness, which is a very *sane* madness, Kierkegaard introduces a third figure, the Knight of Infinite Resignation. Kierkegaard says that Abraham, when we come to really appreciate him, is revealed as a Knight of Faith. But if Kierkegaard (or Johannes de silentio) had been in Abraham's position, similarly tasked with the murder of his child, he would fail the test of faith. The failure, Kierkegaard explained, would not have consisted in his failure to kill. That, however unthinkable, Kierkegaard could do, would do, at God's bidding. If Kierkegaard would have been willing to kill, why fail the test of faith? Is not the killing the test? Nope. Killing is the easy part.

To get a sense for the hard part, Kierkegaard confronted the outright absurdity of what God asked Abraham to do. The story is not what the sermons make it out to be, a pleasant tale of the triumph of faith in the face of adversity. The story is *insane*. Here you are, going about your business, when God comes down and explains that in a few days' time,

[3] For an interesting discussion of *bourgeois* in the context of existentialism, phenomenology, and critical theory, see Peter Gordon, *Adorno and Existence* (Cambridge: Harvard University Press, 2016).

you are going to take your child up a mountain and murder him. Now, it is not the fact of God's showing up on your doorstep that's crazy; God does that. It is what God is telling you to do that is crazy. Kierkegaard conceded that if it had been him in Abraham's position, he would have had little trouble packing up his things, loading his child on the horse for the journey, and setting out on the three-day hike, knowing full-well what would come at the end: a bloody blade. But – and here's where the Knight of Infinite Resignation comes in – it is not only the child's body sacrificed at the end of that blade. It is also Kierkegaard's ability to take pleasure in the human world, ever again. He will forevermore resign to the infinite, banished from the world of the finite, of the particular, of pleasure on earth.

"The moment I mounted the horse," said Kierkegaard, "I would have said to myself: 'Now all is lost; God demands Isaac, I sacrifice him and with him all my joy – yet God is love and continues to be that for me . . . ' "[4] It would not matter for Kierkegaard that at the end, God might gift him the life of his child, excusing the murderous act. It was already over, for once Kierkegaard began the journey, the journey had in its way already ended. With that first step came a total resignation, a surrender to the dissonance between the human world and the world of spirit. Having killed his ability to see a place for himself on earth, this Knight of Infinite Resignation finds himself destined for a solitary life of sadness and strangeness in the world of flesh, waiting only for redemption in the infinite, the universal. He has come to see that while God's love is real and true, it is nevertheless incommensurate with the whole of natural reality. There is no harmony there, just a clashing of devilish tones. Unlike the bourgeois believer who takes his faith on the cheap, the Knight of Infinite Resignation understands the costs of faith in the universal, has borne those costs, and in the process, has become utterly estranged. It is absurd, says the Knight of Infinite Resignation, to enjoy this world as well as the prospect of the next. If you understand faith, really understand it, you'll have your cake, but never take the slightest bite.

Now comes the hard part of the story. Killing Isaac: Yes, Kierkegaard could have done that, and in the process become a Knight of Infinite Resignation. Terrible, but doable. The hard part, the unimaginable part, is to move from the plane of Infinite Resignation to the plane of Faith. And this is what Kierkegaard found so shocking about the Knight of Faith: there he was, eating his cake! But he wasn't eating it as the bourgeois believer eats it, without having paid the price. The Knight of Faith has made the

[4] Kierkegaard, *Fear and Trembling*, supra note 2, at 74.

moves of resignation, just as surely and completely as the Knight of Infinite Resignation. He has drained the antinomian cup and swallowed the impossibility of harmonizing an absurd world. Just like Kierkegaard, his child would have been lost forever from the very first step of the journey. The Knight of Faith's experience of infinite resignation, in other words, is for real. The price has been paid.

It is precisely because the Knight of Faith has paid the price that Kierkegaard regards him with such astonishment. For rather than adopt the asceticism of the solitary monk, forever removed from the world and its pleasures, the Knight of Faith receives his child at the end of the story, just as Abraham did, with joy! Kierkegaard was baffled:

> [W]hen I must think about Abraham, I am virtually annihilated. At every moment I am aware of that prodigious paradox which is the context of Abraham's life; at every moment I am repelled, and in spite of all its passion, my thought cannot penetrate it, cannot make a hairsbreadth of headway. I strain every muscle to get perspective, and at the same instant I become paralyzed ... Abraham I cannot understand; in a certain sense I can learn nothing from him except to be amazed.[5]

As Kierkegaard tells it, Abraham began his journey just as Kierkegaard would have begun: with renunciation. Without delay, Abraham obeyed. And having obeyed, Abraham renounced the world and his love for it, including his love for Isaac. Abraham would have said, just like Kierkegaard, "Once I mounted the horse, all was lost." And yet, it is this very moment that distinguishes renunciation of the natural world from real faith. For even while Abraham renounces materiality in exchange for the world of spirit, Abraham continues to believe that nothing has been lost at all. Abraham exists as a paradox of faith: in virtue of giving up his love for Isaac, he knows that the journey will end with Isaac in his arms, alive and unharmed. But remember, and at least for Kierkegaard, it is not that Abraham has somehow forgotten his travel up the mountain, his realization that the world is pain, and that love only happens in and through God. It is rather that Abraham receives Isaac full of joy and at the very same moment makes the moves of infinite resignation. Faith requires the price of a prior renunciation of the world – you must travel through this critical awareness before you can come back to a belief that begins at exactly the point where reason dies. Faith is madness.

Why end this book's story of liberal legal thought with Kierkegaard's Knight of Faith? Why begin the story with Nietzsche's Madman? For

[5] Id. at 71, 78.

whatever reason, if we include Nietzsche's Madman along with Kierkegaard's three figures, we end up with something like a map of argumentative postures in the history of liberal legal thought. The Madman and the Knight of Faith represent one couplet, and the Bourgeois Believer and the Knight of Infinite Resignation represent another. Each of them illustrates a competing response to the central preoccupation of liberal legal thought: How can we harmonize the twin imperatives of individualism and social interdependence through faith in a naturalizing legal science?

Nietzsche's Madman has a confident response: We cannot. The effort to elevate our experience of contradiction out and away from a painful dissonance, to believe in a force (be it Man or God) that might transform political will into a natural justice, is pure fantasy. The Knight of Faith's more mercurial answer: We can, but the experience of consonance comes with a price only a few are familiar with, and even fewer are willing to pay. What unites the Madman and the Knight of Faith is an appreciation for the warning of the classical pragmatists. Recall that for these American philosophers, the Cartesian formula had run its course. Disenchanted with the naturalizing sensibility, James and Dewey articulated an antinomian stance against those who would seek a harmonious truth in an external, objective universe. Both the Madman and the Knight of Faith arrive at this experience. The Madman has witnessed the folly of reaching for a view of the world that is God's; the Knight of Faith has passed through the experience of infinite resignation. They have both, in other words, encountered the antinomian. But these two figures react very differently in that encounter. The Madman has lost faith, and turns to other games. The Knight of Faith keeps playing, as did James and Dewey, for they suggested that we might nevertheless find truth in the natural world, even after the antinomian experience. This route for moving forward, for reclaiming or claiming anew a harmonious existence with one another and with nature, *demanded a regular confrontation with the antinomian*. Here is the site, embedded in philosophical pragmatism, of what Kierkegaard called "the prodigious paradox." Here is the promise of chiasmus, an antinomian naturalism.

These are two responses to liberal legal thought in its contemporary structure. We follow the Madman and reject it as fantasy or follow the Knight of Faith and accept it and transform it through an ongoing immersion with the antinomian. Today, those who reject liberal legal thought might have a different legal language in mind, perhaps of an Aristotelian or Islamic or Chinese character. Or they might reject it as nothing but politics by other means and without anything ready to put in its place; perhaps this is antinomianism let loose. The effort to transform the structure of liberal legal thought from the inside, neither through surface reform nor through systemic substitution, marshaling its contradictions in an existential roulette, is reflected in the work of the Harvard School and the jurisprudence of style. In this faithful position the jurist believes in law's constitutive power in the construction of the political. In the jurisprudence of style, harmony's law is dissonance.

There are two further responses, reflected in the figures of the Knight of Infinite Resignation and the Bourgeois Believer. These positions are far more suggestive of the structure of liberal legal thought as it is juridically experienced today. As I have noted, liberal legalism underwent a fundamental transformation in the 1970s. As antinomianism flourished in the arts at the turn of the twentieth century, liberal legal thought confronted its own antinomian moment several decades later. Especially for those jurists who participated in those contests and are still working today, the heat of those moments has only partially receded. They remain basically aware of the ideological problems attending any effort to find a harmonious resolution in the dissonance of liberal legalism's foundational features. And as for these masters now at work in the twenty-first century, they suffer from a perennial form of half-belief. The world of liberal legal thought has darkened, and it is only getting darker. Its essential imperatives and modes for harmonizing those imperatives at every level betray a failure to speak with authority. The compromises of the dead govern us for no reason other than that they have died. Nevertheless, these masters of half-belief hobble along, saddened in their roles as purveyors of a system in which they have largely lost faith. In the contemporary structure of liberal legal thought, these are our Knights of Infinite Resignation. Having borne witness to the politics of law, they see no way forward for a law of politics. There is no harmony, only color and sound and violence.

The second group is also aware of the ideology-critique of liberal legal thought. Or, at least, they have heard of it. In any case, they don't take it seriously, and it certainly isn't threatening or generative of the despair plaguing the Knights of Infinite Resignation. Of course, law is not perfect, legal thought (whatever that means) is not perfect, but so long as we focus on the problems in front of us, there is every reason to *believe*, every reason to believe everything will eventually get better. Our practices and tools are better than they have ever been, and once someone figures out cold fusion or better password protection or some such thing, they will get even better still. So long as we have faith in ourselves and our abilities to just make it work, there is no reason to worry over the past, for it has nothing to do with us. It is what it is, and there's no getting around that. These are, of course, victors' murmurs. These victors are the purveyors of the New Normal, adherents of a cultural sensibility that is at once the cutting edge and the poster child for the deaf and the dumb. For them, it is not harmony's law, but rather law's harmony that is American Pragmatism.

The way I see it, the first couplet of responses is operating against the structure of pragmatic liberalism, while the second couplet is working from within it. American Pragmatism has nothing on Nietzsche's Madman and Kierkegaard's Knight of Faith. These guys are lunatics. And there is everything "pragmatic" about the Knights of Infinite Resignation and Bourgeois Believers. They begin their work as jurists in the posture of a chastened faith. Yes, some are more chastened than others. But for each there is a shared commitment to working within the structure of liberal legal thought, either denying in half-belief its ideological formations or just "getting along" by way of a problem-solving mentality taking you from the one point in the Now to the next.

As I recounted in Chapter Nine, pragmatism has its problems. First, there is the illusion of eclectic problem-solving, mystifying and legitimating a "dictatorship of no alternatives." Second, there is the illusion of settled law, rendering invisible a form of structural transformation going beyond the stale choice between reformism and systemic substitution. Third, there is the illusion of the Now, damning us to an everlasting present and blinding us to the constellation of the contemporary. The Madman and the Knight of Faith suggest avenues for seeing and hearing through and beyond these illusions. But it is the path of the Knight and not the Madman that I want to finally encourage, for where the Madman sits in silence, the Knight of Faith speaks. He speaks of individualism and society, of rights and justice, of competition and cooperation. This is not, however, the speech of reconciliation, of mediation, of harmony as consonance. It is a dissonant speech. It is a speech that grapples with the antinomian, churning out chiasma. Perhaps surprisingly, his is also a faith in Harmony's Law, but it is a faith that in dissonance we might yet hear what we've never heard before. And, with some luck, we might find it beautiful.

Index